Negotiating Space

Negotiating Space

Power, Restraint, and
Privileges of Immunity
in Early Medieval Europe

BARBARA H. ROSENWEIN

Cornell University Press / Ithaca

Parts of this book have been published elsewhere; permission is gratefully acknowledged here.

"Association through Exemption: Saint-Denis, Salonnes, and Metz," in *Vom Kloster zum Klosterverband. Das Werkzeug der Schriftlichkeit*, ed. Hagen Keller and Franz Neiske (Munich: Wilhelm Fink, 1997), pp. 68–87.

"Cluny's Immunities in the Tenth and Eleventh Centuries: Images and Narratives," in *Die Cluniazenser in ihrem politisch-sozialen Umfeld*, ed. Giles Constable, Gert Melville, and Jörg Oberste, Vita regularis. Ordnungen und Deutungen religiosen Lebens im Mittelalter 7 (Münster, 1998), pp. 133–63.

"L'espace clos: Grégoire et l'exemption épiscopale," in *Grégoire de Tours et l'espace gaulois. Actes du congrès international, Tours, 3–5 November 1994*, ed. Nancy Gauthier and Henri Galinié, 13th supplement to *Revue Archéologique du Centre de la France* (Tours, 1997), pp. 251–62.

"The Family Politics of Berengar I (888–924)," *Speculum: A Journal of Medieval Studies* 71 (1996): 247–89.

"Friends and Family, Politics and Privilege in the Kingship of Berengar I," in *Portraits of Medieval and Renaissance Living: Essays in Memory of David Herlihy*, ed. Samuel K. Cohn Jr. and Steven A. Epstein (Ann Arbor: University of Michigan Press, 1996), pp. 91–106.

"La question de l'immunité clunisienne," *Bulletin de la Société des Fouilles archéologiques et des monuments historiques de l'Yonne*, no. 12 (1995): 1–11.

First published 1999 by Cornell University Press
First printing, Cornell Paperbacks, 1999

Printed in the United States of America

Library of Congress Cataloging-in-Publication Data

Rosenwein, Barbara H.
    Negotiating space : power, restraint, and privileges of immunity
in early medieval Europe / Barbara H. Rosenwein.
      p. cm.
    Includes bibliographical references and index.
    ISBN 0-8014-3523-4 (alk. paper). — ISBN 0-8014-8521-5 (pbk. :
alk. paper)
     1. Immunity (Feudalism)   2. Europe—Politics and
government—476-1492. I. Title.
JC116.I3R67   1998
320.1′2′0940902—dc21   98-31501

Cornell University Press strives to use environmentally responsible suppliers and materials to the fullest extent possible in the publishing of its books. Such materials include vegetable-based, low-VOC inks and acid-free papers that are recycled, totally chlorine-free, or partly composed of nonwood fibers.

Cloth printing   10 9 8 7 6 5 4 3 2 1
Paperback printing   10 9 8 7 6 5 4 3 2 1

To Tom

For of the Gods we believe, and of men we
know, that by a law of their nature wherever
they can rule they will.

—Thucydides, *Peloponnesian War*

God in heaven forbid
We should infringe the holy privilege
Of blessed sanctuary! not for all this land
Would I be guilty of so deep a sin.

—Shakespeare, *Richard III*

Contents

Illustrations

Maps

Genealogical Tables

Figures

Prefatory Note

THE SPELLING of personal names is regularized here, so that, for example, "Chaino," is always so spelled, even though in the sources he also appears as "Chaeno" and "Chagno." The Latin form of names is normally kept: an example is "Godinus." But this rule is modified in the cases of names that have, by common use, crept into English in shortened form. Examples include "Balthild" (rather than "Balthildis"), "Brunhild" (rather than "Brunechildis"), "Fulrad" (rather than "Fulradus"), and "Leudegar" (rather than "Leudegarius").

In Chapter 5, when the family that will eventually become the Carolingians is introduced, it is called the Carolingians right from the start, even though "the Pippinids" would probably be a more correct (though still modern) designation.

King "Charles *Simplex*" used to be rendered as "Charles the Simple," but I adopt here the better translation of the epithet given by Janet Nelson: "Charles the Straightforward."

The orthography of other words has *not* been regularized. Thus, for example, the same word appears in sources as *dicio*, *dictio*, and *ditio*; the spelling used here follows the particular source quoted.

The names of churches and monasteries are, where possible, given by hyphenating the name of the saint to whom they are dedicated. This practice allows author and reader to differentiate between the saint himself (Saint Denis, for example) and his church (Saint-Denis).

In Chapter 9 the spellings and punctuation of early modern English sources have been modernized for the sake of clarity.

Acknowledgments

FOR THIS book, which ranges over more than seven hundred years and was in the making for about seven more, a great many people have been consulted and large debts accumulated.

I am grateful to several institutions for supporting my research and providing the financial means to make it possible: Loyola University Chicago for leaves in fall 1989 and fall 1996; the John Simon Guggenheim Foundation for a fellowship in 1992; the Newberry Library (Chicago) for a National Foundation for the Humanities-Newberry Library grant for a semester (fall 1997) in residence. A subvention from Loyola University helped defray the cost of this book's illustration program.

Let me turn now to my colleagues. Above all, I want to record a special debt of gratitude to Ian Wood, who read the entire manuscript in draft and whose influence on my ideas and formulations will be evident throughout. Other colleagues read the manuscript as well, and I thank them warmly: Giles Constable, Thomas Head, Ruth Karras, Lester K. Little, Maureen Miller, Alexander Callander Murray, and Cornell's two anonymous readers. Still other colleagues read complete chapters or generously shared their expertise on particular points: Robert O. Bucholz, Wendy Davies, Albrecht Diem, James D'Emilio, Allen J. Frantzen, Patrick J. Geary, Richard Gerberding, Charles Gray, Paul Hyams, William C. Jordan, Theo Kölzer, Élisabeth Magnou-Nortier, Valerie Traub, Cécile Treffort, Stephen D. White, Patrick Wormald, and Élisabeth Zadora-Rio. I want to single out Dominique Iogna-Prat for special thanks; his encouragement and advice nurtured this project from start to finish.

In Fall 1992 I had the opportunity to present my work in various venues. I thank the following along with their students: Alain Boureau and Jean-Claude Schmitt of the École des Hautes Études en Sciences Sociales, Paris; Hartmut Atsma of the Deutsches Historisches Institut, Paris; John Van Engen of the Medieval Institute, Notre Dame. Thanks are also due to Mayke de Jong for the chance to speak at the University of Utrecht in fall

1996; and to Frederick Hoxie and participants of a two-hour seminar devoted to discussing Chapter 9 at the Newberry Library in fall 1997.

Still other experts, too numerous to mention here, are named in the relevant footnotes. Generous colleagues such as these make the profession of medievalist something rare and special.

I thank Lorna Newman, head of Loyola University's Interlibrary Loan Services, and my Loyola students, especially Marc Hanger, Matthew Seeberg, Laura Wilson, and Alan G. Zola for their help.

John G. Ackerman, director of Cornell University Press, awaited this study with patience, intervened when necessary, and generously read and edited the entire manuscript when it was complete. I count myself very lucky to have him as my publisher.

Finally, let me turn to my family. My parents, Roz and Norm, have always encouraged my work and endured my proccupations. My children, Jess and Frank, remain a welcome antidote to a life that at times veers dangerously close to the dull and compulsive Mr. Casaubon's. Moving into their college years, Frank and Jess have made very clear to me what sort of book a student should have to put up with. I have tried to write so that they can read it—if they want to! I dedicate it to my husband, Tom, with whom I discussed its topics large and small over breakfast and dinner and who read it in countless early drafts.

BARBARA H. ROSENWEIN

Evanston, Illinois

Abbreviations

Sources

AASS	*Acta Sanctorum quotquot toto orbe coluntur*, ed. Joannus Bollandus et al., 67 vols. (1640–1940)
AfD	*Archiv für Diplomatik, Schriftgeschichte, Siegel- und Wappenkunde*
Annales: ÉSC	*Annales: Économies, Sociétés, Civilisations*
BÉC	*Bibliothèque de l'École des Chartes*
BHL	*Bibliotheca hagiographica latina*, 2 vols., Subsidia hagiographica 6 (Brussels, 1898–1901) and *Novem supplementum*, Subsidia hagiographica 70 (Brussels, 1986)
CCM	*Corpus Consuetudinum Monasticarum*, ed. Kassius Hallinger, 14 vols. (Siegburg, 1963–)
CCSL	Corpus Christianorum, Series Latina (Turnhout, 1952–)
ChLA	*Chartae Latinae Antiquiores. Facsimile Edition of the Latin Charters prior to the Ninth Century*, ed. Albert Bruckner and Robert Marichal, 46 vols. (Lausanne and Dietikon-Zürich, 1954–1996)
Charles the Bald	*Recueil des actes de Charles II le Chauve, roi de France*, ed. Georges Tessier, 3 vols. (Paris, 1943–55)
Charles the Straightforward	*Recueil des actes de Charles III le Simple, roi de France*, ed. Philippe Lauer, 2 vols. (Paris, 1940)
Cluny	*Recueil des chartes de l'abbaye de Cluny*, ed. Auguste Bernard and Alexandre Bruel, 6 vols. (Paris, 1876–1903)

Conc. Gall.	*Concilia Galliae A.511–A.695*, ed. Charles De Clercq, CCSL 148A (Turnhout, 1963)
CT	*Codex Theodosianus*, ed. Theodor Mommsen et al., 2 vols. (1904; reprint, Dublin, 1971), trans. Clyde Pharr, *The Theodosian Code* (Princeton, 1952)
Cuddihy, "Fourth Amendment-Dissertation"	William J. Cuddihy, "The Fourth Amendment: Origins and Original Meaning, 602–1791" (Ph.D. diss., Claremont Graduate School, 1990)
Cysoing	*Cartulaire de l'abbaye de Cysoing et de ses dépendances*, ed. Ignace de Coussemaker (Lille, 1883)
DBer	*I diplomi di Berengario I*, ed. Luigi Schiaparelli, Fonti per la Storia d'Italia 35 (Rome, 1903)
DBI	*Dizionario biografico degli Italiani* (Rome, 1960–)
DCharles III	MGH, Dip. reg. Ger., vol. 2: *Karoli III. Diplomata*
DGui	*I diplomi di Guido e di Lamberto*, ed. Luigi Schiaparelli, Fonti per la Storia d'Italia 36 (Rome, 1906), pp. 3–68
DHGE	*Dictionnaire d'histoire et de géographie ecclésiastique*
DLamb	*I diplomi di Guido e di Lamberto*, ed. Luigi Schiaparelli, Fonti per la Storia d'Italia 36 (Rome, 1906), pp. 71–111.
DLouis III	*I diplomi Italiani di Lodovico III e di Rodolfo II*, ed. Luigi Schiaparelli, Fonti per la Storia d'Italia 37 (Rome, 1910), pp. 3–92 (Italian diplomas of Louis of Provence)
Documentary History	*The Documentary History of the Ratification of the Constitution* (Madison, Wis., 1976–93)
DRod	*I diplomi Italiani di Lodovico III e di Rodolfo II*, ed. Luigi Schiaparelli, Fonti per la Storia d'Italia 37 (Rome, 1910), pp. 95–141
EHD	*English Historical Documents*
1	Vol. 1: *c. 500–1042*, 2d ed., ed. Dorothy Whitelock (London, 1979)
2	Vol. 2: *1042–1189*, 2d ed., ed. David C. Douglas and George W. Greenaway (London, 1981)

ER	*English Reports* (Edinburgh, 1900–1930)
Ewig, *Gallien*	Eugen Ewig, *Spätantikes und fränkisches Gallien. Gesammelte Schriften (1952–1973)*, ed. Hartmut Atsma, Beihefte der Francia 3, parts 1–2, 2 vols. (Zurich, 1976–79)
Foerster, *LD*	Hans Foerster, ed., *Liber Diurnus Romanorum Pontificum* (Bern, 1958)
GC	*Gallia Christiana*, 16 vols. (1715–1865)
GeM	Paul Warnefrid, *Liber de episcopis Mettensibus*, MGH, SS 2:260–70
Gorze	*Cartulaire de l'abbaye de Gorze*, MS 826 de la Bibliothèque de Metz, ed. A. d'Herbomez, Mettensia 2 (Paris, 1898)
Greg., *Hist.*	Gregory of Tours, *Historiarum libri decem*, ed. Bruno Krusch and Rudolf Buchner, 2 vols., Ausgewählte Quellen zur deutschen Geschichte des Mittelalters 2–3 (Darmstadt, 1977)
Jaffé, *Regesta*	P. Jaffé et al., ed., *Regesta Pontificum Romanorum*, 2d ed., 2 vols. (Leipzig 1885–88; reprint, Graz, 1956)
LD	*Liber Diurnus*
Lorsch	*Codex Laureshamensis*, ed. Karl Glöckner, 3 vols. (Darmstadt, 1929)
Louis III	*Recueil des actes des rois de Provence (855–928)*, ed. René Poupardin (Paris, 1920), pp. 49–124 (Provençal diplomas of Louis of Provence)
Louis IV	*Recueil des actes de Louis IV, roi de France (936–954)*, ed. Philippe Lauer (Paris, 1914)
Mansi	J. D. Mansi, ed., *Sacrorum Conciliorum Nova et Amplissima Collectio* (Florence, 1757–98)
Marculf	*Marculfi Formularum libri duo*, ed. Alf Uddholm (Uppsala, 1962)
MGH	*Monumenta Germaniae Historica*
Cap. reg. Fr.	*Capitularia, Legum Sectio II, Capitularia Regum Francorum*, 2 vols. (Hannover, 1883–97)

Conc.	*Concilia, Legum Sectio* III, 3 vols. (Hannover, 1893–1984)
Dip. Kar.	*Diplomata Karolinorum*, 4 vols. (Hannover/ Munich, 1893–1994)
Dip. Mer.	*Diplomata* [Merovingian Diplomas] (Hannover 1872)
Dip. reg. Ger.	*Diplomata regum Germaniae ex stirpe Karolinorum*, 4 vols. (Berlin, 1934–63)
Epp.	*Epistolae*, 8 vols. (Hannover, 1887–1939)
Epp. sel.	*Epistolae selectae*, 5 vols. (Berlin, 1916–52)
Fontes	*Fontes Iuris Germanici Antiqui in usum scholarum ex Monumentis Germaniae Historicis separatim editi*, 13 vols. (Hannover, 1909–86)
Form.	*Formulae Merowingici et Karolini Aevi, Legum Sectio* V (Hannover, 1886)
Leges	*Leges Nationum Germanicarum*, 6 vols. (Hannover, 1892–1969)
Poet. Lat.	*Poetae Latini Aevi Carolini*, 4 vols. (Hannover, 1881–99)
SRG	*Scriptores Rerum Germanicarum in usum scholarum separatim editi* (Hannover 1871–1987)
SRL	*Scriptores Rerum Langobardicarum et Italicarum saec. VI–IX* (Hannover, 1878)
SRM	*Scriptores Rerum Merovingicarum*, 7 vols. (Hannover, 1885–1920)
SS	*Scriptores*, 30 vols. (Hannover, 1824–1924)
MIÖG	*Mitteilungen des Instituts für Österreichische Geschichtsforschung*
Erg.	*Ergänzungsband*
Modena	*Regesto della chiesa cattedrale di Modena*, ed. Emilio Paolo Vicini, 2 vols., Regesta Chartarum Italiae 16 and 21 (Rome 1931, 1936)
ÖW	*Österreichische Weistümer*
Pardessus	Jean Marie Pardessus, ed., *Diplomata, chartae, epistolae, leges, aliaque instrumenta ad res Gallo-*

	Francicas spectantia, 2 vols. (Paris, 1843–1849; reprint Aalen, 1969)
PL	*Patrologiae Cursus Completus, Series Latina*, ed. J.-P. Migne, 221 vols. (Paris, 1841–66)
Raoul	*Recueil des actes de Robert Ier et de Raoul, rois de France (922–936)*, ed. Jean Dufour and Robert-Henri Bautier (Paris, 1978)
RB	*Regula Benedicti* in *The Rule of St. Benedict in Latin and English with Notes*, ed. Timothy Fry (Collegeville, Minn., 1980)
Reg. Alsat.	*Regesta Alsatiae aevi Merovingici et Karolini, 496–918*, ed. Albert Bruckner, vol. 1, *Quellenband* (Strasbourg, 1949)
RHGF	*Recueil des historiens des Gaules et de la France*, ed. M. Bouquet, vols. 1–13 (Paris, 1738–86); vols. 14–24 (Paris, 1806–1904)
SC	Sources chrétiennes
Statutes of the Realm	*Statutes of the Realm*, 11 vols. in 12 (London, 1810–1828; reprint Buffalo, 1993)
Stoclet, "Fulrad-Dissertation"	Alain Stoclet, "Fulrad de Saint-Denis (v.710–784)" (Ph.D. diss., Toronto University, 1985)
TRHS	*Transactions of the Royal Historical Society*
Vézelay	*Monumenta Vizeliacensia. Textes relatifs à l'histoire de l'abbaye de Vézelay*, ed. R. B. C. Huygens, Corpus Christianorum Continuatio Mediaevalis 42 (Turnhout, 1976)
VT	Donatus, *Vita Trudonis confessoris Hasbaniensis*, MGH SRM 6:264–98
Wattenbach-Levison	*Deutschlands Geschichtsquellen im Mittelalter* 5 vols (Weimar, 1952–73)
Year Book	*Les Reports des Cases . . .* (Year Books 1307–1483) (London, 1674; reprint 1981)
Zimmermann	Harald Zimmermann, ed., *Papsturkunden, 896–1046*, 2d ed., 3 vols. (Vienna, 1988–89)
ZRG	*Zeitschrift der Savigny-Stiftung für Rechtsgeschichte*

GA	*Germanistische Abteilung*
KA	*Kanonistische Abteilung*

Other Abbreviations

arr.	*arrondissement*
B.N.F.	Paris, Bibliothèque nationale de France
ca.	*canton*
ch.-l.	*chef-lieu*
dép.	*département*

Negotiating Space

Introduction

I N T H E waning days of autumn 1095, on an extremely busy and productive trip across the Alps that would include a stop at the Council of Clermont, Urban II visited Cluny.[1] There he consecrated (*sacravit*: the verb is important) the major altar of the new and enormous church that was still under construction; he consecrated (*sacravit*) the second altar; then, at his bidding, other ecclesiastics consecrated (*sacrarunt*) three other altars (see Fig. 1). In an atmosphere heightened by these blessings and the Masses that accompanied them, the pope turned to "the people," just as he would do a month later at the end of the Council of Clermont, and spoke to them, as he would at Clermont, about those who oppressed the Church and about maintaining the peace. At Clermont he would pair the cessation of violence among Christians with the conquest of Jerusalem: "Wrest that land from the wicked race, and subject it to yourselves," he preached, thereby launching the First Crusade.[2] At Cluny, he linked peace to the establishment of a holy and inviolable circle around the monastery, where "no one of whatever condition or power might dare make an attack [*invasio*], whether big or small, or commit arson or pillage or robbery . . . or commit homicide or wound another." Solemnly and methodically he

1. For the trip, René Crozet, "Le Voyage d'Urbain II en France (1095–1096) et son importance au point de vue archéologique," *Annales du Midi* 49 (1937): 42–69 and its pendant piece, idem, "Le Voyage d'Urbain II et ses négociations avec le clergé de France (1095–1096)," *Revue historique* 179 (1937): 271–310. I thank Élisabeth Zadora-Rio for calling these articles to my attention and discussing their implications with me, for which see Chapter 8. For the account of Urban's visit to Cluny, see *Bullarium sacri ordinis Cluniacensis* [ed. P. Simon] (Lyon, 1680), p. 25.
2. Robert the Monk, *Historia Iherosolimitana*, in *Recueil des historiens des croisades*, vol. 2, *Historiens occidentaux* (Paris, 1866), 3:728: "Terram illam nefariae genti auferte, eamque vobis subjicite."

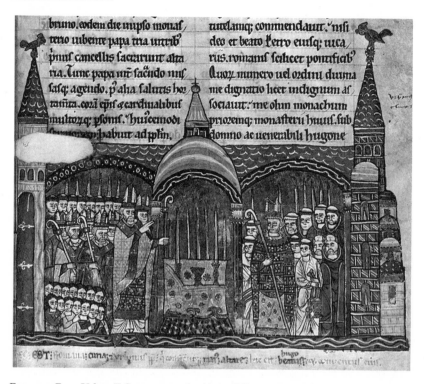

FIGURE 1. Pope Urban II Consecrates the Altar of Cluny. This illumination comes from a manuscript in which important texts and privileges of Cluny were compiled, probably in the late twelfth century, for the monastery of Saint-Martin-des-Champs, a Cluniac monastery since 1079. Pope Urban and his entourage are shown standing on the viewer's left, Abbot Hugh of Cluny (1049–1109) and his monks on the right, as the pope consecrates the high altar of the new church at Cluny. (Paris, B.N.F. lat. 17716, fol. 91, photographed and reproduced by permission of the Bibliothèque nationale de France, Paris.)

named the boundaries of Cluny's sacred "ban," or area of jurisdiction. Starting with a point to the southeast, he ticked off in clockwise order ten different boundary markers. The seventh suggests the model: "Toward Brancion the boundary is the road above Bois de Banan." Now defined and delimited, Cluny's ban was declared by Urban to be *sacratus*—consecrated, like Cluny's altars. Thus the sermon "to the people" at Cluny was itself a kind of blessing, and a territorial circle around Cluny became assimilated to its altars, on which the Eucharist, the central mystery of the Church—a mystery whose importance had been receiving special emphasis from reform popes such as Urban—was celebrated. Urban then turned to his audience and called upon them not to violate the ban; and he prescribed the penalty—excommunication—that would follow if they did.

"Immunity" was the term that the pope used to name what he had created at Cluny: he was assigning, he said, "certain clear limits of immunity and security around the monastery."

How could an eight-kilometer swath of property around Cluny—for that was what it was, including cultivated land, villages, roads, streams, waste, forest, and basins—be consecrated as if it were a high altar, to become itself a "holy land"? Why did the pope think he could declare it such? Had he always declared immunities? Had the word "immunity" always meant what it did in 1095? The historian has only to pose such questions to realize that there must be a history to immunities and sacred places. It is, in large measure, the purpose of this book to trace that history: to begin with the first immunities and to end (after a long, circuitous, and complicated journey) with Urban II's sacred ban.

Immunities and Exemptions as Flexible Tools

The journey is circuitous and complicated because immunities were continually changing, being reinterpreted, and joining with other ideas and strategies. In short, they meant different things at different times. We can give a definition of immunities—historians have done so for years—but only by disregarding their chameleon-like character. That the word "immunity" is a portmanteau term compounds the problem: it refers to a document—initially a *royal* document that prohibited the king's agents from entering onto certain lands to collect taxes and carry out judicial functions. It refers to the privileges embodied in those documents— an "immunity" from taxes, for example. It also refers to the land that was thus made special—Cluny's "immunity," as we saw, was that eight-kilometer circle of land. Finally, the variant noun "immunist" refers to the recipient of the privilege—the holder of the special land.[3]

3. In Latin the corresponding word—*immunitas, inmunitas,* or *emunitas*—had a range of meanings similar to those in English; see J. F. Niermeyer, *Mediae latinitatis lexicon minus,* s.v. *immunitas.*

The Latin word *immunitas* is a compound of *in-* (not), *munus* (a gift as well as a service, such as military service), and *-tas* (denoting an abstraction). Thus it implies in itself the range of meanings in and associations with the ideas of "gift" and "obligation."

It is worthwhile to remark that insofar as one can distinguish between economic immunities (which directly exempted institutions such as churches from commercial tolls and

Early medieval immunities should not be discussed apart from exemptions.[4] They took shape together in the course of the sixth century, emerged in charter form in the seventh, and arose within the same political, social, and religious milieux. Thus it is not surprising that exemptions, too, were chameleons, shifting according to circumstances. The word "exemption" may refer to a document—these were ordinarily issued by bishops or popes to shield monasteries from the entry and normal jurisdiction of their local diocesan bishop. It may refer to the privileges specified in the documents—freedom from episcopal oversight, for example. And the variant adjective "exempt" is used to speak of a monastery that has received an exemption.[5]

taxes) from judicial immunities (which prohibited royal agents from entry onto particular "immune" properties), the emphasis here is on the latter. And of the latter, immunities for churches and monasteries will be the focus, even though immunities for lay people certainly must have existed very early on, since they appear in formulary books such as Marculf 1:82–84, no. 17. Indeed, they may have constituted a regular feature of government in the Merovingian period, even as early as the sixth century; see Alexander Callander Murray, "Immunity, Nobility and the Edict of Paris," *Speculum* 69 (1994): 18–39, esp. p. 32. Because the early immunities for laymen have not left many traces in the extant sources, however, some historians doubt their existence altogether; see Paul Fouracre, "Eternal Light and Earthly Needs: Practical Aspects of the Development of Frankish Immunities," in Wendy Davies and Paul Fouracre, eds., *Property and Power in the Early Middle Ages* (Cambridge, 1995), esp. p. 62.

4. Though this is precisely what most historians have done, with immunities getting most of the attention.

5. The Latin word corresponding to the English "exemption" was *libertas*, which, however, had numerous definitions beyond those of "exemption" outlined above; see Niermeyer, *Mediae latinitatis lexicon minus*, s.v. *libertas*. The Latin word *exemptio* was not the equivalent of *libertas*. In the late Empire it meant the equivalent of "detention" of a person summoned to court; see Charlton T. Lewis and Charles Short, *A Latin Dictionary*, s.v. *exemptio*. Only in the second half of the twelfth century did it come to mean "exemption"; see Kenneth Pennington, *Pope and Bishops: The Papal Monarchy in the Twelfth and Thirteenth Centuries* (Philadelphia, 1984), p. 156. Some historians (as we shall see) refuse to call a document an exemption until it meets certain criteria established in papal bulls of the tenth through twelfth centuries. However, as one of my students, Alan G. Zola, put it, these historians "retain the teleological perspective of understanding the past in the light of its future when they define various papal privilege to be or not be be . . . exemptions based on their similarit[ies to] or difference[s] from a model which postdates them." See also the cautionary remark in Laurent Morelle, "Moines de Corbie sous influence sandionysienne? Les préparatifs corbéiens du synode romain de 1065," in Rolf Grosse, ed., *L'église de France et la Papauté (X^e–XIIIe siècle)—Die französische Kirche und das Papsttum (10.-13. Jahrhundert). Actes du XXVIe colloque historique franco-allemand (Paris 17–19 octobre 1990)* (Bonn, 1993), p. 203: "Le concept d'exemption [in the eleventh century] est encore flou." In this book I use the word "exemption" to refer to a wide variety of privileges that freed monasteries from diocesan episcopal oversight. There were also exemptions for *bishops:* these put bishoprics under the direct jurisdiction of the papacy and freed the bishop from his metropolitan. The phenomenon be-

Certainly the history of immunities and (to a lesser extent) exemptions has been dealt with before—though perhaps never traced in such broad sweep—in elegant and formidably learned studies.[6] Indeed, charters of immunity and exemption formed the cornerstone of nineteenth-century diplomatics, the science of ferreting out authentic documents from forgeries. Yet in part because they are such traditional objects of study, these charters remain largely mired in the assumptions and techniques of pre-Blochian scholarship. And thus, by and large, they have not benefited from the approaches that characterize so many recent studies of medieval history, such as attention to documents as cultural artifacts rather than as seemingly clear windows onto "historical reality"; awareness of how each text presents a "contested site" that may be read in a variety of ways depending on the position of the reader and writer; mindfulness of the need to contextualize documents and to confront and combine them with evidence from different genres.[7]

The second purpose of this book, then, is to bring immunities (and exemptions) back into modern historical discourse: to show how they are rich and polyvalent sources, how they served social and political strategies far beyond their surface meanings, and how the negotiations, conflicts, and accords that they variously embodied, reflected, diffused, and/ or affirmed changed under different circumstances and at different times. Immunities and exemptions, I will argue, were flexible instruments of political and social life.

For years historians thought precisely the opposite. They thought these institutions were unyielding. In particular, they spoke of "the" immunity, as if there were only one.[8] They looked for the "juridical" meaning of the term, the way it functioned as a legal institution. They asked questions

---

gan in the eighth century, but it was not very prevalent. We know of only thirty episcopal exemptions from the eighth to the end of the twelfth century. See Otto Vehse, "Bistums-exemtionen bis zum Ausgang des 12. Jahrhunderts," *ZRG KA* 26 (1937): 86–160. I thank Michel Parisse for reminding me to think about terminology medieval and modern.

6. On exemptions there are Brigitte Szabó-Bechstein, *Libertas Ecclesiae. Ein Schlüsselbegriff des Investiturstreits und seine Vorgeschichte, 4.–11. Jahrhundert*, Studi Gregoriani per la storia della "libertas ecclesiae" 12 (Rome, 1985), and Hans Hubert Anton, *Studien zu den Kloster-privilegien der Päpste im frühen Mittelalter*, Beiträge zur Geschichte und Quellenkunde des Mittelalters 4 (Berlin, 1975). On immunities see the discussion below, pp. 9–18.

7. See the discussion of recent approaches in Jacques Le Goff and Jean-Claude Schmitt, "L'histoire médiévale," *Cahiers de civilisation médiévale, X^e–XIIe siècles* 39 (1996): 9–25.

8. A similar point is raised by Carlrichard Brühl, "Die merowingische Immunität," in *Chiesa e mondo feudale nei secoli X–XII. Atti della dodicesima Settimana internazionale di studio Mendola, 24–28 agosto 1992*, Miscellanea del Centro di studi medioevali 14 (Milan, 1995), pp. 27–43, here p. 29.

such as whether rights of immunity inhered in royal land itself. When they thought of charters of immunity, they had in mind exemplars that appeared in formulary collections, or they recalled the invariable phrases that issued from organized chanceries of the sort that began drawing up immunities under the Carolingian king Louis the Pious (814–40).

Historians believed that such documents gave away power. When kings prohibited their agents from entering lands to carry out public functions, historians (living in nineteenth- and twentieth-century state-centered societies) saw this as conclusive evidence of a profound weakness at the core of the state. Only under post-cold-war conditions can historians easily think differently; for theirs is a world in which public powers can privatize their former functions—the postal service, jails, schools—yet manage all the while to maintain and even enhance their ability to coerce. In the 1990s historians dared to suggest that immunities might have been given out from a position of strength.[9]

The present book builds upon this proposition but deflects the question slightly. The issue in the early Middle Ages was not really the strength or weakness of the state: it was the ability of rulers and others with power to maintain their positions as pivotal and central figures in the lives of key families, friends (*amici*), warriors, and religious figures (the categories overlap). Kings were keen to have power, admittedly: but they gained it largely by manipulating fluid alliances among aristocrats.[10] Their power relied on networks of "consultation" (that is, deference to the nobility), gift-giving, and feuding far more than on bureaucratic institutions.[11] Noble families occupied high positions in both the state (for example, as counts) and the Church (for example, as bishops and abbots). This seemed perfectly natural at the time; and kings, who often thought they too straddled both spheres, were comfortable within such a system.

Clearly the question of state development is proper and indeed unavoidable for the student of immunities, since immunities normally were given out by kings and queens (and exemptions by bishops and popes). At the same time, however, this institutional emphasis has sometimes obscured the following aspects of early medieval royal policy: its inextricable link to piety and religious beliefs; its shifting power base, formed of

9. See Murray, "Immunity, Nobility, and the Edict of Paris," and Davies and Fouracre, *Property and Power*, with summary statement of the point at p. 15.

10. For the following perspective, I am much indebted to the work of recent British historians, such as, for example, Janet L. Nelson, *Charles the Bald* (London, 1992); Paul J. Fouracre, "The Career of Ebroin, Mayor of the Palace, c. 657–680" (Ph.D. diss., University of London, 1981); and Ian Wood, *The Merovingian Kingdoms (450–751)* (London, 1994).

11. Today Japan asserts its "right" to give money to China because it is a "great" power.

social and familial alliances; and its reliance on negotiation to maintain its position.

None of this means that control over resources was unimportant to early medieval rulers. How could a king give out gifts to cement alliances if he had nothing to give? What has seemed unforgivable to historians of immunities is that kings appeared to give away their own jurisdiction—not just land or movables, but the very profits and rights of public power.[12]

Yet however closely tied to gifts in form and intention, immunities were above all sets of prohibitions. These flowed naturally from the entry prohibition, their core feature (though sometimes implicit rather than explicit).[13] Because some commentators consider it simply the "mechanism" by which the rest of the immunity—the fiscal and judicial aspects—worked, the entry prohibition has not excited the interest—even the wonder—that it deserves.[14] For a ruler to restrain his own agents from entering property: does this not seem an ancient precursor of the "liberal" state? More important for the early Middle Ages, does not the very expression of restraint announce the power of the king? This power is of three sorts: first, it is a declaration of self-control; second, it is an affirmation of royal control over public agents and their jurisdiction; third, it is an announcement of control over the configuration of space.[15]

There was another way in which immunities announced power. Based on guarantees of protection, as most later ones were (from the time of Louis the Pious on), they proclaimed the high status of the grantor of the

12. This is in large measure the issue behind the long dispute among historians about whether or not kings gave up their rights to both "high" and "low" justice when they issued an immunity, even though early medieval sources are so laconic in this regard that the dispute may never be satisfactorily resolved; and indeed, even though one may seriously question whether the distinction between high and low justice existed during this early period. See note 49 below.

13. See Brühl, "Die merowingische Immunität," p. 34, for an example of an early immunity (MGH Dip. Mer., pp. 25–26, no. 25) where the entry prohibition is implicit only. Such silences became more usual as immunities became more routine.

14. These words were written before but are nicely complemented by Caroline Bynum's Presidential Address to the American Historical Association Annual Meeting, January 3, 1997, "Wonder," now published in *American Historical Review* 102 (1997): 1–26.

15. The *conception* of space was not modern. Alain Guerreau, "Quelques caractères spécifiques de l'espace féodal européen," in Neithard Bulst, Robert Descimon, and Alain Guerreau, eds., *L'État ou le roi. Les fondations de la modernité monarchique en France (XIVe–XVIIe siècles)* (Paris, 1996), pp. 85–101, argues that space was conceived as discontinuous and heterogeneous, certain points being valorized and set apart from others. Thus, for example, the "parish" was not a coherent district but was conceived of as the church, baptismal font, and cemetery.

immunity.[16] In Germanic and Roman law, men held rights of protection graded by status. This point has been much exploited in the discussion of women in the early Middle Ages, for they were largely understood to be under the protection of their male kin. But dependents of every sort were under the protection of their lords, and the violation of that protection incurred a penalty. The Carolingians in particular exploited this power by explicitly associating the words *tuitio* or *defensio* (both meaning royal protection) with *immunitas*, immunity. Such Carolingian immunities did double duty: they declared a "hands-off" policy while keeping the issuer's fingers very much in the pot. It is not by chance that the Germanic term for protection, *mund*, meant "hand."[17]

Immunities, then, implied not so much strength or weakness as status, power, and influence. Just as nowadays electrical wiring, roads, and bridges are considered part of the essential infrastructure of the state, so in the early Middle Ages, religion and land were considered essential for the proper functioning of society. Immunities combined the two. They set up and cemented alliances between kings, churchmen, and other magnates; and, while doing so, they implicitly declared a reorganization of land use within cities and the countryside by setting certain lands apart and off-limits (at least to certain people for certain purposes.)

Every medievalist comes across immunities, exemptions, and related documents. Every historian of the modern world encounters their vestiges. The word "immunities" figures in the U.S. Constitution,[18] and the state's right to breach an immunity is behind the Constitution's Fourth Amendment.[19] If immunities did not mean what we thought they meant,

16. See Wendy Davies, "'Protected Space' in Britain and Ireland in the Middle Ages," in Barbara E. Crawford, ed., *Scotland in Dark Age Britain*, St. John's House Papers 6 (Aberdeen, 1996), pp. 1–19. It is wrong, however, to consider all immunities as implying protection. Indeed, even after immunity and protection were yoked, they remained conceptually different. See Fredric L. Cheyette, "The Royal Safeguard in Medieval France," *Studia Gratiana* 15 (1972): 631–52, at p. 636.

17. The root of *tuitio* is *tueor*, to "look at"; the root of *defensio* is *defendo*, to "ward off" but also "to cover."

18. *The Constitution of the United States of America*, Article IV, §2, clause 1: "The Citizens of each State shall be entitled to all Privileges and Immunities of Citizens in the several States." The meaning of "immunities" in this context has been elucidated in David S. Bogen, "The Privileges and Immunities Clause of Article IV," *Case Western Reserve Law Review* 37 (1987): 794–861.

19. The Fourth Amendment of the Constitution: "The right of the people to be secure in their persons, houses, papers, and effects, against unreasonable searches and seizures, shall not be violated, and no Warrants shall issue, but upon probable cause, supported by oath or affirmation, and particularly describing the place to be searched, and the persons or things to be seized."

if (as is certainly the case) they meant many things, then it is essential to study them afresh. This book is one step in that process.

Approaches

On the whole, modern studies of early medieval immunities fall into four categories: (1) those concerned with chancery practices; (2) those stressing the fiscal implications of immunities; (3) those emphasizing their administrative and jurisdictional import; and (4) those relating immunities to the movement for church reform and the cry of "church freedom" (*libertas ecclesiae*). There is also a fledgling fifth group, to which the present book belongs: studies that explore the issuance of immunities within their contexts, as elements of the religious politics of medieval rulers.[20]

It goes without saying that these perspectives are not mutually exclusive. Immunities had administrative, economic, and religious implications; that is why they were so important as political instruments. Nevertheless, the contextual approach largely leaves certain traditional issues to one side. Thus, the present book does not concern itself much with whether immunists were (or were not) obliged to give dues and fees to the king, or whether jurisdiction within an immunity was (or was not) exercised on behalf of the king. This is because *these* issues *themselves* constituted subjects of ongoing negotiations. It would require another book— or rather many other books—to explore how particular immunities given to particular recipients worked over time—now as instruments of royal fiscal or judicial administration, now as the basis for independent action on the part of the immunists. *This* book seeks to show the manifold ways in which immunities were conceived, negotiated, and manipulated when they were issued or confirmed, locating these "acts of state" in specific religious, social, and political contexts. This focus shifts, however, in Chapter 9, where the goal is to understand the "afterlife" of immunities in Anglo-American political thought. Here the issuance of immunities is of less importance than the history of their use and interpretation by English officials.

The first scholars to study immunities (and exemptions) were diplo-

---

20. An excellent, but different, overview of the historiography is given in Fouracre, "Eternal Light," esp. pp. 53–68. I had the opportunity to present some of the material that follows at the seminar of Michel Sot, Université de Paris X, Nanterre. I should like to thank Professor Sot, Dominique Iogna-Prat, François Bougard, and the members of the seminar for their comments.

matists—scholars of legal charters. Jean Mabillon (1632–1707), for example, dealt with exemptions in his *De re diplomatica*, where he vindicated the authenticity of the exemptions issued for Saint-Denis and Corbie.[21] Systematic studies, however, awaited the nineteenth century when, under the twin impetus of nationalism and bureaucratization, scholars investigated immunities (but not exemptions) in order to understand royal chancery practices and their development. The father of these studies was Theodor Sickel, who in the 1860s wrote a series of articles on the royal diplomas of Louis the German and, as part of his effort to revise J. F. Böhmer's calendar of royal charters, published the first important research devoted specifically to early medieval—that is, Merovingian and Carolingian—immunities.[22] Sickel's purpose was to identify genuine documents and categorize them. His technique was largely chronological. Setting genuine immunity charters side by side, "from the oldest to the end of the ninth century," Sickel isolated key clauses, then noted their transformation from document to document.[23] So focused was he on these clauses that he refused to consider any not directly tied to the immunity proper; that is, he was interested in the general development of immunities as a formal genre, not in specific immunities for individual houses with special purposes.[24] Because of this "vue cavalière," the year 814 became the essential turning point for Sickel: until that time, immunity clauses had only occasionally been paired with clauses of *tuitio*; after 814 the two were invariably joined.[25]

The legacy of Sickel's work was twofold. First, he set the course for the long series of studies that has by now largely succeeded in winnowing

21. Jean Mabillon, *De re diplomatica*, 2d ed. (Paris, 1709), pp. 11–19.

22. For studies of the diplomas of Louis the German, see Theodor Sickel, "Beiträge zur Diplomatik 1: Die Urkunden Ludwig's des Deutschen bis zum Jahre 859," *Sitzungsberichte der Kaiserlichen Akademie der Wissenschaften, Philosophisch-Historische Klasse* 36 (1861): 329–402; idem, "Beiträge zur Diplomatik 2: Die Urkunden Ludwig's des Deutschen in den Jahren 859–876," ibid., 39 (1862): 105–61. On Carolingian immunities, "Beiträge zur Diplomatik 3: Die Mundbriefe, Immunitäten und Privilegien der ersten Karolinger bis zum Jahre 840," ibid., 47 (1864): 175–277. For a corresponding study of the papal chancery, Hans Hirsch, "Untersuchungen zur Geschichte des päpstlichen Schutzes," *MIÖG* 54 (1942): 363–433.

23. Sickel, "Beiträge zur Diplomatik 3," p. 180.

24. Ibid., p. 194: "Schliesse ich auch hier bei der Prüfung der einzelnen Stücke vor der Hand Alles aus, was ohne mit der Immunität in innerem Zusammenhange zu stehen . . . ist."

25. Ibid., pp. 205–16: discussion of the desultory pairing before 814. Hence Sickel's later installment: "Beiträge zur Diplomatik 5: "Die Immunitätsrechte nach den Urkunden der ersten Karolinger bis zum Jahre 840," *Sitzungsberichte der Kaiserlichen Akademie der Wissenschaften, Philosophisch-Historische Klasse* 49 (1865): 311–410, a search for "ob und in wieweit sich positiv feststellen läßt, welches die Quelle, welches die Bedingungen der Immunität gewesen sind."

out genuine from false charters.[26] The importance and usefulness of this achievement are obvious. But its very strength contains as well the weakness that is the second legacy of his study. Categorized, set forth as part of a lineage of documents leading inexorably from one immunity to the next through time, read as exemplars of scribal practice, immunities have been isolated from other texts.[27] Yet in the early Middle Ages official documents were a fluid genre; in the sixth century, for example, they were mingled with letter collections.[28]

Particularly unfortunate has been the separation of exemptions issued by bishops and popes from immunities granted by kings and queens. As Eugen Ewig recognized in 1973, both forms were often issued for complementary political and religious purposes.[29] Indeed, as we shall see,

26. These include Edmund E. Stengel's study of the development of royal immunities after Louis the Pious and the separate but simultaneous evolution of papal exemptions in his *Die Immunität in Deutschland bis zum Ende des 11. Jahrhunderts* (Innsbruck, 1910; reprint, Aalen, 1964); Léon Levillain's articles on the documents pertaining to Corbie and Saint-Denis in his *Examen critique des chartes mérovingiennes et carolingiennes de l'Abbaye de Corbie*, Mémoires et documents publiés par la Société de l'École des Chartes 5 (Paris, 1902), and idem, "Études sur l'abbaye de Saint-Denis à l'époque mérovingienne," *BÉC* 82 (1921): 5–116; 86 (1925): 5–99; 87 (1926): 20–97, 245–346; 91 (1930): 5–65, 264–300; and François-Louis Ganshof's survey of Merovingian and Carolingian immunities, the footnotes of which provide a nearly exhaustive list of authentic diplomas from the period, in his "L'immunité dans la monarchie franque," in *Les liens de vassalité et les immunités*, 2d ed., Recueils de la Société Jean Bodin 1 (Brussels, 1958), pp. 171–216.

27. The "inexorability" must be qualified. Historians in the Sickel mode have recognized caesuras and mutations as well. For a discussion of the older views, see Brühl, "Die merowingische Immunität," esp. pp. 37–38.

28. Ian Wood, "Writers and Writings between Antiquity and the Middle Ages: The Social Function of Letters" (paper delivered at the University of Maryland, May 8, 1990). I thank Professor Wood for allowing me to see a copy of this lecture. See also his "Letters and Letter-Collections from Antiquity to the Early Middle Ages: The Prose Works of Avitus of Vienne," in M. A. Meyer, ed., *The Culture of Christendom: Essays in Medieval History in Commemoration of Denis L. T. Bethell* (London, 1983), pp. 29–43.

29. Eugen Ewig, "Das Privileg des Bischofs Berthefrid von Amiens für Corbie von 664 und die Klosterpolitik der Königin Balthild" [hereafter "Klosterpolitik"] (orig. publ. 1973), in Ewig, *Gallien*, 2:538–83, takes as its theme the relationship between the royal immunity and the episcopal exemption for Corbie. Ewig was not the first to see the connection between immunities and exemptions. It was understood by Stengel and strongly reinforced by, among others, Hirsch, in "Untersuchungen." Jean-François Lemarignier, *Étude sur les privilèges d'exemption et de juridiction ecclésiastique des abbayes Normandes depuis les origines jusqu'en 1140*, Archives de la France monastique 44 (Paris, 1937), pp. 134–37, saw clear correspondences between ecclesiastical exemptions in Normandy and immunities in the Paris basin, both resulting in a similar kind of jurisdiction for the recipient. Ingrid Heidrich, "Titulatur und Urkunden der arnulfingischen Hausmeier," *Archiv für Diplomatik* 11–12 (1965–66): 71–279, at p. 117, argued for a close relationship between the powers given up by the bishop and those by the king in these privileges. But Paul Fabre, *Étude sur le Liber Censuum*

royal immunities were from the first issued in tandem with episcopal exemptions. Their connection was further signaled by the fact that kings sometimes relied on church councils to declare royal immunities, while exemptions were often issued at royal behest. Finally, some diplomas coupled exemption with immunity.

Exacerbating the isolation of immunities from other sorts of texts has been an overreliance on formulary books. These were medieval collections of a great variety of model legal charters: immunities, letters of introduction from one king to another, exemptions, donations, and the like. We often do not know precisely who put any given collection together, let alone when or why. But scholars have generally assumed that many were compiled to aid scribes, since the models are presented schematically — from bishop X at city Y, for example — to allow the user to tailor them to fit particular circumstances. Thus historians have contentedly analyzed the immunities presented in Marculf, assuming them to be templates of Merovingian immunities, despite the uncertainties of its dating, the circumstances of its genesis, and the immediate uses to which it was put.[30] Reliance on formularies is largely why historians have spoken of "the" immunity and why their discussions have at times been unmoored not only from any particular historical grant but also from any historical circumstance whatever.

The second way in which immunities have been studied is as a window onto early medieval fiscal administration and policy. This, too, is a legacy of nineteenth-century legal and constitutional concerns. In the view of N. D. Fustel de Coulanges, for example, the Merovingian king was absolute, his agents petty tyrants. Hence the exclusion clause, "le point capital" of the immunity, was meant to save privileged persons from oppressive agents.[31] It followed for Fustel de Coulanges that the immunists themselves were obliged to gather the taxes and deposit them into the royal treasury. This argument has many problems. First, it is unlikely that enough immunities were issued to weaken tyrannical agents, if such there were; nor do immunities seem well designed to do the job, since they were not directives to agents but promises to favored recipi-

de l'Église Romaine (Paris, 1892), p. 36, saw not so much a relationship between the two as the supplanting of royal immunities by papal exemptions: "La protection apostolique se substitue à la protection royale."

30. For example, Fustel de Coulanges took Marculf's immunity formula as his key text: N. D. Fustel de Coulanges, "Étude sur l'immunité mérovingienne," *Revue historique* 22 (1883): 249–90 and 23 (1883): 1–27. On the genesis and date of Marculf, Heidrich, "Titulatur und Urkunden," with summary statement on p. 190.

31. Fustel de Coulanges, "Étude sur l'immunité," p. 278.

ents. Second, these same royal agents continued to be used in other aspects of Merovingian administration. Third, royal agents and immunists were not so very distinct; even in the Merovingian period, favored men who received immunities were also part of the king's entourage.

Nevertheless Fustel de Coulanges's view has had a long life. Élisabeth Magnou-Nortier, for example, has more recently argued that immunities granted very restricted fiscal privileges to churches; but, even then, immunists were expected to have their own agents collect and pay the taxes due the king.[32] This argument complements her view that the taxation system of the late Empire persisted virtually unchanged into the early Middle Ages.[33]

Precisely the opposite view—that the fiscal benefits of immunities were substantial—was argued already early in this century by Léon Levillain, for whom the immunity was a real exemption from important public taxes that would normally have gone to the king and his functionaries.[34] Walter Goffart has suggested that such fiscal prerogatives were key to "a conception of personal or corporate dignity" for churches and monasteries. Paul Fouracre, stressing an oft-overlooked portion of the immunity clause, has maintained that the revenues were indeed gained by the beneficiaries and used for one precise and specific purpose: church lighting.[35]

Of what did these revenues consist? Ferdinand Lot's seminal study of the late-imperial land tax set forth the issues, but they remain hotly disputed.[36] On the one hand is Magnou-Nortier, who argues that "fiscal practice hardly changed from the sixth to the ninth century and probably

32. With this point, Brühl, "Die merowingische Immunität," pp. 39–40, agrees: "Echte fiskalische Freiungen oder Schenkungen sind selten."

33. Élisabeth Magnou-Nortier, "Étude sur le privilège d'immunité du IVe au IXe siècle," *Revue Mabillon* 60 (1981–84): 465–512, esp. pp. 474–81; eadem, "Les *Pagenses*, notables et fermiers du fisc durant le haut moyen âge," *Revue Belge de Philologie et d'Histoire* 65 (1987): 237–56; eadem, "La gestion publique en Neustrie. Les moyens et les hommes (VIIe–IXe siècles)," in Hartmut Atsma, ed., *La Neustrie. Les Pays au Nord de la Loire de 650 à 850*, 2 vols. (Sigmaringen, 1989), 1:271–320, with additional bibliography at p. 273 n. 6. Jean Durliat, *Les Finances Publiques de Diocletian aux Carolingiens (284–889)*, Beihefte der Francia 21 (Sigmaringen, 1990), esp. pp. 112–13, sees close similarities between the "finances publiques" of the Roman and barbarian states, but unlike Magnou-Nortier, he also thinks that public powers were held by "new" entities—"roi, duc ou simple évêque devenu autonome"—until the Carolingians restored the "Roman" system.

34. Léon Levillain, "Note sur l'immunité Mérovingienne," *Revue historique de droit français et étranger*, 4th ser., 6 (1927): 38–67.

35. Fouracre, "Eternal Light." The argument that immunities became fiscal privileges in return for prayers is made in Jacques Foviaux, "Les immunités ecclésiastiques (IXe–XIe siècles)," *Histoire médiévale et archéologie*, no. 3 (1991): 47–67.

36. Ferdinand Lot, *L'impôt foncier et la capitation personnelle sous le Bas-Empire et à l'époque franque*, Bibliothèque de l'École des Hautes Études 253 (Paris, 1928). On Merovingian tolls,

beyond that."[37] On the other hand is Walter Goffart, who, writing at about the same time, underlines the discontinuities between forms of late-imperial and Merovingian taxation: the evidence from Marculf is, as he puts it, "disquieting; nothing referred to, including the *redhibitiones* [renders due by tenants], evokes a Roman tax."[38] The *munera* (obligatory public services) survived, but only "at the level of the rural estates," a level previously almost invisible.[39] Thus Merovingian immunities helped suggest to Goffart the hypothesis of a "double-tiered system" for late-imperial taxation: the lower level probably made up of payments in kind, the upper level (the only one in which the imperial treasury was interested) of payments in gold.[40] In Goffart's view, by giving up the latter through royal immunities, the kings also gave up the former, the very taxes on which they depended.

No matter what the content of the revenues, behind both arguments about the fiscal consequences of immunities (the one maintaining that the state gave up little, the other that it conceded a great deal) lurk three assumptions about state power: that it is based on bureaucracy; that it thrives on centralization; and that it attempts to amass and conserve its material resources.[41] The counterpart to this view is that feudalism (that is, fragmented political order and seigneury-based economy) represents a failure of the state. In this light, the question that the immunity raises, above all, is its contribution to feudalism.[42] A few historians, such as

see François-Louis Ganshof, "Les bureaux de tonlieu de Marseille et de Fos," in *Études historiques à la mémoire de Noël Didier* (Paris, 1960), pp. 125–33.

37. Magnou-Nortier, "Étude sur le privilège," p. 466. In eadem, "La gestion publique," she takes up (on pp. 286–88) the question of "Le vocabulaire fiscal."

38. Walter Goffart, "Old and New in Merovingian Taxation," *Past and Present* 96 (1982): 3–21, at p. 5; idem, "From Roman Taxation to Mediaeval Seigneurie: Three Notes," *Speculum* 47 (1972): 165–87, 373–94. This *contra* Lot, *L'impôt foncier*, p. 82, who says that among the Franks, "la terminologie [of taxation] demeure la même que sous l'Empire romain."

39. Goffart, "Old and New," p. 3.

40. A view also underlying the considerations about *hospitalitas* in Walter Goffart, *Barbarians and Romans, A.D. 418–584: The Techniques of Accommodation* (Princeton, N.J., 1980), p. 79 n. 41.

41. Magnou-Nortier, "La gestion publique," p. 281, asks, "Comment ont-ils [the kings] pu travailler avec autant d'assiduité à la destruction de leur propre puissance?" Her answer is that they did *not*; their acts have been misapprehended: "Le contrôle royal est toujours maintenu" (p. 283). Hans K. Schulze, *Die Grafschaftsverfassung der Karolingerzeit in den Gebieten östlich des Rheins*, Schriften zur Verfassungsgeschichte 19 (Berlin, 1973), p. 311, similarly speaks of the "Strebens nach Zentralisierung und Vereinheitlichung."

42. Just as "feudalism" is classically defined by looking at France as archetypical, so too the immunity and its development in Francia have been the focus of historiography. Certainly the formula with entry prohibition appears to be a Frankish invention; however, its evolution in France need not automatically be taken as the only possible one. On immu-

Magnou-Nortier, explicitly deny a direct connection.[43] Indeed, Alexander Murray has taken this view even further. Rather than reflecting or threatening the demise of government, Murray argues, immunities were part of the Frankish kings' way to reorganize jurisdiction. They were one of a number of perfectly sound instruments, used by *strong* monarchs, to grant recompense to those who benefited the realm. "Immunity," Murray writes, "was used as an indirect means of delegating resources to the recipients of the benefit. . . . It was commonly used to offset other valuable services the immunist was performing for the state or to reward him for services already performed."[44] In many ways, Fouracre's observations fit into Murray's picture: public services were not only secular but also religious. Providing for church lighting was the state's way to compensate monasteries for their liturgical services.

The more general consensus, however, represented in Germany by Heinrich Mitteis and in France by Marc Bloch, maintains that immunities were fundamentally responsible for the development of feudalism because they sanctioned the development of areas of private jurisdiction.[45]

---

nities in Italy, the historiography is focused on the devolution of *districtus* (jurisdiction) to Lombard cities; see, for example, Giovanni Tabacco, *The Struggle for Power in Medieval Italy: Structures of Political Rule*, trans. Rosalind Brown Jensen (Cambridge, 1989), p. 156; Chris Wickham, *Early Medieval Italy: Central Power and Local Society, 400–1000* (Ann Arbor, Mich., 1981), pp. 172–73; and Gabriella Rossetti, "Formazione e caratteri delle signorie di castello e dei poteri territoriali dei vescovi sulle città nella langobardia del secolo X," *Aevum* 49 (1975): 243–309. See Chapter 7 below. On immunities as the foundation of the free *Reichstadt* of Metz in Germany, see H. V. Sauerland, *Die Immunität von Metz von ihren Anfängen bis zum Ende des elften Jahrhunderts* (Metz, 1877). On immunities in the Iberian peninsula, Hilda Grassotti, "La inmunidad en el occidente peninsular del rey magno al rey santo," *Cuadernos de historia de España* 67–68 (1982): 72–122; I thank James D'Emilio (University of South Florida) for this and other references. For Byzantium, Rosemary Morris, "Monastic Exemptions in Tenth- and Eleventh-Century Byzantium," in Davies and Fouracre, *Property and Power*, pp. 200–220.

43. Magnou-Nortier, "Étude sur le privilège," p. 470. For her, the connection arises only when forgers begin to use immunities to carve out seigneurial powers (p. 505). Susan Reynolds, *Fiefs and Vassals: The Medieval Evidence Reinterpreted* (Oxford, 1994), p. 60, stresses the fact that ecclesiastical institutions were the normal recipients of immunities, and hence concludes that "the idea that from early on counts or other lay nobles received 'immunities' like those of the great churches and that this was the source of later political fragmentation—'feudal anarchy'—seems to be an over-simplification."

44. Alexander Callander Murray, "*Pax et disciplina*: Roman Public Law and the Frankish State," in *Proceedings of the Tenth International Congress of Medieval Canon Law, Syracuse, N.Y., August 12–18, 1996*, forthcoming. I thank Professor Murray for giving me an advance copy of this article.

45. Heinrich Mitteis, *The State in the Middle Ages. A Comparative Constitutional History of Feudal Europe*, trans. H. F. Orton, North-Holland Medieval Translations 1 (Amsterdam, 1975), which is a translation of the fourth revised edition of *Der Staat des hohen Mittelalters;*

In American college textbooks, feudalism is the *only* topic under which immunities are discussed. A standard formulation goes as follows: "The existence of immunity [in the ninth and tenth centuries] provided, in some cases, the starting point of usurpation. Conversely, usurpation of private jurisdiction was often given a specious legality by later grants of immunity."[46] Here is revealed the assumption that feudalism was a usurpation of the public power that had been handed down from the Roman period. In Maurice Kroell's major study, *L'immunité franque*, Merovingian immunities represented a self-imposed abnegation of public power, explicable by the kings' needs to ensure loyal supporters.[47] Immunities thus joined grants of land as part of a pre-feudal political organization. In Kroell's scheme, the Carolingians tried to halt the process (for example by insisting on royal protection and church advocates); but, in the end, immune lands became part of church patrimony, islands of jurisdiction and public power unto themselves and thus truly feudal.[48]

A variant theory was argued in some twentieth-century German scholarship: in this view judicial power, *Gerichtsgewalt*, was not "public" but rather a subset of domestic power, *Hausherrliche Gewalt*, exercised by Germanic lords in general.[49] According to this argument, royal administration in effect embraced only small islands in a sea of aristocratic lord-

---

Marc Bloch, *Feudal Society*, trans. L. A. Manyon, 2 vols. (Chicago, 1961), 2:362, drawing on the tradition of Fustel de Coulanges. See, for example, Fustel de Coulanges, "Etude sur l'immunité," p. 249: "[One of two reasons to study Merovingian immunities] est qu'elle annonce et prépare le régime féodal des époques suivants."

46. Robert S. Hoyt and Stanley Chodorow, *Europe in the Middle Ages*, 3d ed. (New York, 1976), p. 217. Similarly Katherine Fischer Drew, "The Immunity in Carolingian Italy," *Speculum* 37 (1962): 182–97, relies on the assumption that the immunity is "associated with the development of Italian feudalism" (p. 182).

47. Maurice Kroell, *L'immunité franque* (Paris, 1910). Others making similar arguments: Emile Lesne, *Histoire de la propriété ecclésiastique en France*, 6 vols. (Lille, 1910), 1: 260–66, and Félix Senn, *L'institution des avoueries ecclésiastiques en France* (Paris, 1903).

48. For the Carolingian "moment," see Kroell, *L'immunité franque*, chap. 3, with the title "Subordination de la puissance immuniste au pouvoir royal."

49. For the argument and bibliography, see Schulze, *Grafschaftsverfassung*, pp. 337–39. Part of the argument, adopted by Schulze, relies on the assumption that in the early Middle Ages judicial immunity referred only to low justice ("die niedere Gerichtsbarkeit") (p. 337), here borrowing from Heinrich Brunner, *Deutsches Rechtsgeschichte*, ed. Claudius von Schwerin, vol. 2, 2d rev. ed. (Munich, 1928), § 95, pp. 382–404, esp. pp. 401–3; the same point had been made in the first edition (Leipzig, 1892), pp. 300–302. For the contrary view, see Léo Verriest, *Institutions médiévales. Introduction au corpus des records de coutumes et des lois de chefs-lieux de l'ancien comté de Hainaut*, vol. 1 of *Le Hainaut, Encyclopédie provinciale*, ed. Léon Losseau (Mons, 1946), esp. pp. 89–97, pointing out that Brunner's conclusions rely on extremely laconic sources.

ships. Immunities simply ratified the existing situation of "autogenous" jurisdictions.[50] Both the "public" and "domestic" views of judicial power, however different in outline, had in common the search for the origin of feudalism, the one finding it in the post-Carolingian age, the other seeing it already foreshadowed in the very fabric of the early Germanic polity.

Many historians thus viewed "the immunity" as the institutional ancestor of feudalism. Some also considered it necessary background to the Gregorian reform. In a sense, these views go together: *libertas ecclesiae*, the "liberty of the Church," meant freedom from outside, so-called feudal, control. Historians who concentrate on Church reform, however, tend to look at immunities from the other side, from the point of view of the Church's "liberty" rather than that of the king's "weakness." In Herbert Cowdrey's *The Cluniacs and the Gregorian Reform*, for example, immunities functioned as "the starting-point of the long quest by Frankish monasteries to seek freedom from the temporal claims of outside authorities."[51] They did so because, intentionally or not, they gave ballast to the idea that the Church was off-limits to the state.[52]

The issues of feudalism and eleventh-century church reform are of inestimable interest and importance; and, especially in the case of *libertas ecclesiae*, it is clear that old immunities and exemptions were read and interpreted as authoritative texts that spoke to contemporary, eleventh-century issues.[53] But it is fair to say that if we are interested in what im-

50. The term "autogenous immunity" was coined by Hermann Aubin, *Die Entstehung der Landeshoheit nach niederrheinischen Quellen* (Bonn, 1920; reprint, 1961), p. 223.

51. Herbert E. J. Cowdrey, *The Cluniacs and the Gregorian Reform* (Oxford, 1970), p. 9.

52. E.g., Émile Amann and Auguste Dumas, *L'Église au pouvoir des laïques (888–1057)*, vol. 7, *Histoire de l'Église*, ed. Augustin Fliche and Victor Martin (Paris, 1948), p. 341: "Il y avait plusieurs siècles qu'un mouvement tendait à émanciper les établissements monastiques de toute autorité séculière . . . les chartes d'immunité en étaient la principale manifestation." For the varying notions of "freedom of the Church" and its relationship to the state, see Szabó-Bechstein, *Libertas Ecclesiae*.

But historians agree that in the history of the Gregorian Reform, exemptions were even more important than immunities. See, for example, Jean-François Lemarignier, "L'exemption monastique et les origines de la réforme grégorienne," in *À Cluny, congrès scientifique. Fêtes et cérémonies liturgiques en l'honneur des saints Abbes Odon et Odilon, 9–11 juillet 1949* (Dijon, 1950), pp. 288–340; and in German scholarship, Willy Szaivert, "Die Entstehung und Entwicklung der Klosterexemtion bis zum Ausgang des 11. Jahrhunderts," *MIÖG* 59 (1951): 265–98. Exemptions are largely associated with grants from the pope (though, as we shall see, for a long time they were given out by bishops), and they led to the Gregorian reform (it is commonly thought) by the complementary mechanisms of enhancing papal power and weakening episcopal control. See Cowdrey, *Cluniacs and the Gregorian Reform*, pt. 1.

53. Indeed, one must add forged immunities as key instruments in the development of feudal claims.

munities meant in earlier periods, we ought to be on guard against seeing them as *leading* anywhere in particular, though we will certainly want
to discuss their anticipated and unanticipated historical consequences.

Only recently have historians begun to speak of immunities as part of
religious-political royal and episcopal policy at certain precise moments
in time. Eugen Ewig and Janet Nelson, for example, have explored the
policies of Queen Balthild (d. 680), linking together issues of politics,
church reform, and immunities.[54] Discussing immunities in this way, ex-
ploring how they fit into a particular context, leads to a focus fundamentally different from any we have seen in the other historiographical
schools. For all of the others are, we might say, linear, one immunity
paving the way for or leading to the next; whereas the contextual approach is multilateral, immunities connecting on one side, say, to a power
struggle with bishops, on another to a pious notion of Church liberty.

The contextual approach, adopted by the present book, means that one
must pick and choose examples: even for the early Middle Ages, there are
far too many immunities to begin to compass them all in a survey or even
in multiple volumes. Nor would this be particularly useful: if immunities
must be discussed in their contexts, the context must also make clear the
need to discuss the immunity. Above all, I have looked for "nodal" moments: first, where clusters of texts rather than sole charters exist; and
second, where immunities and exemptions seem to take on new meaning
or at least bear newly critical importance.

Immunities and exemptions were ways to construct space, define boundaries, prohibit entries. Until the tenth century, immunities were royal
documents alone: popes did not issue immunities, nor, at least not often,
did princes.[55] Exemptions, on the other hand, were issued by bishops,

---

54. Ewig, "Klosterpolitik," in Ewig, *Gallien*, 2:538–83; Janet L. Nelson, "Queens as Jezebels: Brunhild and Balthild in Merovingian History," in her *Politics and Ritual in Early Medieval Europe* (London, 1986), pp. 1–48. See further Alain Dierkens, "Prolégomènes à une
histoire des relations culturelles entre les îles britanniques et le continent pendant le Haut
Moyen Age. La diffusion du monachisme dit colombanien ou iro-franc dans quelques monastères de la région parisienne au VIIe siècle et la politique religieuse de la reine Bathilde,"
in Atsma, *La Neustrie* 2:371–94 at 388–93.

55. A point reiterated in Brühl, "Die merowingische Immunität," p. 28 and n. 7. Marculf
2:163–75, no. 1, presents a formula for founding a hospice or monastery by "anyone" (*qui
vult*)—presumably including non-royal lay people—which includes grants of both exemption and immunity, and this is precisely what is contained in Pardessus 2:280–83, no. 475
(709), where the donors stipulate (p. 283): "ut nullus judex vel pontifex de civitate, vel ex

popes, and (sometimes) kings. In both cases, we are clearly dealing with privileges that could be given out only by those in the highest strata of a highly stratified society. One way to understand this "power"—from a statist viewpoint so contrary to commonsense notions of coercion, influence, and exploitation—is to seek its counterpart in other cultures.

Tapu

About seven hundred years after Urban made his way across the Alps to France, the French explorer, J.-F. de Lapérouse, embarked on a far more ambitious voyage around the world.[56] Yet, like Urban, he was concerned about inviolability. When he brought his ship into port at Maui, he feared that the natives would rush on board. Then he hit upon a solution: "I didn't want to allow them to come aboard until the frigate was anchored and the sails were rolled up and secured. I told them that I was *taboo*, and this word, which I knew from English reports, had all the success that I expected."[57] This was no declaration of a sacred ban, but it was meant to have some of the same consequences.

The Polynesian term *tapu*, domesticated as *taboo*, entered European languages from the journals of Captain Cook. It was long a bedfellow of Western chauvinism, the "term of art" for describing prohibitions that seemed irrational, whether in Polynesia or in Europe itself.[58] The concept was grafted by Western writers onto the history of their own culture largely as the archaic set of "don'ts" from which civilized society had advanced.[59] By the twentieth century, anthropologists were using the word in a variety of ways, some of them irreconcilable.[60] In 1934 Margaret

---

ipsa parrochia Virdonense, in ipso monasterio nullam potestatem ad quaslibet redhibitiones aut requisitione exigendi . . . habeat potestatem ingrediendi: quia in ipso praedio, nostro proprio sumptu labore aedificavimus" [that no judge from the city or from the diocese of Verdun may have the right to enter the monastery to exact any renders or requisitions, because we built it on our property and at our own expense]. This is not an entry prohibition against the donors or their men; on the contrary!

56. Robert Borofsky and Alan Howard, "The Early Contact Period," in Howard and Borofsky, eds., *Developments in Polynesian Ethnology* (Honolulu, 1989), p. 252.

57. Jean-François de Lapérouse, *Voyage autour du monde sur l'Astrolabe et la Boussole (1785–1788)*, ed. Hélène Minguet (Paris, 1980), p. 86. See also Borofsky and Howard, "The Early Contact Period," pp. 241–75.

58. P. J. H. Kapteyn, "De sociogenese van het woord 'Taboe' in West-Europa of: De 'Edele Wilde' en de 18de eeuwse burgerij," *Sociologische Gids* 22 (1975): 414–26.

59. See the discussion in Franz Steiner, *Taboo* (1956; reprint, Middlesex, 1967), pp. 50–105.

60. E.g., Sigmund Freud, *Totem and Taboo: Resemblances between the Psychic Lives of Savages and Neurotics*, trans. A. A. Brill (New York, 1946) (originally published in 1913), where

Mead tried to establish order by setting down a simple and precise definition in the *Encyclopedia of the Social Sciences*: taboos were "a negative sanction, a prohibition whose infringement results in an automatic penalty without human or supernatural mediation."[61]

But the definition did not suit all. In 1956 Franz Steiner noted wryly that the Polynesians who whipped a girl for breaking a food taboo had clearly never read their Margaret Mead.[62] Others in the field were unsympathetic to the very enterprise of definition-hunting. Thus, Raymond Firth stressed that Tikopeans themselves refused to deal in abstract generalizations, insisting instead on contextualizing meanings through concrete examples.[63]

In the 1980s, fueled, it seems, by newly intense interest in gender studies and *tapu* as related to females and menstruation, anthropologists began to suggest definitions of the term once again.[64] There is now at least a clear consensus about what *tapu* does not mean: it means neither "sacred" nor "prohibited," and it is too wide to be compassed by the dyad "purity and danger." This time round, anthropologists are careful to test their definitions against the larger cultural context. It is clear, for example, that *tapu* cannot be discussed apart from *mana*.

---

taboos are prohibitions once imposed from without, then internalized by the tribe, and express both the desire to do what is prohibited and the fear of transgression; R. R. Marett, "Is Taboo a Negative Magic?" in *Anthropological Essays Presented to E. B. Tylor* (Oxford, 1907), pp. 219–34; Arnold van Gennep, *Tabou et Totémisme à Madagascar: Étude descriptive et théorique* (Paris, 1904), which, as its title implies, eschews simple definitions in favor of descriptions of usage, but nevertheless sees taboo as an "interdiction religieuse."

61. Margaret Mead, *Encyclopaedia of the Social Sciences*, 1934 ed., s.v. "Tabu." Her definition was adopted by Hutton Webster, *Taboo: A Sociological Study* (1942; reprint, New York, 1973).

62. Steiner, *Taboo*, p. 26.

63. Raymond Firth, "The Analysis of Mana: An Empirical Approach," *Journal of the Polynesian Society* 49 (1940): 483–510, reprinted in idem, *Tikopia Ritual and Belief* (Boston, 1967), pp. 174–94.

64. Nicholas Thomas, "Unstable Categories: *Tapu* and Gender in the Marquesas," *The Journal of Pacific History* 22 (1987): 123–38; Roger M. Keesing, "Conventional Metaphors and Anthropological Metaphysics: The Problematic of Cultural Translation," *Journal of Anthropological Research* 41 (1985): 201–18, esp. pp. 204–5; idem, "Rethinking Mana," *Journal of Anthropological Research* 40 (1984): 137–56. F. Allan Hanson, "Female Pollution in Polynesia?" *Journal of the Polynesian Society* 91 (1982): 335–81; idem, "Method in Semiotic Anthropology or How the Maori Latrine Means," in Hanson, ed., *Studies in Symbolism and Cultural Communication* (Lawrence, Kansas, 1982), pp. 74–89; and idem, "Polynesian Religions: An Overview," in *Encyclopedia of Religion* (1987), pp. 423–32; F. Allen Hanson and Louise Hanson, *Counterpoint in Maori Culture* (London, 1983); Michael P. Shirres, "Tapu," *The Journal of the Polynesian Society* 91 (1982): 29–51; Bradd Shore, "*Mana* and *Tapu*," in Howard and Borofsky, *Developments in Polynesian Ethnology*, pp. 137–73.

Mana is associated with power but always power manifested in some concrete way: in successful enterprises, abundant coconut groves, and the shining, corpulent chiefs who are said to have it. They get it from the gods, the source of all *mana*.

To follow the recent discussion by Bradd Shore: in Polynesian cosmology chiefs wrest generative power (*mana*) from the gods. Potentially destructive and polluting, their newly acquired *mana* is rendered lifegiving by rituals of binding and ordering. Bound *mana* is *tapu*, sacred and powerful because it in turn binds and orders. The chiefs have what Marshall Sahlins calls "personal" *tapu*, but there is another form of *tapu*, economic *tapu*, which is declared by chiefs as part of their control over native resources and productivity. A chief may declare a certain coconut grove *tapu*, for example, in order to protect it from premature harvest or to conserve resources for another occasion.

Being *tapu* is a burden: it is hard on the chief, who in fact is literally bound and immobilized, by thongs on his genitals, by feather cloaks, and by the corpulence he is obliged to suffer as a symbol of fertility. It is also a burden on the community, for a boat or coconut grove declared *tapu* is unavailable for use or exploitation, while other *tapus* enjoin specific, often laborious, tasks.[65]

The medieval West also esteemed power that was both bound and binding. Shackled power was implicit, for example, in certain medieval notions of Christian monasticism and rulership.[66] It was implicit as well in many immunities and exemptions: their very phrases—entry prohibitions and promises against meddling, whether in taxes (immunities) or ordinations (exemptions)—suggested self-restraint on the part of the issuer. In the case of the immunity of Urban II, where the pope was in no way restraining his *own* entry at Cluny, St. Peter's power to bind and loose (the threat of excommunication) was connected to the delimitation of a sanctified zone that could not be penetrated or defiled by violence.

In Polynesian society, the chief's ability to declare something *tapu* demonstrated his power, not only ritually and symbolically but also substantively, because in this way he controlled and channeled productive enterprises. Such control was, in turn, critical to the chiefly enterprise of goods

65. Raymond Firth, *We, the Tikopia: A Sociological Study of Kinship in Primitive Polynesia* (New York, 1936), p. 377, idem, *Economics of the New Zealand Maori* (Wellington, 1959), pp. 148–49.

66. See Barbara H. Rosenwein, *Rhinoceros Bound: Cluny in the Tenth Century* (Philadelphia, 1982), pp. 77–83; for binding the anger of kings and monks, see Barbara H. Rosenwein, ed., *Anger's Past: The Social Uses of an Emotion in the Middle Ages* (Ithaca, N.Y., 1997).

distribution, the major source of his earthly power, privilege, and prestige.[67] Medieval immunities offer parallels. Murray maintains that Merovingian immunities were used as instruments of exploitation and control, despite the fact that the land so designated was declared off-limits to royal agents: the kings used the immunists themselves to catch thieves, for example. Fouracre argues that immunities represented a convenient and efficient means for kings to fulfill their religious functions by directing cash resources to markets selling oil for church lamps. When *tuitio* or *defensio*—protection—was added to the formula of immunities under the Carolingians, royal control was considerably augmented, whether one follows Josef Semmler in thinking that royal protection transformed monasteries into royal properties, or one accepts Goffart's view that, on the contrary, it gave the monasteries certain guarantees against the alienation of their properties.[68]

One difference between areas declared "immune" and those declared *tapu*, though it does not seem essential, is the role of writing in such announcements. Polynesian chiefs did display signs to indicate that a certain area was *tapu*, but they did not describe and promulgate this declaration through written charters of any sort. A more important difference between immunity and *tapu*, however, was that the latter, while making resources for gifts available to the chief for distribution, could not itself be given out as a gift. By contrast, immunities were assimilated with other privileges and grants: they were presented to recipients, as part of (and sometimes indistinguishable from) the "necessary generosity" that characterized early medieval rulership.

Yet the whole scheme of social gift-giving observed, described, and abstracted by anthropologists since the time of Marcel Mauss depended on models from Polynesia.[69] If the two systems, *tapu* and gifts, were separate in the islands of the southern Pacific, why were they not separate in early medieval Europe? The answer appears to lie in notions of the divine and the ruler's relation to it. In the Polynesian view, the gods were capricious and often malevolent. Rulers were forced to wrest *mana* from them; they

67. Marshall D. Sahlins, *Social Stratification in Polynesia* (Seattle, Wash., 1958), p. 3.

68. Josef Semmler, "Traditio und Königsschutz. Studien zur Geschichte der königlichen monasteria," *ZRG* 76, *KA* 45 (1959): 1–33, at pp. 6–8; Walter Goffart, *The Le Mans Forgeries: A Chapter from the History of Church Property in the Ninth Century*, Harvard Historical Studies 76 (Cambridge, Mass., 1966), pp. 12–18, enumerating the various expectations that monasteries had from royal *defensio*, including, importantly, the "prerogative of the sworn inquest."

69. See Maurice Godelier, *L'énigme du don* (Paris, 1996), with excellent bibliography. I thank Dominique Iogna-Prat for calling my attention to this book.

never received it as a gift. Hence, *mana* bound and transformed into *tapu* was not understood as something that could or should be given out or distributed. From the Merovingian period to the eleventh century, Christian ideas about the ruler changed; one cannot suggest a simple formula with which to counter the Polynesian view. Yet it is clear that gift and counter-gift pervaded Christian ideas about human and divine relations in general and royal and divine relations in particular. The earliest immunity that is today extant in the original, issued by the Merovingian king Theuderic III in 688, begins by balancing God's gifts with a necessary counter-gift:

> Since divine piety has allowed us to come to legal age and to succeed to the throne of the kingdom of our ancestors, it is fitting and proper for us to think about the salvation of our soul. So let your diligence know that, for the salvation of our soul, we . . . have conceded the villa called Lagny-le-Sec . . . to the monastery of Saint-Denis . . . where the venerable Abbot Chaino presides together with his many groups of monks . . . to sing the praises of Christ.[70]

The certainties in this document about God, the king, the abbot, and the monks invite modern uncertainty: Why this complex of ideas and images about God's piety and human activity? And why connect them with an immunity, as the rest of the document proceeds to do?

70. *ChLA* 13:90, no. 570. See Appendix 1. Weighing "originals" against "genuine copies," Brühl, "Die merowingische Immunität," p. 32, suggests that too much emphasis has been placed on the former. But prudence dictates that originals be used wherever possible, especially now that we have, thanks to Hartmut Atsma and Jean Vezin, editors of the relevant volumes of the *ChLA*, Merovingian documents that have been reproduced more clearly (through spectacular photographical techniques) than they appear on the original parchment or papyrus.

PART I
Prohibitions

The first charters of medieval immunity and exemption were issued in the early seventh century, during the reign of the Merovingian King Dagobert (Chapter 3). Immunities were soon granted by both kings and queens; they contained a prohibition against the entry of state agents onto certain properties of privileged recipients for judicial and fiscal purposes. Exemptions were issued by bishops; they too contained an entry prohibition, but this time directed at the diocesan bishop himself regarding his monastic duties. In the course of the seventh century (Chapter 4), issuing such documents came to be considered essential to the well-being of the Church and kingdom.

Yet if immunities and exemptions emerged from Dagobert's court, they had long been aborning. During the late antique period, ideas about asylum, new sensitivities to the sacrosanctity of the altar, and increasing emphasis on the inviolability of the monastic enclosure were even more important than Roman immunities for the development of the medieval type (Chapter 1); and in the sixth century attempts to protect religious institutions, carried out with particular finesse by royal women, suggested ideas of exemption (Chapter 2). Although no charters of exemption existed as yet, Queen Radegund's convent of the Holy Cross effectively functioned as if it had such a privilege. We begin, then, in Chapter 1, with the long prelude to the seventh century.

1

Late Antique Traditions

A S F A R as we know, the *word* "immunity" was used for the first time in the kingdom of the Franks in 511 at the Council of Orléans, which met after the defeat of the Visigoths in Aquitaine. One canon, presumably concerned with distributing the property of the heretical Arian Church to the Catholic churches of the conqueror, had the king concede the land with immunity (*inmunitate concessa*). By this was meant (as the canon went on to say) that the taxes from these lands were not to go into the royal treasury but rather were to be put directly to use "for the repair of churches, the alms of the priests and the poor, and the redemption of captives."[1] The provision was reminiscent of the late Roman law that granted immunity to clerics and their men because the revenues would in any event be channeled to provide social services (as, for example, to "benefit the poor").

Roman Immunities

The Roman world knew of immunities; they were important legal privileges.[2] Indeed, the "free and immune cities" of the Roman republican and early imperial periods appear upon first glance to be possible prece-

---

1. Council of Orléans (511), c. 5, *Conc. Gall.*, p. 6.
2. The word "privilege" means a law that applies only to certain individuals or groups; etymologically it derives from *privus* (private) and *legis*, the genitive singular of *lex* (law). Throughout the ancient period and the Middle Ages, immunities were not "rights," though that is what they had become by the time of the writing of the U. S. Constitution.

dents for medieval immunities. Such, for example, were the "free and immune cities" (*civitates liberae et immunes*) of Africa, accorded this privilege because they deserted Carthage and sided with Rome during the Second Punic War.[3] There may have been quite a few of these cities if, as is possible, all "free" municipalities were also, by definition, immune.[4] The so-called *lex Antonia de Termessibus* of 71 B.C. set forth the privileges of one free and immune city: it was allowed to make its own laws and probably to hold its own courts; and it was exempt from the land tax that other cities had to pay to Rome.[5] Over a century ago Theodor Mommsen argued that provincial governors could not enter free cities "in [their] official capacity," and this has been accepted by subsequent historians.[6] But Mommsen's conclusion was based on a passage in Tacitus that described special treatment for Athens: the proconsul entered the city, but with only one lictor.[7] This is hardly an entry prohibition. Even if such prohibitions did exist, these cities could not constitute more than an intriguing parallel to medieval immunities, for municipal privileges eroded in the early Empire, and Diocletian's reforms at the end of the third century rendered distinctions between municipalities moot.[8] There can be no continuity between these immunities and those of the early Middle Ages.[9]

Late Antique immunities, however, are a different matter, and every commentator on the medieval institution must deal with them seriously.

3. See T. R. S. Broughton, *The Romanization of Africa Proconsularis* (Baltimore, 1929), p. 13 and p. 13 n. 4.

4. On the other hand, there is evidence that already in the second century B.C. immunity was separate from liberty. See A. N. Sherwin-White, *The Roman Citizenship*, 2d ed. (Oxford, 1973), p. 179.

5. See Frank Frost Abbott and Allan Chester Johnson, *Municipal Administration in the Roman Empire* (New York, 1968), pp. 40–43.

6. Theodor Mommsen, *Römisches Staatsrecht*, 3 vols., 3d ed. (Leipzig, 1887; reprint 1963), 3:689, and more generally pp. 655–93; and following him, Abbot and Johnson, *Municipal Administration*, p. 42.

7. Tacitus, *Annales* 2.53.

8. Sherwin-White, *Roman Citizenship*, pp. 186–89. See also Claude Lepelley, "Avant-propos. De la cité classique à la cité tardive: continuités et ruptures," in idem, ed., *La fin de la cité antique et le début de la cité médiévale de la fin du IIIe siècle à l'avènement de Charlemagne. Actes du colloque tenu à l'Université de Paris X-Nanterre les 1, 2 et 3 avril 1993* (Bari, 1996), pp. 7–10; idem, "La création de cités nouvelles en Afrique au Bas-Empire. Le cas de la *ciuitas Faustianensis*," in Yann Le Bohec, ed., *L'Afrique, la Gaule, la Religion à l'époque romaine. Mélanges à la mémoire de Marcel Le Glay*, Collection Latomus 226 (Brussels, 1994), pp. 288–99 at p. 291.

9. It is possible, however, that seventh-century scholars knew about these cities from lapidary references in ancient sources such as Pseudo-Caesar, *Bellum Africum* 7.1: "Leptim liberam civitatem et inmunem," or Pliny, *Historia naturalis* 5.23: "immune oppidum." The seventh-century hagiographer Jonas, for one, knew his Pliny. See Jonas, *Vita Columbani, Epistula*, ed. Bruno Krusch, MGH SRM 4: 63.

The precedents outlined by Maurice Kroell in 1910 may serve as the starting point of our discussion:

1. The late Empire had exemptions (*immunitates*) from extraordinary and burdensome services (*munera extraordinaria* and *sordida*). These were granted at certain times to favored categories of persons (such as senators) and corporate persons (such as the Catholic Church), while exemptions from ordinary taxes (*onera canonica*) were accorded to some imperial partisans.[10]

2. In the late Empire, "fiscal" property (that is, the imperial domain) was exempt from some dues and services.

3. At the same time, fiscal property was administered by special agents, known as procurators (*procuratores*), rather than by municipal or provincial governors.

4. The landed domains of great magnates of the Empire (*potentes*) enjoyed a *de facto* (but not *de jure*) exemption from imperial taxation and justice.[11]

Each of these topics is most fruitfully viewed through the lens of the *Codex Theodosianus*. During the reign of Theodosius II (408–50), the Code's composers gathered together and organized various imperial decrees published between 313 and 438. Their purpose was to find the "general laws" of the Empire; but they defined these broadly, as consisting of not only decrees that had originally been promulgated across all the provinces but also more particular directives that, in the eyes of the compilers, set forth principles that could be used in like cases elsewhere.[12] Nevertheless, since the Code was not a systematic exposition of principles but rather a collection of individual directives, some of which contradicted one another, it is impossible to speak of a coherent policy regarding any topic covered by the Code.[13]

The Theodosian Code used the word "immunity" and its variant forms for the privileges of topic (1) above: tax and service exemptions. For example, palace officials were immune from menial compulsory services. The same burdens were lifted from the shoulders of doctors, grammari-

---

10. The word *immunitas* in its original form meant "freedom from public burdens": *in* (not) + *munus* (service or duty). See Introduction, n.3.

11. Kroell, *L'immunité franque*, pp. 1–28.

12. For further discussion, see Jill Harries and Ian Wood, eds., *The Theodosian Code* (Ithaca, N.Y., 1993), pp. 5–6, 25–29.

13. See ibid, p. 96: "Behind the Code was a world of social fluidity and diversity, of tradition interacting with change and of complexities which could not be encompassed by 'general' rules. The contents of the Code provide details from the canvas but are an unreliable guide, in isolation, to the character of the picture as a whole."

ans, and other teachers of literature. Architects, mechanics, and geome-
tricians "rejoiced" in the immunities granted them for their skill and status (*immunitatibus gaudeant*), while other citizens were offered immunities
in lieu of compensation for services rendered, such as shipping grain to
Rome. Clerics were so privileged that they could ply the trade of merchants yet not pay the taxes all other merchants had to pay.[14] These immunities had a charitable purpose: "They [clerics and their men] shall by
no means be subject to the tax payments of tradesmen, since it is manifest
that the profits which they collect from stalls and workshops will benefit
the poor."[15]

These instances well illustrate how and to some extent why Roman imperial immunities were granted as favors, either to privileged classes of
persons or to special individuals. They marked the special, imperial status of the issuers; they indicated the favored status of the recipients; and
they revealed the categories of men that the late Roman state considered
fundamental to its very purpose and structure. Nor did they apply simply to the person of the recipient: they extended to a man's patrimony as
well. Just as late fourth-century churchmen, rhetoricians, and grammarians were legally free from sordid and onerous services, so were their
properties and the people on them:

> If any man is protected by Our law from the performance of such services,
> his patrimony shall not be subject to the duty of preparing meal, shall not
> assume the service of bread baking, shall render no service to the bread-
> making establishments, shall not furnish personal services and artisans;
> its responsibility for burning lime shall cease. Such patrimonies shall not
> be obligated to contribute boards or wood [etc.].[16]

These were lifetime guarantees. They were neither permanently attached
to the patrimony, nor did they exempt it from ordinary dues and taxes.

Exemptions from extraordinary or onerous services also applied directly to one type of property: the imperial "patrimony" or fisc, which
constituted the estates of the imperial treasury.[17] Farmers on fiscal land
were thus always spared "extraordinary burdens," though they certainly
paid taxes.[18] These moneys were normally collected by the procurators

14. On palace officials: CT 6.35.1. Doctors, grammarians, teachers: CT 13.3.1. Architects
and mechanics: CT 13.4.3. Immunities to those who shipped grain to Rome: CT 13.5.32. For
clerics plying the trade of merchants: CT 13.1.11.
15. CT 16.2.10.
16. CT 11.16.18.
17. CT 11.16.1 (immunity of fiscal land in Africa from *extraordinariis oneribus*); CT 11.16.2
(the same in Italy).
18. E.g. CT 11.16.1; and see the discussion in Kroell, *L'immunité franque*, pp. 4–6.

rather than by members of the ordinary municipal and provincial administration.[19] In this sense farmers on fiscal lands were "immune" from provincial governors. But the *word* "immunity" was not used to refer to the fisc's tax exemption or special administration.

When fiscal land was granted out, even ordinary taxes were sometimes abrogated, and here the word "immunity" was used. For example, bare and abandoned tracts were given to cultivators with a *triennii immunitate*—a three-year exemption from the land tax while the farmers coaxed the land back into production.[20] When Constantine's veterans received some vacant fiscal land as a sort of retirement package, they were granted perpetual immunity from the land tax.[21]

Already in the late Empire, then, certain properties pertaining to the state were marked off from others, both by their administration and by their special tax status. Frankish immunities, which also involved the royal fisc, clearly grew out of these precedents in some way. Indeed, some historians, such as Élisabeth Magnou-Nortier, believe that they represent the survival of imperial immunities.

Nevertheless, there are many distinctions between Frankish royal and Roman imperial immunities. Above all, imperial immunities for fiscal properties did not contain entry prohibitions.[22] Moreover, the procurator was not granted the land that he administered. He was not in the position of, say, the abbot of a monastery who received a charter of immunity—however much one might argue that abbots were the agents of Frankish kings. Moreover, it is noteworthy that the special status of the fisc—the fact that it was administered by a procurator rather than a municipal governor—was not marked in Roman sources by the term "immunity." Nor did the fisc become an "immunity" when the procurator took on unusual judicial responsibilities within it, a development that can be traced, in any event, only by using the late (sixth-century) evidence from the Justinian Code. But by that time, immunities were already undergoing an autonomous development in the Frankish world.

There remains the Roman precedent of *de facto* immunities: large domains administered by extremely rich landowners and their agents, without any significant interference by imperial agents.[23] Insofar as this situation really obtained, that is, insofar as it was not negotiated, recognized, obfuscated, or contested, it had nothing whatever to do with early me-

---

19. For procurators of the imperial domain, see *CT* 10.1.17.
20. *CT* 5.11.8.
21. *CT* 7.20.3.
22. But see Goffart, "Old and New," for more subtle differences.
23. See the critique of this view in Fouracre, "Eternal Light," pp. 62–67.

dieval immunities *per se*, which always involved (according to the charters that recorded them) decisions, declarations of mutual interest, and
meetings of minds between kings and their recipients.

Late imperial immunities constitute a fossil record. Some of their elements were passed along to the early Middle Ages. But they should not
be confused with the medieval species.

Episcopal Powers

Unlike immunities, there were no late antique "exemptions," or, to be
faithful to the original Latin, "liberties."[24] On the contrary, the late Empire saw the attempt—admittedly slow and uneven—to establish the
"normal" powers of the diocesan bishop. Only after these powers had
been established would exemptions—in effect reactions against local
episcopal powers—take shape. Although we shall see in Chapter 2 that
ideas later associated with exemptions may be glimpsed as early as the
sixth century, the first clear documents of exemption come from the seventh century.

In order to understand exemptions, it would be good to know the nature of the powers of the diocesan bishop in Late Antiquity. Unfortunately, the canons of the early Church are nothing like the systematic
canonical collections that began to be written, with papal oversight, in
the eleventh century. Early church canons are simply summaries of decisions made at various church councils. They are laconic and sometimes
evasive and contradictory. Above all, they are bound to particular circumstances and contexts that make mining them for "church law" particularly problematic.

One thing is clear: the fathers who assembled for the Council of Chalcedon in 451 attempted for the first time to define the relationship between the bishop and the monk.[25] Three canons are pertinent:

24. See Introduction, n. 5.

25. Most modern commentators of exemption start with the Council of Chalcedon. See
Eugen Ewig, "Beobachtungen zu den Klosterprivilegien des 7. und frühen 8. Jahrhunderts,"
in Ewig, *Gallien*, 2:411–26 at p. 411; Terence P. McLaughlin, *Le très ancien droit monastique de
l'Occident* (Poitiers, 1935), pp. 130–36. Wilhelm Schwarz, "Jurisdicio und Condicio. Eine
Untersuchung zu den Privilegia libertatis der Klöster," *ZRG KA* 45 (1959): 34–98, begins
with an obscure case of possible exemption (he soon disabuses us of the possibility) at Beth-
lehem; but he soon arrives at Chalcedon (pp. 42–45), with, however, a rather different view
than Ewig or McLaughlin, since he emphasizes the restraint rather than extent of episcopal
power inherent in Chalcedon's canons.

Can. 4: No one shall build or establish a monastery or oratory without the knowledge of the bishop of the city. The monks of each city or region shall be subject to the bishop. Let them love quiet, be intent only on fasting and prayer, persevering in the place where they have renounced the world. Nor should they be involved in ecclesiastical or worldly business nor be troubled in any way to leave their own monasteries except perhaps if it is demanded by the bishop of the city on account of necessity. . . . It is indeed the duty of the bishop of the city to exercise appropriate care over the monasteries.[26]

To which must be added canon 8:

Let the clerics who are placed in poorhouses or ordained in monasteries and the basilicas of the martyrs persevere under the power of the bishops of each city, according to the traditions of the holy fathers; nor let them be sundered from their bishop through disobedience.[27]

And finally canon 24:

Once monasteries have been dedicated by the will of the bishop, they are to remain monasteries in perpetuity; and the property that belongs to them is to be kept intact for the monastery; nor may they thereafter become secular houses.[28]

The general thrust of these canons was to subject the monasteries to the bishops.[29] The chief point, expressed in canon 4, was that monks should

---

26. *Canones chalcedonenses* c. 4 in Mansi 7, cols. 374–75: "Placuit nullum quidem usque aedificare aut constituere monasterium, vel oratorii domum, p[r]aeter conscientiam civitatis episcopi, Monachos vero per unamquamque civitatem aut regionem subjectos esse episcopo, et quietem diligere, et intentos esse tantummodo jejunio et orationi, in locis in quibus renunciaverunt saeculo, permanentes: nec ecclesiasticis vero, nec saecularibus negotiis communicent, vel in aliquo sint molesti, propria monasteria deserentes, nisi forte his praecipiatur propter opus necessarium ab episcopo civitatis . . . Verumtamen episcopum convenit civitatis, competentem monasteriorum providentiam gerere." Mansi's Latin translations were made and circulated in the West by about 500; on this point see Schwarz, "Jurisdicio und Condicio," p. 45.

27. Mansi c. 8, col. 375: "Clerici qui praeficiuntur ptochodochiis, et qui ordinantur in monasteriis et basilicis martyrum, sub episcoporum qui in unaquaque civitate sunt, secundum sanctorum patrum traditiones, potestate permaneant, nec per contumaciam ab episcopo suo dissiliant."

28. Mansi c. 24, col. 380: "Quae semel ex voluntate episcopi dedicata sunt monasteria, perpetuo manere monasteria, et res quae ad ea pertinent, monasterio reservari, nec posse ea ultra fieri saecularia habitacula."

29. Canon 8 has been variously interpreted. The first sentence may be understood as saying that the bishop has power (*potestas*) over only the clerical or "ordained" inhabitants of the monastery: see Ewig, "Beobachtungen zu den Klosterprivilegien," in Ewig, *Gallien*, 2:411. McLaughlin, *Le très ancien droit*, p. 131, and Lemarignier, *Étude sur les privileges d'ex-*

attend to otherworldly matters while the bishop attended to the *providentia*, or general welfare, of the monastery.

What rights and obligations were involved in this welfare? Much later, in the twelfth century, canon lawyers would define two categories to encompass the various aspects of episcopal power over the monastery: *ordinatio* and *jurisdictio*. *Ordinatio* referred to a whole series of rights and duties, ranging from ordaining the monks and clerics and blessing the abbot to consecrating the holy chrism and oil, churches, and altars. Part of *ordinatio* included the bishop's right and duty to provide the holy oil for the monastery and to perform the various consecrations there. The importance of these duties can hardly be overestimated: in effect, they made possible the liturgical life, the very *raison d'être* of the monastic round. We have already seen in the Introduction how seriously the monks of Cluny and the pope took the consecrations of the altars, consecrations which suddenly blossomed forth to encompass an eight-kilometer circle of sacred space.

The second category of the bishop's role was his "jurisdiction."[30] Again as defined much later, it included receiving oaths of obedience from all clerics and abbots in the diocese and the right to censure or even excommunicate the members of a religious community, depose its abbot, and interdict its services. The bishop guaranteed his control (or from another point of view, carried out his duty) through regular visitations, during which *dona* (payments) were levied on the monks.

We can tease out some aspects of episcopal practice in Late Antiquity without recourse to such late canon law.[31] The bishop was involved in monastic discipline, since the Council of Chalcedon linked the quiet and

---

emption, p. 1, however, think that the monastic subjection to the bishop was total. This latter view does seem pertinent in light of the next sentence of canon 8 (Mansi 7, col. 375): "Qui vero audent evertere hujusmodi formam quoquo modo, nec proprio subjiciuntur episcopo; si quidem clerici sunt, canonum correptionibus subjacebunt si vero laici vel monachi fuerint, communione priventur."

30. See Ludwig Falkenstein, *La papauté et les abbayes françaises aux XIᵉ et XIIᵉ siècles. Exemption et protection apostolique*, Bibliothèque de l'École des Hautes Études 336 (Paris, 1997). I thank Jean-Loup Lemaître for generously allowing me to see this work prior to its publication. Schwarz, "Jurisdicio und Condicio," however, prefers to *jurisdictio* the word *condicio*, which he defines essentially as taxes owed to the bishop. In his view (p. 41), early "exemptions" were simply freedom from these taxes, not from jurisdiction.

31. For a systematic survey of the provisions of early Gallican councils that treated episcopal oversight of monasteries, see R. Laprat, "Les rapports de Saint Colomban et de la Gaule franque aux VIᵉ et VIIᵉ siècles," in *Mélanges colombaniens. Actes du Congrès international de Luxeuil, 20–23 juillet 1950* (Paris, 1951), pp. 119–41, here at pp. 132–33.

prayers of the monks to episcopal oversight. The same council grounded the foundation, erection, and preservation of each monastery on the will of the bishop; and it implied in the next breath that he would also guarantee the integrity and proper use of monastic property. Gallican church councils emphasized episcopal control over the abbot. At the Council of Orléans (511) the fathers mandated that "the abbots, out of religious humility, be subject to the authority of the bishops; and if they do anything contrary to the Rule, let them be corrected by the bishops."[32] Episcopal supervision could be minute: at the Council of Épaone (517), for example, the abbot was forbidden to sell anything—while at Orléans (511) he was forbidden to solicit benefices—without his bishop's permission.[33] The Fifth Council of Arles (554) reflected Chalcedon, putting monastic discipline itself in the hands of the bishops: "Let monasteries and monastic discipline pertain to the bishop in whose diocese they are established."[34] A nearly contemporary Italian document, however, the Benedictine Rule, listed the diocesan bishop as only one among several outsiders—the others were "abbots or Christians in the area"—who were to intervene should the monks elect a wicked abbot to rule them: "They must block the success of this wicked conspiracy, and set a worthy steward in charge of God's house."[35]

We can also approach the question of episcopal power in Late Antiquity by ascertaining which matters were addressed in charters of exemption when they began to appear in the seventh century. These reveal—by repudiating them!—elements of episcopal power that were current when they were drawn up. Eugen Ewig has defined two groups of such charters. One group, containing very extensive liberties, he called the "grosse Freiheit"—the "big exemption." The second group, slightly less generous in granting freedoms, he dubbed the "kleine Freiheit"—the "little exemption." The "big exemption" guaranteed six liberties:

1. Freedom from the bishop or his agent "usurping or diminishing" the property of the monastery in any way.

---

32. Council of Orléans (511), c. 19, *Conc. Gall.*, p. 10: "Abbates pro humilitate religionis in episcoporum potestate consistant et, si quid extra regolam fecerint, ab episcopis conrigantur."

33. Council of Orléans, c. 7, *Conc. Gall.*, p. 7; Council of Épaone, c. 8, ibid., p. 26.

34. Council of Arles (554), c. 2, *Conc. Gall.*, p. 171: "Vt monastheria uel monachorum disciplina ad eum pertineant episcopum, in cuius sunt terretorio constituta."

35. *RB*, c. 64, pp. 280–81.

2. The right of the monks to choose their own abbot and install him.
3. The free choice of which bishop (*any* bishop, not necessarily the diocesan bishop) would perform the blessings, consecrations, and/or ordinations at the monastery.
4. Exemption from the diocesan bishop's power of jurisdiction and ordination and the dues connected with this power.
5. An entry prohibition: the diocesan bishop could not enter the monastery without the invitation of the abbot; and even if invited, he could not ask for the dues customary during visitations.
6. The right of the abbot alone to discipline the monks. This was the right of *correctio*.[36]

The only difference between this "big" and a "little" exemption involves the third provision. In the "little exemption" the local diocesan bishop *retained* the prerogative to bless the altar and prepare the holy oil each year, though he could not ask for recompense.

Restating these provisions in terms of episcopal *power*—our purpose here—we may say that the pre-seventh-century diocesan bishop normally or at least often (1) had control over the monastic property in his diocese; (2) chose the abbot and installed him; (3) did the blessings and ordinations at the monastery; (4) collected a tax for his services; (5) entered the monastery for regular visitations and collected a tax for that; and (6) corrected the monks if they strayed from the path of right discipline.

Medieval exemptions had no late antique precursors. Exemptions were granted only later, in the seventh century, when the powers of the diocesan bishop came to be seen as impediments to rather than guarantors of monastic independence and integrity.

Sacrosanct Things

In the late Empire three objects or things were already considered sacrosanct, that is, sacred and inviolable.[37] These were churches, altars, and—this was just beginning—certain other enclosures. Let us consider each

---

36. Adapted from Ewig, "Beobachtungen zu den Klosterprivilegien," in Ewig, *Gallien*, 2:418.

37. Anne Ducloux, *"Ad ecclesiam confugere." Naissance du droit d'asile dans les églises (IVe— milieu du Ve s.)* (Paris, 1994), p. 31: "*sacrosanctitas*, qui signifie à la fois sacrosainteté et inviolabilité."

briefly, for the notions of sacred power and space associated with these things made up part of the matrix in which medieval immunities and exemptions took root.

Churches

In the late Empire asylum and immunity were entirely separate concepts. Nevertheless, the law of asylum was an important precedent for later immunities because it prohibited state agents from entering church precincts to apprehend a refugee. Already over a half-century ago, Timbal Duclaux de Martin traced the development of asylum, discovering its origins not in practices associated with pagan temples or shrines, nor in Jewish traditions, but rather in the demands of the Christian Church as it came to define itself in the Roman Empire.[38] Asylum was linked to two episcopal duties: intercession and the administration of penance.[39] The bishops in effect were part of a long series of Roman intercessors—among whom were parents, patrons, friends, and "holy men" outside the hierarchy—whom accused people and criminals beseeched to appeal to the public authorities for clemency. The justification for episcopal appeal was above all to give the criminal time to do penance. In the fourth century, however, episcopal appeals carried no legal weight. Indeed, the Theodosian Code suggests a wholesale reaction at the imperial level *against* the movement toward asylum which had been gathering steam at fourth-century church councils. Consider a constitution of 392: "If public debtors should suppose that they may take refuge in the churches, they shall either be dragged out of their hiding places at once or payment of their debts shall be exacted from the bishops who . . . harbored them."[40]

In the fifth century imperial attitudes changed. A constitution of 419 decreed that "persons who flee for sanctuary to the churches shall be safe within fifty paces outside the doors."[41] And in 431 a constitution allowed "people who were afraid" to find protection in church buildings, not only at the altars and in the oratories but also in the walled-off quarters

---

38. Rights of asylum for temples and shrines were not adopted by the Roman conquerors of the Greek world. Yet it is undeniable that there are striking similarities between, for example, immunities and a law of the Ptolemy Alexander I (95 B.C.), which, as paraphrased by Ducloux (ibid., p. 34 n. 1), "délimite-t-elle avec précision le territoire du temple sur lequel les fonctionnaires royaux ne peuvent entrer pour poursuivre un contribuable ou un justiciable."

39. Pierre Timbal Duclaux de Martin, *Le Droit d'Asile* (Paris, 1939).

40. *CT* 9.45.1.

41. *Constitutiones Sirmondianae* 13, in *CT*. A "pace" was equal to five Roman feet.

that included the priests' cells, houses, gardens, baths, and so on. The seeker of sanctuary had to be unarmed; he was obliged to trust to the protection (*tuitio*) of the designated spaces within the ecclesiastical enclosures (*ecclesiasticis saeptis*). If he arrived with arms and refused the clergy's demands to give them up, then the authorities (including the bishops) were to order armed men to eject him from the church precincts. But if he were unarmed, the authorities could not enter.[42]

Anne Ducloux has asked the key question. Why did imperial attitudes toward asylum change? Why did Roman emperors, so hostile to any relaxation of punishment that they had long ago eradicated the asylum once enjoyed by Greek temples, change their tune in the case of Christian churches? Her answer is that the emperors were forced to bow to popular practice. Already in 343 or 344, the canons of the Council of Sardis had spoken about those who "flee to the mercy of the church." The phrase implies that the practice was in fact widespread by then, though it was not recognized in law. The imperial constitutions at the end of the fourth century, such as the one negating the asylum rights of debtors, reveal that some earlier emperors had begun to tolerate the custom.[43] At the same time religious rhetoric intensified. By the last decade of the fourth century, its discourse was no longer about the duties of bishops or the misery of criminals but the power of God, whose miracles proclaimed the divine right of asylum.[44] In the first two decades of the next century, state authorities showed themselves reluctant to seize fugitives within a church.[45] Their inaction forced the issue: in 419 "the time had come for the legislator to decide officially whether churches were places where earthly law was suspended."[46] This was the context for the first positive law of asylum, promulgated at Ravenna in 419 for the western half of the Empire. As we have seen, it extended the area of protected space to fifty paces, and it ameliorated the misery of the refugees by allowing them to breathe the "open air." Above all, it recognized the violation of the church's sanctity (*sanctitas*) as a sacrilege (*sacrilegii crimen*).

---

42. *CT* 9.45.4.

43. Ducloux, *Ad ecclesiam confugere*, p. 59. In her account, the laws of 397 and 398, promulgated under the baneful influence of Eutropius and denying asylum to Jews and many others, were quickly negated after Eutropius's downfall. Even so, they passed into the Theodosian Code as 9.45.2 and 9.45.3, to which should be added 9.40.16, where clerics and monks were forbidden to harbor (*tenere*) criminals.

44. Ducloux, *Ad ecclesiam confugere*, pp. 86–103.

45. Ibid., p. 182.

46. Ibid., p. 163.

Ducloux thus has placed the curious procession of laws in the section of the Theodosian Code labeled 9.45—constitutions pertaining to "those persons who flee for sanctuary to the churches"—into their proper historical context. She has explained the great shift that is palpable between the first three constitutions in that section—constitutions that *denied* the rights of sanctuary to debtors, Jews, and finally (in 398), to just about everyone—and the fourth constitution, promulgated in 431, which granted asylum to all.

Yet the evidence remains problematic if we seek to understand the long-term impact of these constitutions on the West. There are in fact two great monuments from the "turn-around": the constitutions of November 21, 419, and of March 23, 431. They may not have been as decisive as they seem.

The constitution of 419 was not collected in the Theodosian Code. Was it omitted by chance—the compilers of the Code not knowing about it— or by choice? These kinds of questions are matters of hot debate today.[47] Let us simply be content with pointing out that this monument of the "shift" shows up in the so-called Sirmondian Constitutions. This, like the Theodosian Code, was a collection of Roman laws; but the latest research demonstrates that it was neither imperial nor late antique. Indeed, the best guess is that the Sirmondian Constitutions was compiled in the Frankish kingdom during the Merovingian period, most likely in the early 580s.[48] Thus, delimiting the perimeter of the inviolable church to fifty paces may have been a matter of law in 419, but it was not a preoccupation of the later Empire.[49] The idea made much more sense in the late sixth century, as we shall see in Chapter 2.

The Constitution of 431 seems easier to deal with. Initially it was promulgated for the eastern half of the Empire, but its inclusion in the Theo-

47. They are posed by John Matthews, "The Making of the Text," in Harries and Wood, *Theodosian Code*, p. 32: *his* answer is that missing laws simply could not be found; but Boudewijn Sirks, "The Sources of the Code," ibid., pp. 57–58 and 63, thinks that the laws were deliberately left out, normally because they were no longer valid. But this would mean that when the *CT* was issued the restrictions on asylum from the late fourth century were still in effect.

48. Mark Vessey, "The Origins of the *Collectio Sirmondiana*," in Harries and Wood, *Theodosian Code*, pp. 178–99.

49. Not a preoccupation; but nevertheless, in the *Pactus pro tenore pacis* (511–58), c. 14, MGH Cap. reg. Fr. 1:6, thought was given to the thief who might flee for sanctuary to a church that did not have an *atrium*, or walled-off space. In that case, the area of asylum was to be a square equal to an *aripennis* on each side, namely, about 120 feet, or about half the area of asylum envisioned by the constitution of 419.

dosian Code elevated it to a "general law," applicable to the western half as well. Nevertheless, it was concerned not so much with the right of asylum as such as with the sacrosanctity of the altar.

The Altar

The Constitution of 431 was the first ever to mention the altar; moreover it was unself-consciously written to guarantee the altar's purity. The perimeters of sanctuary were here extended not simply to give fugitives a merciful breath of fresh air; the aim was to keep religious things unpolluted:

> We grant this extent of space for this purpose, namely, that it may not be permitted that any fugitive remain or eat or sleep or spend the night in the very temple of God or on the sacrosanct altars.

And later the point was reiterated even more strongly:

> Hereafter if any persons should flee . . . to the most holy temple of God or to its sacrosanct altar . . . they shall be prevented by the clerics themselves, without any injury to such persons, from sleeping or from taking any food at all within the temple or at the altar. . . . If the fugitive should not agree to these restrictions and should not obey them, reverence for religion must be preferred to humanity, and reckless lawlessness must be driven from these holy places to those that We have mentioned [namely, the other spaces where the refugee could live].

In the Frankish kingdom, these ideas would only later, in the sixth century, be echoed by church councils. The Council of Tours of 567, for example, emphasized the sanctity of the eucharistic sacrifice and feared its defilement by the laity: "At vigils as well as at Mass, let the laity not be permitted to get close to the altar where the holy mysteries are celebrated and mingle with the clergy. Let the space delimited by the chancel toward the altar be open only to the choir of clergy who chant the psalms."[50]
But here we are getting ahead of our story.

50. Council of Tours, c. 4, *Conc. Gall.*, p. 178. In earlier councils the concern was to ensure that the laity not leave the church before the completion of Mass, e.g., at the Council of Orléans (538), c. 32, ibid., pp. 125–26. Archeological evidence supplements textual by revealing the partitions that were erected between laity and clergy officiating at the altar. In the fifth or sixth century, for example, the grand episcopal complex at Geneva included two cathedrals just a few meters away from one another, each constructed with barriers that separated the space around the altar from the rest of the church. See Charles Bonnet, *Les fouilles de l'ancien groupe épiscopal de Genève (1976–1993)* (Geneva, 1993), esp. drawings on pp. 38–39. I thank Professor Bonnet for a splendid guided tour of the complex.

Holy Enclosures

Holy churches and sacrosanct altars were thus both protective and protected in the late Empire. The same was coming to be true for monastic enclosures.

The nuns at Arles practiced the strict enclosure handed down from Lérins via the *Rule for Nuns* of Caesarius of Arles (470–542):

> Above all [says the Rule of Caesarius], to guard your reputation, do not allow any man to enter in the inner precincts [*secreta parte*] of the monastery and the oratories, except for the bishops and the *provisor* [the man who attends to the monastery's physical concerns] as well as the priest . . . [etc.] who, in view of their age and [style of] life, may celebrate Mass from time to time.[51]

Here men were barred. Elsewhere women were the polluters. Gregory of Tours (538–94) tells approvingly of a woman struck dead because she dared to cross "the sacred threshold" to see the pillar of St. Symeon. "And this was quite enough for the people to ensure that no other women would attempt the same thing, since each saw that the worst punishment was inflicted on that woman."[52]

In male monasteries influenced by Lérins, women were not allowed entry. Saint Romain, founder of Condat and other houses in the Jura mountains (today Switzerland), did not want to be buried in any of his monasteries because, as Gregory reported, "I do not want to have my tomb in a monastery, to which access is closed off to women."[53]

But these are Gregory's stories, and Gregory was a sixth-century man living in Frankish Gaul. It is time to follow him there.

---

51. Caesarius of Arles, *Règle des vierges* 33.36, in Caesarius of Arles, *Oeuvres monastiques*, SC 345 (Paris, 1988), p. 219.

52. Gregory of Tours, *Liber in Gloria Confessorum*, c. 26, MGH SRM 1, pt. 2, p. 764 (2d ed., p. 314).

53. Gregory of Tours, *Liber Vitae Patrum*, c. 1 (6), MGH SRM 1, pt. 2, p. 667 (2d ed., p. 217): "Non potest fieri, ut ego in monasterio sepulchrum habeam, a quo mulierum accessus arcetur."

2

Entry and Encroachment

THROUGHOUT THE sixth century, Frankish church councils protested against violators of church property. For example, King Childebert I—scion of the first dynasty of Frankish kings, the Merovingians—called a grand meeting at Orléans in 549 (see Genealogy 1 and Map 1). The fifty bishops who served as signatories to the acts of the council prohibited any person from retaining, alienating, or taking away any of the property of churches, monasteries, or hospices that the church had received in alms: "and if anyone should do this, let him be locked out beyond the boundaries of the church."

"Slayers of the Poor"

The Council of Orléans, like many other Merovingian councils, had a name for someone acting like this: he was a "slayer of the poor" (*necator pauperum*).[1] Some councils not only vilified this "invader" but suggested

---

1. Council of Orléans (549), c. 13, *Conc. Gall.*, p. 152: "Quod quisque fecerit, tanquam necator pauperum . . . ab ecclesiae liminibus excludatur." For this and other Gallican councils, consult Odette Pontal, *Histoire des conciles mérovingiens* (Paris, 1989). The phrase *necator pauperum* was probably borrowed from the Visigothic Council of Agde of 506, c. 4 in *Concilia Galliae A.314–A.506*, ed. Charles Munier, CCSL 148 (Turnhout, 1963), p. 194; see also Charles De Clercq, *La législation religieuse franque de Clovis à Charlemagne. Étude sur les actes de Conciles et les capitulaires, les statuts diocésains et les règles monastiques, 507–814* (Louvain, 1936), p. 34. The phrase "necator pauperum" has a biblical "feel," but its closest analogue appears to be Isaias 3:14: "Vos enim depasti estis vineam, Et rapina pauperis in domo vestra."

GENEALOGY 1. Sixth-Century Merovingian Kings and Queens

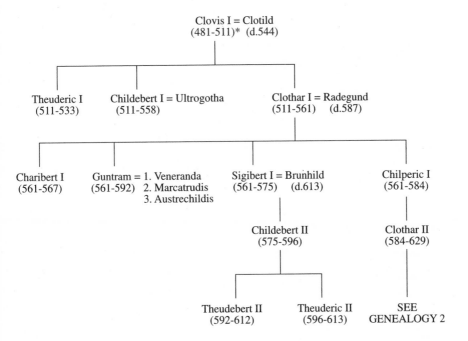

ways to counter him. In 567, for example, the Council of Tours outlined a
ritual procedure to be used against those who persisted in confiscating
church lands: there was to be a convocation of "all the abbots and priests
and clerics who live off of the stipends of their own property; and, as we
have no other arms, let Psalm 108 be chanted at the slayer of the poor
(who invades the property of the church) by the choir of clerics protected
by the help of Christ, so that the curse which came upon Judas may come
upon him."[2]

The invader was not always an outsider. When in 549 the fathers at the
Council of Orléans considered the case of the hospice founded at Lyon by
Childebert I and his wife, Queen Ultrogotha, they accused not just any-

---

2. Council of Tours, c. 25, *Conc. Gall.*, pp. 192–93: "conueniant omnis omnino una coni-
uentia simul cum nostris abbatibus ac presbyteris uel clero, qui stipendiis ex ipso alimento
pascuntur, et, quia arma nobis non sunt altera, auxiliante Christo circumsepto clericali
choro necaturi pauperum, qui res peruadit ecclesiae, psalmos cviii dicatur, ut ueniat super
eum illa maledictio, quae super Iudam uenit." On monastic maledictions such as this, see
Lester K. Little, *Benedictine Maledictions: Liturgical Cursing in Romanesque France* (Ithaca, N.Y.,
1993), esp. p. 23, on the significance of Ps. 108, "perhaps the most maledictory of all psalms."

MAP 1. The Merovingian Kingdoms in the Sixth Century

one but rather, pointedly, the bishop of Lyon himself: "Let the bishop of the church of Lyon not revoke at any time [any of the donations conferred on the hospice] for himself or transfer them to the authority of his church."[3]

Sometimes the *necatores pauperum* were simple clerics: "Let clerics not be allowed to let the property which they received in usufruct from their bishop to deteriorate. If they do this: if he is a junior, let him be corrected by discipline; but if he is senior, let him be treated like a slayer of the poor."[4]

At a council probably convened at Valence in 583–85, these ideas were explicitly connected to the abuse of both royal and ecclesiastical power. King Guntram had called the council to confirm gifts given to the monasteries of Saint-Marcel of Chalon and Saint-Symphorian at Autun: "Let neither *the bishops* of these places nor *the royal power* at any future time presume of their own will to diminish or take away anything. But if anyone presumes to violate or take [anything] away at any time, let him be punished like a slayer of the poor, with the perpetual anathema of divine judgment."[5] Already here, then, limits on royal and episcopal encroachment were in the wind.[6] The calling of the Council of Valence was itself a

3. Council of Orléans (549), c. 15, *Conc. Gall.*, p. 153: "nihil exinde ad se quolibet tempore antestis ecclesiae Lugdunensis reuocet aut ad ius ecclesiae transferat." The Council of Orléans of 538, c. 20, *Conc. Gall.*, pp. 121–22, had already addressed the issue of the bishop's jurisdiction over the property of his priests. On this point see De Clercq, *La législation religieuse*, pp. 24–25, 97–99; and, on the Council of Orléans of 549, ibid., pp. 31–34.

4. Council of Arles (554), c. 6, *Conc. Gall.*, p. 172: "Vt cliricis non liceat facultates, quas ab episcopo in uso accepiunt, deteriorare. Quod si fecerint, si iunior fuerit, disciplina corrigatur, si uero senior, ut necatur pauperum habeatur."

5. Council of Valence, *Conc. Gall.*, p. 235: "neque episcopi locorum neque potestas regia quocunque tempore successura de eorum uoluntate quicquam minorare aut auferre praesumat. Quod si quis hoc quocunque tempore temerare aut auferre praesumpserit, ueluti necator pauperum anathemate perpetuo iudicii diuini plectatur" (emphasis in translation is mine).

6. Indeed, it is possible that already in the sixth century a king had issued an entry prohibition for state agents gathering fiscal dues. The evidence is in the *Praeceptio*, c. 11, MGH Cap. reg. Fr. 1:19, issued by a King Clothar. If issued by Clothar II, as has been the prevailing view until recently, it underlines the importance of entry prohibitions for that seventh-century king (see Chapter 3). But if issued by Clothar I when he reigned as sole king (558–61), as argued by Ingrid Woll, *Untersuchungen zu Überlieferung und Eigenart der merowingischen Kapitularien*, Freiburger Beiträge zur mittelalterlichen Geschichte. Studien und Texte herausgegeben von Hubert Mordek 6 (Frankfurt, 1995), pp. 17–29, it shows that entry prohibitions were more than "in the wind." The key passage reads: "Agraria, pascuaria uel decimas porcorum aecclesiae pro fidei nostrae devotione concedemus, ita ut actor aut decimatur in rebus ecclesiae nullus accedat. Ecclesiae uel cliericis nullam requirant agentes publici functionem, qui avi uel genetoris nostri immunitatem meruerunt." In other words,

kind of gift to the monasteries in question; it added guarantees of inviolability to their patrimony. We do not know exactly what that patrimony was; the council was not concerned with naming places. What we do know—at least a little—is the social side of the story: King Guntram, his Queen Austrechildis (dead by the time of the Council), and his daughters (deceased as well) had given gifts to Saint-Marcel and Saint-Symphorian. To their names, invoked in the written record of the council, were added those of seventeen bishops, signatories to their act of generosity.[7] Thus the guarantees of the council—called, be it remembered, by the king—shielded the newly endowed monasteries from their royal benefactors. The provision against the diocesan bishops (*episcopi locorum*) was, similarly, a restriction at least partially self-imposed: among the bishops signing the document was the diocesan bishop of Chalon, Flavius.

During the papacy of Gregory I (590–604), the pope came into the act. Granting the petitions begged by the dowager Queen Brunhild and her grandson Theuderic II, Gregory wrote three nearly identical letters in November 602 to three separate but equally favored ecclesiastical recipients at Autun: a hospice, a church, and a convent.[8] All had been endowed by the queen and their local bishop, Syagrius. In each case Gregory stipulated that "no kings, no bishops, no one endowed with any sort of dignity, indeed no one at all is to diminish or take away any of those things which were recently given to [variously: the hospice, the church, or the convent] by those aforesaid most excellent royal children of ours."[9] Already in an earlier letter of July 599 to the bishop of Arles, Gregory had confirmed a privilege once given to the monastery there by Childebert II, Brunhild's now-deceased son. At that time, the pope guaranteed the mon-

---

the king conceded fiscal dues by prohibiting his agents from entering (*accedat*) onto church property. I thank Alexander C. Murray for alerting me to Woll's study.

7. Although the record of the council exists only in a sixteenth-century copy, it does not appear to be spurious. See Fredegar, *Chronicle* 4.1, in *The Fourth Book of the Chronicle of Fredegar with Its Continuations*, trans. and ed. J. M. Wallace-Hadrill (London, 1960), p. 4, which mentions a council called by Guntram to confirm the founding of Saint-Marcel.

8. Gregory the Great, *Registrum* 13.9, 13.10, and 13.11, in CCSL 140A, pp. 1004–13. The letters are virtually identical except for a clause in the one to the hospice (13.9, p. 1006) prohibiting any abbot or priest of the hospice from seeking episcopal office. For the resemblance between these letters of Gregory and some *formulae* in the *LD*, see Anton, *Studien zu den Klosterprivilegien*, pp. 51–55.

9. Gregory the Great, *Registrum* 13.9, pp. 1004–5: "nullum regum, ⟨nullum⟩ antistitum, nullum quacumque praeditum dignitate vel quemquam alium de his, quae xenodochio a suprascriptis praecellentissimis filiis nostris regibus iam donata sunt . . . minuere uel auferre." Cf. corresponding passages in ibid., 13.10, p. 1007, and 13.11, p. 1009–10.

astery's control over its property (*in dispositione rerum*) and the ordination of its abbots.[10] The latter, an important prerogative ordinarily claimed by the local diocesan bishop, would become a key provision of subsequent exemptions. In his three letters to Autun, Gregory transferred the rights of election (and ordination!) to the regional king (*rex eiusdem prouinciae*) with the consent of the religious in each house.

Part of the impulse behind these privileges doubtless came from Gregory himself rather than from the Franks. In April 598, some months before his letter to Arles, Gregory had written in a similar vein to Marinianus, archbishop of Ravenna; there was no question of prompting from Frankish royalty here. Gregory wrote that he wanted the properties of the monastery of Saints John and Stephen in Classe to be guaranteed, and he wanted the monks there to elect their own abbot.[11] These were means to an end; they would help the monastery find its necessary quiet and security. Yet the monastery in Classe was not meant to be a kind of template upon which other monasteries and their future exemptions might be constructed. On the contrary, Gregory singled out Classe because it was special, a hardship case: "We know that . . . it endured many harmful and harsh things from your predecessors." Gregory's remedies righted past wrongs, patching up a peace between the monastery and the bishop of Ravenna and setting out terms that would keep them from quarreling in future. It was a nice practical instance of Gregory's desire to snatch perfection from imperfection.[12]

The letters for Arles and Autun were different. There was no adversity to be countered here, but rather glorious foundations to be confirmed and pious acts recognized. Like the bishops at Valence, Gregory was ostensibly granting humble petitions made by illustrious members of his flock, the "most excellent" queen and her grandson. The church fathers at Valence similarly recognized the importance of the royal family. These privileges were created because Merovingian kings, queens, and royal sons and daughters requested them. To understand why, we have to look at more intimate matters.

---

10. Ibid., 9.217, p. 780.

11. Ibid., 8.17, pp. 536–37.

12. Carole Straw, *Gregory the Great: Perfection in Imperfection* (Berkeley, Calif., 1988), e.g., p. 199: "Sometimes only the harsh experience of adversity can recall man to reason, purifying him of selfishness and awakening him to the needs of others." In the case of the letter to Marinianus, the bishop himself must recall the adversity of the monastery and take responsibility for it.

Family Connections

Austrechildis was Guntram's third wife. The couple had at least two sons and two daughters. We learn of the daughters—but not the sons—from the Council of Valence; they had been vowed to the monastic life, but by the time of the council they were both dead. The sons—but not the daughters—figured in the *Histories* of Gregory of Tours, our key source for all the events of the sixth century. The sons, Gregory says, died suddenly in 577, directly after King Guntram had killed the two sons of the magnate Magnacharius. Through juxtaposition Gregory presented the deaths as eye for eye. Literary artifice aside, the two events were connected through Austrechildis. She had been part of the *familia*—a slave—of Magnacharius. Guntram's second wife, Marcatrudis, had been Magnacharius's daughter. After she killed Guntram's first son and lost her own, Marcatrudis "incurred the hatred of the king, was dismissed by him, and died a little while later." Thereafter he married Austrechildis.[13]

None of the wives of this King Guntram was given good press by Gregory; but Austrechildis received the worst. He called her a Herod, anxious to take others with her when she died.[14] She breathed out her last *nequam spiritum*, her vile spirit, in 580; and her husband—carrying out his wife's nefarious dying wish according to Gregory—avenged her death by executing her two doctors.

Thus the verdict of Gregory. But the Council of Valence suggested a different image. Here Austrechildis joined her husband and her two daughters, both consecrated to God (*Deo sacratae*), as the patroness of holy places at Autun and Chalon. What she had given to those monasteries was never to be removed. Janet Nelson has made clear how precarious was the life of a slave-girl-made-queen; but at Valence we see one way in which she might score a success: the privileges recorded in its canons would serve as a memorial to her name and piety, as they would for her daughters.[15]

As we have seen, Autun would later be the focus of the largess of Queen Brunhild and her progeny. Daughter of an Arian Visigothic king, she had converted to Catholic Christianity early in her marriage to Sigibert I.[16]

---

13. Greg., *Hist.* 4.25, 1:226 and 5.17, 1:308.
14. Ibid., 5.35, 1:344.
15. Nelson, "Queens as Jezebels."
16. Greg., *Hist.* 4.27, 1:230–32.

She found among the Franks an already well-worn model of pious royal queens to emulate. Queen Clotild had built (along with her husband, Clovis I) the church of Saints Peter and Paul at Paris; when Clovis died, she lived out her days in semi-retirement "serving at the basilica of Saint Martin at Tours."[17] Queen Ultrogotha co-founded with her husband, Childebert I, a hospice at Lyon. Queen Radegund, a Thuringian princess brought back to the Frankish kingdom as a captive and wed by Clothar I, had "turned to God, changed her garb, and built a monastery for herself in the city of Poitiers."[18] We shall soon see how her monastery prohibited the encroachments of one bishop while fostering the entry of another. Founding, endowing, and living in religious establishments had become part of the repertory of good queenship.

Thus, particularly after the murder of her husband Sigibert in 575, Brunhild might have been expected to do what she did: turn to pious benefactions and establish networks of patronage with churchmen as soon as she could. But at first glance it is puzzling that she would eventually become a patron of Autun. Her husband Sigibert's kingdom had been based in the Merovingian region that later became known as Austrasia; his capital had been Reims, his own royal benefactions had gone to Soissons, where he was buried, although—or perhaps because—this was the capital of his brother Chilperic's kingdom.[19] Autun, in Burgundy, had been part of King Guntram's territory. Brunhild's benefactions there are best understood, then, as an extension of a rapprochement between Guntram and Brunhild that began in 577, after Guntram's sons had died: "Because of the force of my sins it turns out that I must remain childless" (Gregory of Tours tells us that Guntram said), "and so I ask that this nephew of mine [Childebert II, Brunhild's son] be my son."[20]

Guntram and Childebert II were to share their kingdoms "as if under one shield." Yet there was a subsequent period of enmity, not patched up until 584. This was the moment for cementing relations with Autun: it was then that the Council of Valence celebrated the generosity of Guntram and his family there. Guntram himself went to Autun on August 585 to celebrate the feast day of Saint Symphorian. There he found, seeking sanctu-

17. For Clotild, see ibid., 2.43, 1:140. The church of Peter and Paul was the later Sainte-Geneviève. On the model of female asceticism, see Suzanne Fonay Wemple, *Women in Frankish Society: Marriage and the Cloister, 500–900* (Philadelphia, 1981), esp. pp. 58–70.

18. Greg., *Hist.* 3.7, 1:154.

19. Ibid., 4.22, 1:224; 4.19, 1:220.

20. Ibid., 5.17, 1:310.

ary, the leaders of an army he had sent into Spain but which had turned, instead, to plunder the cities of the Midi. Autun was the site of the king's bitter harangue to the assembled bishops and magnates: "How can we obtain victory these days when we don't follow the ways of our fathers: they built churches, 'placing their faith in God' [Ps.78.7]; they honored martyrs and venerated priests."[21]

Brunhild had played a role in this planned invasion of Spain. Her daughter, married to a Spanish prince, had been persecuted by her father-in-law and died in exile in 585. One of Guntram's motives for attacking Spain was likely vengeance on behalf of Brunhild. Before his army had started out, a letter from the Spanish king had been intercepted: "Kill our enemies," it said, "that is, Childebert and his mother"—Brunhild.[22] The abortive military expedition sent out by Guntram, then, was Brunhild's brainchild as well. Their collaboration on the Spanish expedition helps explain Brunhild's later largesse to Autun, so closely associated with Guntram.

In the mid-580s Chalon and Autun served as important focal points of Guntram's piety. When he died on March 28, 593, Childebert succeeded him as king of Burgundy.[23] It is reasonable to assume that Brunhild's gifts to Autun began at this point, continuing the royal tradition of Guntram. Similarly, her work in tandem with Syagrius, the bishop there, reveals that she had inherited Guntram's patronage network, too. Though Syagrius apparently had not been present at the Council of Valence in 583–85, he had been with Guntram and nine other bishops in 589, when news arrived about a scandal at Radegund's convent.[24] In 591, Guntram had summoned him as part of the royal entourage when the king stood as godfather for Clothar II.[25] Brunhild's foundations at Autun and her subsequent request for letters of exemption from Gregory the Great may thus be understood as the continuation of models of piety, Burgundian royal traditions, and personal friendships.[26]

This is not the usual picture of Brunhild. Jonas, writing nearly a half century after the fact, paints her in dark colors, the implacable foe of

---

21. Ibid., 8.30, 2:200.

22. Ibid., 8.28, 2:194. Already at a convocation of nobles earlier in the year, Brunhild had pleaded her daughter's case, though apparently to no immediate avail; see ibid., 8.21, 2:190.

23. Fredegar, *Chronicle* 4.14, ed. Wallace-Hadrill, p. 10.

24. Greg., *Hist.* 9.41, 2:306.

25. Ibid., 10.28, 2:390.

26. At the same time, the letters were part of Gregory's larger program of conversion and reform.

Irish monastic reformer Saint Columbanus.[27] But Jonas, who had his reasons for writing as he did, may well have distorted the reality.[28] In the light of Brunhild's activities at Autun, it is very likely that she and her progeny greeted Columbanus warmly. Indeed, as Ian Wood has noted, Columbanus's foundation at Luxeuil may well have been built on land donated by her grandson, King Theuderic II, who became ruler of Burgundy in 596.[29] Jonas asserted the old saw that Luxeuil had been founded "in a deserted place"; in fact, as he himself revealed, the spot must have been carefully chosen for its dense cultic associations. It was a site shaded by a fortification in ruins, well supplied with baths, and jammed with pagan stone images.[30] It was a notorious and sacred place.

Despite the paucity of evidence, therefore, it seems clear that by the beginning of the seventh century, kings, queens, and bishops were giving out special privileges to certain religious institutions to supplement general fulminations against usurpers of church property. Particular ecclesiastical properties were singled out for special attention, guaranteed their quiet and security, and declared off-limits to royal and episcopal encroachment. The sacred places so favored were certainly not randomly chosen. Nor did they depend on the intrinsic prestige of the particular church or monastery involved. Rather, they tended to be newly founded places with special political, religious, social and familial associations for certain members of the royal Frankish house. The nature of the favored institution seems to have mattered less than the location: at Autun Brunhild distributed her largess almost as if she wished to touch every possible sort of establishment: a community of nuns dedicated to the Virgin, a church dedicated to Saint Martin, a hospice for lepers and the poor. As Polynesian chieftains used declarations of *tapu* to demarcate certain crop reserves, so did sixth-century Frankish rulers use phrases of prohibition to mark off particular saintly spaces.

These royal prohibitions were from the first linked to their episcopal counterparts. The mixture was signaled by the fact that kings called upon church councils to declare restraints on royal power, while the papacy invoked Frankish royalty when imposing episcopal restraint. These prohi-

---

27. Wood, *Merovingian Kingdoms*, p. 185.

28. Ian N. Wood, "The *Vita Columbani* and Merovingian Hagiography," *Peritia* 1 (1982): 63–80.

29. Ian N. Wood, "Jonas, the Merovingians and Pope Honorius: *Diplomata* and the *Vita Columbani*," in *After Rome's Fall: Narrators and Sources of Early Medieval History. Essays in Honour of Walter Goffart*, ed. Alexander Callender Murray (Toronto, 1998), pp. 99–120.

30. Jonas, *Vita Columbani* 1.10, MGH SRM 4:76.

bitions were a shared effort in another way as well: they were inspired as much (and sometimes more) by queens as by kings.

Radegund's Convent

While no doubt unusual, the experience of Queen Radegund's monastery, the Holy Cross at Poitiers, provides a telling example of one way that tensions between episcopal "rights" and "encroachments" led to entry prohibitions. Like the Council of Valence, it provides an early example of "negotiating space." But at Holy Cross, the negotiators took advantage not only of fears of the poor-slayer in their midst but also of the cult of relics and the sacrosanctity of the altar.[31]

This is not the place to recount in detail the history of the convent of the Holy Cross at Poitiers, founded by Queen Radegund and chronicled in two *vitae* of the saint as well as in the writings of Gregory of Tours.[32] Here we need simply to show that the nunnery ended up functioning in some ways as an exempt monastery later would do, despite the protests of both Gregory of Tours and Baudonivia (the author of one of the *vitae* of Radegund) that the nuns welcomed the intervention of the local diocesan bishop, Maroveus. In brief, Radegund became the wife of King Clothar I but not long afterward fled to the monastic life. At Poitiers she founded a monastery, soon called Holy Cross for the precious relic that she obtained for it. This was a "woman's" relic. It had been discovered by Helena, mother of Constantine, and in the monastery of Radegund, where it joined a cache of other precious relics, it was off-limits to the public and even to most men, as we shall see below.

The monastery of the Holy Cross was supported by Clothar from the

31. The connection between episcopal-monastic tensions at the monastery of the Holy Cross and seventh-century exemptions was already signaled by Edward James, *The Origins of France: From Clovis to the Capetians, 500–1000* (London, 1982), pp. 109–10. Much of the argument made below may be found, with some supplementary evidence, in Barbara H. Rosenwein, "L'espace clos: Grégoire et l'exemption épiscopale," in Nancy Gauthier and Henri Galinié, eds., *Grégoire de Tours et l'espace gaulois. Actes du congrès international, Tours, 3–5 November 1994* (Tours, 1997), pp. 251–62, in English as "Inaccessible Cloisters: Gregory of Tours and Episcopal Exemption," in *Gregory of Tours*, ed. Kathleen Mitchell and Ian Wood (Leiden, forthcoming).

32. Most recently discussed in detail, with excellent bibliography, in Raymond Van Dam, *Saints and Their Miracles in Late Antique Gaul* (Princeton, N.J., 1993), pp. 28–41. See also Yvonne Labande-Mailfert, "Les débuts de Sainte-Croix, 1: La fondation," in Y. Labande-Mailfert et al., eds., *Histoire de l'abbaye Sainte-Croix de Poitiers. Quatorze siècles de vie monastique* = Mémoires de la Société des Antiquaires de l'Ouest, 4th ser., 19 (1986–87): 25–69.

start, and the royal princesses Basina and Clotild were sent there to live as nuns. One might say that it was a kind of royal cloister, though not the "property" of the king. Georg Scheibelreiter's formulation is best: it was under royal protection.[33] It was also (and this must be the main point here) under episcopal protection, but *not* the protection of the *local* bishop, even when he was apparently willing to serve. Rather, most often the bishop of Tours was called in. Sometimes other bishops intervened, but they did so almost always under the *aegis* of the bishop of Tours or in the name of his patron, Saint Martin (ca. 316–ca.397). The latter's polyvalent importance is signaled by his many roles: he had been the first bishop of Tours and the father of monasticism in Gaul; he remained the patron saint of his church and was a special cult figure for Frankish kings and queens.

From the first, Radegund used her political and social connections to go over the head of her local diocesan bishop, the bishop of Poitiers.[34] For example, when Radegund chose Agnes to be abbess of her monastery, which must have been very early on, she turned to Bishop Germanus of Paris to perform the abbess's consecration; and although the appointment of Agnes was made with the consent of the bishop of Poitiers, Radegund gathered the consent of other bishops as well.[35] Again, when her husband, King Clothar, wanted to "repossess" her, threatening to come in person to the cloister, Radegund did not turn for protection to her diocesan, nor to the bishop of Bordeaux (the metropolitan of the bishop of Poitiers), but rather once again to Germanus, who was at the time—and this is significant—at Tours.[36] Solemnly abasing himself at the tomb of Saint Martin there, Germanus prevailed upon the king to give up his impious wish, and then Germanus went to Radegund, right into the oratory

---

33. Georg Scheibelreiter, "Königstöchter im Kloster. Radegund (†587) und der Nonnenaufstand von Poitiers (589)," *MIÖG* 87 (1979): 1–37, at pp. 12–13, 35.

34. Wood, *Merovingian Kingdoms*, pp. 137–38, stresses the peculiarity of a monastery run by a queen. Note that our sources for Radegund cannot be taken at face value. We shall explore below some of the ways in which Gregory was an "interested party" in the history of her monastery. Fortunatus wrote the first book of her *Vita* (MGH SRM 2:358–77) when he was bishop of Poitiers; he was interested in extolling her heroic virtues but decidedly underplayed the special prerogatives of her monastery; Baudonivia wrote the second book of Radegund's *Vita* (MGH SRM 2:377–95) at some point during the first two decades of the seventh century: for her Radegund was above all the patron and guarantor of monastic privileges. For further discussion, see the illuminating study of S. Gäbe, "Radegundis: sancta, regina, ancilla. Zum Heiligkeitsideal der Radegundisviten von Fortunat und Baudonivia," *Francia* 16, pt. 1 (1989): 1–30. See also Isabel Moreira, "Provisatrix optima: St. Radegund of Poitiers' Relic Petitions to the East," *Journal of Medieval History* 19 (1993): 285–305.

35. Greg., *Hist.* 9.42, 2:312.

36. Baudonivia, *Vita Radegundis* 2.7, p. 382.

of the monastery, to beseech her to forgive her husband. In Baudonivia's narrative, Martin's tomb was not incidental to the story: its looming presence explained why Germanus's petitions had their desired effect upon the king and why the king's evil counselors, who had encouraged him to go to Poitiers and take Radegund, were struck down.

In a letter, sometimes called Radegund's Testament, written when Maroveus was bishop of Poitiers, Radegund nevertheless appealed over his head to an unnamed bishop to protect her monastery from the brigands and despoilers of the poor who might appear after her death. Listed among these potential enemies was the "bishop of this place"—Poitiers.[37] Here Radegund was clearly drawing upon traditions that condemned the *necator pauperum*. In the same letter, she "adopted and chose" new (outside) episcopal protectors "to be my patrons in God's cause," charging them to appeal to whichever king ruled Poitiers "on behalf of this institution which has been commended before the Lord to your care [*pro re vobis ante Dominum conmendatam*]." Thus using the contemporary vocabulary of dependency and subordination (*commendare*), Radegund placed the monastery under the protection of outside bishops as well as of kings.[38]

Upon Radegund's death, when Maroveus was again absent (whether intentionally or inadvertently), Gregory (bishop of Tours as well as historian)—whether at his own initiative, the nuns' request, or the mourners' entreaties—undertook to bring the queen to her final resting place.[39]

Thus outside bishops played the role of "invited bishops" at the con-

37. For the Testament, Greg., *Hist.* 9.42, 2:310–16. It is addressed to bishops (in the plural): "dominis sanctis et apostolica sede dignissimis in Christo patribus." Then toward the middle Radegund speaks directly to one bishop (but whom?): "te quoque, beati pontifex, successoresque vestros."

38. Ibid., p. 314. Baudonivia, *Vita Radegundis* 1.16, p. 389, says that the queen "praecellentissimis enim dominis regibus et serenissimae dominae Bronichildi reginae . . . et sacrosanctis ecclesiis vel pontificibus eorum . . . suum commendavit monasterium." This implies royal and episcopal protection, but not of the local bishop. For the use of *commendatio* and related words, see, for example, Greg., *Hist.* 4.46, 1:260–62: Andarchius, who "se patrocinio Lupi ducis . . . commendavit." Similarly, ibid., 7.20, 2:112: Queen Fredegund sends a cleric to pretend to ingratiate himself with Queen Brunhild: "Veniens igitur clericus, cum diversis ingeniis se eidem commendavit." For further discussion, see François-Louis Ganshof, *Feudalism*, trans. Philip Grierson, rev. ed. (New York, 1964), p. 6.

39. Nuns request Gregory to do the burial in Baudonivia, *Vita Radegundis* 2.23, pp. 392–93; in Gregory of Tours, *Liber in Gloria Confessorum*, c. 104, MGH SRM 1, pt. 2, p. 815 (2d ed., p. 365), Gregory goes to Poitiers on his own volition; when he suggests speeding up the funeral even though Maroveus is not there, he is prevailed upon by "cives et reliqui viri honorati" to do the burial himself.

vent of the Holy Cross. In a letter written to Radegund, apparently responding to her request, seven bishops, including Eufronius of Tours and Germanus of Paris, but *not* any bishop of Poitiers, called the queen a second Saint Martin. She was, they said, an apostle to her nuns, who "abandoning their families . . . attach themselves voluntarily to you and make you their mother in God's grace." The bishops pointed with pride to the many women from their dioceses who flocked to Radegund's monastery: if any dared try to leave it after taking their vows, "let them be excluded from our communion and struck with the wound of awful anathema."[40] In this way, the bishops took the nuns, led by another "Saint Martin," under their external, non-diocesan spiritual charge.

The tensest confrontations between Radegund and Bishop Maroveus took place over the issue of relics. When she wanted some for her monastery, Radegund once again went over the head of her diocesan and did not seek his permission. Instead, she turned to King Sigibert I.[41] Nor did Radegund seek out local and well-known relics but rather hunted down exotic ones—such as the finger of Saint Mammas at Jerusalem—and exceptionally rare and potent ones, notably the fragment of the True Cross. Baudonivia called the cross "the wood where once hung the salvation of the world," and this is exceptionally important for the way in which this relic helped negotiate space in Radegund's monastery.[42] For the cross was coming now to be associated with the sacrosanctity of the altar.[43] The Council of Tours in 567 wanted "the body of the Lord [to] be placed on the altar not in a figurative manner but in the image of the cross."[44] This

40. Greg., *Hist.* 9.39, 2:298–302. The date of this letter is uncertain: the bishops are precisely those who attended the Council of Tours of 567, and this is the date adopted for the letter by Bruno Krusch in MGH SRM 7:342. But Luce Pietri, *La ville de Tours du IVe au VIe siècle. Naissance d'une cité chrétienne*, Collection de l'École française de Rome 69 (Rome, 1983), p. 232 n. 247 and p. 234 n. 253, dates the letter later, squarely in the context of the altercation with Maroveus. See Van Dam, *Saints and Their Miracles*, p. 31 n. 98, with further bibliography. That the letter responds to the queen's request is clear from Greg., *Hist.* 9.39, 2:300: "inspicientes etiam vestrae petitionis epistulam libenter a nobis exceptam." That Radegund is a "Saint Martin": ibid., p. 298.

41. Baudonivia, *Vita Radegundis* 2.16, p. 388.

42. Ibid., p. 388. For the finger of Saint Mammas, ibid., pp. 386–87. Moreira, "Provisatrix optima," p. 296, stresses the "lengthy process" involved in Radegund's search for relics.

43. That Radegund herself considered the holy cross exceptionally potent may be inferred from a passage in her letter to the bishops in Greg., *Hist.* 9.42, 2:314, where she threatens any who would contravene the conditions set forth with the judgment of God, the holy cross, and Mary (in that order).

44. Council of Tours, c. 3, *Conc. Gall.*, p. 178: "Vt corpus Domini in altari non imaginario ordine, sed sub crucis titulo componatur."

was the same council that prohibited the laity from mingling with the celebrating clergy. The altar cross marked the sacrosanct place from which the laity was excluded at the most awesome moment—the Mass. Radegund's cross, once installed in her monastery, was exceptionally powerful—and largely off-limits![45] How could it be otherwise, when the nuns practiced the strict enclosure enjoined by the Rule of St. Caesarius? They could not venture outside the walls of their monastery, nor could others come inside.

The inaccessibility of the relic of the holy cross may help to explain why Maroveus objected to presiding over its installation: he may have been concerned about the relationship between relics and his flock. We know that he was sensitive to the needs of the common people. It was at his request that King Childebert reviewed the tax lists for Poitiers, for "many of the inhabitants had died, and therefore the burden of the tax fell upon the widows, the orphans, and the weak."[46] When King Guntram's hostile army came to Poitiers, Maroveus "broke a golden chalice among the church vessels, melted it into money, and thus ransomed himself and the people."[47] In refusing to install the relics, Maroveus reflected not simply the self-interest of a man devoted to the cult of his own cathedral rather than to the holy cross but also the general antagonism of the Poitevins, who, "playing the role of the Jews," in the words of Baudonivia, "rejected the world's ransom and refused to receive [the holy cross] in the city."[48] When Radegund died, Maroveus was not on hand to bury her because he was "visiting his parishes."[49] This bishop was not a slacker; but he was willing to exclude the holy cross from his ministrations.

Maroveus did not draw up an exemption for the convent of the Holy

45. The miracles of the holy cross that Gregory of Tours recounts concern only the community of nuns or Gregory himself in special audience with the queen; see Gregory of Tours, *Liber in Gloria Martyrum,* c. 5, MGH SRM 1, pt. 2, pp. 490–92 (2d ed., pp. 39–42). In fact, Gregory may not have actually seen the holy cross; his description of it is incorrect, as noted by May Vieillard-Troiekouroff, *Les monuments religieux de la Gaule d'après les oeuvres de Grégoire de Tours* (Paris, 1976), p. 228. Baudonivia, *Vita Radegundis* 2.16, p. 389, claims greater accessibility: "Quisquis a quacumque infirmitate detentus ex fide venerit, per virtutem sanctae crucis sanus redit." But in fact her miracles do not ordinarily involve seeing the relic.

46. Greg., *Hist.* 9.30, 2:280.

47. Ibid., 7.24, 2:122.

48. Baudonivia, *Vita Radegundis* 2.16, p. 388. No doubt this is why Baudonivia went on to ask rhetorically (ibid., p. 389), "Quis queat dicere, quantum et quale donum huic urbi beata contulit?"

49. Gregory of Tours, *Liber in Gloria Confessorum,* c. 104, p. 815 (2d ed., p. 365).

Cross.[50] But we can see how royal or nearly royal monasteries such as Radegund's might well suggest to a late-sixth-century bishop that his wisest course would be to remain aloof. At Radegund's monastery a number of the factors leading to episcopal exemption came together. Its cult of relics and the particular sanctity of the cross intensified the expectation of asylum there, a fact made clear when Leubovera, its new abbess, "demanded to be brought near to the casket with the holy cross" as soon as she heard that rebellious nuns had sent a band of assassins after her.[51] It is significant, too, that the first miracle Gregory recounts about this relic concerned a divine light that "appeared before the altar," enhancing the pious vigils of the nuns on Good Friday.[52] The exclusivity of the convent—typified by this liturgical miracle performed only for the nuns—and its new-style enclosure, based on the Rule written by Saint Caesarius, set it off from the surrounding community and its bishop. The convent nurtured this isolation by discouraging interference from the nearby bishop and sought protection for its property and way of life from outside agents: kings, relics, and bishops in other dioceses.[53]

The convergence of these disparate developments was utterly new in the age of Gregory of Tours. Disjunctions between the new reality and the old norms may account in part for the evasiveness with which Gregory handled his narratives of Radegund's monastery. Gregory condemned Maroveus; but he was also entirely ready to take advantage of the new opportunities offered by appeals for his aid. He blessed the altar in Radegund's cell, escorted her body to its final resting place, and blessed the burial spot, leaving (perhaps) the funeral Mass and the covering of the tomb to Maroveus.[54] Despite Gregory's conception of a "universal episcopacy" (which Martin Heinzelmann has brought to light), there was no "legal" justification yet for doing what Gregory did. We

50. After Radegund's death, to fulfill his vow to act as "patrem earum" to the nuns, Maroveus "ut habiens ad Childeberthum regem praeceptionem elicerit, ut ei hoc monastyrium, sicut reliquas parrochias, regulariter liceat gubernare (Greg., *Hist.* 9.40, 2:304)." This suggests that Maroveus needed a special royal mandate to justify his future activities at Holy Cross.

51. Ibid., 10.15, 2:358.

52. Gregory of Tours, *Liber in Gloria Martyrum*, c. 5, p. 490 (2d ed., p. 40).

53. The rebellious nun Clotild was following this pattern when she went first to Tours to speak with Gregory and thence appealed to King Guntram: Greg., *Hist.* 9.39, 2:296.

54. Gregory of Tours, *Liber in Gloria Confessorum*, c. 104, p. 816 (2d ed., p. 366); but in Baudonivia, *Vita Radegundis* 2.23, p. 393, Gregory "eam [sc. Radegund] cum digno sepelivit honore."

have seen how church councils generally inveighed against episcopal encroachment while nevertheless continuing to enjoin oversight.[55] Gregory (and Baudonivia) had thus to blame Maroveus in order to justify intervention from Tours.[56]

It would take only a small nudge to end this predicament; and that was provided by the advent of a new political regime and the influence of a new religious sensibility.

55. Martin Heinzelmann, *Gregor von Tours (538–594). "Zehn Bücher Geschichte," Historiographie und Gesellschaftskonzept im 6. Jahrhundert* (Darmstadt, 1994), p. 68. Adriaan H. B. Breukelaar, *Historiography and Episcopal Authority in Sixth-Century Gaul: The Histories of Gregory of Tours Interpreted in Their Historical Context*, Forschungen zur Kirchen- und Dogmengeschichte 57 (Göttingen, 1994), pp. 188–89 n. 6, claims that Gregory had the legal right to intervene in church affairs at Poitiers: although the ecclesiastical metropolitan of Poitiers was supposed to be the bishop of Bordeaux, royal administration placed Poitiers in the same region as Tours. In the case of the Holy Cross convent, according to Breukelaar, "royal geography prevailed over the ecclesiastical: the nunnery belonged to the royal estates, not to the ecclesiastical, and Poitiers belonged to Sigebert's kingdom." But the nature of Merovingian jurisdiction was perhaps not as clearly defined as Breukelaar claims, since the bishop of Bordeaux *did* intervene in the case of the rebellious nuns at Holy Cross during the reign of Childebert, successor of Sigibert: see Greg., *Hist.* 9.41, 2:306.

56. On other ways in which Gregory sometimes shaped his narrative to fit his political predicament, see Ian N. Wood, "The Secret Histories of Gregory of Tours," *Revue Belge de Philologie et d'Histoire*, fasc. 2: *Histoire Médiévale, Moderne et Contemporaine* 71 (1993): 253–70.

3
The "Secret Enclosure"

THE YEAR 613 marked a political revolution in the Frankish kingdom. Theudebert II, Brunhild's grandson, was killed, and his brother, Theuderic II, died. The aristocracy of Burgundy and Austrasia deserted Brunhild and handed all parts of the kingdom to the Neustrian Clothar II (see Genealogy 2).

The brutal dismemberment of Brunhild signaled the end of the old order.[1] Shortly thereafter, king and court announced the agenda of their new regime at Paris. We have two documents from the meetings that took place there, one in the form of canons, the other an edict. The conservative character of the proceedings was announced by the preface to the canons, which called for a renewal (*renovatio*) of old laws; and many of the canons were in fact lifted word for word from a church council that had been held at Lyon in 567–70.[2] The Paris edict largely confirmed and repeated the canons, but it also made some additions, and here a tidy bit of historical revision took place. In effect, the line of Brunhild was wiped out: "Regarding the *toloneus* [transportation toll on merchandise]: it ought to be collected in these places and on the merchandise on which it was exacted [in the time] of preceding princes, that is, until the passing of kings Guntram, Chilperic, and Sigibert, our lords and ancestors of good repute."[3]

1. Fredegar, *Chronicle*, 4.42, ed. Wallace-Hadrill, p. 35.

2. Council of Paris (614), pref., *Conc. Gall.*, p. 275: "pro renouandis antiquorum canonum statutis"; for the Council of Lyon, ibid., pp. 201–3.

3. *Chlotharii II Edictum [Edict of Paris]* (614), c. 9, MGH Cap. reg. Fr. 1:22: "De toloneo: ea loca debeat exegi vel de speciebus ipsis, quae praecidentium principum, id est usque tran-

GENEALOGY 2. Later Merovingian Kings and Queens

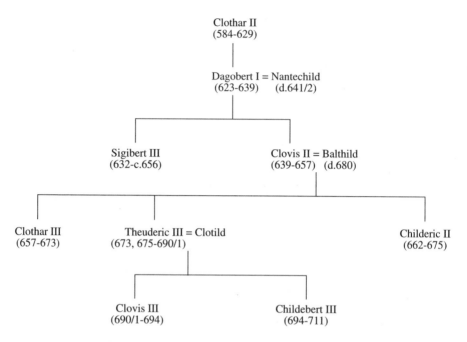

Clothar II
(584-629)

Dagobert I = Nantechild
(623-639)   (d.641/2)

Sigibert III
(632-c.656)

Clovis II = Balthild
(639-657) (d.680)

Clothar III
(657-673)

Theuderic III = Clotild
(673, 675-690/1)

Childeric II
(662-675)

Clovis III
(690/1-694)

Childebert III
(694-711)

Thus did Clothar stake his claim: not to the Burgundy of Brunhild's son or grandson, but to the "good old days" of Guntram. The edict also contained a provision about immunities. It began by invoking the same "pure" line of kings, then continued: "Let the property of churches, priests, and the poor—who cannot defend themselves—be defended by public agents [*iudices publici*] prior to a court hearing according to the law, but without violating the immunity granted by the preceeding lords [Kings Guntram, etc.] to the Church or magnates . . . to bring about peace and discipline."[4]

situm bone memorie domnorum parentum nostrorum Gunthramni, Chilperici, Sigiberthi regum est exactum." The Edict is found in a single manuscript. It has a long historiography of interpretation, for it is taken as a window onto the early medieval polity. For Mitteis, *The State*, p. 51, it "marked the surrender of political power to the Frankish landowning aristocracy." For Alexander Murray (most recently in "*Pax et disciplina*: Roman Public Law and the Merovingian State"), on the contrary, it shows how the Merovingian state "rested on notions derived from Roman public law."

4. *Chlotharii II Edictum*, c. 14, p. 22: "Ecclesiarum res sacerdotum et pauperum qui se defensare non possunt, a iudicibus publecis usque audientiam per iustitiam defensentur, salva emunitate praecidentium domnorum, quod ecclesiae aut potentum vel *cuicumque visi* [reconstructed by the editor, Boretius] sunt indulsisse pro pace atque disciplina facienda."

This was an important passage. First, it suggested that immunities had regularly been given out by kings of good repute and that it was thus appropriate for the new king and his heirs to grant such privileges. Second, it associated immunities with the activities of royal agents (*iudices publici*), who were to protect the property of those who could not defend themselves. Finally, it made clear that the purpose of immunities was to ensure peace and order (*pro pace atque disciplina facienda*). Under the new regime, immunities found their place in the welfare of both kingdom and Church.

Though, as we have seen, privileges called immunities existed in the sixth century, the reigns of Clothar II (584–629) and his son Dagobert I (623–39) saw the development of a new kind of immunity, granted by charter and emphasizing the pious, religious meanings of entry prohibitions. To understand why this happened when it did obliges us to examine their context, the new court milieu out of which these immunities grew.

Columbanian Disciples

Around Clothar and his son was a coterie of talented and largely aristocratic young men on the rise. Their careers mingled Church and court. They included Desiderius, royal treasurer and later bishop of Cahors; Audoin, referendary (a sort of proto-chancellor) under Dagobert and later bishop of Rouen; Eligius, favorite goldsmith of the king and later bishop of Noyon; Paul, later bishop of Verdun; and Sulpicius, later bishop of Bourges.[5] Their fraternity was tightly bonded; even when apart the men kept up a long-distance correspondence.[6] Their solidarity was nourished by old memories and hopes of reunion: "Let us support one another with mutual prayers so that, just as we were friends [*socii*] at the court of a terrestrial prince, so we may merit to live together in the palace of the high king of heaven."[7]

The key figure was Audoin.[8] He was born c. 603 into a rich, powerful,

5. For the careers of these men, see Horst Ebling, *Prosopographie der Amtsträger des Merowingerreiches von Chlothar II (613) bis Karl Martell (741)*, Beihefte der Francia 2 (Munich, 1974), and Wood, *Merovingian Kingdoms*, pp. 150–51.

6. See Desiderius of Cahors, *Epistulae*, ed. Dag Norberg, Acta Universitatis Stockholmiensis, Studia Latina Stockholmiensia 6 (Uppsala, 1961), with, as examples, letters to Audoin (1.11, 2.4), Paul (1.12), Sulpicius (2.1), Eligius (2.6).

7. Ibid., 1.11, p. 30.

8. Indeed, Richard A. Gerberding dubs the seventh century "The Age of Saint Audoin" as the title of chapter 5 of *The Rise of the Carolingians and the "Liber Historiae Francorum"* (Ox-

and extended family and patronage network, with landholdings blanketing the region of Meaux and Soissons and further afield as well.[9] Two "poles" of this network—Chagnericus, patriarch of the family called (by later historians) the Farones, and Autharius, father of Audoin—attracted the Irish monastic reformer Columbanus (c. 540–610) as he made his way, self-exiled from his island, across the Continent.

The effects of the interaction between Columbanus and this aristocratic group gradually unfolded in Audoin's generation. Chagnoaldus, son of Chagnericus, became a disciple of the holy Irishman. His sister, Burgundofara, founded the monastery of Faremoutiers and became a nun herself. Burgundofaro, very likely another member of this family, was at first at home at Dagobert's court (he was the king's referendary), but was also, later, bishop of Meaux; and he helped found the monastery of Rebais.[10] Autharius's children were equally touched by the Irish reformer. Audoin himself was the chief founder of Rebais. Ado, his older brother, built the monastery of Jouarre. Their younger brother, Rado (who, like Audoin, spent much of his career as court referendary), was the founder of yet another monastery, "Radolium," at Reuil-en-Brie.[11]

Hitherto the monasteries of the Merovingian kingdom had sprung up around holy men; or they had been founded by bishops or members of

---

ford, 1987). For Audoin, see *Vita Audoini Episcopi Rotomagensis*, MGH SRM 5: 553–67, written c. 688; Jonas, *Vita Columbani*, 1.26, p. 100 (where he is called Dado); and Elphège Vacandard, *Vie de Saint Ouen, évêque de Rouen (641–684). Étude d'histoire mérovingienne* (Paris, 1902).

9. The properties have been surveyed by Alexander Bergengruen, *Adel und Grundherrschaft im Merowingerreich. Siedlungs- und Standesgeschichtliche Studien zu den Anfängen des fränkischen Adels in Nordfrankreich und Belgien*, Vierteljahrschrift für Sozial- und Wirtschaftsgeschichte, Beihefte 41 (Wiesbaden, 1958), pp. 75–78. Bergengruen argues for kinship ties between Autharius and Chagnericus on the basis of convergent property holdings (esp. p. 66 n. 31) and some hagiographical hints. But in the *Vita Agili*, c. 5, *AASS*, August VI, p. 584, Agilus, who clearly *was* related to Chagnericus, was allied by *amicitia*, not blood, to Audoin: "Audoenus . . . satagebat . . . amicitiae foedere illum [Agilum] sibi conjungere."

10. For Chagnoaldus, see Jonas, *Vita Columbani* 1.17, p. 85; for Burgundofara, ibid., 1.26, p. 100, and 2.7, p. 121. For her testament, Jean Guérout, "Le Testament de Sainte Fare: matériaux pour l'étude et l'édition critique de ce document," *Revue d'histoire ecclésiastique* 60 (1965): 761–821. The evidence for Burgundofaro's participation in the foundation of Rebais comes from the *Vita Agili*, c. 6 [*recte*, 4], p. 582: "cum beato Farone episcopo ecclesiae fundamenta locaret." See also his role in the wooing of Agilus to become abbot of Rebais: ibid., c. 5, p. 584. His participation is also implied by his role in the episcopal exemption and royal immunity there; see Eugen Ewig, "Das Formular von Rebais und die Bischofsprivilegien der Merowingerzeit," in Ewig, *Gallien*, 2:456–84 and below. On the impact of Columbanus in Gaul, see the papers in H. B. Clarke and Mary Brennan, eds. *Columbanus and Merovingian Monasticism*, BAR International Series 113 (Oxford, 1981).

11. On Jouarre and Rebais, see Jonas, *Vita Columbani* 1.26, p. 100; for "Radolium," see *Vita Agili*, c. 6 [*recte* 4], p. 582.

royalty.[12] If they attracted patrons, these had been (by and large) kings, queens, or churchmen. The generation of aristocrats who came under Columbanus's spell cracked this monopoly. They took a newly intense and active role not only in founding and endowing monasteries, but also in redefining the nature of that endowment: it would consist not just of property but also of inviolability.

Royal and Aristocratic Monastic Patronage

The kings of the seventh century participated in the aristocratic court culture of their officials and its fierce devotion to monasticism. Clothar II called Saint Denis—the first bishop of Paris, whose relics rested just outside his city in a basilica named for him—his "particular patron."[13] It was a term of close friendship and deference, once used by Audoin, for example, to refer to his fellow courtier Desiderius.[14] But when Clothar died, he was buried at the church of Saint-Vincent (later Saint-Germain-des-Prés), as his father had been.[15]

Clothar's son Dagobert, however, linked the very identity of the royal house with Saint-Denis. He reformed the daily round carried out by the monks living there, instituting the liturgy of the prestigious monastery of Saint-Maurice d'Agaune, where the relics of the first martyr-king of the West lay.[16] Dagobert bedecked Saint-Denis with jewels, donated property

12. See Ian N. Wood, "A Prelude to Columbanus," in Clarke and Brennan, *Columbanus and Merovingian Monasticism*, pp. 3–32.

13. *ChLA* 13:6–7, no. 550 (584–629), and ibid., pp. 16–17, no. 552 (625).

14. Desiderius, *Epistulae* 2.4, p. 48 (from Audoin, bishop of Rouen, and Constancius, bishop of Albi, to Desiderius).

15. Childebert I had built Saint-Vincent and was buried there: Greg., *Hist.* 4.20, 1:222. Clothar I, who took over Childebert's kingdom patronized Saint-Medard of Soissons, however, and was buried there (ibid., 4.21, 1:224). Chilperic I revived Saint-Vincent as a family necropolis. He was buried there (ibid., 6.46, 2:84), as were his sons Clovis and Merovech on order of Guntram: ibid., 8.10, 1:171–72. The burial of Clothar II at Saint-Vincent (Fredegar, *Chronicle* 4. 56, ed. Wallace-Hadrill, p. 47) may thus be interpreted as another sign of his claim to the traditions of Guntram. On these necropoleis and their significance, see Eugen Ewig, "Résidence et capitale pendant le haut moyen age," in Ewig, *Gallien*, pp. 362–408, esp. p. 388, and Patrick Périn, "Saint-Germain-des-Prés, première nécropole des rois de France," in *La mort des grands (Vᵉ–XIIᵉ siècles) = Médiévales* 31 (1996): 29–36.

16. *ChLA* 13:36–37, no. 558. Dagobert's reform was apparently not successful: see Fredegar, *Chronicle* 4.79, ed. Wallace-Hadrill, p. 68: "Sallencium ibidem ad instar monastiriae sanctorum Agauninsium instetuere [Dagobert] iusserat; sed facilletas abbatis Aigulfi eadem instetucionem nuscetur refragasse." On Agaune, see most conveniently Friedrich Prinz, *Frühes Mönchtum im Frankenreich. Kultur und Gesellschaft in Gallien, den Rheinlanden und Bayern am*

to it, and enlarged its west end.[17] He also transformed it into the new royal mausoleum. When his son Clovis II confirmed a privilege for Saint-Denis, he noted who rested in the basilica: the three martyrs who served as its patron saints, to be sure; but also his own mother and father![18]

Meanwhile, the men who surrounded these kings, most of them part of the far-flung network of Columbanus's disciplines, were ending the ambivalence about diocesan episcopal control still evident in the writings of Gregory of Tours. From this circle came the first charters of exemption.

Columbanus and Exemption

To understand why this took place, it is first necessary to raise doubts about a widely held assumption: that the idea of episcopal exemption was introduced—as if something Irish and foreign—into the Frankish kingdom by Columbanus himself. J. M. Wallace-Hadrill, for example, writes:

> Columbanus broke every Gallic conciliar decree on the right relationship of monks with diocesans; and these decrees had unimpeachable canonical tradition behind them. He meant to claim, and did claim, a degree of exemption from diocesan supervision that was hitherto unknown in Francia and even brought with him an Irish bishop to carry out episcopal functions for his own monks.[19]

Arnold Angenendt has described just what that bishop did:

> At Luxeuil the blessing of the altar was carried out by a bishop who was evidently Irish and probably should be understood as a *Klosterbischof.*[20]

Beispiel der monastischen Entwicklung (4. bis 8. Jahrhundert), 2d ed. (Munich, 1988), pp. 102–7. On Agaune's prestige, see Frederick S. Paxton, "Power and the Power to Heal. The Cult of St. Sigismund of Burgundy," *Early Medieval Europe* 2 (1993): 95–110. See also references in Chapter 4, note 6.

17. Dagobert's original donation charter is lost, but there is a confirmation of it in *ChLA* 13:28–31, no. 556. On Dagobert's contribution to the architecture of Saint-Denis, see Patrick Périn, "Quelques considérations sur la basilique de Saint-Denis et sa nécropole à l'époque mérovingienne," in Jean-Marie Duvosquel and Alain Dierkens, eds., *Villes et campagnes au Moyen Âge: Mélanges Georges Despy* (Liège, 1991), pp. 599–624. I thank Patrick Périn for sending me a copy of this paper in advance of its publication.

18. *ChLA* 13:36, no. 558; Fredegar, *Chronicle* 4. 79, ed. Wallace-Hadrill, p. 67.

19. J. M. Wallace-Hadrill, *The Frankish Church* (Oxford, 1983), p. 66.

20. A *Klosterbishof,* a "monastic bishop," was attached to a monastery rather than to a diocese. He carried out episcopal functions within the monastery, such as blessings and consecrations. Sometimes he was also abbot. See *Lexikon des Mittelalters* 5:1223–24.

Luxeuil's exemption from episcopal jurisdiction would soon be made good by an episcopal privilege which, of course, is no longer extant.[21]

What are the bases for these assertions? The notion that Columbanus's entourage included a bishop who consecrated the altar at Luxeuil comes from a letter written c. 610 by the exiled Columbanus to his disciples. In this letter, Columbanus expressed the hope that those he left behind would remain united and true to his teachings:

> Whoever are rebels, let them make their exit; whoever are obedient, let them become my heirs. Observe these things, you and whoever are fully mine. And for the sake of unity and humility, . . . let all look to him who ministers to God near the altar which holy bishop Aidus blessed.[22]

The passage is opaque. It certainly speaks of an altar blessed by Aidus and symbol of the unity of the disciples. But was the altar necessarily at Luxeuil?[23] Did its blessing by Aidus mean that he had been part of Columbanus's entourage? Or that his blessing of the altar defied the canonical rights of the episcopal hierarchy? Certainly Aidus was an "Irish" name; and no one by that name served as diocesan bishop of any of Columbanus's Gallican foundations. But G. S. M. Walker has suggested that the "altar [might have been] a portable stone, blessed in Ireland, and carried thence to France."[24] Even if an outside bishop had indeed been brought in to bless the altar, he might have done so in the same way that the bishop of Tours intervened at Holy Cross. Columbanus's foundations, like Radegund's, were special, royally sponsored ventures.[25]

The organization of the Irish church, with its subordination of bishops

21. Arnold Angenendt, *Das Frühmittelalter. Die abendländische Christenheit von 400 bis 900* (Stuttgart, 1990), p. 215. Though I differ with Fr. Angenendt on this point, I have enjoyed and learned much from conversations with him about it and related matters.

22. Columbanus, *Epistula 4*, in *Opera*, ed. and trans. G. S. M. Walker, Scriptores Latini Hiberniae 2 (Dublin, 1957), p. 30: "Quicumque sunt rebelles, foras exeant; quicumque sunt obedientes, ipsi fiant heredes. Haec tu observa et quicumque mei sunt ex integro; et propter unitatem et humilitatem . . . ad eum, qui iuxta altare quod sanctus Aidus episcopus benedixit Deo servierit, omnes aspiciant."

23. Pierre Riché, "Columbanus, his Followers and the Merovingian Church," in Clarke and Brennan, *Columbanus and Merovingian Monasticism*, pp. 61–62, suggests that the altar was at Annegray. It is true that a memorial book from Luxeuil contains the name of a bishop Aeduus. For a discussion of this point, and of the identity of bishop Aidus and bibliography on the question, see Laprat, "Saint Colomban," pp. 121–22 n. 10.

24. Columbanus, *Opera*, p. 31 n. 1.

25. Laprat, "Saint Colomban," p. 134 and n. 76, thinks that Luxeuil was built on part of the fisc. The extent of the royal role in Columbanus's foundations is made clear in two articles by Ian Wood: "The *Vita Columbani* and Merovingian Hagiography" and "Jonas, the Merovingians and Pope Honorius."

to abbots, *might* have suggested an institution resembling exemption to one of its members, though recent research suggests that bishops had more jurisdiction in sixth-century Ireland than had been thought previously.[26] Columbanus himself did not seem much concerned with the matter. True, he appealed over the heads of Gallican bishops to Pope Gregory the Great when his calculations for the Easter celebration came under attack. True, again, he "dared not" (as he put it) attend an episcopal church council to which he was summoned on the matter.[27] Nevertheless, none of this spelled out a *policy* of limited episcopal jurisdiction. Indeed, as we have seen, it was Queen Brunhild, the supposed enemy of Columbanus, who appealed to Pope Gregory to favor the churches at Autun with the first rudiments of such limits. The only reason to assume that Luxeuil received an exemption in the time of Columbanus is that the extant episcopal exemption charter for Rebais—the first that is (by and large) authentic—names Luxeuil as precedent. But the exemption for Rebais may itself have been reinterpreting Luxeuil's and other monasteries' status to conform to its own, new conception of privilege.

It is clear from the example of Radegund's convent of the Holy Cross that even if Columbanus *had* used the services of an "outside bishop," there was already precedent in Gaul for it. This is the main point. We have seen a number of indigenous factors, some going back to Late Antiquity, which converged by the end of the sixth century, perhaps even before Columbanus's arrival on the Continent, to make exemptions a logical "next step," whether or not he had a hand in them.

The Next Generation

If we shift the date of the first exemptions from Columbanus's lifetime to the era of his disciples—that is, to the next generation—the facts fall into

26. See Kathleen Hughes, "The Celtic Church: Is This a Valid Concept?" in eadem, *Church and Society in Ireland*, A.D. 400–1200, ed. David Dumville (London, 1987), paper 18, p. 2, and Richard Sharpe, "Some Problems Concerning the Organization of the Church in Early Medieval Ireland," *Peritia* 3 (1984): 230–70.

27. Letter to Pope Gregory the Great (603), in Columbanus, *Epistula* 1, in *Opera*, pp. 2–12. Letter to the Gallican bishops in *Epistula* 2, ibid., pp. 12–22 (on p. 18 he says he did not dare come to the council: "Ego autem ad vos ire non ausus sum"). Friedrich Prinz, "Columbanus, the Frankish Nobility, and the Territories East of the Rhine," in Clarke and Brennan, *Columbanus and Merovingian Monasticism*, pp. 73–87, emphasizes that Columbanus's monasteries were in the countryside, far from cities and their bishops. From Jonas, *Vita Columbani*, it

place. It was Bertulfus, Columbanus's disciple and abbot of Bobbio (a northern Italian monastery founded by Columbanus), who obtained the first *papal* exemption ever issued when in 628 Pope Honorius freed Bobbio from the jurisdiction of its diocesan bishop, Probus of Tortona.[28] It was Audoin—that "model" of the second generation—who requested that Bishop Burgundofaro grant Rebais the first extant authentic *episcopal* exemption, granted in 637.[29] This charter, which followed Dagobert's immunity of 635 for the same monastery, illustrates once again the close relation between the two sorts of privileges.[30] The text of the immunity is suspect, but the exemption has been vindicated by the studies of Ewig. Let us look at it closely.

would seem that Columbanus set up his monasteries without reference to episcopal oversight. On the other hand, we should beware accepting Jonas's account, written c. 643, at face value; see below at note 37.

28. Jonas, *Vita Columbani* 2.23, pp. 144–45; see Carlo Cipolla, ed., *Codice diplomatico del monastero di S. Colombano di Bobbio fino all'anno MCCVIII*, vol. 1, Fonti per la storia d'Italia 52 (Rome, 1918), p. 100, no. 10; and Anton, *Studien zu den Klosterprivilegien*, pp. 55–57, who sees the privilege as "nichts anderes als die Formel 77 des L[iber] D[iurnus]," which he dates to the seventh century (ibid., p. 2).

29. Jean Guérout, "Les origines et le premier siècle de l'abbaye," in *L'abbaye royale Notre-Dame de Jouarre* (Paris, 1961), pp. 41–44, gives arguments for its authenticity, though recognizing an interpolation (p. 42). Ewig has shown that the exemption for Rebais was used as the model for episcopal grants of "grosse Freiheit," thus vindicating it as an *essentially* authentic document, and he has countered Guérout on the question of the interpolation as well: see Ewig, "Das Formular von Rebais," in Ewig, *Gallien*, 2: 456–84 (on the interpolation, p. 463 n. 36), and "Beobachtungen zu den Klosterprivilegien," in Ewig, *Gallien*, 2:411–26. The most extended criticism of the exemption's authenticity is in Léon Levillain, "Le formulaire de Marculf et la critique moderne," *BÉC* 84 (1923): 21–91, esp. pp. 32–47, 51, though Franz Beyerle, "Das Formelbuch des westfränkischen Mönchs Markulf und Dagoberts Urkunde für Rebais a. 635," *Deutsches Archiv für Erforschung des Mittelalters* 9 (1951): 43–58, esp. p. 46 n. 7, has also cast doubt on it. No one has seen the congruence of vocabulary between the exemption for Rebais and the *Vita Columbani*, as argued below. I do not claim that all of the phrases in the extant exemption for Rebais are authentic; but I do claim that the sense of all of its provisions are more or less so.

30. The purported diploma is published in MGH Dip. Mer., pp. 16–18, no. 15, and in V. Leblond and Maurice Lecomte, *Les Privilèges de L'abbaye de Rebais-en-Brie* (Melun, 1910), pp. 51–53. Burgundofaro's exemption is edited there as well, at pp. 53–56. Strongly challenging the authenticity of the immunity is Beyerle, "Das Formelbuch," pp. 43–58. His argument is that the Rebais immunity published by Mabillon from an "original text" (since lost) must have been written *after* Marculf's formulary was drawn up. Since the latter, in Beyerle's view, was written for Landeric, bishop of Paris 643/53–57, the Rebais privilege cannot be an authentic document from 635, as it pretends. Beyerle's argument has been accepted by Guérout, "Les origines," pp. 40–41, and by Ewig, "Das Formular von Rebais," in Ewig, *Gallien*, 2:463 n. 36. Even so, it remains very likely that Dagobert issued an immunity for Rebais, later copied and revised in the light of Marculf.

The exemption was addressed to Burgundofaro's co-bishops in the form of a privilege granted at the petition of Audoin.[31] Invoking the precedents of Saint-Maurice d'Agaune, Lérins, Luxeuil, and Saint-Marcel of Chalon, the exemption for Rebais nestled itself within a seemingly comfortable early tradition. Yet this ancient *libertas*, although possibly real, has not left many traces. The invocation of earlier exemptions in the Rebais charter may have been a reinterpretation of older materials based on a new view of the monastery's role in the body politic—a fictive reconstruction of the past that served to embed the privilege in a venerable tradition.[32]

Burgundofaro's exemption granted Rebais virtual autonomy from the diocesan bishop—Burgundofaro himself. In Chapter 1 we saw, in effect, an outline of its provisions in Ewig's model of the "big exemption":

1. No cleric, bishop, or king was to "usurp or diminish" any property that had been given (or in future would be given) to the monastery.
2. When the abbot died, the congregation was to elect his successor.
3. "If the time is right to bless the altars or consecrate the chrism or ordain a priest, let [the monks] have the right to have it done by any bishop they choose."
4. No one, "not we, nor our archdeacons nor our successors" is to have authority over [the monastery's] property or ordination [of its clerics] or is to appropriate the dues gathered by the monks from their dependents.
5. No bishop is allowed entry into the "secret enclosure" of the mon-

31. Although giving Audoin pride of place, the exemption says that he "pariterque Chado et Rado, ejus germani . . . basilicam . . . loco nuncupato Resbaco construxerunt" (Leblond and Lecompte, *Les Privilèges*, p. 54).

32. Ewig, "Beobachtungen zu den Klosterprivilegien," in Ewig, *Gallien*, 2:419 follows Guérout, "Les origines," pp. 40–43 and n. 38, in assuming that the Rebais exemption was based on an earlier one, drawn up for Luxeuil (see also Angenendt, as above, n. 21). This is very unlikely. It is more likely, as Albrecht Diem argues in his dissertation-in-progress, that pronouncements of particular Gallican church councils were taken out of context and understood in the light of the new mid-seventh-century sensibilities about the inviolability of the monastery. Diem has noted, for example, some echoes of the third Council of Arles (449–461) (which met to discuss a conflict between the abbot of Lérins and the bishop of Fréjus) in the provisions of the Rebais exemption; the council's canons are in *Concilia Galliae*, CCSL 148: 131–34. Similarly, the Council of Valence (583–585), *Conc. Gall.*, p. 235, may have suggested the "free" status of Saint-Maurice d'Agaune and Saint-Marcel; see Barbara H. Rosenwein, "One Site, Many Meanings: Saint-Maurice d'Agaune as a Place of Power in the Early Middle Ages," in *Topographies of Power in the Early Middle Ages*, ed. Mayke de Jong and Frans C. W. J. Theuws (Leiden, forthcoming).

astery unless invited "by the congregation or its abbot"; and if a bishop is so invited, he is to carry out his tasks without requiring payment.

6. If the monks' behavior requires it, "let them be corrected by their abbot."

While granting the importance of all of these provisions, we must consider the first and fifth in particular. Echoing the canons of Frankish church councils, the first provision summarized the various forms of church property—land, dependents, sacred books—that had been given to the monastery by pious donors, including Audoin and Dagobert. It then turned to condemn the potential violators: "Let no cleric, bishop, or king (*regalis sublimitas*) presume to take anything from there for his own use or to diminish it."[33] Like the church canons, this statement connected royal and ecclesiastical power: it restrained the king alongside the bishop. Whether or not Dagobert ever issued a formal immunity for Rebais (and it seems likely that he did, even though the extant one is not authentic), the exemption itself named him as a benefactor of the monastery and at the same time drew him into the process of defining its inviolability.

The formula of the entry prohibition, the fifth item, was something new.[34]

And unless we have been invited by the congregation or its abbot, let none of us be allowed to go into [*adire*] or enter [*ingredi*] the secret enclosure [*secreta septa*] of the monastery. But if the bishop has been asked by them and has entered [*accesserit*] in order to supplement their prayers or be useful to them, let him be sure to leave immediately after the divine mystery has been celebrated and finished, without demanding any gift [*absque ullo requisito dono*].

Although emphasizing the entry prohibition through the use of three different verbs meaning "to enter"—*accedere, adire,* and *ingredi*—Burgundofaro's exemption did not set up an absolute taboo. A bishop's role vis-à-vis a monastery was complex: unlike a royal agent, the bishop might be necessary—to celebrate Mass for example. Nevertheless, resources were

33. Leblond and Lecompte, *Les Privilèges,* p. 55: "nullus sibi exinde . . . clericorum aut pontificum, vel regalis sublimitas aliquid suis usibus usurpare aut minuere presumat." Where I have put elipses, Leblond and Lecompte suggest "[aliquid]"; but Alexander Murray kindly called my attention to the fact that this extra *aliquid* is not needed.

34. Ewig, "Beobachtungen zu den Klosterprivilegien," in Ewig, *Gallien,* 2:418.

conserved within the parameters of a partial taboo: the bishop had no right to profit materially from "requisitions," the *requisita dona*.

By reiterating words of entry and the necessity of invitation, Burgundofaro stressed the autonomy and initiative of the monastery; the bishop became its passive servant. But the use of the term *secreta septa* implied more than this: it implied the sacrosanctity of asylum.[35] A contemporary source suggests that it meant even more.

The *Vita Columbani*

Jonas, the author of the *Vita Columbani* (the *Life* of Columbanus), was, like Audoin and Burgundofaro, a member of the "second generation."[36] He wrote not long after Burgundofaro's exemption was issued, at a time, that is, when the line of Clothar II was well established and Jonas was eager to dissociate his hero from the disgraced progeny of Brunhild.[37] He depicted Columbanus arriving on the Continent from Ireland, settling in Burgundy, founding a number of important monasteries—Annegray, Luxeuil, Fontaines—and immediately coming into conflict with the aged Queen Brunhild and her grandson Theuderic II.

Whatever really happened between these rulers and the Irishman (see Chapter 2 for the suggestion that he depended on their support), the important point here is that it was recalled and interpreted in a certain way by Jonas c. 639–43. In *his* account, a dramatic confrontation pitted Columbanus against the queen. The scene opened with Columbanus's arrival at the royal court. Brunhild brought out her great-grandchildren— Theuderic's progeny—to be blessed. Columbanus refused and prophesized that they would never become kings because they had been born to concubines.[38]

35. Indeed, the constitution of 431 (CT 9.45.4), so important for establishing asylum (see Chapter 1) used the phrase *in ecclesiasticis saeptis*.

36. He was a disciple not of Columbanus directly but of Bertulfus and Athala, both abbots of Bobbio: Jonas, *Vita Columbani*, pref., pp. 61–62.

37. Wood, "Jonas, the Merovingians, and Pope Honorius." Thus the *Vita Columbani* must be read not "only" or even primarily for the information it gives us about Columbanus but for the insight it gives us into the "new mood" of his followers.

38. Jonas, *Vita Columbani* 1.19, p. 87. On the importance of prophecy in the *Vita Columbani*, see Wood, "The *Vita Columbani* and Merovingian Hagiography," esp. p. 71. Note that Brunhild confronted Columbanus in the *aula*; that was her "space." See the remarks on the *aula* in Philippe Ariès and Georges Duby, eds., *A History of Private Life*, vol. 2, *Revelations of the Medieval World* (Cambridge, Mass., 1988), pp. 15–16. Later (see note 39 below) her grandson would challenge Columbanus's right to limit access to the *septa* of his monastery. In

This set the stage, in Jonas's text, for an inverted confrontation between Theuderic and Columbanus. For now it was the king's turn to visit Columbanus at Luxeuil, where Theuderic accused the abbot of departing from the customs of the region: not the custom of royal concubinage, which surely was at issue in the minds of all present, but the custom of allowing all Christians to enter the monastery's "very secret enclosure," *septa secretiora*.[39] Here the use of the very vocabulary of Burgundofaro's exemption betrays not textual dependency—though it would appear to argue further for the authenticity of the exemption—but above all congruence of concerns.

In Jonas's view, royal entry and royal monastic patronage were inextricably connected, but in extremely complex ways. He had the king threaten: "If you want to get the gifts of our generosity and the supplies of our aid, your entrance will be open to everyone everywhere."[40] Columbanus turned the threat on its head: "If you try to violate that which up to now has been closed under the firm rules of discipline, I will not in future accept your gifts or your help."[41] Refusing the king's gifts was a way to dishonor him; Jonas's Columbanus was playing on the prestige of the king as patron.[42] Uninvited, he could not violate the portals of the monastery.[43]

The next episode raised the dispute to its highest pitch: the king defied the abbot. Theuderic entered the refectory—then ran out, terrified. In the dramatic structure of Jonas's narrative, the king could neither open the monastery to others nor will his own entry. It was God, through Columbanus, who declared the monastery "closed." In such a context it surely behooved a wise king to promulgate—of his own free will and power—the immunity of a holy place.

Jonas's narrative, triumph over Brunhild extended even to trumping her domestic domain: the holy man could enter her space and say what he would, but the king could not enter the holy man's.

39. Jonas, *Vita Columbani* 1.19, p. 88.

40. Ibid.: "'Si,' inquid, 'largitatis nostrae munera et solaminis supplimentum capere cupis, omnibus in locis omnium patebit introitus.'"

41. Ibid.: "'Si, quod nunc usque sub regularis disciplinae abenis constrictum fuit, violare conaris, nec tuis muneribus nec quibusque subsidiis me fore a te sustentaturum.'"

42. For other instances in which gifts are rejected, see Ian Wood, "The Irish and Social Subversion in the Early Middle Ages," in *Irland. Gesellschaft und Kultur VI*, ed. Dorothea Siegmund-Schultze (Halle a. S., 1989), pp. 263–70, esp. p. 266.

43. For a further episode of this sort, see Jonas, *Vita Columbani* 2.17, p. 137, where Jonas recounts the invasion of Faremoutiers, Burgundofara's monastery, by Aega, to whom King Dagobert had commended his son and kingdom. Aega violated the confines (*termini*) of the monastery and died by divine vengeance.

Jonas constructed scenes with Columbanus's aristocratic supporters in the Meaux region as inverse images of these hostile confrontations. Fleeing the kingdom of the Franks, Jonas's Columbanus met Chagnericus, who was in a position to provide Columbanus access to the court of the king.[44] At the same time, Chagnericus was anxious to keep Columbanus with him "to ennoble his home." Columbanus blessed his house and vowed Burgundofara to the Lord. (She fulfilled the vow by becoming a nun.)

Directly thereafter, Columbanus met Autharius, Audoin's father. This episode was constructed as a reversal of Columbanus's meeting with Brunhild. Arriving at Autharius's villa, Columbanus was greeted by Audoin's mother, who (like Brunhild) immediately brought out her young children to be blessed by him. "Seeing the faith of the mother," wrote Jonas, "he consecrated the children with his benediction."[45] Then Jonas recounted Audoin's founding of Rebais under the Rule of St. Columbanus.

In these three episodes of blessing, the first (which was spurned) functioned as a curse; the second sanctified a space (that is, a house); and the third prophetically led to the foundation of Rebais. The exemption for Rebais was issued by a bishop whose ancestral home had been blessed and whose sister's life had been consecrated to God by Columbanus. The bishop acceded to the request of the illustrious founder of the monastery, claimed to follow a long-hallowed tradition, granted *libertas* as it was then understood, added to this a curb on his own right of entry, and gave up all "gifts." If we take seriously Jonas's constructed interchange between Columbanus and Theuderic, we can see that these sacrifices gave Burgundofaro moral stature of the sort that accrued to a Polynesian chieftain: bound by thongs, restrained in his own movement, prevented from "grasping," he guaranteed the integrity of the secret enclosure. Moreover, he thereby tapped into monastic resources: by guaranteeing the "quiet" of the monks, Burgundofaro ensured their prayers for Church, king, and country.[46]

Bugundofaro's exemption reveals that in the late 630s and early 640s there was a meeting of minds between king and aristocrats. Dagobert declared his solidarity with the Columbanian sensitivity to sacred space; he

44. Ibid., 1.26, p. 99.
45. Ibid., p. 100. "Videns ille matris fidem, infantulos sua benedictione sacravit."
46. Leblond and Lecomte, *Les Privilèges*, p. 55: "quatenus monachi . . . de perfecta quiete valeant . . . exultare et . . . pro statu ecclesiae et salute regis vel patrie valeant plenius deum exorare."

would participate in limiting access to it. At the same time, the Columbanians declared their solidarity with the Neustrian dynasty of Clothar II by creating the myth—it is already well developed in Jonas's *Vita Columbani*—of an evil, fornicating, ungodly Austrasian royal line.

In the ancient world the countryside had been, as people of the time understood it, populated by dieties. These were transformed into demons in the early Christian period. But by the end of the sixth century, the countryside had become sacred once again, purged by the presence of dispersed and carefully housed relics of saints.[47] The monasteries of Saint Columbanus were constructed outside the ancient city centers; they tapped into the powers of this newly Christianized rural landscape. The exemption granted to Rebais and subsequent seventh-century immunities and exemptions were one means by which kings and bishops recognized, honored, organized, and allied themselves with these new sources of divine power.

47. See Peter Brown, *The Rise of Western Christendom: Triumph and Diversity*, A.D. 200–1000 (Oxford, 1997), chap. 6

4

The Heyday of Merovingian Immunities

THE SO-CALLED do-nothing kings who followed Dago-
bert's death did nothing because they didn't have to: the political system
worked without fuss.[1] In many ways, the period 640–70 was the high
point of Merovingian rule, particularly in Neustria (see Map 2). Although
aristocratic factions there fought over the highest office that the court had
to offer— "mayor of the palace" (*maior domus*)—King Clovis II (d. 657)
and his wife Queen Balthild (d. 680) kept all sides happy by giving them
access to the royal ear, ensuring in that way that the court remained the
focus (hence linchpin) of aristocratic strivings. Whereas the magnates
touched by Columbanus orchestrated monastic reform in the period
620–40, the Merovingians regained much of the initiative thereafter.

Recapturing the Initiative: Clovis II and Balthild

Early in his reign Clovis II granted Saint-Denis his royal protection
(*sermo*), and in 654 he asked its diocesan bishop, Landeric of Paris, to grant

1. Paul Fouracre and Richard A. Gerberding, *Late Merovingian France: History and Hagiography, 640–720* (Manchester, 1996), p. 16. For the persistence of the idea of the *rois fainéants*
and their role in French identity today, see Patrick J. Geary, *Before France and Germany: The
Creation and Transformation of the Merovingian World* (New York, 1988), pp. 221–26. I thank
Richard Gerberding for reading this chapter and making many pertinent suggestions.

MAP 2. Neustria in the Seventh Century

it an exemption.[2] The extant copy of Landeric's document is interpolated; but we have Clovis's confirmation of it in the original, its papyrus only slightly worn and tattered even today.[3] The court circle of Desiderius's day still showed life: among the many witnesses, the aged Eligius signed his name in grand capital letters to the left of the king's monogram, while Rado, brother of Audoin, signed to the right. The confirmation emphasized the property of the monastery: neither the bishop of Paris nor anyone else was to take away anything from the monastery against the will of its monks or without the permission of the king himself: "[The bishop] ought not to dare to take away or diminish or carry off to his city either the chalices or the crosses or the altar cloths or the sacred books or gold or silver or any sort of precious stuff that has been or will be given to the same place."[4] Janet Nelson has already called attention to the "redistribution of resources" that this document was meant to ratify.[5] The exemption allowed the king to control access to wealth as well as to balance the fiscal demands of old episcopal sees with the acquisitive interests of new monastic centers. Indeed, the king's permission was placed on a par with that of the congregation; Saint-Denis had become a "royal monastery." This significance was underlined when Clovis reinstituted there the demanding "day and night" liturgy associated with Saint-Maurice d'Agaune, which was a model for monasteries created as "acts of state."[6]

The particular objects that were named and numbered in Clovis's confirmation had symbolic significance. The chalices and crosses were as-

2. *ChLA* 13:26–27, no. 555 is the grant of royal protection. Because only a fragment survives, its attribution is problematic. Léon Levillain, "Un diplôme mérovingien de protection royale en faveur de Saint-Denis," *BÉC* 72 (1911): 233–44, argues persuasively that it was issued by Clovis II, but Clovis III is also possible.

3. *ChLA* 13:36–43, no. 558; for Landeric's exemption, see Pardessus 2:95–97, no. 320. Ewig has been able to tease out much that is genuine in the latter in "Klosterpolitik," in Ewig, *Gallien* 2:538–83, esp. pp. 575–76.

4. *ChLA* 13:37: "aut calices uel croces seo indumenta altaris uel sacros codeces, argentum aurumue uel qualemcumque speciem de quod ibidem conlatum fuit aut erit auferre aut menoare uel ad ciuetate deferre non debeat nec praesumat."

5. Nelson, "Queens as Jezebels," p. 39. Compare this with the episcopal custom of taking one-half of the oblations of the altar: Council of Orléans (511), c. 14, *Conc. Gall.*, p. 9: "ut de his, quae in altario oblatione fidei conferentur, medietatem sibi episcopus uindicet," though in some instances his portion was reduced to one-third; see De Clercq, *La législation religieuse*, p. 98.

6. *ChLA* 13:37. The liturgy of Saint-Maurice is generally called the *laus perennis*, but this seems to be a modern name, based on an assumed connection with the Akoimetoi (Sleepless Monks) of the Eastern Empire; see Barbara H. Rosenwein, "Perennial Prayer at Agaune" (forthcoming). For the association between St. Maurice and monarchy, see Wood, "Prelude to Columbanus," in Clarke and Brennan, *Columbanus and Merovingian Monasticism*, p. 17.

sociated with the altar. Some time before this confirmation, Clovis had already convened a council at Chalon, a focal point (as we know) for Merovingian piety. The canons recorded a particular concern about the "inner sanctum" of the churches. To the usual provisions against despoilers of church property was added a diatribe against men and women who, crowding into the churches for dedications and feasts, sang "filthy and disgusting songs": "Whence it is right that the priests of those places ought to keep and fence off those people from the enclosures [*septa*] and the porticos of their basilicas and even from the atria; and if they do not want to pay the penalty voluntarily [the priests] ought to excommunicate them or control them with the sting of discipline."[7] Having Landeric draw up an exemption was thus part of the attempt, already begun long before (as we have seen), to limit access to the holy spaces of the churches. But now the initiative for this drive was very clearly royal. That Saint-Denis should become central to the history of exemptions was inevitable once it became important to the Neustrian monarchs.

The bishop seems to have lost much. He gave up his jurisdiction over the monastery's property, and he sacrificed his ability to requisition its holy and precious objects. But it would be wrong to view this exemption simply as demonstrating royal advantage. Hitherto, the assumption has been that bishops were pretty well forced to write their exemptions: Landeric even seems to complain that he issued his grant "because the request of King Clovis is for us like a command that is very difficult to resist."[8] But advantages are complicated; "the king's wish" had its benefits for Landeric, too. The very act of issuing the exemption was recognition of his control over episcopal access. Furthermore, by delimiting his own rights, he entered the gift network that bound Saint-Denis to its generous donors. The episcopal exemption willed (in neat reversal, like Burgundofaro's exemption) a blow to episcopal prestige that thereby redounded to it.

At the end of his life Clovis's identification with his "particular patron" grew so intense that he "cut off the arm of blessed Denis the martyr."[9] The king kept it near him, just as the remainder of the "saint's precious

7. Council of Chalon (647–53), c. 19, *Conc. Gall.*, p. 307: "Vnde conuenit, ut sacerdotes loci illos a septa basilicarum uel porticus ipsarum basilicarum etiam et ab ipsis atriis uetare debiant et arcere et, si uoluntarie noluerint emendare, aut excommunicare debeant aut disciplinae aculeo sustinere."

8. Pardessus 2:96, no. 320. See Nelson, "Queens as Jezebels," pp. 38, 41, and Ewig, "Klosterpolitik," in Ewig, *Gallien*, 2:577 n. 88, both of whom cite this passage to make this point.

9. *Liber Historiae Francorum*, c. 44, MGH SRM 2:316: "Eo tempore Chlodoueus brachium beati Dionisii martyris abscidit."

body" lay with Clovis's dead parents.[10] His mayor of the palace, Erchinoald, did much the same thing; he held onto the corpse of Saint Fursey for thirty days in order to place it in a church he was building on his property at Peronne.[11] Related to the royal house, Erchinoald was eager to ape its strategies for success.[12]

Clovis's death in 657 left Balthild acting as regent for Clothar III. She was aided by Audoin and Ebroin (a mayor of the palace who represented a faction opposed to Erchinoald).[13] According to the author of the earliest version of the *Life* of Queen Balthild (*Vita Balthildis*), written shortly after the queen's death in 680, Balthild quickly brought peace to the three kingdoms of the Franks so that she could set about reforming the Church.[14] This *Vita*, like that of Jonas for Columbanus, is best read as an artifact of its period; we shall want to explore aspects of its design and underlying assumptions when we come to the reign of Theuderic III (d. 690/91). Nevertheless, like the *Vita Columbani*, it is also the chief quarry for facts about its subject. Of particular importance here is Balthild's "wholesale" granting of immunities as part of her policy of monastic reform:

> Throughout the "senior" basilicas of the saints—of Lord Denis and Lord Germanus and Lord Medard and Saint Peter and Lord Anianus and also Saint Martin and wherever her written notice applied—she commanded the bishops and abbots, persuading them for the love of God, and she sent letters to them saying that the brethren staying in these places ought to live under the holy order of a Rule. And in order for them [the monks] to acquiesce willingly, she ordered that a privilege [of exemption] be granted them, and she even granted them immunities, so that they would better like to pray for the mercy of Christ, the highest king of all, on behalf of the king and for peace.[15]

10. The phrase "ubi ipse preciosus domnus [Denis] in corpore requiescere uedetur," though slightly varied from time to time, was essentially formulaic: cf. *ChLA* 13:10, no. 551; ibid., p. 78, no. 568; ibid., p. 90, no. 570.

11. *Vita Fursei Abbatis Latiniacensis*, c. 10, MGH SRM 4:439.

12. He was related to Dagobert's mother, according to Fredegar, *Chronicle* 4.84, ed. Wallace-Hadrill, p. 71.

13. She was helped as well by Chrodobertus, bishop of Paris. See *Vita Balthildis*, c. 5, MGH SRM 2:487.

14. There are two *Vitae Balthildis*, the first, A, written c. 680, the second, B, a ninth-century attempt to supplement and "clarify" the Merovingian prototype (see Krusch's comments in MGH SRM 2:478–79, and Fouracre and Gerberding, *Late Merovingian France*, pp. 114–16). The A version will be the only one cited here. On Balthild, see Fouracre and Gerberding, *Late Merovingian France*, pp. 97–114; Ewig, "Klosterpolitik," in Ewig, *Gallien*, 2:538–83; Nelson, "Queens as Jezebels"; and Prinz, *Frühes Mönchtum*, pp. 171–77.

15. *Vita Balthildis*, c. 9, pp. 493–94: "per seniores basilicas sanctorum domni Dionisii et

It is no accident that the first house on the list was Saint-Denis. Indeed Clovis's confirmation of its exemption had already linked liturgical and religious reform there with its specific privileges. Saint Martin's place at the end of the list is connected with renewed royal interest in his cult center at Tours.[16] To the royal relic collection, where the first, most prized possession had been the arm of Saint Denis, Balthild or her son Theuderic III added the precious cloak (*cappa*) of Saint Martin.[17]

We may get a fair idea of the immunities of which Balthild's *Life* speaks from sources concerned with Corbie, a monastery that Balthild and Clothar III founded between 657 and 661. We have two important documents. One is an immunity issued by Clothar, the other an episcopal exemption drawn up at royal request by Corbie's diocesan bishop, Berthefridus of Amiens.[18]

The first document is an immunity from tolls. It prohibited royal agents from exacting or requiring customary tolls and duties from Corbie's merchants and agents. The charter echoed the phrase in the *Vita Balthildis* quoted above: it was issued so that "on account of this benefit the holy

---

domni Germani vel domni Medardi et sancti Petri vel domni Aniani seu et sancti Martini, vel ubicumque eius perstrinxit notitia, ad pontifices seu abbates suadendo pro zelo Dei praecepit et epistolas pro hoc eis direxit, ut sub sancto regulari ordine fratres infra ipsa loca consistentes vivere deberent. Et ut hoc libenter adquiescerent, privilegium eis firmare iussit, vel etiam emunitates concessit, ut melius eis delectaret pro rege et pace summi regis Christi clementiam exorare."

16. Eugen Ewig, "Le culte de Saint Martin à l'époque franque," in Ewig, *Gallien*, 2:355–70, esp. p. 367.

17. Ewig, "Klosterpolitik," in Ewig, *Gallien*, 2:581, suggests that Balthild may have been behind the acquisition of the *cappa*, though extant documentation does not place it at the royal court before the reign of Theuderic III: *ChLA* 13:76, no. 567: "in oraturio nostro, super cappella domni Martine."

18. The royal diploma: MGH Dip. Mer., p. 35, no. 38; the exemption: Pardessus, 2:126–28, no. 345, and Bruno Krusch, "Die Urkunden von Corbie und Levillains letztes Wort," *Neues Archiv* 31 (1906): 337–75, text on 367–75. Neither of these documents survives in original form, and there is a long history of disputation regarding their authenticity. The chief opposition was between Bruno Krusch and Léon Levillain. The latter's *Examen critique*, pp. 26–59, argues for their authenticity; Krusch's introduction to the *Vita Balthildis* insists that they are all forgeries. For further bibliography, see the notes to Krusch, "Die Urkunden von Corbie." More recently, Ewig, "Klosterpolitik," has fairly conclusively demonstrated the authenticity of the episcopal exemption, seconded by Laurent Morelle, "Le statut d'un grand monastère franc. Corbie (664–1050)," in François Bougard, ed., *Le christianisme en Occident du début du VIIᵉ siècle au milieu du XIᵉ siècle. Textes et documents* (Paris, 1997), pp. 209–15, with a translation of the exemption on pp. 205–9. There is a third document for Corbie from the same period: MGH Dip. Mer., pp. 36–38, no. 40. The research of Theo Kölzer suggests that the latter is a forgery. I am extremely grateful to Professor Kölzer, who generously answered my inquiries about all of these documents and supplied me with the results of his studies in advance of their publication.

congregation may love even more to pray for the mercy of the Lord for the stability of our kingdom."[19]

The episcopal exemption for Corbie, probably issued in 664, underlined the close connection between royal and episcopal entry prohibitions.[20] Indeed, the exemption provided, in its own words, both *libertas* (exemption) and *emunitas* (immunity). The signatories included some of the old guard—Audoin and Burgundofaro.[21] Ewig has discussed the charter type undergirding the clauses and organization of this exemption. It belonged to the tradition of the "little exemption"; behind its clauses stood Landeric's exemption for Saint-Denis, which must have been the model as well for the bishops who drew up exemptions for Saint-Pierre-le-Vif in 660 and for Sithiu (Saint-Bertin) in 663.[22] The diplomatic similarities betray more than formulaic connections; they point to the policies alluded to in the *Vita Balthildis*. It is almost certain that Saint-Pierre-le-Vif was the Saint-Peter referred to in the *Life's* list of "senior" basilicas.[23]

All these "little" exemptions of the 660s were connected explicitly with monastic reform, royal safety, the stability of the kingdom, and redistribution of its resources. The bishops who were present when Berthefridus had his exemption drawn up made clear that, given the persistent requests of queen mother and son, "our hearts would have considered it irreligious not to grant their petition."[24] Like Landeric, they were relinquishing much. But they were also thereby establishing and maintaining alliances: with one another; with the royal house that nurtured and (at the same time) deferred to them; with the saints and martyrs in whose honor Corbie was constructed; and with its abbots and monks.[25] They were also defining religious space: prohibitions against seizure and entry demarcated privileged territory and tested episcopal discipline and virtue. It is

19. MGH, Dip. Mer., p. 35, no. 38: "quo potius delectat ipsa sancta congregatione pro ipso beneficio pro stabilitatem regni nostri Domini misericordiam exorare."

20. For the date, see Levillain, *Examen critique*, pp. 164–65.

21. On the witness list, see ibid., pp. 160–65 and 295–99, no. 37.

22. Ewig, "Klosterpolitik," in Ewig, *Gallien*, 2:566–76. See also Levillain, *Examen critique*, p. 158.

23. Ewig, "Klosterpolitik," in Ewig, *Gallien*, 2:577, 582–83. See also Nelson, "Queens as Jezebels," p. 40.

24. Pardessus 2:126: "ut petita non concedere . . . noster animus inreligiosum fore putaret."

25. In the *Vita Balthildis*, c. 4, MGH SRM 2:485–86, the queen is both mother and daughter to the men at court: "ut domino et principibus se ostendebat ut mater, sacerdotibus ut filia, iuvenibus sive adolescentibus ut optima nutrix." This is the web of relations into which the bishops were woven.

no accident that the final clause of Berthefridus's charter explicitly condemned and set the penance for any bishop who might violate it. Finally, these exemptions were declaring the connection between privacy and living rightly: "The books of Saint Augustine . . . teach that monks who live peacefully according to a rule should reside without the interference of priests or bishops."[26]

Ewig has connected all these little exemptions—for Saint-Denis, Saint-Peter, Sithiu, and Corbie—with Balthild's "monastic politics" (*Klosterpolitik*). In his view, the court under Balthild used exemptions to further Columbanian monasticism against the greater part of the episcopacy and its prerogatives.[27] Nelson has shown how these policies did even more: they associated the royal house with sources of supernatural power.[28] Immunities and exemptions made it clear how that association was to be defined: precisely by disavowals of contact between royal agents and monastic officers and, marking this hands-off policy, gifts of the tolls and taxes that would normally be due at the boundary points where royal and monastic power would have met outside the monastery; and by the creation of an entry taboo in the case of bishops, this too marked by a gift, or rather by the ostentatious rejection of hitherto obligatory "gifts" due to the diocesan bishop from the monks. Though the "little exemption" institutionalized regular contact between the diocesan bishop and the monks—when the bishop blessed the altar and when, each year, he prepared the holy oil—the prohibition of a return gift sanitized even this transaction.

Seeking the Stable Center

In the 680s the most important event for Neustria was not the passing of Balthild and Audoin, but rather, ironically, the fall of the *Austrasian* court. From then on Austrasian aristocrats looked to Neustria—its court and its elite—for favors and power. In the process, they added their own interests and arms to an already turbulent brew.

---

26. Pardessus 2:126, no. 345: "sancti Augustini . . . libri . . . doceant monachos sub quiete regulariter viventes, absque inquietudine clericorum vel episcoporum residere." Compare the nearly identical passage in Landeric's privilege for Saint-Denis, in Pardessus 2:95–96, no. 320: "sancti Augustini libri . . . doceant monachos sub quiete regulariter viventes suâ singulari lege debere quiescere, et ab omni infestatione clericorum intrepidos permanere."

27. Ewig, "Klosterpolitik," in Ewig, *Gallien*, 2:579.

28. Nelson, "Queens as Jezebels," p. 41.

We see this turbulence in two key texts written in the 680s: the *Vita Balthildis* and the *Passio Leudegarii* (Martyrdom of Leudegar).[29] They announce less a world of partisans (though the *Passio Leudegarii* does that) than of stable centers. In the *Vita Balthildis* the queen is portrayed as the source of all action and gift-giving. In the *Passio Leudegarii* the bishop Leudegar, the queen's appointee, is the still point around which alliances shift.

In the *Vita Balthildis* royal gifts are potent tools for good, but gifts given by others are the glue of unholy alliances. As wife of Clovis, Balthild is the distributor of royal treasure to pious causes.[30] As widow, she brings peace to the kingdom and then turns immediately to religious reform. Here she becomes (in the hands of her biographer) fairly obsessed with accepting, prohibiting, and giving gifts. At the behest of "good priests" Balthild turns against the polluting crime of simony (the crime of "buying"—or giving gifts—for ecclesiastical offices). She forbids it as an impious sin.[31] In the same breath, the hagiographer praises Balthild for forgoing her own receipts: she remits the poll taxes customarily due the royal treasury.[32] At the same time, Balthild's own bequests are lavish: she hands over lands and great forests, whole manors, and untold wealth to religious cells and monasteries. She gives away fiscal lands, establishes the nunnery of Chelles, founds and endows Corbie, gives gold and silver and even her own "royal belt" to the monastery at Moutiers-au-Perche, concedes important gifts to the monastery founded by Burgundofara, and hands over to the basilicas and monasteries of Burgundy and Paris "great and many villas," enriching them with "many gifts."[33] Prohibitions against simony were thus matched, in the economy of the *Vita*, by an alternative, indeed overwhelming, distribution of gifts. "What more?"

29. For a similarly contextual approach, see Jacques DuBois, "Sainte Bathilde vers 625– 680, Reine de France 641–655, Fondatrice de l'abbaye de Chelles," *Paris et Ile-de-France. Mémoires* 32 (1981): 13–30. Fouracre and Gerberding, in *Late Merovingian France*, pp. 118–32 and 215–53, supply translations of both texts.

30. *Vita Balthildis*, c. 4, p. 486: "largasque elemosinas distribuens singulis" and with Bishop Genesius, her *fidelis* and *famulus*, she "pascebat egenos et induebat vestibus nudos studioseque sepelire ordinabat mortuos, dirigens per ipsum ad coenobia virorum ac virginum auri vel argenti largissima munera."

31. Ibid., c. 6, p. 488. On these reforms, which affected local aristocratic rather than royal pocketbooks (a point stressed by Nelson in "Queens as Jezebels," p. 32), see the Council of Chalon (647–653), c. 16, *Conc. Gall.*, p. 306.

32. This has been treated as evidence of the persistence of the *capitation* in Merovingian Gaul in the seventh century, e.g., Lot, *L'impôt foncier*, p. 89 n. 6.

33. *Vita Balthildis*, cc. 7–8, pp. 489–92.

asks Balthild's hagiographer, continuing, "As we said, we cannot recount everything; we can hardly tell half the story."[34]

Indeed, it was less than half; for all these gifts, in the structure of the *Vita*, were but the prelude to Balthild's monastic policies: her reform of the "senior basilicas" and their endowment with immunities and exemptions. For the hagiographer, these privileges were "freedoms" indeed, paired immediately with Balthild's practice of redeeming slaves, both by buying their freedom and by sending them into monasteries "to pray for her." Yet these freedoms, too, were above all gifts: the chapter in which they appear concludes by describing the length of Balthild's reach: "Straight to Rome, all the way to the basilicas of blessed Peter and Paul, and to the Roman poor, she repeatedly sent many and large gifts."[35]

Composed at about the same time as the *Vita Balthildis*, the *Passio Leudegarii* was interested less in gifts than in the contrast between Leudegar's steady probity (*justitia*) and the shifting alliances for good and evil that swirled about him.[36] Balthild makes a cameo appearance in Leudegar's *Passio* as the good queen who, inspired by God, places the saint on the episcopal seat at Autun. After her retirement to Chelles, Ebroin, her mayor of the palace, is corrupted by evil men and bribes and becomes the villain of the story. First he turns against Leudegar.[37] Then, when Theuderic III is raised to the Neustrian throne in 673, Ebroin, puffed up with the spirit of pride, turns back the nobles who had arrived for the ceremony and denies them their customary role in the royal elevation. Fearing this "tyrant Ebroin" and the king he serves, the nobles call upon Childeric, Theuderic's brother, to be king. Leudegar and other bishops save Ebroin's life by convincing the magnates to exile him to Luxeuil; Theuderic is sent to Saint-Denis.

Leudegar remains the stable moral center thereafter as well. The nobles bring in Childeric but many are soon disenchanted with him; now it is the new king who is the labile foil to the bishop. Leudegar takes on the

34. Ibid., c. 8, p. 493.

35. Ibid., c. 9, p. 494: "Etiam ad Romam usque ad beati Petri et Pauli basilicas vel ad Romensis pauperes plura ac larga sepius direxit munera." The theme of munificence ends with Balthild's entry into Chelles; thenceforth her *humilitas* is the watchword.

36. *Passio Leudegarii Episcopi Augustodunensis I*, MGH SRM 5:282–322. Leudegar was killed in 679, and the first *Passio* (I) was written shortly thereafter. See Fouracre and Gerberding, *Late Merovingian France*, pp. 194–96.

37. That is, in the view of the author of the *Passio*. I make no attempt here to draw "ein bild der persönlichkeit Ebroins" as in Johannes Fischer, *Der Hausmeier Ebroin* (inaugural dissertation, Bonn, 1954), p. 76.

thankless role of upbraiding Childeric for his inversion of custom and his incestuous marriage bed. Put into custody—at Luxeuil, alongside Ebroin—Leudegar is depicted as another Peter about to be handed over to his persecutors to die (Acts 12:3–4). He is saved by the intervention of an abbot. Later, when Childeric is killed, both Ebroin and Leudegar emerge from Luxeuil, the former to take up his evil ways once again, the latter to return to Autun, where he preaches eternal verities and defiantly lectures even Ebroin's men. They take him as a willing hostage, torture him over a long period of time, then "suddenly" decapitate him.[38]

These texts reveal the strivings of aristocratic groups at court, some allied to the "old guard" (including Ebroin and Audoin) and others to Leudegar.[39] Soon a new faction would make a dramatic entrance. At Tertry in 687 Pippin II, a rich landowner in Austrasia and leader of a powerful faction of aristocrats there, won a battle against the Neustrians (see Genealogy 3). From hindsight we know that Pippin's heirs would eventually take over Neustria and become the "Carolingian" dynasty of kings. It used to be thought that 687 marked their rise.[40] More recently, Pippin's victory at Tertry has been downgraded to a skirmish in his real battle for alliances within the Neustrian aristocracy.[41] This new view is borne out by another important text from the 680s: the earliest immunity extant in its original form (see Fig. 2). It was issued by Theuderic III in 688—thirteen years after he emerged from Saint-Denis to take the throne again, and one year after Tertry. Like the *Vita Balthildis*, his immunity portrays a Merovingian at the center, giving gifts; like the *Passio Leudegarii*, it deals with the aristocratic factions of Ebroin and Leudegar—and it adds that of Pippin. But unlike the *Passio*, it portrays the king as the stable center.

Indeed, like a satin veil drawn over eddied sand, Theuderic's immunity of 688 reveals not a trace of political tumult. Instead, it expresses con-

---

38. *Passio Leudegarii*, c. 35, p. 317: "huius caput subito amputasset."

39. Gerberding, *Rise of the Carolingians*, convincingly insists on the crucial role of these factions on both sides, rather than of royal centralizers vs. regionalist nobles, and on p. 77, he speculates that Ebroin, who was not himself from a great family, may have been Audoin's "agent." The participation of Audoin is known from the account in the *Liber Historiae Francorum* c. 45, MGH SRM 2:318–19.

40. Even recent surveys repeat this view. See Stéphane Lebecq, *Les origines franques. V^e–IXe siècle*, Nouvelle Histoire de la France Médiévale 1 (Paris, 1990), p. 169.

41. Paul J. Fouracre, "Observations on the Outgrowth of Pippinid Influence in the 'Regnum Francorum' after the Battle of Tertry (687–715)," *Medieval Prosopography* 5 (1984): 1–31, esp. p. 13: "What we see in 687–715 may be the continuation of an old regime, not the establishment of a new one."

GENEALOGY 3. The Early Carolingians (simplified)

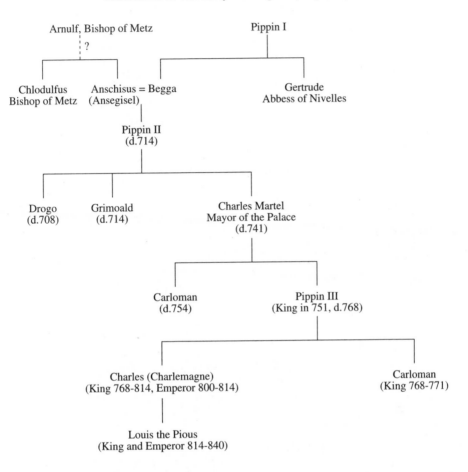

tinuity, amity, and cooperation. It is worth quoting; for clarity I present it in full summary rather than in literal translation.

> King Theuderic, who has been allowed by divine piety to come to legal age and succeed to the throne of the kingdom of his ancestors, finds it fitting and proper to think about the salvation of his soul. For this purpose he has come together in council with his bishops and nobles to cede the *villa* (estate) called Lagny-le-Sec, in the Meldois. This villa had belonged to Ebroin, Waratto, and Ghislemarus, all former mayors of the palace, and it reverted to the royal fisc after Waratto's death. At the suggestion of the

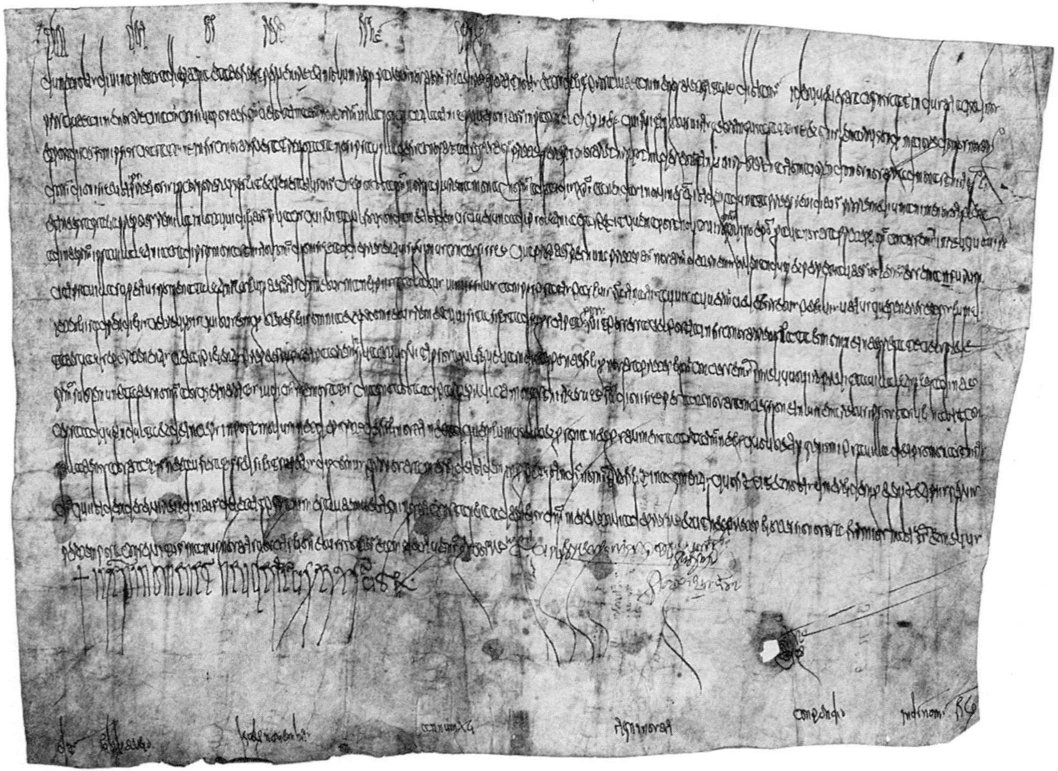

FIGURE 2. The Immunity of King Theuderic (October 30, 688). This is the earliest immunity still extant in its original form. Written on parchment, its first line is in *litterae elongatae*, a script characteristic of Merovingian and Carolingian royal documents and designed to impress even illiterate "readers." (Document K3, no. 2, reproduced by permission of the Centre Historique des Archives Nationales à Paris, whose Atelier de Photographie supplied the photograph.)

queen, Clotild, and of Bercharius, the present mayor, the king cedes the villa to the monastery of Saint-Denis. There Abbot Chaino and his community of monks sing the praises of Christ.

Lagny-le-Sec is ceded fully, except for a piece of property called Silly-le-Long. Silly once belonged to Arulfus, but afterward [perhaps when Lagny belonged to the mayors] it was part of Lagny. The king now gives Silly to Godinus, bishop of Lyon, while he gives Lagny to Chaino.

Thus Lagny is ceded, including all its land, houses, slaves, tenants, vineyards, woods, fields, meadows, pasture, mills, water and water courses, cattle, with all its adjacent land and properties except for Silly, which belonged to Arulfus and which by the king's edict now goes to the bishop of Lyon. Lagny is conceded under the title of immunity—whereby royal judges have no right of entry—to Chaino, who represents Saint-Denis, for lights for its basilica.

And henceforth let that villa not be in any way alienated or taken from the monastery by the royal fisc, either by charter or any device, to benefit someone else. But let it prosper there for the king's eternal reward; and let it be pleasing to those servants of God who labor there to pray very industriously for the salvation of the king's soul and the stability of his kingdom.[42]

Read one way, this is a document about rending and making whole again. Lagny-le-Sec, whole and integral, had included Silly-le-Long; but Silly could also be broken off from it, as in the days of Arulfus. Now, once again divided, Lagny served to unite, in one moment of gift-giving, two disparate factions. One was that of Ebroin. Eleven years before, Theuderic had given Chaino, then a deacon, property near Lagny: two pieces were near Provins, another probably near Meaux.[43] The mayor of the palace at that time was Ebroin, whose name appeared in Tironian notes (an elaborate shorthand) at the bottom of the charter. Now, in 688, Ebroin's name was invoked again in a gift to Chaino, who had meanwhile become abbot of Saint-Denis. At the same time, Silly was broken off Lagny to go to Go-

42. *ChLA* 13:90–91, no. 570. In giving a "full summary," I follow here the technique of Paul Fouracre, "'Placita' and the Settlement of Disputes in Later Merovingian Francia," in Wendy Davies and Paul Fouracre, *The Settlement of Disputes in Early Medieval Europe* (Cambridge, 1995), pp. 23–44. For the full Latin text, see Appendix 1.

43. *ChLA* 13:71–75, no. 566: property at Sancy-lès-Provins and Monceaux-lès-Provins (both *dép.* Seine-et-Marne, *arr.* Provins, *ca.* Villiers-Saint-Georges) and at *Alniti*, which is probably Aulnoy (*dép.* Seine-et-Marne, *arr.* Meaux, *ca.* Coulommiers). These places are close to each other; but it is possible that *Alniti* is Aulnay-sous-Bois (*dép.* Seine-Saint-Denis, *arr.* Le Raincy, *ch.-l. ca.*), which is near Paris.

dinus, bishop of Lyon, who represented another faction, that of Pippin.[44] We find Godinus as a bishop for the first time in this charter of 688. Subsequently he played a major role both in the Church and at court, ending up as abbot of Jumièges.[45] The simultaneous gifts of Lagny and Silly thus were meant to express a rapprochement between these two factions— Ebroin's and Pippin's—of Frankish aristocrats.

Not all factions were represented, however. There was another group, that of Leudegar. It was pointedly left out. We have seen how the *Passio Leudegarii* handled the enmity between Leudegar and Ebroin. Modern historians have a more jaundiced view of the matter. As soon as Childeric was killed (675) the two rivals "burst out of Luxeuil and each made a bid for power."[46] Leudegar backed Leudesius (Erchinoald's son) as mayor, but Ebroin immediately lured the new mayor to a deadly ambush. The fact that Leudesius was not part of the parade of mayors in the immunity of 688 suggests that one of its purposes was to write Leudegar's group out of the story.[47] Because immunities were part of a gift network, they did not just reorder space, like Polynesian taboos. They cemented and ruptured alliances as well.[48]

44. For Godinus, see Jean Laporte, "Les listes abbatiales de Jumièges," in *Jumièges. Congrès scientifique du XIIIe centenaire, Rouen, 10–12 June 1954* (Rouen, 1955), pp. 435–66; Alfred Coville, *Recherches sur l'histoire de Lyon du Vme siècle au IXme siècle (450–800)* (Paris, 1928), pp. 424–28.

45. In *ChLA* 14:11–14, no. 576, for example, he was present at a judicial hearing (*placitum*) held in 692 or 693 at the behest of Pippin's appointee as Neustria's mayor of the palace, Norbertus. Around the same time he mingled his church's land with the fisc, giving Nassigny, in Berry, to the royal fisc in exchange for Villeurbanne, in the vicinity of Lyon; see *ChLA* 14:15–19, no. 577: "quem apostholicus uir domnus Godinus, Lugduninsis urbis episcopus, de parti aecclisiae suae, pro alia uilla nuncopanti uilla Orbana, tempora bone memoriae germano nostro Chlodouio, condam rige, ad parti fisci, in conmutacionis titulum, uisus fuit dedisse." The transaction must have taken place between 690 and 694, the dates of Clovis's reign. We know (see LaPorte, "Les listes," p. 451) that someone named Godinus was abbot of Jumièges in about 710. If, as is likely, this was Godinus the bishop, then he was no doubt a Pippinid appointee; see Gerberding, *Rise of the Carolingians*, p. 98.

46. Fouracre and Gerberding, *Late Merovingian France*, p. 22.

47. Lagny-le-Sec was in an area associated with this group. In the *Vita Fursei*, Saint Fursey, welcomed by Clovis II and Erchinoald, builds a monastery at Lagny, in the vicinity of Meaux; see *Vita Fursei* c. 9, MGH SRM 4:438; this Lagny is *dép*. Seine-et-Marne, *arr*. Meaux, not far from Lagny-le-Sec, which is *dép*. Oise, *arr*. Senlis.

48. At one point, Leudesius and Ebroin had not been enemies. Leudesius was Ebroin's *compater*, which means that one of them had stood as godfather to the other's child. Fredegar [Continuator], *Chronicle*, c. 2, ed. Wallace-Hadrill, p. 82: "[Ebroinus] conpatri suo insidias praeparans ipsum Leudesium interficit." On the significance of this relationship, see Gerberding, *Rise of the Carolingians*, p. 77. More generally on the alliances that godparenthood generated, see Joseph H. Lynch, *Godparents and Kinship in Early Medieval Europe* (Princeton, N.J., 1986), esp. pp. 237–51; Bernhard Jussen, "Le parrainage à la fin du moyen âge: Savoir

One other group needs to be considered: those who were named as the petitioners for the immunity of 688. The gift of Lagny was ceded to Saint-Denis at the suggestion of the queen, Clotild, and the mayor of the palace, Bercharius. Bercharius's position seems straightforward enough: he was successor to the mayoral series Ebroin-Waratto-Ghislemarus, but he sacrificed the property that once came with the office.[49] Presumably he did so for the stability (*constancia*) of the kingdom. But what was Clotild's interest in Lagny? We know nothing more than her name; but that is suggestive. Levillain has speculated that she was of royal blood, possibly related to the Clotild who, in 673, founded and endowed a monastery for women at Bruyères-le-Châtel, south of Paris.[50] What is more certain is the model of queenship she was following: we have seen that the *Vita Balthildis*, written during the same decade, presented a royal benefactress who worked with her palace mayor to distribute gifts properly and thereby bring peace.

The Tenacity of the Merovingian System

That peace would hold.[51] The great "change" of the 690s was simply that the Carolingians became part of the system. The first of the still-extant original immunities of Theuderic's son Childebert III, issued in 694, was given to Abbot Chaino of Saint-Denis. Ornately displayed (and sublimely hidden) at the bottom of the charter was written in Tironian notes: "by order of Pippin, mayor of the palace."[52] The immunity ceded the *villa* of Nassigny to Chaino.[53] Its fiscal worth was finely calculated: Nassigny was given in exchange for two annual rents. The 200 *solidi* formerly given

public, attentes théologiques et usages sociaux," *Annales: ÉSC* 47 (1992): 467–502; and idem, *Patenschaft und Adoption im frühen Mittelalter: Künstliche Verwandtschaft als soziale Praxis* (Göttingen, 1991), esp. pp. 221–25 and 271–311.

49. He married into the family of Waratto's wife, Ansflidis. According to Fredegar [Continuator], *Chronicle*, c. 5, ed. Wallace-Hadrill, pp. 84–85, he was Ansflidis's son-in-law. According to *ChLA* 14:32–35, no. 581, the record of a *placitum*, he married Ansflidis, for there he was father-in-law (*socer*) of Drogo, Pippin's son, who married Ansflidis's daughter.

50. *Dép.* Essone, *arr.* Palaiseau, *ca.* Arpajon. See Léon Levillain, "Études mérovingiennes. La charte de Clotilde (10 mars 673)," *BÉC* 105 (1944): 5–63, esp. pp. 17–23.

51. See Fouracre and Gerberding, *Late Merovingian France*, pp. 25–26.

52. *ChLA* 14:19, no. 577.

53. The charter notes that Nassigny, given to the fisc by Godinus, was conceded to the *vir inluster* Pannichius, after whose death it reverted to the fisc, to be given out again, this time to Saint-Denis. Unfortunately, we know nothing further about Pannichius: see Ebling, *Prosopographie*, pp. 197–98, no. 250.

to Saint-Denis from the public purse and the 100 *solidi* previously handed over yearly to its agents by the king's agents at Marseille were now to go to the royal fisc. This marks a clear break with royal tradition: prior kings had granted the rents to Saint-Denis, which was now admonished not to claim them.[54] Yet the continuities are more striking: under the Carolingians, as under the Merovingians, immunities were used to reallocate resources.[55]

That the Carolingians were largely playing by Neustrian rules is also likely in Childebert's confirmation of a full immunity for all the property of the monastery of Tussonval, granted in 696.[56] The document harked back to a now lost immunity of Theuderic III. Nothing was said of fiscal land or specific properties: instead, every piece of property held by the monastery then and in the future was given immunity. Such a "blanket" immunity was unusual: it recalled the general entry prohibition of exemptions rather than immunities, but added the specific restraints on royal agents (*judices*) characteristic of immunities alone. No agent could hear cases, exact fines, collect dues of lodging, requisition victuals, or gather any sort of taxes on the lands of Tussonval; no agent could "presume to have ingress or entrance at all" on any of its property; rather, all the fines and dues were granted to the abbey for its lighting.

Why was Tussonval so favored? The answer seems to be that it represented an enclave of Neustrian aristocrats in the Chambliois that Pippin was wooing.[57] Tussonval had been founded and endowed on family lands by Chardericus, the abbot of Saint-Denis c. 677–88. He had dedi-

---

54. That the rents had indeed been given to Saint-Denis by earlier kings, beginning with Dagobert, is confirmed by the evidence in *ChLA* 14:6, no. 574.

55. Gerberding, *Rise of the Carolingians*, p. 105 and n. 78, sees no evidence of Pippin's influence in royal dealings with Saint-Denis until the time of Charles Martel. But perhaps Pippin made his presence felt in this reallocation of resources that the exchange of Nassigny for rents seems to imply. We might then understand the diploma of Chilperic II (*ChLA* 14:63–65, no. 589) drawn up in March 716 to restore to Saint-Denis the very rents exchanged for Nassigny, as part of the strategy fashioned by the *major domus* Raganfrid and other nobles among the Neustrian *Franci* to counter Charles Martel, son of Pippin, just before the battle of Amblève in April of the same year. On these events in *Liber Historiae Francorum*, cc. 51–52, see Gerberding, *Rise of the Carolingians*, pp. 129–30; Josef Semmler, "Zur pippinidisch-karolingischen Sukzessionskrise 714–723," *Deutsches Archiv für Erforschung des Mittelalters* 33 (1977): 1–36, esp. pp. 7–13.

56. *ChLA* 14:23, no. 579. See Gerberding, *Rise of the Carolingians*, p. 104.

57. The "Chambliois," or territory (*pagus*) of Chambly, was an irregularly shaped region about thirty kilometers wide at its widest point, centering on Chambly and cut, at its southernmost part, by the Oise river. See Map 2 and Auguste Longnon, *Atlas historique de la France depuis César jusqu'à nos jours* (Paris, 1889), plate 8. The landholdings of the Neustrian faction discussed here extended from this region northward (though still within the present *dép.* Oise).

cated the new monastery to Saint Denis and set up his nephew, Magnoaldus, to be its abbot.[58] Magnoaldus was already a landowner in the vicinity, and one of his neighbors was a man by the name of Godinus.[59] We know of three men of this name at this time, and all were associated with Pippin.[60] It seems that we have come upon a territorial enclave of which Pippin, too, was aware.

This is further borne out by evidence from two "fictive disputes" of the 690s. Such showcase trials began at about this time; they should be seen as part of the political and social strategies of both the Carolingians and "native" Neustrian factions either to "announce" their power or to make a show of their capitulation. Fictive cases used the form of the *placitum*—the recorded judgment of a royal convocation at which one party presented a claim against another—to ratify property ownership arrangements to which all parties were already agreed.[61] While fictive in "proving" property ownership, the court sittings were real in acting out clashes or potential clashes of interests and their resolution. Two of them concern the Chambliois faction. They demonstrate how Pippin was forced to make—and to be seen making—concessions after Tertry.

In the first (691), Abbot Chaino of Saint-Denis came to a moderately-

58. The information is in *ChLA* 14:23, no. 579. The date of the foundation is not known, nor is the monastery's location, other than that it was "in pago Camliaciacinse"—the Chambliois.

59. In about 691 (when he was already abbot of Tussonval), he and Landebertus, the abbot of Saint-Germain-l'Auxerrois at Paris, exchanged some family lands about fifty kilometers to the north of the Chambliois. The transaction was a friendly one, allowing both men to consolidate the patrimony of their kinfolk: see *ChLA* 13:60–62, no. 563. The consolidation can be seen from the border description: Magnoaldus gave up land at "Francorecurte" (not identified) that bordered on property belonging to Landebertus and his heirs; Landebertus did the same for Magnoaldus and his heirs at Rocquencourt (*dép. Oise, arr. Clermont, ca. Breteuil*).

60. Present at the *placitum* of Clovis III (*ChLA* 14:11–14, no. 576), which concerned land just north of the Chambliois (Bayencourt [*dép. Oise, arr. Compiègne*]) were three men named Godinus. One was the bishop of Lyon; another signed next to Norbertus, Pippin's "representative" in Neustria; the third, a count (*grafio*), signed next to Sigofredus, who subsequently became *auditor* for Grimoald, Pippin's son. (For Norbertus, see Ebling, *Prosopographie*, p. 196, no. 248; for two of the men named Godinus, see p. 163, nos. 192–193; for Sigofredus, see pp. 216–17, no. 280.) Thus, although the *bishop* Godinus was probably not Magnoaldus's neighbor at Rocquencourt (since no title follows his name in that document), the other landowners in the vicinity with the name Godinus seem also to have represented Pippin's men or those he was wooing, given that one became a functionary for his son while the other signed next to one of his followers.

61. These fictive disputes were first identified and analyzed in Werner Bergmann, "Untersuchungen zu den Gerichtsurkunden der Merowingerzeit," *Archiv für Diplomatik* 22 (1976): 1–186, esp. pp. 93–102; see further, Fouracre, "Placita," in Davies and Fouracre, *Settlement of Disputes*, pp. 23–44, esp. p. 26 and nn. 13–14.

sized gathering of king, magnates, and bishops to claim that a *villa* in the Chambliois, Noisy-sur-Oise, had been given to him and his monastery by a woman named Angantrudis and her husband Ingobertus, deceased by the time of the hearing.[62] Written evidence concerning this property was introduced into court; Angantrudis confirmed the donation; and Clovis III awarded Noisy to Chaino, barred Angantrudis and her heirs from making claim to the property, and called upon them to oppose zealously anyone who might attempt to do so. This was clearly a prearranged outcome.

The second *placitum*, a grand affair attended by numerous lay and ecclesiastical leaders, took place in 697. It, too, concerned Noisy.[63] Magnoaldus, the abbot of Tussonval, claimed that King Theuderic had dipped into the royal fisc to give Noisy, which had once belonged to Gaerinus (count of Paris and brother of Leudegar) to Tussonval. But, said Magnoaldus, the agents of Drogo, Pippin's son, had stolen from and wasted the property. Then Drogo made his case. He did not exactly dispute the history of Noisy presented by Magnoaldus. But he claimed that the abbot had subsequently exchanged Noisy with his father-in-law (*socer*)— Bercharius, mayor of the palace. The land had then gone by right and law to Adaltrude, Bercharius's daughter and Drogo's wife.[64] Magnoaldus admitted that he had once discussed making such an exchange with Bercharius, but nothing had ever come of it.[65] For his part, Drogo was unable to buttress his claim with documentation, and the court ruled against him.

There are a number of reasons to think that this was a showcase trial that announced in a graphic manner just how much Pippin was willing to concede to the interests of one Neustrian faction. Pippin was present in court at the king's side, named right after the bishops and before the great magnates (*optimates*). His own son Grimoald stood amid the latter group. Drogo, the unsuccessful defendant, was also Pippin's son, and was clearly identified as such in the written account. The family was out in

---

62. ChLA 14:8–10, no. 575.

63. ChLA 14:32–35, no. 581: here Noisy is first called *curte . . . nuncopanti Nocito, que ponetur in pago Camiliacinse*; later it is called *ipsa uilla, ipsa curte, loco Nocito,* and *rem Nocito.* In ibid., no. 575, the earlier court case, it is first called *uilla nuncopanti Nocito sitam in pago Camiliacinse,* and thereafter, consistently, *villa Nocito.* The fact that the words *villa* and *in pago Camiliacinse* are used at both court procedings strongly suggests that they concern the same unit of property.

64. These are the relationships reported in the *placitum.* It is likely that Bercharius had *not* been Drogo's father-in-law (see note 69 below).

65. ChLA 14:34, no. 581: "Intendebat aecontra ipsi Magnoaldus, quasi conlocucione et conuenencia exinde apud ipso Berchario habuissit, ut ipsa inter se conmutassent; sed hoc numquam ficissent nec de ipsa curte ipsi Berecharius mano uestita numquam habuissit."

force. Yet Drogo was unable to produce written evidence to support his position. He and his brother and father must have known that written documentation was required by these royal courts.[66] It seems that they were there to capitulate ostentatiously.

There are other anomalies in the account of the *placitum* that may also be explained by supposing that the court was not terribly interested in all the facts of the case. First, if the Noisy of Angantrudis's *placitum* and that of Drogo's were the same (as seems to be the case), then the two proceedings presented rather different histories of ownership. Yet there was a considerable overlap of magnates present at the two *placita* (although the meeting of 697 was indisputably larger), and many of the participants would have heard both stories.[67]

Second, the *placitum* pretended that Drogo's relationship with Bercharius was close. This is very odd indeed, considering that Bercharius was a discredited man. Some Neustrian magnates had disliked him as soon as he became mayor of the palace in 686. That is why they encouraged Pippin's foray into Neustria the next year.[68] Bercharius promptly lost the ensuing Battle of Tertry. In 688, he was killed in a plot orchestrated by Ansflidis, who was probably his mother-in-law. Surely Pippin had been working behind the scenes, for shortly thereafter his son Drogo married Ansflidis's widowed daughter.[69] Why rehabilitate Bercharius as a "father-in-law" and emphasize his "lawful" handing down of Noisy if not to placate remnants of the "old guard?"

If we assume that the *placita* of 691 and 697 were related and that the

66. Fouracre, "Placita," in Davies and Fouracre, *Settlement of Disputes*, e.g., at p. 35.

67. Five men were present at both: Constantinus, Grimo/Gribo/Gripho, Ursinianus, Madelulfus, and Benedictus. The *placitum* of 691 had only seven others present. The number of magnates at the *placitum* of 697 cannot be counted, since the list ends with "and all our fideles." Presumably the men who had participated at both meetings would have recalled that at the first Chaino had been awarded Noisy.

68. Fredegar [Continuator], *Chronicle*, c. 5, ed. Wallace-Hadrill, p. 85; *Liber Historiae Francorum*, c. 48, MGH SRM 2:322.

69. According to Fredegar [Continuator], *Chronicle*, c. 5, ed. Wallace-Hadrill, p. 85, Bercharius was *gener*, son-in-law, of Ansflidis. According to the *Annales Mettenses Priores*, ed. B. von Simson, MGH SRG (Hannover, 1905), p. 16, Drogo was Ansflidis's son-in-law; he married her daughter, Anstrude/Adaltrude. (Ewig and others consider it probable that the name Adaltrude was changed by the writer of the *Annales* to Anstrude: see Eugen Ewig, "Die fränkischen Teilreiche im 7. Jahrhundert," in Ewig, *Gallien*, 1:227 n. 218.) The conclusion accepted by most commentators is that Anstrude/Adaltrude married Bercharius; after his death (arranged by her mother and Pippin), she married Drogo. Drogo's court case, however (ChLA 14:34), presents Bercharius as the *father* of Drogo's wife, Anstrude/Adaltrude, and says that Noisy reverted to her from him by law: "iustisseme ad partem coniuge sui [Drogo's] Adaltrute ligibus reddeberitur."

defendants in both cases and on all sides were reconciled to the very verdicts in fact arrived at, we can begin to understand the dynamics behind both the vagaries of Noisy and Childebert's immunity for Tussonval of 696. Let us begin with the relationships recalled in 691. Angantrudis's father, Ebrulfus, had been among the dignitaries present when, in the early part of his reign, Clovis II confirmed Saint-Denis's possession of land in the Chambliois.[70] His position in the charter next to Wandalbertus, *dux* in the Chambliois, suggests that he, too, was an official there.[71] In Dagobert's confirmation of Landeric's exemption for Saint-Denis, Ebrulfus's name had been placed next to Gaerinus, who was count of Paris and brother of Leudegar. The juxtaposition was more than happenstance: Ebrulfus married his daughter, our defendant Angantrudis, to a man close to the Leudegar group.

Angantrudis's husband, Ingobertus, figures in a key primary source for the period, the *Liber Historiae Francorum*, as a ringleader of the conspirators who plotted against Childeric, elevated Leudesius to the mayoralty, and found support in the circle represented by Leudegar and Gaerinus.[72] In a spurious diploma, which is nevertheless perhaps correct in this detail, Ingobertus was a "top man" (*optimas*) under Theuderic III.[73]

To sum up: the evidence suggests that a circle of Chambliois magnates—including Chardericus, Magnoaldus, Angantrudis, and Ebrulfus—partially intersected with another, older faction that included Leudegar, his brother Gaerinus, and Ingobertus. The relationship of both groups to the king's court was in the process of redefinition after Tertry. We have already seen how, in 688, Leudesius was passed over in a parade of named mayors. In the 690s silence was abandoned in favor of reconfiguring alliances. In 691 Chaino, abbot of Saint-Denis since 688 and, as we have seen, a man agreeable to making adjustments between his basilica and the royal house, claimed Noisy. Since his predecessor, Chardericus, had endowed Tussonval and dedicated it to Saint Denis, Chaino's claims (in Chardericus's place and on behalf of the proper saint) had validity even if, as we learn later, Tussonval had a claim on it as well. But the point of Chaino's claim was more than to document ownership. He arrived speaking against (*adversus*) Angantrudis. He invoked a story (surely the truth, but not the whole truth) about Noisy: how it had been hers and her hus-

---

70. *ChLA* 13:28–29, no. 556: property "in pago Quamliacense," that is, the Chambliois.
71. For Ebrulfus, see Ebling, *Prosopographie*, p. 134, no. 151; for Wandalbertus, pp. 231–32, no. 305.
72. *Liber Historiae Francorum*, c. 45, MGH SRM 2:318.
73. MGH Dip. Mer., p. 190, no. 74.

band's *villa*, obtained by them through both inheritance and acquisition, and then given to Saint-Denis. At the end of the *placitum* the shades of the past were joined by future generations: Angantrudis and her heirs would henceforth defend Saint-Denis's claims to the property. Thus the procedings against Angantrudis, held in a royal court with Norbertus sitting in for Pippin, reenacted enmity and effected reconciliation with a Neustrian family that apparently found it to be in its own interest to readjust its alliances.

The next stage that we can glimpse in the realignment of the Chambliois group is in the document we have been following for several pages—the 696 confirmation of Theuderic's immunity for Tussonval issued by Childebert III. We do not know what Theuderic's now lost immunity contained. But it is certainly clear that by 696 Chardericus, Magnoaldus, and their foundation at Tussonval were being linked indissolubly to royal largesse. The history of Tussonval was reviewed; the king's role in its freedom and integrity made clear; and the obligations of the community to "pray ceaselessly for the stability of our kingdom" set forth. This was another immunity that, behind its formulaic phrases, hid the negotiation of a new alliance.

In 697, as we have seen, Magnoaldus brought claims against Drogo. This *placitum* associated Noisy explicitly with the various parties whose rapprochement was ritually enacted in it: the Merovingian house, the Carolingians, and the Chambliois faction. Saint-Denis's stewardship of Noisy was immaterial in this particular context.[74] Here still another partial history of Noisy was set forth: that it had been part of the royal fisc, that it had once belonged to Gaerinus (Leudegar's brother, let us remember), and that it had been conceded to Tussonval by King Theuderic himself. The enmity between these Neustrian groups and the Carolingians was expressed through the medium of the *placitum*; and we may imagine that Drogo did indeed make claim to the property in question and had a right (of some sort) to do so. But now the Carolingians were ready to make concessions. Drogo countered the charge against him with a story about Bercharius, in the process invoking close relations and even a kind of right of inheritance from the man who had lost a battle to Drogo's father and a wife to Drogo himself! Further, even if Bercharius had made a trade with Magnoaldus, Drogo's method of demonstrating it—without written evidence—was calculated to fail. Thus the Chambliois faction, repre-

---

74. This may explain why here Chardericus is referred to as lord (*domnus*) and former bishop, not as abbot of Saint-Denis.

sented by Magnoaldus, made their peace with the Carolingians. Let the matter henceforth remain a "sleeping claim" (*subita* [= *sopita*] *causacio*) are the last words of the *placitum*.

We can now summarize the history of Noisy as it emerges from the sources. A royal fisc, it was probably given to Gaerinus when he became count at Paris.[75] Later it became part of the "patrimony" of Ingobertus, whose relationship with Gaerinus we have noted. Indeed, Ingobertus may have succeeded Gaerinus as count at Paris precisely because he had control of Noisy.[76] He and his wife, Angantrudis, later gave Noisy to Saint Denis (that is, the saint and his churches). This must have been a complicated transaction, involving the participation of the king (Theuderic III), Abbot Chaino, and Magnoaldus (abbot of Tussonval). Magnoaldus and Bercharius later made some sort of agreement concerning Noisy. Though nothing may have come of it, the agreement gave Drogo a pretext to make claim to Noisy through his wife. The history of Noisy gave it a social significance of unusual richness: it could rightly be claimed by numerous groups. Thus it served as an especially potent focal point for negotiating alliances and realliances. The needs of the moment dictated which elements of the story would be selected for retelling at any one time.

Thus the 696 immunity for Tussonval was part of a social and political process of realignment.[77] If we survey the immunities issued by the Merovingians between the 650s and the 690s we see clearly that they were issued and used as multivalent political instruments. There is nothing wrong with speaking about *the* purpose of immunities—charitable, administrative, fiscal—but it seems more correct to recognize that they were all these things and more: by the late seventh century they had become key instruments in the politics of negotiation.

75. *ChLA* 14:54, no. 586 (709 or 710): "Gairinus, qondam, loce ipsius Parisiace comis."

76. Ebling, *Prosopographie*, p. 175, no. 215.

77. The similarities between the name Angantrudis and Adaltrude/Anstrude (the element -trude/trudis = -thruth) suggest kinship between the women involved.

PART II
Control

The Carolingian coup of 751 is better known than that staged by Clothar II in the seventh century, and it brought with it a more profound transformation. The new Carolingian conception of government modeled the ruler on the kings of the Old Testament, who instituted God's law and ruled by God's grace. The Carolingians had the contrary of a "hands-off" policy vis-à-vis churches and monasteries. But by the time they came to power, immunities could not simply be jettisoned; they were part and parcel of a well-run kingdom. Instead, they were transformed. The key to this transformation was one small word: *tuitio*—protection. It came to be paired with the word "immunity," as in the phrase *sub nostra defensione et inmunitatis tuitione*—"under our defense and the protection of immunity." Protection meant that kings would be actively involved in ecclesiastical and monastic business. Exemptions underwent similar modifications.

We see the change beginning already in the mid-eighth century, with Bishop Chrodegang of Metz and his foundation of the monastery of Gorze (Chapter 5). The political and religious uses of the new type of charter are explored in detail by looking at an immunity *cum* exemption for the monastery of Salonnes (Chapter 6).

5

"Playing a New Tune": The Carolingians

THROUGHOUT THE first third of the eighth century, bishops and kings continued to issue restrictions against their own or their agents' incursions.[1] By the middle of the century, however, *tuitio*, protection, was sometimes added to privileges of immunity. The modification betokened nothing less than a sea change—from prohibition to control.

The new development reflected transformations at the top of both Church and kingdom. Rulers and bishops alike claimed the new rights and responsibilities of protection. Sometimes, especially at first, in the time of Boniface and Charles Martel, competing claims resulted in clashes. But the close working relationship with, and indeed control over, the Church that the Carolingians cultivated meant that most often clerics and rulers found common ground.

With Pippin's son Charles Martel, who seized the mayoralty in 715 against his father's wishes, a new political order was set in place. In general, the Carolingians did not just favor and reform monasteries: they saw themselves as arising *from* monasteries and churches. They claimed, for example, that Pippin II was the nephew of the saintly Abbess Gertrude of Nivelles and grandson of Bishop Arnulf of Metz.[2] When Pippin III became the first Carolingian king in 751, he marked the occasion by receiv-

---

1. Laymen also restricted the entry of bishops and royal agents in their charters. See examples in Heidrich, "Titulatur und Urkunden."

2. For the relation to Gertrude: *Vita sanctae Geretrudis*, c. 1, MGH SRM 2:454, where she is daughter of Pippin I; for the relationship to Arnulf, see below, Chap. 6 n. 41.

ing a holy anointment intended to graft his dynasty onto the line of Old Testament priest-kings. The Carolingians were part of the Church. Indeed, when Pope Stephen II crossed the Alps to beg the aid of Pippin III in 753–54 and to anoint him once again, the Carolingians appeared to "rule" the Church. Already Pippin III claimed to govern "by grace of God"; he was the custodian of the ecclesiastical order.[3] In this atmosphere, monasteries and churches were rightly under the king's control.

Charles Martel marks the start of this development. Long considered a despoiler of churches, his image is currently being rehabilitated.[4] The "new history" of Charles's mayoralty emphasizes his attempts at Church reform. His efforts were not, admittedly, in the severe style of his contemporary, the Anglo-Saxon missionary Boniface (675–754). Nevertheless, they were real and pragmatic.[5] The most serious accusation against Charles used to be that he alienated church property. He was associated with precarial arrangements, the so-called *precariae verbo regis*—the king's forcible transfer of church lands into theoretically temporary land grants (*precariae*) to reward his followers. The new historiography, however, points out that the sources attesting to such a policy are few, mostly late, and sometimes forged.[6] Precarial (that is, temporary) grants were given out by churches and monasteries, but not because of Charles. They were part of local networks of gift exchange in which benefactors and their families routinely received their donations back again in precarial grants. If the palace mayor and his men took advantage of the practice, there was nothing remarkable in the fact.[7] From their point of view, they were

---

3. MGH Dip. Kar. 1:33, no. 24 (768), is apparently the first royal diploma to use the formula "gratia dei rex Francorum." However, it is not extant in the original. The earliest extant original royal diploma to use this formula is one for Carloman, issued in 769: ibid., no. 45, p. 65.

4. See the papers in Jörg Jarnut, Ulrich Nonn, and Michael Richter, eds., *Karl Martell in seiner Zeit*, Beihefte der Francia 37 (Sigmaringen, 1994). The older view is well summed up in Alain Bondroit, "Les 'precariae verbo regis' avant le concile de Leptinnes (a. 743)," *Revue d'Histoire Ecclésiastique* 1 (1900): 41–60, 249–66, 430–47.

5. See Timothy Reuter, "'Kirchenreform' und 'Kirchenpolitik' im Zeitalter Karl Martells. Begriffe und Wirklichkeit," pp. 35–59, at pp. 46–50, and Hans-Werner Goetz, "Karl Martell und die Heiligen. Kirchenpolitik und Maiordomat im Spiegel der spätmerowingischen Hagiographie," pp. 101–17, both in Jarnut, Nonn, and Richter, *Karl Martell in seiner Zeit*.

6. Reuter, "Kirchenreform," pp. 44–45.

7. Herwig Wolfram, "Karl Martell und das fränkische Lehenswesen. Aufnahme eines Nichtbestandes," in Jarnut, Nonn, and Richter, *Karl Martell in seiner Zeit*, pp. 61–77, esp. pp. 67–68; Ian N. Wood, "Teutsind, Witlaic and the History of Merovingian *Precaria*," in Davies and Fouracre, *Settlement of Disputes*, pp. 31–53. Hans Josef Hummer, "Monastic Property, Family Continuity and Central Authority in Early Medieval Alsace and Southern Lotharingia" (Ph.D. diss., UCLA, 1997). I thank Hans Hummer for providing me with a copy of his study.

rightly sharing, even participating, in the wealth of the Church. At the same time, as Walter Goffart has pointed out, they were announcing a new idea: that churches should be allotted only as much property as they needed to carry out their duties. The ruler's "protection" would guarantee the necessary minimum.[8] The Carolingians intended to be the stewards of ecclesiastical wealth.

But another view of the matter came from the circle of church reformers such as Boniface, who placed new emphasis on *episcopal* control over the property of the Church. We can see their program clearly in the canons of church councils held under his aegis.[9] The assembled fathers no longer spoke about bishops threatening to alienate, deteriorate, diminish, or subtract from the property of churches.[10] On the contrary, they were preoccupied with establishing the bishop's control over the religious institutions in his diocese.[11] If church property was abused, it was the fault of laymen. In a letter written in 747, Boniface spoke of "the layman or emperor or king or official or count" who snatches a monastery "from the power of a bishop, an abbot, or an abbess and begins to reign there in place of the abbot and has monks under him and takes possession of the wealth that was obtained through Christ's blood": *that* man is a murderer of the poor (*homicida pauperum*).[12]

Chrodegang of Metz

Thus, in reformist circles, bishops were no longer seen as potential abusers of church property. Indeed, they were the "shepherds," the protectors,

8. See Goffart, *Le Mans Forgeries*, pp. 9–11, adding to Wallace-Hadrill, *Frankish Church*, p. 139. The principle that this *necessary* property should not be alienated is expressed (as Goffart points out) in 768 in a capitulary for Aquitaine: MGH Cap. reg. Fr. 1:43. Goffart, *Le Mans Forgeries*, p. 12, connects this new idea with the growth of royal protection.

9. For the church councils of the eighth century, see MGH Conc. 2, pt. 1, and some of the capitularies in MGH Cap. reg. Fr. 1.

10. Such unconcern about episcopal abuse would continue until the reign of Louis the Pious (814–40). When it became an issue once again in the ninth century, however, it was not handled through episcopal exemptions, as it had been in the Merovingian period; see Janet Nelson, "Making Ends Meet: Wealth and Poverty in the Carolingian Church," in W. J. Sheils and Diana Wood, eds., *The Church and Wealth* (Oxford, 1987), pp. 25–35.

11. Summed up in Wilfried Hartmann, *Die Synoden der Karolingerzeit im Frankenreich und in Italien* (Paderborn, 1989), pp. 50–67.

12. Boniface, *Epistola 78*, ed. Michael Tangl, in *Die Briefe des heiligen Bonifatius und Lullus*, MGH Epp. sel. 1:169: "Illud autem, quod laicus homo vel imperator vel rex aut aliquis prefectorum vel comitum seculari potestate fultus sibi per violentiam rapiat monasterium de potestate episcopi vel abbatis vel abbatissae et incipiat ipse vicę abbatis regere et habere sub

of churches. And protection meant control. The career of Chrodegang of Metz (d. 766) demonstrates this new view in action. But Chrodegang also illustrates how church reform and episcopal control could serve the interest of the king too, as long as both bishop and ruler were linked by family ties, land-ownership, oaths of fidelity, and common goals.

A man of both the palace and the Church, Chrodegang served as referendary under Charles Martel.[13] He rose with the Carolingians. The center of their power was Metz, long a royal residence, and also the resting place of Saint Arnulf, bishop of Metz, whom the Carolingians would later claim as the illustrious ancestor of their dynasty.[14] Chrodegang was appointed bishop of Metz by Pippin III in 742.

Within a few years of his consecration as bishop, Chrodegang founded a monastery within his diocese at Gorze, about thirteen kilometers southwest of Metz.[15] From the start, it was closely tied to the patronage of Chrodegang's cathedral church. He received permission from Pippin, whom he styled his "lord" (senior), to donate numerous properties belonging to the patrimony of his cathedral church of Saint Stephen at Metz to the patron saints of the new church at Gorze: Saints Peter, Stephen (as at Metz), and others.[16] The patrimony was meant to provide the monks with necessities only: "food and clothes and other comforts" (victum et vestitum

---

se monachos et pecuniam possidere, quę fuit Christi sanguine conparata, talem hominem antiqui patres nominabant raptorem et sacrilegum et homicidam pauperum."

13. According to Paul the Deacon in GeM, p. 267; but Heidrich, "Titulatur und Urkunden," pp. 205–9, suggests that Paul's terminology is anachronistic here, though Chrodegang was doubtless a high official in the royal scriptorium.

14. On Metz, see Ewig, "Résidence et capitale," in Ewig, Gallien 1:362–408, here 385–86; Otto Gerhard Oexle, "Die Karolinger und die Stadt des heiligen Arnulf," Frühmittelalterliche Studien 1 (1967): 250–364. Heidrich, "Titulatur und Urkunden," p. 223, calls Metz the "Metropole" of the Austrasians. On the date of Chrodegang's consecration, Eugen Ewig, "Saint Chrodegang et la reforme de l'église franque," in Ewig, Gallien, 2:232–59, here p. 234 and n. 3. Chrodegang was not from the Moselle (or Metz) region but rather from the Hesbaye (around Liège). The evidence is in GeM, p. 267: "ex pago Hasbaniensi oriundus, patre Sigramno, matre Landrada." But he was consanguineus of Cancor, count in the Rheingau (see Lorsch 1:266), who, together with his mother, Williswinda, was founder of Lorsch in the Moselle region. She was the widow of Ruopertus comes (ibid., 1:265), probably Robert, duke in the Hesbaye. Perhaps Chrodegang's mother, Landrada, was related to Robert: see Karl Glöckner, "Lorsch und Lothringen, Robertiner und Capetinger," Zeitschrift für die Geschichte des Oberrheins, n.s., 50 (1937):301–54, at 312.

15. On the diocese of Metz, see GC 13:826–957; for Gorze, pp. 875–93.

16. The charters of Chrodegang for Gorze were copied into the twelfth-century MS 826 Bibl. municipale Metz = Gorze, where Chrodegang's donations are nos. 1–3; issues of authenticity are raised on pp. 365–78: some of the places named in Chrodegang's bequest may be interpolations.

vel aliam consolationem). It was to be a reformed monastery in the new, pared-down style.

The meaning of "reform" was made still clearer when, in 757, Chrodegang gave Gorze a privilege, but decidedly not an exemption. The document, a clear break from the past, reflected Chrodegang's growing importance in the political and religious life of the Frankish kingdom. It may well have been he, rather than Boniface, who first anointed Pippin king. Certainly he was one of the prelates who escorted Pope Stephen II across the Alps to reanoint Pippin. He received the *pallium*—a scarf that symbolized special ties to Rome—upon the death of Boniface in 754 and with it succeeded to Boniface's archiepiscopal position.[17] Around the same time, he published a *Rule* for canons, an unprecedented blueprint that (among other things) set up a way of life (*ordo*) for his canons (priests serving the cathedral) at Metz parallel to the *ordo* for monks everywhere else. The Council of Ver in 755, where Chrodegang presumably presided, decreed that all men who had taken the tonsure but still held their own properties and estates were to be "either in a monastery under the order of a rule or under the control of the bishop under the order of canons," that is, under Chrodegang's rule.[18]

Chrodegang's privilege for Gorze was issued in the course of another synod held two years later (757) at Compiègne. In some ways it was a counterpart to Ver: just as the fathers at the earlier council had attempted to describe and control a great variety of lay marital practices, so the privilege for Gorze tried to anticipate, confine, and control the monastic life. Although echoing some of the phrases of exemption in the Merovingian formulary book of Marculf, for example, the Gorze privilege turned the key ideas of Merovingian exemption on their head. What Chrodegang issued in 757 was, in effect, an anti-exemption. A comparison of the relevant passages in his privilege with its "model" in Marculf is instructive. (See Appendix 2 for a systematic analysis. The numbers in parentheses here refer to the clause numbers in Appendix 2).[19] Both documents

17. For convenient summaries of the facts, see Angenendt, *Das Frühmittelalter*, pp. 288–91, and Josef Semmler, "Chrodegang von Metz," in *Theologische Realenzyklopädie*, 8:71–74.

18. Council of Ver, c. 11, MGH Cap. reg. Fr. 1:35: "placuit ut in monasterio sint sub ordine regulari aut sub manu episcopi sub ordine canonica."

19. The formula is Marculf 1.1, pp. 18–24. Chrodegang's privilege is in MGH Conc. 1:60–63, and *Gorze*, no. 4. I am grateful to Professor Michel Parisse for kindly sharing with me his view that Chrodegang's privilege is authentic. While it clearly relies on passages that are also in Marculf, this does not necessarily mean that the formulary was available to Chrodegang's scribes; it may mean that this privilege relied on one or more similar privileges now lost. Indeed, Chrodegang's privilege refers to a previous (and now lost) "constitutionem, quam eis instituimus," which may have contained some of the same passages. How-

announced the same purpose, to ensure monastic peace, but took entirely different paths to this goal. In Marculf, the key was exemption:

> (2) Let no one disparage us, thinking that he sees us playing a new tune here; for from ancient times, in conformity with episcopal regulations for royal decrees, innumerable monasteries clearly existed under privileges of liberty.

Chrodegang's charter inverted the liberty:

> (2) Let no one disparage us, thinking that he sees something new here; for from ancient times, in conformity with episcopal practice, other monasteries were subjected to, preserved by, and secure in bishops in all matters.

Marculf's formulary prohibited all episcopal powers over the monastery:

> (5) Neither we nor our episcopal successors nor archdeacons nor other deputies or any other person from the [episcopal] city should presume to have any other right at all over this monastery: not over its property, its ordinations, or the estates that have been given or will be given there by royal or individual gift, or over any other of its holdings. Nor should [any of us] hope for or take anything from this monastery by way of remuneration as [we do] from the diocese or other monasteries. Nor should we presume to take what has been given by God-fearing people or offered on the altar, whether sacred volumes or objects of any kind that have been or will be given in future to adorn the divine office.

Chrodegang's charter echoed the provision against spoliation of monastic lands, but pointedly left out the provisions against ordination and remuneration:

> (3) It is fitting that we preserve their quiet and order and tranquillity for them so that they not be disturbed or plundered or despoiled against the order of reason—not by us nor our archdeacon or other delegate of Saint-Stephen [of Metz] or anyone at all. Rather, let them hold and possess their property in quiet. Nor should we take away what we gave and confirmed to the monastery or what was given and confirmed by God-fearing people or given as a gift or placed on the altar, whether sacred volumes or precious objects of any kind to adorn the divine office.

---

ever, Marculf *could* have been a model, for Heidrich, "Titulatur und Urkunden," pp. 175–90, has pointed out that it was first clearly utilized as a formulary book in the time of Charles Martel.

Indeed, the bishop's visitations, to be made when he pleased, were envisioned as a regular feature of life at Gorze, though done *gratis*:

> (6) And if, when it pleases him, the aforesaid bishop comes to the monastery to give them the benefit of prayer or visit the brethren . . . let him return without requiring any earthly gift.

This last provision not only struck against the entry prohibition of episcopal exemptions but did so deliberately, by changing, leaving out, and adding a few words to the model, which read:

> (6) And unless we have been asked by the congregation or its abbot to give them the benefit of prayer, none of us should be allowed to enter the *secreta septa* of the monastery. . . . But if the bishop is asked . . . let him leave without seeking any required gift.

Here was an inversion indeed. It is therefore not surprising that Chrodegang's charter modified the exemption's provision that promised free election of the abbot; the Gorze monks had to be sure that the election would be in accord with (5) "the consent and will" of the bishop.

The key new words in the Gorze charter were "subjection" and "protection." They were paired in a clause that set forth the monastic purpose:

> (4) And let this monastery be subject to the protection and safeguard of the church of Saint Stephen of Metz, so that [the monks] will be pleased to pray for the Lord's mercy for the life and safety of the king, for the stability of the kingdom of the Franks, for their bishops, and for those placed under them.

To sum up: Chrodegang's privilege for Gorze was protective rather than liberative. It emphasized the control that the bishop of Metz had over his monastery rather than prohibitions on his rights. True, he would not despoil it of its property; but he would exercise his *pontificium* of blessing and consecrating (without exacting a fee), and his consent would be necessary whenever a new abbot was chosen. Chrodegang knew that he was flying in the face of the by now standard "big liberty." We can be sure of this not only because his charter so flagrantly tampered with its formulae but also because he himself had once participated in the granting of just such an "old-fashioned" liberty. This happened about a decade before the foundation of Gorze (746), when a disciple of Pirmin, Bishop Heddo of Strasbourg, affirmed an exemption of the old sort for the monastery of Arnulfsau-Schwarzach. We know that Chrodegang was there: he signed the charter.[20]

Chrodegang's privilege for Gorze was in fact an amalgam of old and new.[21] By affirming the rights of the bishop over the monastery, it harked back to the council of Chalcedon. But it mitigated this reactionary flavor with a provision that was just coming into vogue in public administration. Envisioning a relationship of intimate dependency, Chrodegang placed Gorze under the protection (*mundeburdium* and *defensio*) of the church of Saint Stephen.[22]

Protection

By the time Chrodegang drew up his privilege, popes had been taking monasteries under their protection for over a century. We have seen in Chapter 3 that in 628 Honorius I freed Bobbio from the jurisdiction (*dicio* and *auctoritas*) of every ecclesiastic (*sacerdos*) except that of the pope himself: *sub iurisdictione sanctae nostrę*.[23] Extant only in a tenth-century copy, the authenticity of this key passage is nevertheless very likely. First, it

20. *Reg. Alsat.*, pp. 97–100, no. 166. The document is clearly based on the same model as *ChLA* 19:5–7, no. 671, and is certainly genuine: see Eugen Ewig, "Entwicklung der fränkischen Reichskirche," in Ewig, *Gallien*, 2:224.

21. Ewig, "Entwicklung der fränkischen Reichskirche," pp. 222–28, explained the great shift between 746 and 757 as the reconciliation of three major episcopal circles: the followers of Pirmin, the disciples of Boniface, and those who had been marginalized by both reformers. Yet it is not clear how the precise provisions of the privilege of Gorze helped effect such a rapprochement. Pirmin "stood for" monastic exemption and Boniface for episcopal control: see Arnold Angenendt, "Pirmin und Bonifatius. Ihr Verhältnis zu Mönchtum, Bischofsamt und Adel," in Arno Borst, ed., *Mönchtum, Episkopat und Adel zur Gründungszeit des Klosters Reichenau* Vorträge und Forschungen 20 (Sigmaringen, 1974), pp. 251–304. It is true that Eigil, *Vita Sturmi*, c. 20, in *Die Vita Sturmi des Eigil von Fulda*, ed. Pius Engelbert (Marburg, 1968), p. 155, speaks of a privilege from the Apostolic See, which (from its context in the *Vita*) apparently freed Fulda (which was founded by Boniface) from the jurisdiction of the bishop of Mainz. In a private discussion with me, Professor Angenendt suggested that Boniface allowed this because he was archbishop and could therefore displace the diocesan without violating the hierarchy of the Church.

22. Once he did so, everyone followed. Even bishop Heddo, whose privilege for Arnulfsau echoed the great freedoms of Pirmin's Murbach, would soon (in 762) draw up a testament for Ettenheim that borrowed freely from the letter and spirit of Chrodegang; see Angenendt, "Pirmin und Bonifatius," pp. 301–4; on Murbach and its significance, idem, *Monachi peregrini. Studien zu Pirmin und den monastischen Vorstellungen des frühen Mittelalters* (Munich, 1972), pp. 81–96, 175–86; on Arnulfsau, ibid., pp. 104–6.

23. Jaffé, *Regesta*, no. 2017 = Cipolla, *Codice diplomatico del monastero di S. Colombano di Bobbio*, pp. 101–3, no. 10.

corresponds to Formula 77 in the *Liber Diurnus* (*LD*) a formula book likely used by the papal chancery. This correspondence, while not decisive, suggests its considerable antiquity.[24] Second, its gist was summarized by Jonas's account of it in the *Vita Columbani*.[25] Finally, as Hans Hubert Anton has shown, it was one in a line of similar privileges extended by the papacy to the monasteries of Farfa, Chertsey, Malmesbury, Bermondsey/Woking, and Saint-Denis.[26]

Although the significance of the word *dicio* is problematic and no doubt multilayered, almost certainly one of its meanings was protection. In the late 1950s Wilhelm Schwarz vigorously disputed the hitherto general view that Honorius's document and *LD* 77 gave "exemptions."[27] For Schwarz, exemptions existed only when the provisions of a privilege explicitly prohibited the diocesan bishop from his spiritual oversight and rights of consecration. These, for Schwarz, were not implied by *dicio*, which, he argued, meant protection for the temporal holdings of the monastery only. Honorius's privilege, in this view, removed Bobbio's *property* from the potential exploitation of its diocesan but in all other ways left the monastery firmly within the episcopal orbit. This argument, embedded as it was in a denial of *any* exemptions in the Merovingian period, went too far. As we have seen, in a series of important articles written between 1968 and 1973, Ewig demonstrated the existence of both big and little episcopal exemptions.

Nevertheless, we may learn from Schwarz's wariness when we com-

24. It must be admitted that the *LD* is neither securely dated nor is its purpose clear. It was certainly a formulary book; but who used it? The uses and significance of the *LD* (or, indeed, of various versions of the *LD*) have been hotly disputed since its discovery; the controversies and hypotheses are nicely summarized through the 1950s in Hans Foerster's edition of the *LD*, pp. 9–36. More recently, Leo Santifaller, *Liber Diurnus. Studien und Forschungen*, ed. Harald Zimmermann, Päpste und Papsttum 10 (Stuttgart, 1976), pp. 59–66, 167–68, has argued that the *LD* was not very important for the papal chancery. However Anton, *Studien zu den Klosterprivilegien*, p. 2, has adduced evidence that the *LD* was the "päpstlichen Formularbuch" and *LD* 32 and 77 "sicher auf das 7. Jahrhundert zurückgehen."

25. Jonas, *Vita Columbani* 2.23 MGH SRM 4:145: "privilegia sedis apostolicae largitus est, quatenus nullus episcoporum in praefato caenubio quolibet iure dominare conaretur."

26. Anton, *Studien zu den Klosterprivilegien*, esp. p. 79 and n. 89.

27. Schwarz, "Jurisdicio und Condicio." The revolutionary nature of Schwarz's interpretation of the word is clear when we compare it with the discussion by Heinrich Appelt, "Die Anfänge des päpstlichen Schutzes," *MIÖG* 62 (1954): 101–11, writing five years before Schwarz. In Appelt's view, the *LD* used *jurisdictio* "im Sinne der frühesten Form der Exemtion aber noch keine Verbindung der letzteren mit dem Schutz." For Schwarz the chronology was protection first, exemption later (eleventh century); for Appelt, exemption was early and protection developed in the course of the ninth century. More recently, Falkenstein, *La papauté*, has considered a monastery as "exempt" when the diocesan bishop cannot excommunicate its monks. By this definition, Merovingian liberties were not exemptions.

pare early papal privileges (or the passage in *LD* 77) with Merovingian episcopal exemptions. Whether or not they hoped to save particular monasteries from full episcopal jurisdiction or simply from episcopal exploitation of their temporal property, the popes who issued these privileges most certainly were not limiting their own powers in the way that Merovingian bishops were doing around the same time. The *provisions* of their exemptions contained some themes in common with Merovingian episcopal grants and royal immunities.[28] Nevertheless, the *context* of their grants was entirely different. The popes were not issuing exemptions against their own encroachment or that of their officials but rather against the power of others. In this way, papal *dicio* arrogated power to the issuers themselves.

That contemporary monks considered this *dicio* to be benevolent is suggested, for example, by the vocabulary that the Anglo-Saxon monk Bede used when speaking of papal privileges. Like Jonas, he thought of them as a gift: "Benedict [Biscop] brought not a paltry gift, a letter of privilege received from venerable pope Agatho [678–81] . . . by which the monastery that he founded was protected [*tutum*] in perpetuity."[29] The privilege given by Sergius I to Malmesbury, c. 701, speaks of the monastery as being "under the jurisdiction and protection" (*sub jurisdictione atque tuitione*) of the Roman see.[30] Farfa's privilege from John VII also placed it under papal *tuitio*.[31] Though of uncertain authenticity and therefore individually inconclusive, taken together, such examples suggest that by the late seventh or early eighth century, papal protection, whatever its specific content, was actively sought by and handed out to special monasteries.

At just about the same moment that Chrodegang's charter for Gorze was issued (757), Pope Stephen II gave an extraordinary privilege to Abbot Fulrad of Saint-Denis. The authenticity of Pope Stephen's bull has

---

28. E.g., the privileges quoted in Anton, *Studien zu den Klosterprivilegien*, p. 78 n. 88 and p. 79 n. 89.

29. Bede, *Historia abbatum*, c. 6, in *Venerabilis Baedae opera historica*, ed. Charles Plummer, 2 vols. (Oxford, 1896), 1:364–87, at p. 369: "Benedictus non uile munus adtulit, epistolam priuilegii a uenerabili papa Agathone . . . qua monasterium, quod fecit, ab omni prorsus extrinseca irruptione tutum perpetuo redderetur ac liberum." See Anton, *Studien zu den Klosterprivilegien*, pp. 62–63 n. 60, for further examples.

30. Jaffé, *Regesta*, no. 2140 = *Cartularium saxonicum*, ed. Walter de Gray Birch, 3 vols. (London, 1885–93), 1:153, no. 105. Anton, *Studien zu den Klosterprivilegien*, p. 67, dates it c. 695.

31. Jaffé, *Regesta*, no. 2144 (705) = Jean Mabillon, *Annales ordinis S. Benedicti* (Lucca, 1739), 2:703–4, no. 78: "Idcirco vestra religio hanc apostolici privilegii tuitionem indeptam, fructuosum atque laudabile concessum beneficium demonstret ante omnia in psalmis, & hymnis, & canticis spiritualibus diebus ac noctibus, permanentes."

long been debated, but certainly, as Karl Hauck has remarked, it is authentic in its essentials.[32] The privilege gave Fulrad license to construct monasteries on any of his properties in the Frankish kingdom. These monasteries were to be placed under the jurisdiction of the papal see; no other bishop would have *dicio* over them or would be able to ordain any of their monks as deacons or priests or say Mass in them unless invited to do so by the ruling abbot. These provisions echoed the formulae of *LD* 32 and are certainly genuine.[33] The last disposition gave Fulrad the right to appeal (*reclamare*) all his cases to the pope. This provision is not in *LD* 32, but it, too, has contemporary echoes: it is precisely parallel to the provisions in documents of royal *tuitio* from Fulrad's time. Let us turn to them for a moment.

Lay and royal protection (expressed early on in the latinized German word *mundeburdium* and later by other words) grew up independent of, but alongside, papal *dicio*.[34] By the seventh century, the term or its synonyms were appearing in royal documents.[35] We have already seen that Clovis II took Saint-Denis into his *sermo*, that is, under his protection.[36] At about the same time (647–55), Desiderius wrote to Pippin II's son Grimoald, then mayor of the palace in Austrasia, asking him to receive a monastic foundation "as commended to you in every way" and to care for it so devotedly that the mayor would be sure to reap an eternal reward.[37] In

32. Karl Hauck, "Paderborn, das Zentrum von Karls Sachsen-Mission 777," in *Adel und Kirche. Gerd Tellenbach zum 65. Geburtstag dargebracht von Freunden und Schülern*, ed. Josef Fleckenstein and Karl Schmid (Freiburg, 1968), pp. 92–140, at p. 115 n. 141. There are two versions of the privilege (Jaffé, *Regesta*, no. 2331). A new edition of the first, A, which is largely authentic, is in Alain Stoclet, "Fulrad de Saint-Denis (v. 710–784), abbé et archiprêtre de monastères 'exempts,'" *Le Moyen Age* 88 (1982): 205–35, at pp. 234–35. Stoclet, "Fulrad-Dissertation," pp. 401–17, analyzes its provisions in detail. The second version of the privilege, B, is clearly interpolated; it is printed in PL 89, cols. 1014–17.

33. Further proof is provided by Stoclet, "Fulrad, abbé et archiprêtre," p. 223.

34. Appelt, "Anfänge des päpstlichen Schutzes," reviews the older historiography, where the growth of papal notions of protection was taken as evidence of the penetration of "Germanic" ideas into the Roman see. Appelt argues, on the contrary, that ideas of protection were inherent in the very Roman notion of *jurisdictio* and came to the papacy via that route. However, he allows for the penetration there of "feudal" ideas (p. 102).

35. The evidence in Niermeyer, *Mediae latinitatis lexicon minus*, s.vv. *mundiburdis, mundium*, and Charles du Fresne Du Cange, *Glossarium mediae et infimae latinitatis*, s.vv. *mundiburdus, mundium*, suggests that *mundeburdium* does not appear in any documentation prior to the seventh century.

36. *ChLA* 13:26, no. 555, and Chapter 4, at note 2.

37. Desiderius, *Epistulae*, 1.2, p. 12. Compare the use of *commendare* in Marculf, Ad. 2 (Carta de mundeburde), p. 354: "abba . . . tam se quam et ipso monasterio cum omnes rebus suis ad Nos sibi plenius comendavit." On Desiderius's letter in the context of requests for "Schutz," see Schwarz, "Jurisdicio und Condicio," p. 74. See also (in Chapter 2 above, note

706 Pippin II and his wife made clear by charter that the monastery of Echternach was under their protection and defense.[38]

The formulary of Marculf provided several variants on this theme. One of its two models for a charter of protection (*mundeburdium*) for a church or monastery began with the bestowal of protection (*tuitio*) by the royal power.[39] Here the words *tuitio* and *sermo* were paired (*sub sermonem tuicionis Nostre*) to describe the nature of royal protection from "the unlawful attacks of evil men." *Mundeburdium, defensio,* and like words guaranteed that a church and its property would either be left in peace or its case would be defended at a comital or royal court. This active defense was normally the role of the mayor of the palace rather than of the king himself.[40] But such distinctions could blur. In the second formula of *mundeburdium* in Marculf, the king or prince warmly received an abbot, his monastery, and his dependents under his protection and promised to defend them against all claims.[41] This formula was followed by a general protective decree directed to all magnates and royal functionaries: that they "not presume to disturb or lay waste or diminish any of [the church's] property at all." Claims that could not be settled locally without injury to the protected church were to come before the prince or king.

Not very different was the notion of protection in Charles Martel's letter of recommendation for Boniface. Directed to bishops, dukes, counts, and other royal officials, it gave Boniface a safe conduct: "Wheresoever he may go, he is to be left in peace and safety by our love and under our *mundeburdium* and *defensio* . . . And if any dispute or necessity should arise against him that cannot be determined according to law, he should be left in peace and safety until he comes before our presence."[42]

---

38) the early use of the term *commendare* in connection with the monastery of the Holy Cross.

38. Camillus Wampach, *Geschichte der Grundherrschaft Echternach im Frühmittelalter,* 1/2 Quellenband (Luxemburg, 1930), p. 43, no. 15.

39. Marculf 1.24, pp. 98–101.

40. Heidrich, "Titulatur und Urkunden," pp. 127–29.

41. Since Marculf, Ad. 2, pp. 354–57, was used by Charles Martel in his letter of commendation for Boniface in 723 (see below, note 42), it must have been written prior to this time, but not necessarily much before. As Heidrich, "Titulatur und Urkunden," pp. 186–90, notes, although Marculf was substantially completed by 690, it was continually reworked and mingled with other forms. As examples of later additions she includes Marculf 1.24 and Ad. 2.

42. Boniface, *Epistola* 22 (723), ed. Tangl, MGH Epp. sel. 1:36–38: "ut ubicumque, ubi et ubi, ambulare videtur, cum nostro amore vel sub nostro mundeburdio et defensione quietus vel conservatus esse debeat . . . Et si aliqua causatio vel necessitas ei advenerit, quę per legem definiri non potuerit, usque ante nos quietus vel conservatus esse debeat." Heidrich has reconstructed the model (the "*Hausmeierschutzbrief*") behind this letter for Boniface (and also

Two extant original charters from the 770s offered royal protection to individuals. In 772 Charlemagne bestowed his protection on a *presbyter* named Arnaldus. Closely following the first formula in Marculf discussed above, the king took Arnaldus, with all his property and dependents, under his *mundeburdium* and *defensio* against "the unlawful attacks of evil men," to live in peace for the rest of his days. That "evil men" might very well be the "loyal men" (*fideles*) to whom the document was addressed is clear from the royal order that neither they nor their "agents nor successors should presume to disturb or act unreasonably against Arnaldus." Here, too, any claims that might be brought against Arnaldus were to be judged by the king's court if they could not be resolved at the local level.[43] This was the royal counterpart to the papal license to appeal cases before the see of Saint Peter.[44]

Royal protection was separate from immunity and, indeed, in some ways conceptually contrary to it. Immunity emphasized nonintervention, whereas protection celebrated and imposed jurisdiction. Nevertheless, granting protection to someone (or something) was close to offering him immunity from everyone else. The same complaints against usurpers of property lay at the base of both impulses, and this is no doubt what made it possible to pair them.[45] In a privilege issued to Saint-Calais in 760, Pippin III assigned the *mundeburdium* and *defensio* of the monastery to his son Charlemagne, while he himself took responsibility for its *tuitio* and *immunitas*, its protection and immunity.[46] This is the earliest extant pairing of the words; and since the document exists today only in a seventeenth-century copy, an interpolation might be suspected. But the same phrase

---

behind *ChLA* 2:98, no. 158, discussed below at note 43) in Ingrid Heidrich, "Die Verbindung von Schutz und Immunität. Beobachtungen zu den merowingischen und frühkarolingischen Schutzurkunden für St. Calais," *ZRG GA* 90 (1973): 10–30, with the reconstructed model, pp. 11–13 n. 6.

43. *ChLA* 2:98, no. 158.

44. On this right of appeal, see Heidrich, "Die Verbindung," p. 25 and n. 68 with further bibliography.

45. See Heidrich, "Die Verbindung," p. 26: "Das Ziel der Besitzsicherung ist wohl der Grund für das Koppelung von Schutz und Immunität." For Heidrich, the two hitherto independent notions of immunity and protection came together now because immunity had been too limited a safeguard: it applied only to formerly royal property. (We have seen, however, with Tussonval, that this was not always the case.) In Heidrich's view, protection provided the same function as immunity but applied generally to *all* the property of a monastery. But despite the similarities between protection and immunity, it is hard to escape the conclusion that *tuitio* represented a promise of benevolent jurisdiction, not a hands-off policy.

46. MGH Dip. Kar. 1:19–20, no. 14. The phrase is "sub sermone tuitionis nostrae vel emunitatibus."

appears in a near-contemporary privilege for Echternach with an entirely different and independent manuscript tradition.[47]

A Familial Model

The addition of one small word, "protection," made a big difference. Chrodegang's privilege for Gorze, for example, brought the monastery under his control. Kassius Hallinger called the monastery, bluntly, an *Eigenkirche*, a proprietary church.[48] But Chrodegang did not claim unbounded proprietorship. He stated in his privilege that he had no right to take away the property he had given to Gorze; it was no longer his to alienate. The property of the church of Metz had been donated to create the monastery; now he and the canons of his cathedral could enjoy the spiritual benefits of their largesse, but they could not reclaim the gift.

Here church property worked "double duty," belonging to Gorze but at the same time benefiting the church at Metz. An arrangement for property sharing also came up in Chrodegang's Rule for canons, which in fact was probably written around the time of the Compiègne synod and the Gorze privilege.[49] Chrodegang had the canons turn over all their property to the church of Saint Paul (the canonry of the Metz cathedral) but retain the usufruct while they lived.[50] The church of Metz became their heir; but the bishop returned their former patrimony to them in the form of precarial grants that they could enjoy as if their own.[51] Because they held these grants in trust, they could not diminish or sell or exchange anything, just as the bishop of Metz could not alienate any of the property of Gorze. In both cases the model was "family inheritance." The can-

47. For Echternach, see MGH Dip. Kar. 1: 41–42, no. 30, as recorded in the thirteenth-century *Liber aureus*. See Heidrich, "Die Verbindung," p. 13.

48. Kassius Hallinger, "Zur Rechtsgeschichte der Abtei Gorze bei Metz (vor 750–1572)," *Zeitschrift für Kirchengeschichte* 83 (1972): 325–50, esp. pp. 325–28.

49. The body of the Rule was written c. 755–56: see Gaston Hocquard, "La Règle de saint Chrodegang. État de quelques questions," in *Saint Chrodegang. Communications présentées au colloque tenu à Metz à l'occasion du douzième centenaire de sa mort* (Metz, 1967), pp. 55–90, at p. 66. Martin Claussen, "Community, Tradition, and Reform in Early Carolingian Francia: Chrodegang and the Canons of Metz Cathedral" (Ph.D. diss., University of Virginia, 1991), suggests that cc. 31–34 of Chrodegang's Rule were written later, during the period 757–62. I thank Martin Claussen for discussions about Chrodegang and for sending me parts of his dissertation.

50. Claussen, "Community, Tradition, and Reform," chap. 5, traces with exactitude Chrodegang's use of Julian Pomerius in arriving at this nevertheless quite original formulation.

51. Chrodegang, *Rule for Canons*, c. 31, ed. Jean-Baptiste Pelt, *Études sur la cathédrale de Metz*, vol. 1, *V^e–XIIIe siècle* (Metz, 1937), p. 24.

ons gave their property to their new heirs, the community of Saint-Paul. Chrodegang identified so closely with Saint-Stephen of Metz that he included his donations from that church to Gorze—gifts of land, people, and tithes that had belonged to Saint-Stephen—in what he called a *testamentum*, a will.[52]

The familial character of this bishop's notion of control was expressed even more clearly when his kinsman Cancor and Cancor's mother, Williswinda, gave their new foundation of Lorsch to Chrodegang, "not subjecting it to the law or dominion of a bishop or any church but . . . to a relative, Chrodegang, archbishop of Metz, at the same time commending it by charter to the man most knowledgeable in the ways of God to bring it to fruition and to govern it."[53] Chrodegang became its first abbot, while remaining bishop of Metz; then in 765 he turned the abbacy over to his brother Gundelandus.[54]

In 762 Chrodegang gathered around him at Attigny the first prayer association declared by a synod.[55] Abbot Fulrad of Saint-Denis was there, as was Lull (Boniface's successor at Mainz), and Bishop Heddo of Stras-

---

52. *Gorze*, pp. 1–5, no. 1. The *testamentum* of the seventh and eighth centuries was much changed in form and function from its Roman precursor: see Ulrich Nonn, "Merowingische Testamente. Studien zum Fortleben einer römischen Urkundenform im Frankenreich," *Archiv für Diplomatik* 18 (1972): 1–129; Goswin Spreckelmeyer, "Zur rechtlichen Funktion frühmittelalterlicher Testamente," in Peter Classen, ed., *Recht und Schrift im Mittelalter*, Vorträge und Forschungen 23 (Sigmaringen, 1977), pp. 91–113; and Patrick J. Geary, *Aristocracy in Provence: The Rhône Basin at the Dawn of the Carolingian Age*, Monographien zur Geschichte des Mittelalters 31 (Stuttgart, 1985), pp. 27–33.

53. *Lorsch* 1:266: "Ruotgango, Metensis ęcclesię archiepiscopo . . . tradiderunt, nullius quidem episcopii seu ciuislibet ęcclesię iuri aut dominio subicientes, sed quia minus id per se poterant, tamquam consanguineo, et tum in dei rebus uiro spectatissimo perficiendum gubernandumque sub traditionis titulo commendantes." Lorsch was in the diocese of Mainz, and this vague if general exemption took the monastery away from the jurisdiction of that bishop in favor of the governance of Chrodegang, a family member. In 772 Charlemagne took Lorsch "in mundeburdem uel defensionem nostram" (*Lorsch* 1:274–75, no. 4 = MGH Dip. Kar., 1:105–6, no. 72); this provided for the election of the abbot by the monks themselves from their own number and warned the diocesan bishop not to "inquietare aut constringere, uel contra rationis ordinem facere presumat"—another vague gesture at exemption.

54. For Chrodegang's abbacy, see *Lorsch* 1:267, no. 1 (12 July 764): "ubi preest uir uenerabilis Ruodgangus archiepiscopus et abbas"; for Gundelandus, who had been abbot of Gorze (*Gorze*, no. 6), see *Lorsch* 1:270–71: "cum ipsius monasterii curam gubernationemque per se éxequi [Chrodegang] non posset . . . Gundelandum germanum suum . . . eidem loco prefecit." Gundelandus was a local landholder, as we learn from his donation: *Lorsch* 2:495, no. 2002 (May 17, 772): "Gundelandus abb. . . . dono . . . in pago Nachgowe in Vffiliubesheim" = Hüffelsheim, just southwest of Kreuznach, about sixty-five kilometers from Lorsch.

55. MGH Conc. 2, pt. 1, pp. 72–73; Hartmann, *Synoden*, pp. 79–81; Karl Schmid and Otto Gerhard Oexle, "Voraussetzungen und Wirkungen des Gebetsbundes von Attigny," *Francia* 2 (1974): 71–122, esp. p. 85.

bourg. Despite the seemingly ideal amity that prevailed between abbots and bishops—each owing Masses, psalms, and prayers to the others upon their deaths—the abbots were not quite the equal of bishops. Like "infirm or impeded" bishops, they were incapable of saying the requisite thirty masses and had to ask a bishop to act as their proxy.[56] Nevertheless, the abbots were not required to turn to their *diocesan* bishops. For all his concern about the subjection of Gorze to its local bishop, Chrodegang was still comfortable within a flexible system. Even as this system hardened in the direction of increasing royal control, it could still be negotiated to benefit multiple interests.

56. MGH Conc. 2, pt. 1, p. 72: "Ipse autem episcopus per se XXX misas impleat, nisi infirmitate aut aliquo inpedimento prohibeatur. Tunc roget alterum episcopum pro se cantare. Abbates vero, qui non sunt episcopi, rogent episcopos, ut vice illorum ipsas XXX misas expleant." Schmid and Oexle, "Voraussetzungen," p. 85, point out that the bishops have the key role.

6

A Meeting of Minds

THE PAIRING of protection and immunity opened up immense new political possibilities. Paul Hyams has called private charters reports of accommodations between parties.[1] Much the same could be said of royal diplomas, though because they are extremely formulaic, they do a better job of hiding the negotiations that went into them. Occasionally, however, they do reveal how different parties asserted and readjusted their positions. We have already been able on occasion to glimpse such bargaining under the placid surface of some Merovingian charters. In the Carolingian period the sources are more plentiful; we can in some cases—though certainly not all—tease out not only partisan interests but also articulated attitudes and assumptions. Let us follow out one such case: the immunity that Charlemagne granted to Fulrad, abbot of Saint-Denis, for the monastery of Salonnes on December 6, 777 (see Map 3).[2]

Some Diplomatic Texts

In full summary, the diploma, issued from Aachen, reads as follows:

> Charles, by grace of God king of the Franks and the Lombards and patri-
> cius of the Romans, considers that it is fitting to his serenity to grant what

1. Paul Hyams, "Observations on the Charter as a Source for the Early English Common Law," *Journal of Legal History* 12 (1991): 173–89, at p. 174.
2. Some of the arguments in this chapter may be found in somewhat different form in Barbara H. Rosenwein, "Association through Exemption: Saint-Denis, Salonnes, and Metz,"

is requested justly and rationally by his loyal men [*fideles*] in return for the service and fidelity that they showed to him and to his father, King Pippin. Therefore he makes known to all his *fideles*, both present and future, that Fulrad, his palace chaplain and abbot of Saint-Denis, came to him and brought to his attention a privilege in favor of Saint-Denis; it had been issued by a church council held at Paderborn in the ninth year of Charlemagne's reign with the solemn agreement of Bishop Angilram and Archbishop Wilcharius. It concerned the property of Fulrad at Salonnes, where a monastery had been built in honor of the Holy Mother of God and blessed martyrs, confessors, and virgins and where the relics of Saint Privatus, the martyr, and Saint Hilary, the confessor, rested. The king found that the privilege contained the provision that neither Bishop Angilram nor his successors nor any archdeacons or *missi* [agents] from his church at Metz could exercise the bishop's right [*pontificium*] to do ordinations or bless the chrism and altars at Salonnes unless asked to do so by the abbot of Saint-Denis. The king asked Bishop Angilram whether he had himself consented to this privilege, and he did not at all deny it. Rather, he made the privilege known exactly as it had been issued by the synod where his bishops agreed to it.

Therefore the king decrees the following decree and confirmation on behalf of Saint-Denis: that henceforth no bishop at all, neither Angilram nor his successors, may touch the monastery of Salonnes. Rather it is to be under the immunity and privilege of Saint-Denis, in accordance with the Rule, like the other churches that belong to the house of Saint-Denis and the estates which Angilram and Fulrad exchanged in the district of Salonnes. And similarly, the king decrees and confirms that Saint-Denis, along with its monastery at Salonnes, is to be under the protection [*tuitio*] and defense [*defensio*] of the king and his leading men without impediment from the bishop of Metz. The king confirms by his authority that whatever might be added or conferred by royal exchange or by popular gift or offering or which Fulrad might give to Salonnes from his own property should remain under the immunity and defense of Saint-Denis forever. This is done so that the congregation of Saint Denis and Saint Privatus and Saint Hilary may be the better pleased to pray even more attentively for the Lord's mercy for the king, his heirs and his wife.[3]

This diploma has several striking features, some of which have already been recognized by commentators. In the first place, it jumbles together

---

in Hagen Keller and Franz Neiske, eds., *Vom Kloster zum Klosterverband. Das Werkzeug der Schriftlichkeit*, Akten des Internationalen Kolloquiums des Projekts L 2 im SFB 231 (22.–23. Februar 1996), Münstersche Mittelalter-Schriften 74 (Munich, 1997), pp. 68–87.

3. *ChLA* 19:28–33, no. 679. For the Latin text, see Appendix 3.

MAP 3. The Rhine-Moselle-Meuse Region, Late Eighth Century

immunity, exemption, and royal protection. If the first two had already
been paired (as we have seen), the appearance of all three together was
something new. Using the most traditional of formulae, the immunity of
777 mixed a variety of very heady privileges into one impressive mé-
lange of protection, defense, exemption, and immunity. In the second
place, the charter is unusually descriptive, even dramatic: it narrates a
lively interchange between king, bishop, and abbot—all taking place at
the *placitum*, or meeting, where the privilege was granted. In the third
place, it mentions a synod at Paderborn for which there is no other evidence. There the assembled bishops under Angilram's leadership issued
an exemption for Saint-Denis. Paderborn surely happened, as Karl Hauck
has shown.[4] Thus, in effect, we have two texts, one extant, the other
known only by report. How are we to understand them?

In Hauck's view, these diplomas reveal the very heart of Charlemagne's
Saxon strategy. In brief, Hauck argued that in 777 Charlemagne and his
advisers were filled with exultation at their defeat of the Saxons. Unable to anticipate the coming setback (the Saxons would turn around
and trounce them in 778), they set about to complete what they took to
be their Roman apostolic mission. This meant, in part, organizing the
Church in Saxony along Roman lines.[5] The privilege for Salonnes, Hauck
argued, revealed how Fulrad hoped to orchestrate this new Church.
As the king's archchaplain, he held a politico-religious position of extraordinary power; as abbot of Saint-Denis he was head of the premier
monastery in the kingdom. Fulrad wanted to minimize local episcopal
prerogatives over his monastery and its cells.[6] He knew well how military victories might go hand in hand with new privileges: at some point
between 772 and 776 he had taken advantage of Carolingian conquests in
Bavaria and Lombardy to gain liberties for his cell at Herbrechtingen.[7] In
late 776 or early 777, anticipating the Carolingian thrust into Saxony,
worried about its success, fearful of his own demise, he gave his proper-

---

4. Hauck, "Paderborn," pp. 103–7 deals with formal issues; pp. 109–16 deals with
content.

5. But see Eckhard Freise, "Das Mittelalter bis zum Vertrag von Verdun (843)," in Wilhelm Kohl, ed., *Westfälische Geschichte*, vol. 1, *Von den Anfängen bis zum Ende des Alten Reiches*
(Düsseldorf, 1983), pp. 275–335; at p. 305 Freise expresses doubt that the Synod at Paderborn divided Saxony into bishoprics. He suggests that it simply defined regions for missionary work.

6. If Charles confirmed the privilege for Salonnes, it meant for Hauck, "Paderborn,"
p. 127, that "Karl selbst wünschte die Mitwirkung Fulrads an der Sachsen-Mission."

7. *ChLA* 16:51, no. 627.

ties to Saint-Denis.[8] This is the moment when Salonnes came under its patronage. Once victory was declared in Saxony, Fulrad went to Paderborn to ensure, along with Wilcharius and Charlemagne himself, that the new Saxon church would be linked to Rome and Saint-Denis through its patron saints and that Saint-Denis's cell at Salonnes would be the launching pad for Carolingian missionary activity to the north.[9]

This is an important and worthy argument, though it shifts Fulrad's activities from the east and south, where they had previously been concentrated, to the north, where he had hitherto shown no interest. But because Hauck's thesis concentrates exclusively on Fulrad, it fails to comprehend the full significance of the diploma for Salonnes and its many curious features. Hauck treats the privilege as the brainchild of Fulrad and, to a lesser extent, of Charlemagne and Wilcharius; he ignores the other character in the drama: Angilram.

A year after Hauck's study appeared, Otto Gerhard Oexle published an article that did put the emphasis on Angilram. For Oexle the documents were proof of a dispute (*Streit*) between Angilram and Fulrad that was in effect resolved finally in favor of Fulrad.[10]

The Aachen diploma suggests that Oexle was on the right track, especially if we change "dispute" to "negotiation." The latter word helps stress Angilram's importance. Indeed, the Aachen diploma says nothing at all about Fulrad's presence at Paderborn, though perhaps it is not too much to imagine, with Hauck, that he had been there. Angilram was the key person to agree to the exemption for Salonnes at Paderborn. Indeed, the Aachen diploma suggest that Angilram, not Fulrad or anyone else, orchestrated the terms of the Paderborn synod, since it speaks of Angilram's bishops (*episcopi sui*) making the synodal decisions. That the royal privilege makes this point and then reinforces it with Angilram's assent at Aachen are further proofs of the diocesan bishop's importance for the privilege for Salonnes. (Contrast this with Charlemagne's privilege for the monastery of Saint-Véran at Herbrechtingen, where freedom from *pontificium* did not require the consent of a bishop.)[11]

The Aachen charter suggests, in fact, three sets of negotiations: first (in time) were those between Angilram and Fulrad which culminated in

---

8. *ChLA* 16:16–37, nos. 622–24. For further discussion of this testament, see below, note 24.
9. Hauck, "Paderborn," pp. 128–29.
10. Oexle, "Die Karolinger," p. 296.
11. *ChLA* 16:51, no. 627; see below, note 21.

an exchange of land at Salonnes;[12] second were the negotiations and agreements determined at Paderborn; and third were the dialogues at Aachen between king, bishop, and abbot about those prior arrangements and about the agreements that the new royal document was meant to announce.

The chief question for our inquiry is why Angilram agreed to and drafted up an exemption that diminished his own authority. We have seen that Merovingian bishops did this sort of thing, often in tandem with or at the behest of royal authority. But Angilram was no Merovingian bishop; indeed he was the kinsman and episcopal successor of Chrodegang at Metz. His tradition, as we saw in the last chapter, was one of exercising *pontificium* over the monasteries in his diocese. Indeed, he was present at Compiègne when Chrodegang issued the charter for his own episcopal protection of Gorze.[13] Very likely Angilram was at that time a cleric at Metz, and very likely he was there because of his familial ties to Chrodegang.[14] How can the Aachen document represent a real negotiation when it seems to point to Angilram's abject defeat?

Let us be clear about one thing: both Fulrad and Angilram were important and powerful people. As for the other *dramatis personae*: Wilcharius was at the Paderborn synod but was not the diocesan concerned; Charlemagne was not at the synod and simply (though surely not ingenuously) confirmed the agreement reached there.[15] The key figures were Fulrad and Angilram. Let us consider them separately in order to un-

12. The importance of this exchange is underlined by the fact that it is noted not only in the diploma for Salonnes but also in Fulrad's testament, *ChLA* 16:24, no. 623: "tam illas commutationes, que cum Angalramno episcopo feci." This phrase is repeated in one of the contemporary abbreviated copies of this document, *ChLA* 16:32, no. 624.

13. He signed the document (MGH Conc. 2, pt. 1, p. 63) in twenty-sixth place, right after Sadrius, bishop of Angers.

14. *GC* 7, col. 224, and *GC* 13, col. 708, claim that Angilram was the son of Chrodegang's brother. On this point, see Oexle, "Die Karolinger," pp. 293–94 n. 87; Glöckner, "Lorsch und Lothringen," p. 312; and Josef Fleckenstein, *Die Hofkapelle der deutschen Könige*, pt. 1, *Grundlegung. Die Karolingische Hofkapelle*, Schriften der MGH 16, pt. 1 (Stuttgart, 1959), p. 49 n. 29.

15. Josef Fleckenstein, "Fulrad von Saint-Denis und der fränkische Ausgriff in den süddeutschen Raum," in *Studien und Vorarbeiten zur Geschichte des großfränkischen und frühdeutschen Adels*, ed. Gerd Tellenbach = *Forschungen zur oberrheinischen Landesgeschichte* 4 (1957): 9–39, at p. 29, argues that the privilege for Salonnes of 777 was part of Charlemagne's "Kirchenpolitik" to tie the Alemannian and Bavarian churches to the Neustrian core; Salonnes served as a link between Saint-Denis and Alemannia. Stoclet, "Fulrad-Dissertation," p. 412, adds one other document to the list of privileges foreshadowing the exemption for Salonnes: the diploma of Stephen II for Fulrad (see above, Chap. 5, n. 32). In Stoclet's view the synod of Paderborn carried out the provisions of Stephen's bull.

derstand how the privilege at Aachen represented a mutually agreeable arrangement.

Fulrad

Since at least 757—thus for fully two decades before the Aachen meeting—Fulrad had been busily gaining privileges of special protection for the monasteries and churches belonging to him or (what was in his view the same thing) Saint-Denis.[16] As we saw in Chapter 5, he succeeded in gaining an extraordinary letter of grand intent from Pope Stephen II in 757: this letter gave Fulrad the right to found monasteries on his properties, and it put them all under direct papal jurisdiction, bypassing their local bishop. At another time (when, we do not know), Fulrad donated his entire inheritance to Pippin for safe-keeping because he thought—wrongly, in the event—that he was on his deathbed.[17] Then he turned tables and obtained from Pippin, on the *latter's* deathbed, a privilege echoing Dagobert's ancient confirmation of Saint-Denis's exemption from the bishop of Paris.[18] He received a privilege from Pope Stephen III (768–72) giving the "monastic bishop" at Saint-Denis *pontificium* not only at Saint-Denis but at its other monasteries and churches.[19] Even the "simple" gifts that Fulrad received from Charlemagne were couched in phrases reminiscent of immunities, as for example in a donation charter to Salonnes in 775, where the king forbade his *fideles* and agents to trouble the monastery or bring any claims against it.[20] When Charlemagne gave the fisc at Herbrechtingen to the monastery of Saint-Véran, built by Fulrad on his property, the king proclaimed the same prohibition, then added that no

16. This is apart from his efforts to gain confirmations of property and of regular—we might say old-fashioned—immunities for Saint-Denis, as in *ChLA* 15:3–5, no. 595; ibid., p. 9, no. 596; ibid., pp. 16–17, no. 598; ibid., p. 35, no. 602; ibid., p. 47, no. 604, etc.

17. Ibid., p. 35, no. 602.

18. Ibid., p. 47, no. 604 (September 23, 768), echoing *ChLA* 14:59, no. 588. Pippin died the next day; see Stoclet, "Fulrad-Dissertation," p. 528.

19. The privilege is not extant, but the confirmation of Hadrian was included in the Formulary of Saint-Denis, MGH Form., p. 504, no. 13, the full text of which is printed as Adrian, *Epistola* 53, PL 96, cols. 1211–12. On its authenticity, see Levillain, "Études sur l'abbaye de Saint-Denis," *BÉC* 87 (1926): 263 and n. 2 as well as pp. 333–34; Hieronymus Frank, *Die Klosterbischöfe des Frankenreiches*, Beiträge zur Geschichte des alten Mönchtums und des Benediktinerordens 17 (Münster, 1932), p. 49.

20. *ChLA* 16:8, no. 620.

one should exercise *pontificium* over the abbot and the monks.[21] After the same king gave Fulrad property in the Valtellina—prime real estate in the newly conquered kingdom of Lombardy—he granted it an immunity as well.[22] Perhaps then or slightly later, Hadrian I issued a privilege to Saint-Denis for a church in the Valtellina, exempting it from the jurisdiction of its diocesan (the bishop of Como) and putting it under the jurisdiction of no one (*sub nullius jure*)![23]

Then came 777, the year in which Fulrad's concerns rose to fever pitch (or were, at least, so documented). Late in 776 or in 777 he wrote a testament bequeathing his property to Saint-Denis. The charter was copied at least twice at the time it was drawn up; Fulrad was leaving nothing to chance.[24] Josef Fleckenstein has shown how most of the property named in this testament was newly acquired rather than inherited. Perhaps, as Fleckenstein argues, Fulrad feared that these properties were more liable to dispute than family lands; or perhaps, as Alain Stoclet suggests, he was here disposing of "residual" properties that remained to him after his heirs had taken the rest.[25] There were other purposes as well, as we shall see.

For during this same period, Fulrad had been anxious not just to ac-

21. *ChLA* 16:51, no. 627 (772–76): "et nullus ex iudiciaria potestate aut qualibet persona predicto Folrado, abbate, nec sancto Uarano neque iuniores aut successoribus suis de memorata rem inquietare nec contra racionis ordine uel calomniam generare quoque tempore pontificium non habeant." Stoclet, "Fulrad abbé et archiprêtre," p. 222, notes that this document and that for Salonnes of 777, "font écho . . . au privilège d'exemption." Nevertheless, in the case of Saint-Véran the provision is very vague.

22. *ChLA* 15:95, no. 616; the immunity follows almost to the letter (with the exception of the place names) *ChLA* 15:47, no. 604, namely, Pippin's confirmation of the immunities of Saint-Denis issued in 768. The Valtellina is the valley of the Adda river to the north and east of Lake Como.

23. Jaffé, *Regesta*, no. 2443.

24. *ChLA* 16:16–37, nos. 622, 623, 624 (the first two with autograph of Fulrad). The editors have annotated the documents in detail, with full bibliographies to 1986. The most significant additions since then are Stoclet's "Fulrad-Dissertation" and idem, *Autour de Fulrad de Saint-Denis (v. 710–784)*, École pratique des Hautes Études, Sciences historiques et philologiques 5, Hautes Études médiévales et modernes 72 (Geneva, 1993), and for place names, Wolfgang Haubrichs, "Fulrad von St. Denis und der Frühbesitz der Cella Salonnes in Lotharingien. Toponomastische und besitzgeschichtliche Überlegungen," in *Festschrift zum 65. Geburtstag von Hans-Walter Herrmann* (Saarbrücken, 1995), pp. 1–29.

25. Stoclet, "Fulrad-Dissertation," p. 35, and *Autour de Fulrad*, pp. 35–57; Fleckenstein, "Fulrad von Saint-Denis," p. 14. Patrick Wormald hypothesizes that Anglo-Saxon wills concerned precisely the land that would not automatically go to the customary heir: Patrick Wormald, "The Boundaries of Family Property in Pre-Conquest England" (paper delivered at Loyola University Chicago, September 6, 1991).

quire and control property but also to give away and exchange property with others. He is very likely the "Folradus" who gave vineyards in the Wormsgau and arable land in the Enzgau and Maingau to the monastery of Lorsch.[26] He exchanged some land with Peter, the bishop of Verdun, at an unknown date but certainly before October 781, when he exchanged Peter's land with Eufemia, abbess of Saint-Pierre of Metz; in return Eufemia gave him some property in the Saulnois (or Seillegau—the region just to the southeast of Metz).[27] Similarly, Fulrad exchanged land with Bishop Angilram at Salonnes, also in the Saulnois.

These exchanges with Angilram—there seem to have been more than one—figured in both the 777 privilege for Salonnes and in Fulrad's testament. They are therefore worth considering carefully. Fulrad begins his testament with a general statement about having received various properties in exchange transactions. He announces that he is giving to Saint-Denis all the property that he obtained by exchange and gift. In fact, however, his exchanges with Angilram are the only ones that he particularizes. Moreover, their placement in the charter context is significant.[28] The charter's threefold scheme sandwiches a statement of spiritual purpose between two lists of properties:

(First layer): The names of Fulrad's properties and their donors in the Bliesgau, Alsace, and the Ortenau, ending with properties in the Saulnois;

(Middle layer): Spiritual statement: "[I give all these things] to Saint-Denis from the present day for my soul and that of my father Riculfus

26. *Lorsch* 2:426, no. 1560 (765), and 2:469, no. 1836 (771–72): vineyards in the Wormsgau; 3:25, no. 2358 (767): arable land in the Enzgau; 3:131, no. 3417 (769–782): arable land in the Maingau. Stoclet includes these in his Fulrad *Regesta*, "Fulrad-Dissertation," pp. 527–28, 531, 536, which should be consulted for further examples, e.g., of Fulrad's participation in transactions at the monastery of Saint-Gall.

27. *ChLA* 16:55, no. 628, a confirmation involving land in Filstroff, where, in November 777, Charlemagne had himself given land to Salonnes (*ChLA* 16:8, no. 620). For Eufemia, see Nancy Gauthier, *L'évangélisation des pays de la Moselle. La Province Romaine de la Première Belgique entre Antiquité et Moyen Age (IIIe–VIIIe siècles)* (Paris, 1980), pp. 295–99.

28. That the order of properties as listed in the charter (*ChLA* 16:24, no. 623) is important has already been appreciated. Fleckenstein, "Fulrad von Saint-Denis," esp. pp. 29–32, has seen it as chronological, revealing Fulrad's "push" into Alemannia and Alsace. But chronological organization seems unlikely, for the other monasteries that follow Salonnes in the testament appeared on the scene at about the same time. We know about Salonnes from 775 (*ChLA* 16:8, no. 620), Saint-Hippolyte from 774 (*ChLA* 15:78–79, no. 613), Herbrechtingen from 772–76 (*ChLA* 16:51, no. 627). For further criticism of Fleckenstein, see Stoclet, *Autour de Fulrad*, pp. 54–57, and idem, "Fulrad-Dissertation," pp. 64–67. Stoclet (ibid., p. 34) suggests that the charter is organized by geographical region. I propose that it is organized with Salonnes as the focal point.

and my mother Hermengardis and my brothers Gausbertus and Bonefacius and my sister Uualdradane and for my family [*genelogia mea*] so that by the intercession of Saint Denis with his associates we may merit to obtain eternal life."

(Last layer): The names of Fulrad's monastic cells, their saintly patrons, and how they were acquired. The first cell mentioned is Salonnes, and the first thing said about it is that exchanges with Angilram took place there: "That cell ought to belong to Saint-Denis, along with the exchanges which I made with bishop Angilram and the other exchanges." [29]

There had been other exchanges at Salonnes, but only one was made explicit: the one that made the connection between Salonnes and Angilram, perpetuating the memory of that connection even as it was being modified. It was no accident that this cell came first, directly after the "spiritual statement." Salonnes's placement complemented the "first layer" on the other side. That series of donors and properties had ended in the Saulnois; the new series picked up right there, where Salonnes was located. The testament thus betrays an ongoing and important relationship with Angilram. It does not imply that Angilram was in Fulrad's power or that their relationship was hostile. Rather, the evidence suggests that Fulrad and Angilram had converging interests; what they did with land at Salonnes they did because it was to their mutual advantage. A few months after the testament was drawn up, the immunity for Salonnes was confirmed. We return to our initial question: how did Angilram profit?

Angilram

As Chrodegang's kinsman, Angilram came from the highest reaches of the Frankish aristocracy. He followed his illustrious relative to become bishop of Metz in 768. Eventually he garnered fame of his own, receiving the title archbishop.[30] Like Chrodegang, Angilram spent time at the king's side, and the whole royal family joined him when he consecrated Lorsch in 774.[31] He was with Charlemagne in 775 to receive an immunity for his

29. *ChLA* 16:24, no. 623: "a partibus sancti Dionisii ipsa cella debeat aspicere, tam illas commutationes, que cum Angalramno episcopo feci, quamque et reliquas commutationes."

30. On his accession: *GC* 13, col. 708; on his title of archbishop: MGH Dip. Kar. 1:218, no. 161. See Oexle, "Die Karolinger," p. 296.

31. *Lorsch* 1:282; the account is certainly plausible but it has problems, not least being that Queen Hildegardis is said to be there with her three sons, including Louis, who was born in

cathedral church of Saint-Stephen at Metz and its properties south of the Loire.[32] An extant copy of Charlemagne's *Epistola de litteris colendis* (dated 780–800), a capitulary that connected religious belief to literacy, was made from an original parchment sent to Angilram.[33] Finally, at some time between 784 and 788, Angilram went beyond the legacy of Chrodegang to become Fulrad's successor as chaplain of the royal court.[34]

We know more than the bare facts about Angilram; indeed, we can reconstruct some of his thoughts from a whole series of extant texts that he commissioned or wrote himself. By and large, their dates are uncertain; most commentators put them after he became chaplain, but there is no clear reason why this should be so.[35]

Without exception, everything that Angilram commissioned or wrote celebrated Metz. If he wrote an addendum to Chrodegang's Rule, it was directed specifically to the canons serving Saint Stephen, the patron of

---

778. Its general historicity is accepted by Oexle, "Die Karolinger," p. 296, and Fleckenstein, *Hofkapelle*, p. 283.

32. MGH Dip. Kar. 1:131–32, no. 91. Its general authenticity is certain, but it is taken from the late-twelfth century Gorze cartulary and appears to have some interpolations. See Wilhelm Levison, *Aus rheinischer und fränkischer Frühzeit. Ausgewählte Aufsätze* (Düsseldorf, 1948), pp. 156–57.

33. MGH Cap. reg. Fr. 1:78–79, no. 29. See Wattenbach-Levison, 2:201 n. 106.

34. Fulrad died July 16, 784: see Stoclet, "Fulrad-Dissertation," p. 537, with references. The first document attesting to Angilram's position as *capellanus* (chaplain) is MGH Dip. Kar. 1:218, no. 161, (June 11, 788), but it is likely that he functioned in the new capacity before that time. The same document (from the Gorze cartulary) styles Angilram "archiepiscopus." It is clear that at some point in the 780s Angilram began to wear three hats: bishop of Metz, archbishop (but not attached to any city), and *capellanus*.

35. The full inventory of texts is as follows:

(1) A small addition to chapter 20 of Chrodegang's Rule (a mitigation of fasting during Lent); see Pelt, *Études sur la cathédrale de Metz*, p. 18.

(2) A list of monetary tips due to the various participants (deacons, subdeacons, cantors, etc.) during the liturgy of major feasts at Metz, written perhaps 787–91; see Michel Andrieu, ed., "Réglement d'Angilramne de Metz (768–791) fixant les honoraires de quelques fonctions liturgiques," *Revue des Sciences religieuses* 10 (1930): 349–69.

(3) A *Liber de episcopis Mettensibus* (modern commentators style it the *Gesta episcoporum Mettensium* and it is abbreviated here *GeM*), written for Angilram by Paul the Deacon.

(4) The *Versus de episcopis Mettensis civitatis quomodo sibi ex ordine successerunt*, MGH Poet. Lat. 1:60–61, possibly composed by Angilram himself: see Karl Neff, ed., *Die Gedichte des Paulus Diaconus. Kritische und erklärende Ausgabe*, Quellen und Untersuchungen zur lateinischen Philologie des Mittelalters 3, no. 4 (Munich, 1908), pp. 186–90 (with new edition of the text). Neff dates it after the *GeM*. The poem seems to date itself, for it combines Angilram's episcopacy at Metz with Charlemagne's conquest of Italy (774).

(5) A *Vita* of Saint Trudo (here *VT* = *BHL* 8321), written by one Donatus at Angilram's behest.

Metz cathedral.[36] If he devised a scheme to tip the clerics as they manned their liturgical posts, it was in order to support the liturgy of "stations" that Chrodegang had established at Metz in imitation of practices at Rome.[37] If he wrote laudatory verses about the bishops of Metz, he did not hesitate to compare himself, the latest in a long line of shepherds of souls, to Charlemagne, the conqueror of Italy. The king's fate, just like Angilram's, depended (he declared) on Saint Stephen of Metz![38]

Angilram also commissioned a work in praise of the deeds of the bishops of Metz, the so-called *Gesta episcoporum Mettensium*. It has been much interpreted.[39] Like his poem about the Metz bishops, the *Gesta* too attempted to meld episcopal history with the fate of the Carolingians.[40] Indeed, it made Metz the "ancestral home" of the royal house. Interposed within a series of biographies of the bishops of Metz was a catalog of Carolingian rulers, emphasizing their warlike victories—and their "clement moderation" wherever they conquered. The interposition was justified by kinship. The *Gesta* connected the Carolingians to Bishop Arnulf of Metz by blood: Arnulf was father of Chlodulfus (who became bishop of Metz) and Anschisus (who became the father of Pippin II). This section of the *Gesta* began with a fable about father and sons:

> Since he was merciful and always intent on doing works of piety, Arnulf tried to persuade both his sons to agree that he could distribute all his property for the use of the poor. Then the older son, Chlodulfus, entirely denied he could do it, that is give away the portion that should come to him from his father; but the younger son, Anschisus, trusting that more things would be given to him from Christ's piety, freely promised to obey

36. Pelt, *Études sur la cathédrale de Metz*, p. 18.

37. On these stations, see T. Klauser and R. S. Bour, *Un document du IXe siècle. Notes sur l'ancienne liturgie de Metz et sur ses églises antérieures à l'an mil*, in *Annuaire de la Société d'Histoire et d'Archéologie de la Lorraine* 38 (1929): 497–639. For the tips, see above, note 35, text (2).

38. Neff, *Die Gedichte des Paulus Diaconus*, p. 190: "Iam nunc tricenus pastorque octavus herili / Auxilio fultus trahit ad pia pascua vitae / Angelramnus oves: quo tempore maximus armis / Rex Carolus sensu formaque animoque decorus / Italiae accepit Christi de munere sceptrum. / Quos simul excelsi, Stephano poscente beato, / Protegat atque regat felices dextra per aevum."

39. *GeM*. Wattenbach-Levison, 2:218, claims that it "provides the first example of episcopal history north of the Alps." But Walter Goffart, "Paul the Deacon's 'Gesta Episcoporum Mettensium' and the Early Design of Charlemagne's Succession," *Traditio* 42 (1986): 66, disputes this, and Ian Wood suggests (personal communication) that the last chapter of Greg., *Hist.*, has probably the best claim to the distinction. For modern interpretations of the *GeM*, see the survey in Rosenwein, "Association through Exemption," pp. 77–78.

40. See Rosenwein, "Association through Exemption," pp. 78–80, for details.

all his father's wishes. The venerable father gave thanks to his son and predicted that he would get more than he gave up. Moreover, he blessed him and all his posterity that would be born. And that's what happened.[41]

The tale is a metaphor for generosity to the Church.[42] On the one hand, the royal line, which gives its property to the poor—above all to God's poor, the clergy—is blessed, thrives, gains back more than it gives away in conquests so startling that it can afford to temper victory with moderation.[43] On the other hand, Chlodulfus, who cannot bring himself to give up his portion of the property, becomes the leader of Metz; his response to his father is a metaphor for his church's land, which may not be alienated but only amassed. Thus the *Gesta* presents a vision of two intertwined careers springing from the seed of Arnulf: bishop of Metz and king of the Franks. Allied by common purpose, they triumphed in each other's victories and found protection in the same saintly patron. They diverged only, but fundamentally, in their use of property. We are nearly ready to return to Salonnes and the events of 777.

Saint-Trond

We have not yet, however, explored the text perhaps most important for our purposes, the *Vita* of Saint Trudo (c. 620/30–c. 693), written for Angilram by one Donatus.[44] It forms the counterpart, as it were, of the *Gesta*, so admiring of Anschisus; for in the *Vita* it is the other brother, Chlodulfus, who is the central figure. Here the consequences of his stance toward patrimony loom large.

41. *GeM*, p. 264: "quoniam erat misericors et ad pietatis opera semper intentus, utrisque filiis suis coepit suadere, ut ei assensum praeberent, quatinus omnes suas facultates ad usus pauperum dispertiret. Tunc maior filius, id est Chlodulfus, se hoc posse facere, id est ut portionem sibi debitam patri largiretur, omnimodis denegavit; at vero minor filius, id est Anschisus, fidens de Christi pietate sibi pluriora condonari, ad omnia quae pater vellet, se libenter obedire promittit. Agit venerandus pater gratias filio, et praedicit ei, pluriora eundem quam reliquerat habiturum; insuper benedixit eum eiusque cunctam progeniem nascituram in posterum. Factumque est."

42. For a different interpretation, see Goffart, "Paul the Deacon's 'Gesta Episcoporum Mettensium,'" pp. 92–93.

43. We need look no further than Julianus Pomerius, invoked in Chrodegang's *Rule* itself, for the idea that the Church and the poor were one: Julianus Pomerius, *De vita contemplativa*, 2.9, PL 59, cols. 453–54.

44. See note 35, text (5).

Presented as the driving force of Saint Trudo's life and an organizing principle of his *Vita* is his vow, taken as a child, to build a church on his inheritance. A second organizing principle is exile; for in order to fulfill his vow, Saint Trudo must first leave his *patria* (the Hesbaye) and travel to Metz, then leave Metz to return home. Viewed in this way, the *Vita* may be divided into five parts, following a prefatory dedication to Angilram:

1. The vow is made.
2. Saint Trudo is sent to Metz to fulfill his vow.
3. During his stay Trudo gives his inheritance to Saint-Stephen of Metz and becomes a priest.
4. Trudo returns home and builds his church.
5. Miracles occur (a) while Saint Trudo is alive, and (b) at his grave.

Let us look first at the nature of the vow. Trudo the child is said to be extraordinarily generous, giving away all that he has to the poor and needy.[45] His largesse presages the charity to come; having constructed a "play church" from rocks in a field, "he vowed to God that if the interval of life was given to him to become heir of his parents, he would build a church on his very own inheritance."[46]

The fulfillment of the vow entails divinely mandated travel. Donatus has Trudo go first to the local bishop, Remaclus, here styled the head of the episcopal see of Liège. In fact Remaclus was the "abbot-bishop" of Stavelot-Malmédy.[47] The error in the *Vita* is significant and possibly intentional. For Donatus has *his* Remaclus fly in the face of what a diocesan bishop would normally do: his Remaclus tells Trudo to give his future church to Metz. In effect, Remaclus gives Trudo an anticipatory exemption: "Therefore, my son, go on happily to Chlodulfus, bishop of the city of Metz, and give over to Saint Stephen, protomartyr of Christ, all your possessions and everything that you have in these parts into [Chlodulfus's] hand and make [Saint Stephen] heir to your earthly possessions."[48]

45. *VT*, c. 2, p. 276.
46. *VT*, c. 3, p. 277: "vovit Deo, quod, si ei spatia vitae dedisset, ut parentum suorum heres extitisset, in sua propria hereditate ęcclesiam aedificaret."
47. *Vita Remacli episcopi et abbatis*, MGH SRM 5:88.
48. *VT*, c. 7, p. 280: "Perge igitur, fili mi, feliciter ad Chlodulfum Metensis urbis episcopum omnemque possessionem tuam et cuncta, quae habere visus es in his partibus, per manus ipsius trade sancto Stephano prothomartyri Christi facque illum heredem tuae terrenae possessionis."

Thus "like Abraham" setting out on the road to distant Canaan, so Trudo makes the long journey to Metz. The analogy to the patriarch should be taken seriously: the distance of the Hesbaye from Metz is crucial to Donatus's story. When Trudo arrives at "the glorious church of Saint Stephen," the custodian immediately sees him for the stranger he is. And when he meets with Chlodulfus, the first question the bishop puts to him is: "What can be the reason that you have visited us from such remote parts?"[49] Trudo had jumped borders and so would his gift. That this is a major point for Donatus should not be surprising: we have already seen that Angilram secured an immunity for the property of Metz situated outside of his diocese.[50] The *Vita Trudonis* makes the case for extra-diocesan interests.

Handing over the property from the Hesbaye did not, of course, fulfill Trudo's vow. After a hiatus in the story, while Trudo becomes learned in Scripture and is ordained priest at Metz, Chlodulfus himself initiates the final step. He sends Trudo home "for the utility of blessed Stephen or rather for the benefit of all the inhabitants of the Hesbaye."[51]

Returning, Trudo converts the local population; establishes his church (later Saint-Trond; today Sint Truiden in Belgium); fills it with "many sons of very noble men who, despising the prosperity of this world, shave off their hair" to become monks; works many miracles; and dies.[52] Miracles follow. Among them—their consequence, really—is a donation by Pippin II, son of Anschisus. Donatus stresses, as did the *Gesta*, the rich rewards awaiting a dynasty that practices virtue by giving away property: "[Pippin] gave at [Trudo's] tomb whatever he possessed in a villa called Exel and in another villa called Ham. And so, as we believe, he merited to receive an eternal reward from the Lord and, as is clear to all, his progeny gained perpetual benediction."[53] Thus Arnulf's desire to

---

49. Custodian: *VT*, c. 9, p. 282: "'Ubi tuae nativitatis sumpsit exordium, frater, aut unde itineris tui, ut huc venisses, exstitit inceptio?'"; Chlodulfus: *VT*, c. 10, p. 283: "'Quaenam,' inquit, 'fili karissime, causa extitit, ut de tam remotis partibus nos visitasses?'"

50. See note 32 above.

51. *VT*, c. 13, p. 285: "ob utilitatem beatissimi Stephani, immo ob profectum cunctorum habitantium Hasbaniam."

52. *VT*, c. 16, p. 288: "Itaque factum est, ut multi nobiliorum hominum filii, istius seculi prospera dispicientes, comam suam deponentes, cum invicto milite Christi soli Domino deservirent."

53. *VT*, c. 23, pp. 292–93: "tradidit ad tumulum ipsius, quicquid habere visus est in villa quae cognominatur Ochinsala et in altera villa quae dicitur Ham; indeque, ut credimus, mercedem aeternam a Domino suscipere meruit, et perpetuam, ut omnibus patet, benedic-

give away his property, as presented in the *Gesta*, was fulfilled (and its meaning rendered unambiguous), in the *Vita Trudonis*.

Saint-Trond was ruled by Metz. Donatus took pains to make the point on the occasion of a visitation by Chrodegang: "The monastery of Saint Trudo was, as we said, properly ruled by the bishop of Metz."[54] Yet the episode in which this claim was made manifest illustrates the sort of *self-restraints* that were expected from a pious bishop in the position of ruler. He might preside over the monastery; he might enter its precincts; but he could not violate the sanctuary of the altar:

> [When Chrodegang was at Saint-Trond] one of his servants committed not a little fault. [The bishop] was aroused, and he ordered him to be dragged outside to be beaten. His officers [*ministri*] got [the servant] outside, but he broke away from their hands and fled from them to the altar of Saint Trudo. Then the officers, in great fear of their lord, pursued [the servant] there and were trying to pull him away from the altar. But while they were doing this, suddenly, by divine command, the candles around the altar lit up. The officers were truly amazed; and, leaving behind the servant, who was terrified with great fear, they fled and told the miracle to the blessed bishop. Then that most religious high priest, Chrodegang, went in haste to the church and prostrated himself in prayer before the tomb of the blessed father, begging for [Trudo's] mercy. And rising from his prayer, he immediately pardoned the servant's fault.[55]

Salonnes and the Politics of Control

The privilege of Salonnes was not the first to combine a royal immunity with an episcopal exemption; nor was it the first time that royal *tuitio* had been granted at the same time as royal immunity. But because it combined all of these uses, and because it survives in an original charter whose production in the late eighth century cannot be doubted, it signals for our purposes a critical turning point in the meaning and manipulation of property and public power in the Frankish world.

---

tionem sua progenies adepta est." Anschisus is here (as often elsewhere) styled "Ansigisus." The editor of the *VT*, Levison, notes (p. 292 n. 2) that Donatus's prose here echoes the style of charters.

54. *VT*, c. 28, p. 295–96: "Nam quadam die, dum idem venerandus episcopus in monasterio sancti Trudonis fuisset, quod proprium est ad regendum, ut diximus, Metensis urbis episcopis."

55. Ibid., p. 296.

The new views that it conveys belonged to a circle of highly influential churchmen and courtiers—Fulrad, Chrodegang, Angilram—and the king as well. For Fulrad, securing special status for his properties was a lifelong task. He was not content with immunities and exemptions alone, though he was careful to get them renewed. But their renewal meant something different in the context of the protection (*dicio*) that Fulrad obtained from the pope for any monasteries he might construct on his properties. After Fulrad gave those properties to Saint-Denis, he sought to make sure that *its* jurisdiction—like the pope's—would jump borders. The Aachen privilege for Salonnes was an attempt to guarantee this control. It removed Salonnes and, let us remember, "the other churches that belong to the house of Saint-Denis," from the power of the diocesan bishop, placing them "under the immunity and the protection of Saint Denis" (*sub emunitate et defensionem sancti Dionisii*). This is a marvelously ambiguous phrase: the king gives the *immunitas* and *defensio* (Saint-Denis itself cannot grant them), but Saint-Denis henceforth has them to use. That is, Saint-Denis has jurisdiction over Salonnes and the other churches; and the king's *tuitio* and *defensio* guarantee it. Royal *tuitio* has the potential to be active; the king's court is the court of appeals, and the king's judgment, which is rendered there, is final. In this context *immunitas* does not mean that public power is restrained; combined with protection—*defensio, tuitio*—it means that this power has been extended in order to guarantee special privileges and unusual property arrangements. At the same time, like barnacles, the old meanings of immunities stuck to the new. In the Carolingian period, monasteries were still *tapu* in many ways: royal agents were forbidden to enter, diocesan bishops needed an invitation to carry out their blessings. But at the same time they were not *tapu* in that they were "touched" directly by the royal *Mund*—the king's hand.

Chrodegang and Angilram seconded these initiatives. Like Fulrad, they too were interested in controlling their own foundations and believed this could best be accomplished in alliance with royal power. Chrodegang made certain that Gorze was founded with the concurrence of Pippin. Angilram sponsored texts that celebrated the entwined history of Metz's bishops and the Carolingian kings. The *Vita* of Saint Trudo he commissioned portrays a hero who was as concerned as Fulrad to carve out a special status for his property. Like Fulrad, Trudo put his property into the "hand" of Chlodulfus; in Trudo's case, though, protection came from Metz rather than from the Holy See.

With developments such as these, we have entered a new world, where episcopal exemption has been replaced by its opposite—claims of jurisdiction—and where immunities, once pledges of state restraint, have become promises of direct protection.[56] Episcopal exemptions were not issued by many *bishops* in the Carolingian period; they were issued by kings. And after Charlemagne's time, immunities were so tightly bound to royal protection that, from the time of Louis the Pious, the formula was almost always *immunitas atque tuitio*, immunity *and* protection.

What were the causes of this change? It is certain that they were manifold. Under the Carolingians, the king and his churchmen were bound together through strengthened family ties and other alliances. Bishops merged their patrimony into their episcopal endowment and, consequently, they identified the one with the other. Some churches felt the "shock" of precarial arrangements and the call to tighten their purse strings; naturally they looked around for new sources of protection. Nevertheless, none of these reasons comes to the fore in the documents and texts that we have just reviewed.

The one issue that does is at first a surprise: episcopal jurisdiction. We saw in Chapter 5 how Chrodegang put the old exemption on its head to arrive at one that gave him *mundeburdium*. He was part of a wider movement, whose general outline was long ago traced by Émile Lesne.[57] Under Boniface, Lesne points out, church councils elaborated a clear ecclesiastical hierarchy; in Neustria the establishment (or, as Boniface saw it, re-establishment) of a metropolitan system seemed to be under way. Nevertheless, around 751 Boniface complained that Pippin had retreated on the issue. Under Chrodegang at the Council of Ver in 755, the bishops were told to submit to the bishops of metropolitan cities.[58] The Council of Ver also dealt explicitly with the hierarchical position of the bishop within his diocese: "Let every bishop have power in his diocese to correct and emend [the actions of] priests, monks, and the laity."[59] In Lesne's view

56. It is perhaps significant that royal criminal jurisdiction figures in the *VT*, c. 29, p. 297. A thief steals the treasury of Saint-Trond: "Iudicante ergo clementissimo rege Pippino, ille latro suspensus est in patibulo [by the judgment of the most clement King Pippin, that robber was hanged on the gibbet]."

57. Émile Lesne, *La hiérarchie épiscopale. Provinces, métropolitains, primats en Gaule et Germanie depuis la réforme de saint Boniface jusqu'à la mort d'Hincmar, 742–882* (Lille, 1905), pp. 30–79.

58. Council of Ver, c. 2, MGH Cap. reg. Fr. 1:33: "Episcopos quos in vicem metropolitanorum constituimus, ut ceteri episcopi ipsis in omnibus oboediant." At this time bishops of metropolitan cities did not themselves need to have metropolitan status.

59. Council of Ver, c. 3, MGH Cap. reg. Fr. 1:33: "Ut unusquisque episcoporum potestatem habeat in sua parrochia, tam de clero quam de regularibus vel secularibus, ad corregendum et emendandum."

the debate between old and new ended in 779, at Herstal, where suffragan bishops were made subject to metropolitans, and where priests were placed under the power of their diocesan. But despite the general validity of Lesne's schema, we can see that negotiations about monastic jurisdiction did not end. Though no one still advocated old-style Merovingian exemptions, where "any" bishop could be invited to do blessings and so on, nevertheless royal "protection" opened up possibilities previously unanticipated. In the first place, the papacy discovered new opportunities and became more important actors on the Frankish stage than hitherto. We can see Rome's new role clearly in the exemptions sought by Fulrad, who simply bypassed *all* local bishops in favor of the pope.[60] But in the second place, "protection" offered new possibilities to Frankish bishops who, like Angilram, were willing to trade control over one monastery (say, Salonnes) in order to assure the subjection of another (such as Saint-Trond).

To men whose properties lay scattered throughout the kingdom, as was the case for Carolingian aristocrats, a diocese was a paltry and confined thing. These were men comfortable with the titles of "archpriest" and "archbishop" unattached to any particular metropolitan see. They were content to establish monasteries on their own land or on the lands of their churches without imagining there was a difference and without abandoning their control. They were pleased to link episcopal shepherding with royal victory in Italy.

Thus, when Angilram issued the privilege at Paderborn for Saint-Denis's monastery of Salonnes, he was affirming a vision of the church to which he himself subscribed. He had not lost a fight, nor was he the weak tool of the abbot. He had not been manipulated to set up a "post" for Saint-Denis on the way to Saxony. He intended to issue the privilege; Charlemagne's confirmation says so explicitly. For his exemption set up just the sort of extra-diocesan control to which he himself was committed. If he had not anticipated the king's addition to the privilege—the offer of royal immunity and protection—he could not have been sorry to see it. For in his view the fates of the royal line and the bishops of Metz were inextricably and gloriously intertwined. Charlemagne's immunity for Salonnes redounded to the domination of the king, but it promised power as well to the bishop of Metz. It represented a happy meeting of minds for all concerned.

60. Schwarz, "Jurisdicio und Condicio," for one, would call these "emancipations" rather than exemptions.

The Carolingian combination of protection with immunity changed the rules of the political game as hitherto played.[61] *Mundeburdium* meant protection but also control. Not every bishop was like Angilram, able to find a happy *quid pro quo* in the new order: Maurinus, the bishop of Auxerre, for example, could not have been satisfied to "get back" some small monasteries in his diocese while the great house of Saint-Germain d'Auxerre remained under Charlemagne.[62] But immunities had never been delights to all who traded in them: we have already seen that Bishop Landeric could hardly contain his displeasure at the king's request to issue an exemption in the mid-seventh century. Immunities from the first offered certain possibilities for a meeting of minds; but they could also be manipulative, uncomfortable, and discordant. Carolingian immunities, simply because they had more elements to play with, were richer in such possibilities. At the same time, the new emphasis on "protection," which they reflected, allowed the papacy, long the issuer of privileges of this sort, to become a more important player. Thus, not only were Carolingian privileges more polyvalent, but the issuers were more diverse. To succeed in this new world, as R. W. Southern remarked in a somewhat different context, "the whole secret lay in knowing the ropes, and in sensing how far one could go."[63]

61. See Appendix 4 for a discussion of another possible Carolingian innovation: the confounding of immunity with asylum.

62. The source is the late ninth-century *Gesta Pontificum Autissiodorensium*, c. 33, MGH SS 13:394–400, at p. 395. Though it must be read as a source of its own period, its general account of the earlier episcopal domination of Auxerre followed by royal "takeover" and finally partial restitution is accepted by Josef Semmler, "Episcopi potestas und karolingische Klosterpolitik," in Borst, *Mönchtum, Episkopat und Adel*, pp. 305–95, at p. 351; Yves Sassier, "Les Carolingiens et Auxerre," in *L'École carolingienne d'Auxerre de Murethach à Remi, 830–908*, ed. Dominique Iogna-Prat, Colette Jeudy, and Guy Lobrichon (Paris, 1991), pp. 21–36. For a convenient summary of early biographies in the *Gesta Pontificum*, see Constance B. Bouchard, *Spirituality and Administration: The Role of the Bishop in Twelfth-Century Auxerre*, Speculum Anniversary Monographs 5 (Cambridge, Mass, 1979), pp. 5–8. Charlemagne's immunity for Saint-Germain is not extant but is attested to in later documents. See Reinhold Kaiser, *Bischofsherrschaft zwischen Königtum und Fürstenmacht. Studien zur bischöflichen Stadtherrschaft im westfränkisch-französischen Reich im frühen und hohen Mittelalter*, Pariser historische Studien 17 (Bonn, 1981), p. 357 and nn. 1314 and 1315.

63. R. W. Southern, *The Making of the Middle Ages* (New Haven, Conn., 1953), p. 134.

PART III
Divergence

The tenth and eleventh centuries saw extraordinary experimentation with the forms, ideas, and uses of immunities. King Berengar I of Italy incorporated them into a conception of kingship founded on gift-giving (particularly of castles and walls) and on his belief in the sacral character of all royal acts (Chapter 7). Shortly thereafter, the papacy and the Cluniac monks together found a new definition of immunities that allowed them to be declared by popes (Chapter 8). Eventually the amalgamation of immunities and exemptions in papal charters and pronouncements led to the idea of a "sacred ban." Immunities underwent still another evolution in England, where they were immediately drawn into the tightly meshed network of royal law and administration (Chapter 9). Eventually they and the institutions created to deal with them were brought into play during the early modern period, when the aphorism that "a man's house is his castle" became a basis for legal and political action.

7
A Gift-Giving King

FOR THE Carolingian kings who followed Louis the Pious (814–40), immunities were routine affairs. The familiar diplomas were still given out, in regular and measured doses, generally to confirm old ones and thus to maintain a royal tradition that now stretched back to a mythologized past.[1] They still carried prestige, conveying in their by now utterly formulaic way the panache of royal self-restraint, charitable religious behavior, and benevolent protection. They still cemented personal relations, papered over conflicts, and signaled agreements. Clearly they were fulfilling important functions; but there is nothing much new to say about them.

Thus in one of the first acts of his reign, Charles the Bald (840–77) renewed a diploma of Louis the Pious for the monastery of Saint-Maur-des-Fossés, borrowing word for word nearly all the provisions of the earlier document, which had been brought to him for just this purpose by the abbot of Fossés.[2] To read Charles's confirmation is to be overcome by royal filial piety: its first section evokes Louis's diploma and Charles's gracious willingness to renew it; the second section is the old immunity recopied. The text breathes a sense of order, tradition, and satisfaction with the status quo.

By the end of the ninth century, however, two important developments

1. On the mythic past, see Amy G. Remensnyder, "Legendary Treasure at Conques: Reliquaries and Imaginative Memory," *Speculum* 71 (1996): 884–906.

2. *Charles the Bald* 1:12–15, no. 4 (841). The model on which it is based, a diploma of Louis the Pious, is published in *RHGF* 6:491–92, no. 51 (816).

were taking place. As we shall see in Chapter 8, one was that immunities were becoming redefined and, in their new guise, were associated with the papacy, with declarations of the Peace of God, and with the creation of sacred precincts and jurisdictions. The second, as we shall see in this chapter, was that they were subsumed and to some extent supplanted by new kinds of gifts and royal entry prohibitions: licenses to construct castles and walls into which no royal agent might enter; and grants of *districtus* or *bannus*, rights of legal and fiscal jurisdiction over territory.[3]

Some of the charters of Charles's grandson and namesake, Charles the Simple or Straightforward, moved in this latter direction (see Genealogy 4). In 898 Charles acceded to the requests of friends of the monks of Saint-Denis to grant that monastery an immunity within its newly constructed fortification.[4] A few years later he confirmed a whole panoply of privileges for Corbie, recalling the ancient ones of Queen Balthild and Bishop Berthefridus, renewing the immunities of his grandfather, Charles the Bald, and finishing with a flourish of new privileges for the monks' new castle (*castellum*): "Let no public agent have any right to judge or administer or command anything as if by force within the castellum constructed at the monks' own expense and initiative within the very walls of their monastery."[5] In 911 he gave Stephen, bishop of Cambrai, the right to have a castellum and a market at the villa of Lestorf and for both to be under the "defense of our immunity" in perpetuity. Here as elsewhere, a new-style immunity—one that included fortifications and perhaps some form of jurisdiction—was justified by crisis: Lestorf was under attack by the barbarians from without (*barbarę gentis*, certainly a reference to Vikings) and unnamed enemies from within.[6] Meanwhile the monks of Corbie had lost their store of previous charters—hence their new charter in which the old ones were reaffirmed "on account of the attacks of the pagans."[7]

3. This, rather than the development taken up in Chapter 8, is stressed in the traditional historiography, as in Amann and Dumas, *L'Église au pouvoir des laïques*, pp. 223–31; Jean-François Lemarignier, "La Dislocation du 'pagus' et le problème des 'consuetudines' (Xe–XIe siècles)," in *Mélanges d'histoire du Moyen Age dédiés à la mémoire de Louis Halphen* (Paris, 1951), pp. 401–10.

4. *Charles the Straightforward* 1:16, no. 10 (898): "immunitatem infra castellum ejusdem loci a novo constructum."

5. Ibid., p. 90, no. 41 (901): "ut nullus judex publicus in castello propriis sumptibus ac juribus infra ipsa monasterii moenia constructo, nullam ibi quasi potestative licentiam habeat discutiendi aut ordinandi aliquod aut disponendi."

6. Ibid., p. 151, no. 67 (911).

7. Ibid., p. 90, no. 41 (901).

GENEALOGY 4. The Later Carolingians (simplified)

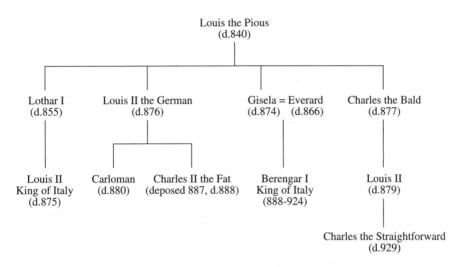

Louis the Pious
(d.840)

| Lothar I (d.855) | Louis II the German (d.876) | Gisela = Everard (d.874)   (d.866) | Charles the Bald (d.877) |

| Louis II King of Italy (d.875) | Carloman (d.880)   Charles II the Fat (deposed 887, d.888) | Berengar I King of Italy (888-924) | Louis II (d.879) |

Charles the Straightforward
(d.929)

Crisis indeed is what one sensitive and learned student of the Carolingian scene makes of Charles the Straightforward's reign, but not primarily because of attacks by outsiders or even insiders: "The royal palace was ceasing to operate . . . as powerhouse, as clearing-house, as distribution-centre for *honores* [great estates; fiefs] and largesse. What was new was not the passing of *honores* from one holder to his close kinsman, but the by-passing of the palace in that transfer, the cutting-out of the king from the transmission-process."[8] This was indeed the kiss of death. Immunities were part of the politics of negotiation. If a king no longer functioned as a gravitational center for alliances, gift distribution, and declarations of self-restraint and protection, then both the king and his charters became disengaged. The documents might spin out all the old lines, but they would do so in a void. Could the new-style immunities and other entry prohibitions charm, cajole, and keep magnates in the fold? Could they be used as part of a reconfigured political landscape in which the king could still function at the center of alliances and enmities? The answer is that they could and they did. But the clearest example is not with kings of the old Frankish heartlands, constrained by traditions of form and meaning, but rather with a king on the periphery: Berengar I of Italy.

8. Nelson, *Charles the Bald*, p. 259.

Carolingian Italy

After 774, when Charlemagne took the Lombard crown, the kingdom of Italy (comprising northern and central Italy down through the March of Spoleto) became part of the Carolingian empire. While Charlemagne and his successors generally were "absentee monarchs," they brought in their wake contingents of Frankish settlers.[9] Beginning in about 834, under the auspices of Louis the Pious, a whole ruling class of outsiders and their underlings came to Italy to live on lands confiscated from churches, Lombard magnates, and the Lombard royal fisc.

Among the families that found new fortune in Italy were the so-called Unruochings in Friuli (Berengar's direct ancestors), the Widonen at Spoleto (the dynasty of Berengar's early rivals, Kings Wido and Lambertus), and the Supponids at Parma (the family of Berengar's first wife, Bertilla).[10] Some of these families sought the crown of Italy; it was not only a prize in itself but a stepping-stone to the even loftier position of emperor. All of these families consolidated their positions in Italy through their control of property; canny alliances of friendship, lordship, and marriage; and careful cultivation of Carolingian ties and traditions.

Suppo II (see Genealogy 5) suggests the importance of the Carolingians to the magnates of Italy. When the emperor and king of Italy Louis II died, Suppo supported the east Frankish faction represented by Louis the German and his sons Carloman and Charles the Fat, maintaining in this way both the interests of his sister (the widow of Louis II) and his own "imperial" standing. In 880, for example, he accompanied Emperor Charles the Fat to hear a court case at Pavia.[11] Neither Suppo nor any of his sons attempted to obtain the Italian crown.

Wido, who not only tried but succeeded in becoming king of Italy (889–95), may serve as the counterexample to Suppo. He was hardly at-

9. The term "absentee monarch" is Chris Wickham's in *Early Medieval Italy*, p. 47. For narratives and overviews of late Carolingian Italy, see also Eduard Hlawitschka, *Franken, Alemannen, Bayern und Burgunder in Oberitalien (774–962)* (Freiburg im Breisgau, 1960), pp. 67–94, supplemented by Jörg Jarnut, "Ludwig der Fromme, Lothar I, und das Regnum Italiae," in Peter Godman and Roger Collins, eds., *Charlemagne's Heir: New Perspectives on the Reign of Louis the Pious (814–840)* (Oxford, 1990), pp. 349–62.

10. Adding the endings *-en*, *-ings*, and *-ids* to refer to clans is an artifact of modern historiography. These family groups or clans did not have one name; and it is only for convenience, to designate in a rough and ready way a political / familial / party / group / alliance, that terms such as Widonen are used here.

11. Cesare Manaresi, ed., *I Placiti del "Regnum Italiae,"* vol. 1, Fonti per la Storia d'Italia 92 (Rome, 1955), pp. 315–18, no. 88; pp. 318–22, no. 89.

GENEALOGY 5. The Supponids

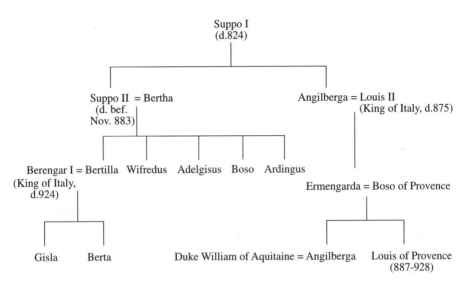

tached to the Carolingians, though some of his charters clearly depended on Carolingian forms.[12] With the deposition of Charles the Fat in 887 and the election of Berengar by a faction of the Italian nobility in 888, Wido briefly attempted to claim the *west* Frankish crown. Unsuccessful there, he gathered an army of Frankish supporters and beat Berengar back to his home base in the Italian northeast.

In many ways Berengar was a maverick.[13] As Suppo's son-in-law he inherited the support of Suppo's sons and the alliances that Suppo had forged with the east Frankish house.[14] Yet unlike either Suppo or Wido, Berengar broke with his non-Italian roots and cultivated only local Italian ties. He gave up his interest in his inheritance in the Hesbaye, for ex-

---

12. On the Widonen, see Wolfgang Metz, "Miszellen zur Geschichte der Widonen und Salier, vornehmlich in Deutschland," *Historisches Jahrbuch* 85 (1965): 1–27; Julia M. H. Smith, *Province and Empire: Brittany and the Carolingians* (Cambridge, 1992), pp. 52–53. Wido's charters are in DGui; see DGui., pp. 21–24, no. 9, for a charter that invokes the precedent of Charlemagne and is based on a diploma of Charles the Fat.

13. On Berengar, see G. Arnaldi, "Berengario," in *DBI* 9: 1–26; Barbara H. Rosenwein, "The Family Politics of Berengar I, King of Italy (888–924)," *Speculum* 71 (1996): 247–89; eadem, "Friends and Family, Politics and Privilege in the Kingship of Berengar I," in Samuel K. Cohn Jr. and Steven A. Epstein, eds., *Portraits of Medieval and Renaissance Living: Essays in Memory of David Herlihy* (Ann Arbor, Mich., 1996), pp. 91–106.

14. *Gesta Berengarii imperatoris*, bk. 2, ll. 78–84, ed. Ernst Dümmler (Halle a. S., 1871), p. 101.

ample.[15] He hardly ventured out of Italy; he certainly never sought the west Frankish crown.

Yet Berengar was more "Carolingian" than either Suppo or Wido. He was, in fact, a scion of the Carolingians through his mother, Gisela, sister of Charles the Bald. Names were an important signal by which medieval people declared their ties and allegiances, and it was not by accident that Berengar named one of his two daughters Gisla, thereby recalling not only his mother but also a sister of Emperor Louis II.

But Berengar was Carolingian in more than family matters. Extant today in the library of Monza cathedral, for example, is a sacramentary that was used in Berengar's chapel. A contemporary hand added Berengar's name and that of his queen to the prayers that followed the Exultet during the Holy Saturday service.[16] The addition suggests that Berengar was consciously imitating the kingship of Lothar I.[17] There is more: Aldo Settia has demonstrated how the idea of the *murus ecclesiae*, the rampart of the Church, came to be a key image in Carolingian royal ideology after Lothar I and Louis II authorized the construction of a defensive wall around Saint Peter's basilica at Rome.[18] Not only the fortification, but also the ruler who ordered it, was the *murus ecclesiae*. The poet Sedulius Scottus used the phrase when he referred to Lothar; and it was also his sobriquet for Everard, Berengar's father, who was marquis of Friuli.[19] Berengar would take the image and reify it: he would bestow on favored recipients the privilege of licenses to build walls and defensive structures.

Throughout his reign, Berengar issued diplomas modeled on old Carolingian forms. Nevertheless, they were modified to suit the new conditions of a local king (see Map 4). He gave out and confirmed donations,

15. The land was willed to him by his parents in *Cysoing*, no. 1, pp. 1–4.

16. Monza, Biblioteca Capitolare 7 B 15/98, fol. 48r. I thank Dott. Giuseppe Chichi for allowing me to view this manuscript at nearly a moment's notice. The description of the manuscript in Francesco Frisi, *Memorie storiche di Monza e sua corte*, 3 vols. (Milan, 1794), 3:66–75, is still extremely useful, since some passages are now illegible.

17. *Die älteste erreichbare Gestalt des Liber Sacramentorum anni circuli der römischen Kirche (Cod. Pad. D 47, fol. 11r–100r)*, ed. P. Kunibert Mohlberg and Anton Baumstark, Liturgiegeschichtliche Quellen 11–12 (Münster, 1927), p. xxxiii.

18. Aldo A. Settia, "Églises et fortifications médiévales dans l'Italie du nord," in idem, *Chiese, Strade e Fortezze nell'Italia Medievale*, Italia Sacra: Studi e documenti di storia ecclesiastica 46 (Rome, 1991), pp. 81–94; see also idem, *Castelli e villaggi nell'Italia padana. Popolamento, potere e sicurezza fra IX e XIII secolo* (Naples, 1984), pp. 45–47.

19. For Lothar: Sedulius, *Carmina* 2.25, MGH Poet. Lat. 3:192; for Everard: *Carmina* 2.53, ibid., p. 212; and to an anonymous poet writing c. 900, even Christ ought to be a *murus* like the one around His church at Modena: *Carmina mutinensia* 1, ibid., p. 704: "Tu murus tuis sis inexpugnabilis, / . . . Tu cinge nostra haec, Christe, munimina." See DGui, pp. 28–32, no. 11 (891).

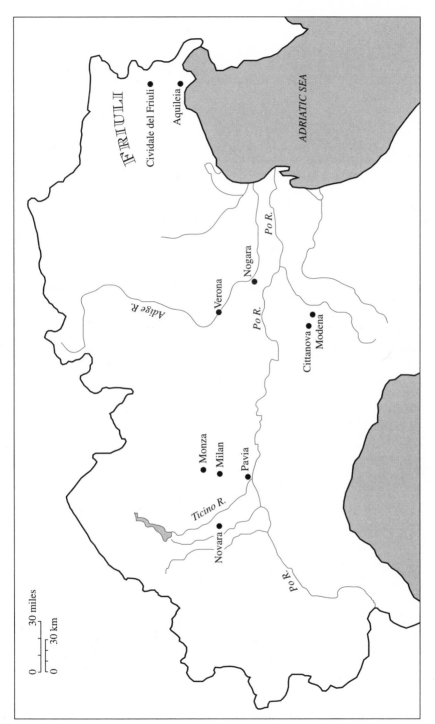

MAP 4. Northern Italy in the Time of Berengar I

immunities, and grants of protection; he conceded tolls, market dues, and other public revenues; he permitted certain people to dig moats, build along public routes, construct walls, and set up castles; he gave away *districtus*—the right to punish and the fines and revenues associated with it—to specific recipients. The net effect of these concessions was to blur the boundaries between immunities and other gifts.

Blurring the Boundaries

To Risinda, abbess of the monastery of Santa Teodota at Pavia, Berengar issued a charter conceding the right to build castles wherever it seemed most useful and best:

> We also receive Abbess Risinda and her castles and all the property of her monastery together with the serfs and slaves, semi-free and free peasants dependent on her under the charter of our immunity and defense such that no duke, count, viscount, sculdahis, gastald, decanus [these last three being public officials] or anyone great or small may requisition the right of lodging within those castles, or enter there by force to hold court, or collect the teloneum [toll], or collect public taxes within those castles, but let all be under the power and dominion of this same Abbess Risinda and her successors, remote from encroachment by all public parties.[20]

In this charter, as in many others, immunities were connected with castles, their perimeters defined by the castle walls. Other charters, however, though essentially identical to immunities in all other respects, dropped the word "immunity." Consider Berengar's privilege to his *fidelis* Folcoino in 900:

> We establish and order that no count, viscount, sculdahis, or any power may enter into that fortified place [*castrum*] by force, nor hold court or take by force the toll [*teloneum*] or any pledge within it, but let [Ful-

20. DBer, pp. 225–26, no. 84 (912): "Quam etiam Risindam abbatissam et sua castella omniaque sui monasterii predia una cum servis et ancillis, libellariis, colonis suisque commendaticiis sub nostre emunitatis atque defensionis praeceptum recepimus, ut nullus dux, comes, vicecomes, sculdassio, gastaldio, decanus aut aliqua magna parvaque persona infra castella ipsius monasterii mansionaticum faciat, nullusque inibi potestative ingrediens placitum custodiat, neque teloneum exquirat, aut infra ipsa castella publicas exigat functiones sed omnia sint in potestate et dominio eiusdem Risindae abbatissae suisque successoribus, amota totius publicae partis contradictione."

coino] . . . hold that estate [*curtis*] and said fortification built at Gropello without any molestation or diminution.[21]

The word "immunitas" does not appear in this charter. Nevertheless, the phrases are clearly patterned on an immunity, including an entry prohibition connected, in the "new style," to a fortification.

In other charters, the formulae characteristic of immunities were embedded into gifts that did not contain explicit entry prohibitions at all, though such prohibitions were implied. Consider the privilege that Berengar gave to the deacon Audebertus in 906. Since its cast of characters will be subject to some close analysis later, I provide a full summary here:

In the name of God, Lord eternal. King Berengar makes known to the devoted astuteness of all the *fideles* of the holy church of God and his own, present and future, that Ardingus, most reverent bishop [of Brescia] and beloved archchancellor of the king humbly begged the clemency of his serenity to make a concession on account of the incursion of the pagans: that the king deign to give in perpetuity license to Audebertus, deacon of the holy church at Verona, to build a castle at Nogara, between Duas Robores and Tillioano, above a bank of the Tartaro river, and to transact business around this castle and within this castle and to build a market. Acceding to these worthy requests, the king permitted Deacon Audebertus to build at the aforesaid place a castle with redoubts, crenelations, moats, and every sort of fortification, and he decreed it be affirmed by this diploma. And thus Audebertus, confident in the king's royal authority, was to surround the castle with redoubts, fortify it with ramparts, add to it every fortification; and he was to construct a market there with the king's license. The king granted and conceded as the deacon's own property the tolls, mooring dues, taxes, and all tributes and jurisdictional fines [*districtiones*]; and whatever else that once pertained to the king was given in full to the deacon by proprietary right. Likewise no count, viscount, sculdahis, gastald, decanus or anyone, great or small, of whatever dignity or order might presume to hold court in that castle or exact or lay claim to anything within it for the king or presume to requisition lodging by force or compel anything to be paid from its market to the public treasury. Rather, Audebertus would possess everything by proprietary right, re-

21. DBer, p. 97, no. 32 (900): "Statuentes itaque iubemus, ut nullus comes nec vicecomes neque sculdassio aut aliqua potestas in ipso castro potestative ingrediatur, neque placita celebret, nec tholoneum aut aliquod pignus inibi potestative accipiat, nec mansionaticum aut aliquam functionem inibi exigatur, sed liceat predictum Fulcoinum . . . nostrum fidelem eandem cortem atque pretaxatum castrum in loco Graupello fundatam sine molestatione et diminoratione atque invasione alicuius tenere."

mote from the disturbance and diminution of every power. If anyone should be tempted to rise up audaciously against this concession to prevent its being carried out, he should pay thirty pounds of the best gold, half to the royal palace treasury and half to Deacon Audebertus.[22]

This was a hefty concession to give to a mere deacon. Charters such as this have given Berengar a bad name; they suggest that he scattered gifts and privileges about, mindless of the consequences.[23] We seem far from Dagobert's negotiations with the most powerful clans of the Meaux valley or the high-level accommodations between Fulbert, Angilram, and Charlemagne. Yet a closer look reveals that Berengar, too, was manipulating tight alliance networks—only his were more local and had more filaments. Moreover, like Dagobert and Charlemagne, he was carrying out his own understanding of the religious role of the king. Let us consider each of these points in turn.

Alliance Networks

As I have shown elsewhere in detail, Berengar did not in fact disperse his privileges widely.[24] Although many different people are mentioned in his charters, they represent closely interlocking factions. Berengar was chiefly intent on negotiating with three groups: women related to him by blood or marriage; his courtiers, especially men at Verona, where he had set up a fortified base; finally, his enemies, who were also, sometimes, his friends. This last network was centered chiefly at Pavia.

Audebertus may have been "only" a deacon at the church of Verona, but he was a key man in the entourage of the king. The charter itself links him to Ardingus, its petitioner: *he* was Berengar's brother-in-law, and thus tied by blood to the first group of Berengarian supporters: his female kin. Audebertus also belonged among the second group of supporters, the courtiers. He was himself based at Verona, and he was close to Anselmus, count of Verona between c. 901 and c. 913. Anselmus was a pivotal figure, for he was both the king's *compater* and *compater* of Audebertus.[25] *Compatres* were spiritual relatives because the one was parent and

22. DBer, pp. 177–78, no. 65 (906). For the text, see Appendix 4.
23. For the traditional argument that these concessions were acts of a weak king, and my rebuttal, see Rosenwein, "Family Politics."
24. Ibid., and Rosenwein, "Friends and Family."
25. For the spiritual co-parentage of king and count, see DBer, pp. 151–53, no. 53; for the same of count and deacon, see ibid., p. 236, no. 88 (913).

the other the baptismal sponsor of the same child. Although we do not know the specific relationships in the case of Berengar, Anselmus, and Audebertus—who was the biological father? who the spiritual?—we do know that the very title *compater* made a public statement about mutual goals and obliged the parties to conduct themselves as associates.[26] Thus, even before the diploma for the castle at Nogara had been drawn up, Anselmus, styled "our most glorious count, dear *compater* and *fidelis*," petitioned Berengar to give the chapel of Saint Peter and other property near Verona to Deacon Audebertus.[27] Then, two years after he received the right to construct the castle at Nogara, Audebertus gave half of it to Anselmus.[28] In turn Anselmus gave *his* half and much else besides to the monastery of Nonantola "for the soul of Lord Berengar most pious king and for the soul of Count Anselmus himself and their relatives."[29] Thus the seemingly isolated concession of a castle was in fact part of a complex series of gifts that associated Berengar, Nonantola, and two men at Verona in a social, political, and finally spiritual network.

In this way Berengar's concessions helped hold together alliances at Verona; but did they work as well with the third group, the one largely based at Pavia? The simple answer is no, since this group began to break away from Berengar around 918, when it invited two powerful men— first Hugh of Arles and then Rudolf, king of Trans-Jurane Burgundy—to seize the crown from Berengar. But we shall see that Berengar's concessions worked very well for a time; the defection of 918 was the consequence not of his policy but rather of its cessation.

At Pavia, Berengar negotiated with magnates in the context of a lively real-estate market. The swelling trade of the Po valley and Pavia's place as an administrative center combined to make it an unusually popular place in which to live—and invest. Pietro Vaccari has drawn up an impressive list of episcopal and monastic cells located within the city: they included outposts of the churches of Milan, Lodi, Cremona, Bergamo, Tortona, Genoa, Piacenza, and Reggio, as well as cells of the monasteries of Sant'Ambrogio of Milan, Bobbio, Santa Giulia (San Salvatore) of Brescia, Nonantola, and so on.[30] This dense population generated a highly

---

26. For royal participation in and the political uses of spiritual parentage, see Arnold Angenendt, *Kaiserherrschaft und Königstaufe. Kaiser, Könige und Päpste als geistliche Patrone in der abendländischen Missionsgeschichte*, Arbeiten zur Frühmittelalterforschung 15 (Berlin, 1984), esp. pt. 2.

27. DBer, pp. 151–53, no. 53 (905).

28. DBer, pp. 235–39, no. 88 (913).

29. DBer, p. 304, no. 117 (918).

30. Pietro Vaccari, *Pavia nell'alto medioevo e nell'età comunale. Profilo storico* (Pavia, 1956), p. 38.

competitive real estate market, in which men and women sought to enhance their position within the city landscape through purchases, exchanges, and, of course, royal grants.

Bishop Dagibertus of Novara was one such investor.[31] Already in 887, as a young acolyte at Pavia, he purchased houses and land there, near the monastery of San Senatore. A dozen years later, now a subdeacon, he purchased more property bordering on San Senatore, extending and consolidating his earlier purchases. Dagibertus began his episcopal career in 905 by showing Berengar's then rival, Louis of Provence, the diplomas that his church had received from earlier kings. He came home with Louis's confirmation of his church's possessions, a guarantee of immunity for his church at Novara, and royal protection.[32] In 908, when Dagibertus shifted his allegiance to Berengar, he orchestrated (largely, however, from behind the scenes) some of that king's most generous concessions. Let us look in some detail at the one given to Leo, Dagibertus's *vicedominus* at Novara.

Leo was *iudex domni regis* as well as *vicedominus* for the church of Novara, which meant that he worked for both the state and the Church: the *iudices* constituted a kind of proto-civil service for the Italian kings; the *vicedominus* was the man responsible for administering church property. In 911 Leo headed up a group of twenty-nine men at Novara: they petitioned the king "on account of the persecution of the pagans and evil Christians" to give them license to build a castle on their property.[33] Bristling with towers and parapets, it was meant to stave off not only the "pagans" but also the incursions of public power:

> Let no count, viscount, sculdahis, public servant, nor anyone great or small presume to distrain[34] or molest those aforesaid men or their heirs or requisition anything [from them] in any way contrary to law or justice: but let those who reside in the castle live quietly, without public interference, for the salvation of our soul; and let no one dare distrain them in that castle, or enter violently, or hold court hearings inside, or try to occupy their houses against their will; but let them live and remain quietly under our protection for our soul's reward.[35]

---

31. The point is made, and particulars given, in Rosenwein, "Family Politics," p. 269.
32. DLouis III, pp. 58–61, no. 21.
33. DBer, pp. 208–10, no. 76 (July 19, 911).
34. *Distrain* (from Latin *distringere*) is a term of law referring to the right to seize and hold property in order to compel payments or reparations, e.g., of debts. *Distraint* is its noun form.
35. Ibid.: "ut nullus comes, vicecomes atque sculdassio nullusque publicus [minister] vel quelibet magna parvaque persona predictos homines suorumque heredes super hoc dis-

We have seen the connection drawn here between the quiet, ordered life and the king's immortal soul in the very first immunities and exemptions of the Merovingian period. But those privileges had been given to religious institutions. Leo's group of twenty-nine, by contrast, was made up of family men, lay inhabitants of the region who planned to build a fortification and live within it. Even Leo was a family man, as we learn when, a month later, Berengar took him under his royal protection (*defensio*) along with his wife, sons, daughters, and dependents, "remote from all public dues," confirmed all their possessions, including castles, and prohibited public functionaries from daring to "dispossess" them of anything without legal judgment.[36] These privileges did not touch monks or churchmen. Nevertheless, the diploma treated the tranquillity of twenty-nine householders as an act of piety and the protection of their possessions from distraint by public officials as an act of state. A decade or so thereafter, the ecclesiastics at Novara considered these privileges so useful that they copied them into a special scroll.[37]

That the privileges granted Leo were based on old immunities is clear from the formulaic vocabulary, the enumeration of public taxes such as the *teloneum*, and the granting of royal *mundeburdium*—the protection that, since 814, had been a regular feature of immunities. But the convergence of these clauses with guarantees of familial, domestic privacy was original: houses (*mansiones*) were now to be protected from the incursion of royal agents.[38] The homes of the men of Novara were clearly within a castle; and the public power stopped before their door. Here we find for the first time the association between a castle, a man's residence, and governmental restraint. In theory, immunities *could* have led to the idea that "a man's house is his castle against the king," but, as we shall see in Chapter 9, they did not.

Probably around this same time—certainly before 915—Berengar gave Leo license to build more castles on his properties at Pernate, Terdobbiate, Cameri, and Galliate (none more than twenty kilometers from No-

---

tringere, molestare, aut aliquid exquirere quod iniustum aut contra legem videtur aliquo modo presumat, sed liceat eis in ipso castro residentibus pro mercede anime nostre quiete vivere absque publica inquietudine; ita ut nullus audeat in ipso castro eos pignorare, aut violenter intrare, aut placitum inibi tenere, aut in eorum mansionibus sedere absque eorum voluntate pertemptet, sed liceat eis sub nostro mundburdo pro mercede anime nostre quiete vivere et manere."

36. DBer, pp. 212–14, no. 78 (August 19, 911).

37. See Rosenwein, "Family Politics," appendix 2.

38. DBer, pp. 213–14: "nemo [after a listing of public functionaries] etiam per vim in suas mansiones ingredi audeat."

vara).[39] It was also about this time that he gave Bishop John of Pavia, another associate of Dagibertus, the right to build a fortification at Cilavegna (also near Novara).[40] It is likely that Bishop Dagibertus hoped eventually to obtain all of these properties; that, at least, would explain why in the 920s the ecclesiastics at Novara sewed copies of these charters together in the scroll referred to earlier.

Why, then, did Dagibertus and many others who were benefiting from the king's largess abandon Berengar in the early 920s? It would seem that whereas elsewhere in Berengar's kingdom royal and aristocratic relations tended to be fairly stable—we have seen an example at Verona—the situation around Pavia was extremely volatile. Landowners there negotiated with Berengar for privileges, but they also cast about for other royal patrons. Berengar satisfied the Pavian group for only so long; between about 908 and 915 he gave them what they wanted—land, castles, walls, and immunities. Then, in 915, he had himself crowned emperor, and the flow of gifts subsided to a trickle.

From King to Emperor

As king, Berengar conceived his primary duty to be gift-giving. This was a far more precise tool for negotiating, balancing factions, and making alliances with churchmen and others than it might at first seem. Bluntly, gifts bound recipient and giver in the tight clasp of mutual obligation. There were conventions of gift-giving and receiving, shame in not carrying them out, honor in doing so. There were also religious reasons to give gifts. Berengar had in his library at least one copy of Isidore of Seville's *Synonyma*.[41] He could certainly read; he must have read it.[42] Isidore

39. DBer, pp. 266–68, no. 102. On the date of the charter, see Rosenwein, "Family Politics," p. 168 n. 109; for a map of the places around Novara, ibid., p. 260.

40. DBer, pp. 268–69, no. 103.

41. We know some of the books in his library because they were willed to him by his parents; see *Cysoing*, pp. 1–5, no. 1. He received 17 of the 62 books named; but it is very likely that he also inherited the 16 books that had originally been intended for his older brother, Unroch, who died c. 874. The books are identified in Pierre Riché, "Les bibliothèques de trois aristocrates laïcs carolingiens," *Le Moyen Age* 69 (1963): 87–104; see also Rosamond McKitterick, *The Carolingians and the Written Word* (Cambridge, 1989), pp. 245–48. If Riché's identifications are correct, Berengar was given two copies of the *Synonyma* and ended up, when he inherited his brother's library, with three.

42. Even the women in this family were literate. Berengar's mother had a psalter specifically "for her own use" (*ad opus suum habuit*); and his sisters were willed books such as the *Enchiridion* of Saint Augustine. It is just possible that Berengar's mother had the bene-

pitched part of his treatise to a man like him: the powerful. Such men were victims, Isidore said, victims of wealth! "Their riches lead them to danger; their riches drag them to ruin."[43] The remedy was to give gifts: "Share with everyone, give to everyone, offer to everyone."[44] Of course, Berengar did not take this literally; he did not share with everyone, even though some historians have thought that he did. As we have seen above, he worked within a tight network. But he put everything into his gifts: not just properties, not just immunities, but rights like holding court and collecting tolls. He had, as the historian Giovanni Tabacco has nicely put it, an "allodial conception of power and jurisdiction, conceived in connection with visible goods and property."[45]

But to leave it at that is to miss Berengar's essentially religious conception of gift-giving. In many of his charters, Berengar's *clementia*, clemency—his gentleness, mercy, and kindness—was associated with the clemency of God.[46] Berengar, these charters announced, was king by divine clemency; in turn, he gave gifts out of his own clemency; and in turn again, he would himself be rewarded for his clemency with eternal life.

The imperial title, however, obliged Berengar to respect different models of rulership. It meant taking seriously the universalist meaning of *imperium*; the emperor must look beyond the boundaries of a paltry kingdom, intervening, for example, in the episcopal affairs of Liège.[47] It demanded a new sort of domestic life, leading the king to reject his Supponid consort in favor of a Byzantine wife.[48] It meant that Berengar would present himself differently, donning the jewels and robes of the Byzan-

---

fit of learning from Walafrid Strabo, tutor of her brother, Charles the Bald. The fact that Walafrid was chosen for Charles by *his* mother, Judith, suggests that education of sons was forwarded through mothers; see Nelson, *Charles the Bald*, p. 82.

43. Isidore, *Synonyma* bk. 2, PL 83, col. 865: "Divitiae usque ad periculum ducunt, divitiae usque ad exitium pertrahunt."

44. Ibid., col. 866: "Omnibus communica, omnibus tribue, omnibus praebe."

45. Tabacco, *Struggle for Power*, p. 159.

46. Of the thirty-eight original charters in which the king's *clementia* is invoked, twenty-two (58%) speak of his being king or emperor "by the favor of divine clemency (divina favente clementia)"; or to look at the matter from the other side, of the forty-one original charters in which Berengar is said to be king "by the favor of divine clemency," twenty-two (54%) speak of the *clementia* of the king. There are a total of seventy-three extant original diplomas, not counting *placita*; the pairing, then, occurs in a bit over a quarter of them.

47. Zimmermann 2:81, no. 48; Rudolf Hiestand, *Byzanz und das Regnum Italicum im 10. Jahrhundert* (Zurich, 1964), pp. 134–35. For the universal idea implicit in the emperorship, see Stephen Fanning, "Bede, Imperium, and the Bretwaldas," *Speculum* 66 (1991): 1–26.

48. On the Byzantine origins of Berengar's second wife, Anna, see Carlrichard Brühl, *Deutschland-Frankreich. Die Geburt zweier Völker* (Cologne, 1990), pp. 517–18, with further bibliography.

tine emperor.[49] Finally it necessitated his taking on a newly aloof, stationary, "eternal" persona.[50] The majesty of the emperor might still give out gifts, but it was moved to do so much less often than before.[51] This is why the men at Pavia abandoned him.

Competitive Generosity

Gift- and privilege-giving were bolstered by implicit social and ideological structures that determined the "rules of the game," nurturing the reasonable expectations of all the players about why and what kings should give, and to whom; and what they might expect in return. Among these structures were the known and assumed traditions of previous kings and sometimes the need to ape or indeed rival them in generosity.

Consider the example of Berengar's gifts to Bishop Gotfredus. Gotfredus had constructed a castle near Cittanova before his accession to the bishopric of Modena (904?).[52] We can understand why he would have been anxious to have Berengar confirm the fact that he had given this castle to the church of Modena, especially since six of the ten still extant acts drawn up by this bishop were written at the site of that fortification, while another—this one after Berengar's death—was drawn up at a different stronghold.[53] Castles were clearly the focal point of this bishop's public activity.

It is less easy to understand why Berengar gave Gotfredus what he wanted. The bishop was no particular supporter of that king: less than a year after receiving diplomas from Berengar, he used the regnal year of Berengar's rival, Louis of Provence, to date a charter pertaining to Cittanova.[54] Not that there is evidence that Gotfredus was a particular partisan of the Provençal king either; there are no recorded concessions from Louis to Gotfredus.

To this hesitant and lukewarm bishop, then, Berengar conceded that "no duke, count, viscount, sculdahis, no agent of public power or anyone

49. On the model that Berengar followed as emperor, see ibid., pp. 516–18, and Hiestand, *Byzanz*, pp. 128–37.

50. Sabine G. MacCormack, *Art and Ceremony in Late Antiquity* (Berkeley, Calif., 1981), pp. 55–56; Geneviève Bührer-Thierry, "'Just Anger' or 'Vengeful Anger'? The Punishment of Blinding in the Early Medieval West," in Rosenwein, *Anger's Past*, chap. 4.

51. See Rosenwein, "Family Politics," p. 254, Table 2, and p. 258, Table 3.

52. See DBer, pp. 132–34, no. 46 (904).

53. *Modena*, pp. 66–67, no. 44 (July 927).

54. *Modena*, pp. 57–58, no. 38 (May 10, 905).

small or great carrying out public functions may exercise any power in said fortification and castle."[55] Why did he do this? The answer seems to be that privileges to Modena were part of Berengar's conception of the royal purpose. Above all, in this case, he sought to match the gifts made by Wido, Berengar's earlier rival.[56]

Already in 891, Wido had given the church of Modena a confirmation that drew in form and substance upon the diplomas of Charlemagne, Louis the Pious, and Louis II.[57] But it went beyond those models in authorizing the church to "dig moats, construct mills, build gates, and fortify [*firmare*] the territory within the radius of a mile around the church for its safety and defense and that of its canons; to open and close watercourses without any public contradiction."[58] Berengar gave concessions to Modena even before Gotfredus became bishop there: on December 7, 898, he granted it a privilege that repeated with few changes the words of a diploma that Lambertus, Wido's son, had drawn up on behalf of the same church only a month and a half before.[59] Clearly Modena was a beneficiary of a tradition of royal gift-giving. Gotfredus must have been delighted to be at the center of such munificence. From the point of view of Berengar, however, this particular bishop was incidental to the larger purpose: to follow the traditions of kings in giving away the symbols and substance of fortified edifices. As the *arenga* (introductory flourish) of one of Berengar's privileges for building castella put it: "If [the king's] royal munificence protects the holy churches of God and venerable places with temporal safekeeping [then] he will equal the traditions of his predecessors and will be received by the Lord into eternal joy and perpetual stability."[60] A kind of competitive generosity is invoked here, whereby kings strive to equal one another in their generosity by protecting holy places

55. DBer, p. 133, no. 46 (904): "ut nullus dux, comes, vicecomes, scudassio, nullusque rei publicae minister seu quaelibet parva magnaque persona publico ministerio fungens in iam dicta firmitate atque castello potestatem ullam exerceat."

56. On precedents favoring the church of Modena, the origins of which can be traced back to Pippin in 755, see Giovanni Tabacco, "L'allodialità del potere nel medioevo," *Studi medievali*, 3d ser., 11, pt. 2 (1970): 565–615, esp. pp. 568–81.

57. DGui, pp. 28–32, no. 11, with analysis of the models on p. 28; the diploma itself emphasizes how the king is imitating his predecessors ("morem . . . predecessorum regum sequentes").

58. Ibid., p. 31, borrowing here in part from the felicitous translation of Tabacco, *Struggle for Power*, p. 154.

59. DBer, pp. 72–74, no. 24; compare with DLamb, pp. 96–99, no. 11.

60. DBer, p. 225, no. 84 (912): "Si regalis munificentia sanctas Dei ecclesias et venerabilia loca temporali custodia protegit, morem suorum predecessorum equiperat et perpetua stabilitate in aeterna gaudia a Domino suscipitur."

not just with the promise of royal *defensio* but by authorizing material fortifications. Their reward is eternal salvation and parity with their predecessors in status and image.

As at Modena, the privileges that Berengar granted elsewhere, even when personal relations were of utmost importance, revealed elements of this competitive generosity. For a final example of this "overdetermined" gift-giving, let us look at the church of Aquileia, which Berengar endowed partly because of personal relations and partly in conscious imitation of his illustrious predecessors. To these motives, which were very much political in this context, we must add the even more overtly political fact that the marquis of Friuli (or, later, the king based in the eastern wing of Lombardy) was obliged to cultivate the friendship of the patriarch of Aquileia, his metropolitan.[61] Already before 850 Berengar's father, Everard, had twice interceded before Lothar I on behalf of the patriarch of Aquileia.[62] He may have acted similarly when Louis II came to the throne.[63]

For a time, the Unruochings's active intervention on behalf of the patriarch ceased. The patriarch Walpertus (d. c. 900) appeared in person before Carloman to ask for an immunity, even though he and (then Marquis) Berengar were in contact.[64] But as soon as the next patriarch, Federico (d. c. 922), had occupied his see, Berengar began to give privileges to the church of Aquileia. In November 900, calling Federico his "spiritual father," Berengar granted the church of Aquileia a stretch of waterway with its fishing rights, mills, marshes, and annual dues (including those from judgments concerning mercantile disputes) in return for prayers for his soul and those of his descendants.[65] By 911 Berengar had given the Aqui-

61. On Aquileia's status as a metropolitan see and its fluctuating jurisdiction, see Heinrich Schmidinger, *Patriarch und Landesherr. Die weltliche Herrschaft des Patriarchen von Aquileja bis zum Ende der Staufer* (Graz, 1954), esp. pp. 1–13.

62. MGH Dip. Kar. 3:192–93, no. 76 (843); see Harald Krahwinkler, *Friaul im Frühmittelalter. Geschichte einer Region vom Ende des fünften bis zum Ende des zehnten Jahrhunderts* (Vienna, 1992), pp. 251–52. Everard interceded on behalf of the patriarch another time, in a lost diploma: MGH Dip. Kar. 3:348–49, no. 186 (834–50).

63. MGH Dip. Kar. 4:98–99, no 17. The charter as a whole is a forgery, but the editor, Konrad Wanner, points out parts that are genuine. Its authenticity is accepted by Krahwinkler, *Friaul*, pp. 258–59 n. 68.

64. They were together, for example, at a church synod (c. 885) when Aimo of Belluno thanked the marquis for his help; see Krahwinkler, *Friaul*, p. 272 n. 138. For Walpertus's direct petition to Carloman, see MGH Dip. reg. Ger. 1:316–18, no. 22 (879). On the dating of the patriarchs, see Ernst Klebel, "Zur Geschichte der Patriarchen von Aquileja," in *Festschrift für Rudolf Egger. Beiträge zur älteren europäischen Kulturgeschichte*, vol. 1 (Klagenfurt, 1952), pp. 396–422, esp. pp. 406–9, 419.

65. DBer, pp. 98–100, no. 33: "Fredericum . . . nostrum videlicet spiritalem patrem." On the privileges to Aquileia, see Krahwinkler, *Friaul*, pp. 285–89; Schmidinger, *Patriarch und*

leian church property at Cividale and had confirmed all of its privileges.[66] There was then a hiatus; but toward the end of his reign, Berengar turned back to Aquileia. During the period 921–24, when he gave out only six privileges, Aquileia received two of them. In the first, dated 921, Federico gained the castle of Pozzuolo, its territory, and its *districtus* covering a circle one mile in radius.[67] A year later the emperor gave permission to Peter, a *presbyter* at Aquileia, to fortify his castle at Savorgnano.[68] These privileges seem less exceptional when viewed in the light of the long-term involvement of Berengar's family in the fortunes of the Aquileian church and its traditions of gift-giving there. Berengar might have considered gift-giving beneath an emperor's "decorum," but at Aquileia a competitive momentum, driven by the gifts of former kings and the gifts he himself had given—a kind of potlatch where the rivals were both living and dead—impelled Berengar to larger and more spectacular concessions.

Thus we see in Berengar's kingship a radical reification of abstract rights and public duties and their incorporation into an intricate network of gifts. Here was a king who could give out *districtus* with the same vocabulary of gracious generosity as when he offered up landed properties. By incorporating everything into the language of material gift-giving, by interpreting that gift-giving as the mirror image of divine practice, by following the models of Isidore's ideal and of past kings, Berengar fashioned his charters into monuments to his piety, self-discipline, and restraint.

"I shall sing of Berengar," wrote the author of the *Gesta Berengarii*, an epic poem in praise of the king, "to whom the High Power gave the proud nobility of Italy, to curb them by war and wealth."[69] The radical reorganization of resources and the setting up of taboos against his own and his agents' entry bridled Berengar; in turn he was fit to curb the magnates of Italy. Like a Polynesian chief, Berengar projected an image of power immobilized and thereby, paradoxically, proclaimed.

Landesherr, pp. 42–43, and Pio Paschini, *Storia del Friuli*, vol. 1: *Dalle origini alla metà del Duecento*, 2d ed. (Udine, 1953), pp. 172–76.

66. The concessions to the church are contained in two diplomas from around the same time: DBer, pp. 142–43, no. 49 (904?), and pp. 143–46, no. 50 (904); the gift to the deacon is in DBer, pp. 216–17, no. 80 (902–11).

67. DBer, pp. 348–51, no. 136 (921).

68. DBer, pp. 351–54, no. 137 (922).

69. *Gesta Berengarii imperatoris* 1, ll. 11–13, p. 80: "Ergo Berengarium genesi factisque legendum / Rite canam, frenare dedit cui celsa potestas / Italię populos bello glebaque superbos," where the gloss (probably by the poet) to "populos superbos" is "nobiles" and to "gleba" is "divitiis."

8

The Making of the Sacred Ban

MORE THAN two centuries after Berengar's death, a scholar named John Beleth produced a treatise on the nature of the Church. The first topic he took up was the category of places appropriate for prayer. "Holy places," he wrote, using a form of the Latin word *sanctus*, the same term used for saints, "are called places of immunity around monasteries . . . where . . . safety is offered fleeing criminals."[1] In the twelfth century, then, immunities were not only associated with holy places: they *were* holy places. And not only that but, as we shall see in the case of the ban around Cluny, they could also be "sacred" (from the Latin *sacer*) and "consecrated"(from *sacratus*).

Not kings but rather princes, monks, bishops, and popes created this idea—a hybrid of royal immunity, church asylum, and liturgically consecrated space. How they did so is certainly not just the story of the monastery of Cluny; we shall see how important, for example, were ideas first elaborated at the monastery of Fleury. But Cluny was the expert at using and elaborating on the elements at hand.

Cluny's Foundation

It used to be thought that Cluny's foundation was utterly unique, as if its eventual renown and power had been present at its inception. The histo-

1. John Beleth, *Summa de ecclesiasticis officiis*, c. 2, ed. Heriberto Douteil, Corpus Christianorum Continuatio Mediaevalis 41A (Turnhout, 1976), p. 6. Beleth's terminology was borrowed from Justinian's *Digesta* 1.8. I thank Michel Lauwers for calling my attention to this text.

riography of the last twenty years has rightly undermined that view.[2] Without trying to undo this work, which is certainly correct in seeing Cluny as a product of its time, it is, however, necessary to point out that certain aspects of Cluny's foundation were indeed unusual.

The best place to begin is Cluny's foundation charter of 910, which contained at least three striking elements connected with control over the monastery.[3] First, the monastery was placed by its founder, William, duke of Aquitaine, under the *tuitio* and *defensio* not only of the pope (which, as we have seen, was fairly common) but also of the apostles Peter and Paul, to whom control (*dominatio*) over the *villa* of Cluny and the rest of its property was given. Second, Berno, Cluny's first abbot, was to have power and control (*potestas* and *dominatio*) over the monks and all their property; and after his death the monks were to choose another abbot "without our interference or that of any other powerful person." Finally, the monastery was to be free from the "yoke" (*jugo*) of the founder and all other earthly rulers and its property was to be protected from attack, usurpation, and diminution caused by every possible category of powerful persons, including the pope himself: "I pray that no worldly prince, count, bishop, or pope of the above-mentioned see of Rome . . . may usurp the property of these servants of God, or sell, diminish, or exchange it, or grant it out in benefice, or constitute any prelate over them against their will."[4] These were declarations of intent, not fact, and other monastic founders had sent up similar prayers. Yet they had not put the matter in quite the same way. As precedent for Cluny's relationship to the papacy, scholars have cited, for example, foundation documents for reli-

<hr />

2. See the historiographical review in Barbara H. Rosenwein, "La question de l'immunité clunisienne," *Bulletin de la Société des Fouilles archéologiques et des monuments historiques de l'Yonne*, no. 12 (1995): 1–11, at pp. 1–2.

3. Paris, B.N.F. Coll. Bourg. 76 no. 5 = *Cluny* 1:126, no. 112. On the authenticity of this foundation charter, see Hartmut Atsma and Jean Vezin, "Cluny et Tours au Xe siècle. Aspects diplomatiques, paléographiques, et hagiographiques," in Giles Constable, Gert Melville, and Jörg Oberste, eds., *Die Cluniazenser in ihrem politisch-sozialen Umfeld*, Vita regularis. Ordnungen und Deutungen religiosen Lebens im Mittelalter 7 (Münster, 1998), pp. 121–32. Atsma and Vezin have reviewed the evidence for the date of the charter; 910 appears most likely.

4. *Cluny* 1:126, no 112: "neque aliquis principum secularium, non comes quisquam, nec episcopus quilibet, non pontifex supradicte sedis Romane . . . deprecor invadat res ipsorum servorum Dei, non distrahat, non minuat, non procamiet, non beneficiet alicui, non aliquem prelatum super eos contra eorum voluntatem constituat." I take *invadere* to mean "occupy illegally," as in the charter of a *placitum* presided over by Queen Ermengarda, mother of Louis of Provence, where Berno, then abbot of Gigny, complains that Bernard, one of the queen's vassals, "eorum res injusto ordine invadendo possedisset, hoc est Balmam cellam," while Bernard replies that "per donum Ludovici predictas res se tenere credere," that is, that he had just title to them; see *Louis III*, no. 28, pp. 50–51.

gious houses at Lucca, Saint-Gilles du Gard, Aurillac, and Vézelay. Close examination reveals important differences from Cluny.

In the case of the convent at Lucca, the relationship with the papacy was one of subjection and overlordship: if the monastery had no one (such as the founder) to lead it, then (wrote the founder), "I will and establish that that church, with all the property pertaining to it, come under the power [*potestas*] of Saint Peter at Rome or [*vel*] of the pope, to order and govern it [*ordinandum et gubernandum*] in all matters."[5] For Aurillac, we have only the brief account by Abbot Odo of Cluny in his *Life* of Gerald of Aurillac, which is perhaps colored by his own monastic understanding. Odo wrote that Gerald, founder of Aurillac, gave his monastery to Saint Peter with all its appurtenances; and every year he paid an annual tribute (*census*) at the "urn of St. Peter" at Rome.[6] Saint-Gilles is an interesting case, whose status has been clarified by Ulrich Winzer.[7] In brief, although under the control of the bishop of Nîmes until the late ninth century, it was claimed as a papal monastery (*monasterium apostolice sedis*) by John VIII, who then entrusted it to Leo, the abbot of Saint-Gilles, and to Amelius, the archdeacon of Uzès, "to rule and protect and make prosper" (*ad regendum et tuendum et bene hedificandum*)."[8] Rule, govern, order: these are strong words. In Cluny's foundation charter, they were used only in connection with Saints Peter and Paul and Abbot Berno.

Vézelay, too, is different from Cluny. When Count Gerard and his wife gave their property to found two monasteries—Pothières for men, Vézelay for women—they subjected (*subdidimus*) them to the apostolic see.[9] At the same time the founders remained closely attached to these houses, retaining the *tuitio* and *defensio* of the monasteries for themselves. The emphasis in their foundation charter was on control of the monasteries by outside forces: the founders were protectors with an active role; the pope held the monasteries in order to rule, order, and dispose of them (*ad regendum, ordinandum . . . disponendumque*) as he would, though he could

5. Text cited in Fabre, *Étude sur le Liber Censuum*, pp. 38–39 n. 3.

6. Odo, *Vita Sancti Geraldi* 2.4, PL 133, cols. 672–73.

7. Ulrich Winzer, *S. Gilles. Studien zum Rechtsstatus und Beziehungsnetz einer Abtei im Spiegel ihrer Memorialüberlieferung*, Münstersche Mittelalter-Schriften 59 (Munich, 1988), esp. pp. 41–47.

8. *Bullaire de l'abbaye Saint-Gilles*, ed. F. Goiffon (Nîmes, 1882), no. 4, p. 14. On the authenticity of this and related documents, such as no. 3, pp. 5–13, see Winzer, *S. Gilles*, esp. p. 27 n. 2, with extensive bibliography.

9. The foundation charter of Vézelay is not extant in the original. It was included in Auxerre 227, fol. 22–24v, a twelfth-century manuscript, and is published in *Vézelay*, pp. 244–48. See Appendix 6 for the key passages of Cluny's foundation charter and their counterparts in the foundation charter of Vézelay.

not give their property away. Furthermore the pope had the right to approve the choice of abbot or abbess, while the king and pope together had the responsibility of condemning and punishing anyone who acted against the foundations.

By contrast, the foundation charter of Cluny was profoundly ambivalent about the pope. As King Raoul observed in 927, William "subjected Cluny to the Apostolic See for protection, not domination."[10] The radical dissociation of Cluny from any earthly power whatsoever apart from the abbot—who was not entirely worldly himself, since he ruled in place of Christ in the monastery—was therefore something new.[11] To understand how it came about, we need to understand its political context.

Historians have dismissed out of hand the possibility that William had Sergius III in mind when he founded Cluny. Rosalind Berlow has observed:

> No one intent on religious reform at that date could seriously consider involving Pope Sergius III (903–911). Sergius is perhaps best remembered as the lover of Marozia by whom he was alleged to have fathered the future Pope John XI. His term, which began with the strangulation of rival claimants to the title, supposedly at his instigation, represents the nadir in the history of the papacy.[12]

Morals aside, we should take note of the fact that Sergius's much maligned liaison with Marozia, whether true or not, was an indication of his extremely close relations with the most important family at Rome, that of Theophylact and Theodora, Marozia's parents. Furthermore, he owed his position as pope—indeed his very access to Rome—to Alberic I, duke of Spoleto. The latter had been an effective opponent of King Berengar, wounding him on the battlefield and preventing him from entering Rome to claim the imperial crown in 906.[13] By 915 Alberic was known as a "fe-

10. *Raoul,* p. 51, no. 12 (927): "apostolicae sedi ad tuendum non ad dominandum subjugavit." The formula was repeated, e.g., in *Louis IV,* p. 31, no. 10 (939).

11. *RB,* c. 2, p. 172. Cluny's foundation charter may be read as explicitly associating the abbot's power with his following the Rule; see *Cluny* 1:126, no. 112: "Sintque ipsi monachi cum omnibus prescriptis rebus sub potestate et dominatione Bernonis abbatis, qui, quandiu vixerit, secundem suum scire et posse eis *regulariter* presideat" (emphasis mine). Earlier in the text (p. 125) the Rule of St. Benedict is specifically mentioned.

12. Rosalind K. Berlow, "Spiritual Immunity at Vézelay (Ninth to Twelfth Centuries)," *Catholic Historical Review* 62 (1976): 573–88, at p. 575. What follows below on the political context of Cluny's foundation was published in French and in somewhat different form in Rosenwein, "La question de l'immunité clunisienne," pp. 4–8.

13. G. Arnaldi, "Alberico di Spoleto," in *DBI* 1:657–9, from which is taken the biographical information that follows.

rocious lion" (*leo fortissimus*) against the Saracens. At the same time he married Marozia; their son was Alberic II. We know that Abbot Odo of Cluny (927–42) would mediate between that younger Alberic, "prince of Rome,"and Hugh of Arles, king of Italy in the 930s. Odo also reformed the monasteries in and around Rome at Alberic's request.[14] The active role of Cluny's second abbot in Roman affairs makes no sense unless it is understood as part of a long-term relationship between the monastery and the most important political faction at Rome, a relationship initiated by the foundation charter itself.[15]

Nor was Sergius a political fool; he knew well how to garner friends and punish enemies. In 904 he wrote a scathing letter to Amelius, once archdeacon, now bishop of Uzès, upbraiding him for "rehabilitating" Pope Formosus and reminding him of the "stipend"that he owed Saint Peter from the monastery of Saint-Gilles, which (as we saw above) had been given to Amelius by John VIII. If Amelius did not pay up, the pope intended to take the monastery away from him.[16] In 907 he wrote to the abbot of Nonantola, rejoicing in the reconstruction of his monastery's church, confirming its status under papal *tuitio*, and specifying that the abbot might invite only one of three bishops to consecrate it: John of Pavia, Wido of Piacenza, or Elbung of Parma.[17] The timing of the charter, coming right after Alberic had blocked Berengar from Rome, suggests its political purposes: the chosen bishops were men ready to be wooed away from the king. In fact, we know that Wido joined at least one conspiracy against King Berengar later on, while Elbung of Parma never supported the king at all.[18] John of Pavia was, around this time, the king's emissary (*missus*) at a court hearing held at Pavia, but we hear nothing more of him in Berengar's charters up to his death in 911.[19] Nor was this the end of

---

14. Gregory of Catino, *Destructio Monasterii Farfensis*, in *Il Chronicon Farfense di Gregorio di Catino*, ed. Ugo Balzani, Fonti per la storia d'Italia 33 (Rome, 1903), pp. 39–40.

15. Moreover, that relationship bore fruit in Provence. Hugh of Arles and his son Lothar, kings of Italy, made their first and only donation to Cluny during their contest with Alberic; see *Cluny*, 1:403–4, no. 417 (934). Thereafter, following their example, members of the Provençal aristocracy began to donate their own properties to Cluny as well; see Barbara H. Rosenwein, "Les bienfaiteurs de Cluny en Provence (v. 940–v. 1050)," in *Saint Mayeul et son temps. Millénaire de la mort de saint Mayeul 4ᵉ abbé de Cluny, 994–1994. Actes du Congrès International, Saint Mayeul et son temps, Valensole, 12–14 May 1994* (Digne-les-Bains, 1997), pp. 121–36.

16. Zimmermann 1:33–34, no. 20.

17. Ibid., pp. 44–45, no. 25 (907).

18. Rosenwein, "Family Politics," p. 274.

19. For the *placitum*, DBer, pp. 188–92, no. 70. It used to be thought that John was bishop of Pavia until 924 (e.g., those are the dates still given in Zimmermann 1:45 n. 5), but this is unlikely. The John who was favored by Sergius is now known as John II, while his succes-

Sergius's interventions in the political life of Italy. In 910 he wrote another angry letter, this time about Albuinus, count of Istria, who was seizing the land and dependents of the church of Ravenna. The pope wanted all the property restored; and he threatened to withhold the imperial crown from Berengar "unless he promises to take the march away from Albuinus and give it to another, better person."[20] Then, looking beyond Italy, that same year Sergius intervened in the affairs of the church of Lyon.[21]

Thus, as a political actor, Sergius was not the worst person in whom to confide the protection—though not the control—of a monastery. The question that remains is why William did so when he did. The situation in Provence suggests an answer.

At the end of the ninth and the very beginning of the tenth century, there was a rapprochement between two groups contending for power in Provence: the "Guillelmids" (members of William's family and his *fideles*) and the "Bosonids" (who, in fact, became hereditary kings of Provence). William married the sister of Louis of Provence, a member of the Bosonid family; and William and his *fideles* figured prominently in the early charters of the young king's reign. Indeed, the very first charter issued by Louis was a judgment on behalf of Abbot Berno of Gigny.[22] This was the Berno who would later be William's choice to be abbot of Cluny. An even more telling document was drawn up two years later when, at William's request, Louis gave Saint-Martin d'Ambierle to two of his *fideles*, Teutbertus and Bernard.[23] That these men were *fideles* of William as well cannot be doubted (why else would he intervene for them?), and the point is reinforced when we find their names next to each other as witnesses in Cluny's foundation charter. Until 908, Teutbertus was one of the most important figures around Louis, intervening in numerous privileges.[24] In 903, he and Count Walo asked Louis to give Bishop Amelius of Uzès property in the county of Avignon and the church of Saint-Remy near Arles.

---

sor, John III, became bishop in 911 or 912. The former date is the most likely, following Erwin Hoff, *Pavia und seine Bischöfe im Mittelalter. Beiträge zur Geschichte der Bischöfe von Pavia unter besonderer Berücksichtigung ihrer politischen Stellung*, vol. 1, *Epoche: Età imperiale* (Pavia, 1943), pp. 17 n. 65 and pp. 29–34, 133, 380–83. It is possible, however, that John II was still alive in 912, in which case he was present at another *placitum* with Berengar, but not as *missus*; see DBer, pp. 222–24, no. 83.

20. Zimmermann 1:53, no. 30 (910).

21. Ibid., pp. 53–55, no. 31 (910).

22. *Louis III*, pp. 50–51, no. 28 (890).

23. Ibid., pp. 77–78, no. 41.

24. They are inventoried and Teutbertus's career is discussed in Georges de Manteyer, *La Provence du premier au douzième siècle*, vol. 1 (Paris, 1908), pp. 95–98. It is clear that Teutbertus *fidelis* is identical to the Teutbertus *comes* in the charters, as Manteyer shows.

Walo also would be a witness for Cluny's foundation charter. Before 908, certainly, William could not have welcomed Sergius's condemnation of Amelius, who was a favorite of Louis. But matters would soon change.

Teutbertus disappeared from Louis's entourage after 908, though (as we have seen) he and other *fideles* remained with William. So too did his son, also Teutbertus. In these former supporters of Louis of Provence we probably have the personages behind the series of names that appear at the end of Cluny's foundation charter: *Teotbertus, item Teotbertus, Bernardus, Walo.*

After 908, Hugh of Arles took Teutbertus's place at Louis's side. At about the same time some of William's *fideles* (in fact, relatives of Cluny's third abbot, Majolus) fled Narbonne and made their way to Mâcon, a few kilometers from the *villa*—not yet the monastery—of Cluny. The crisis continued. Around 913, the bishopric of Narbonne was given to a member of the family of Bishop Amelius of Uzès. Not long afterward, following the assassination of Majolus's father, Majolus and his mother fled Provence for the Mâconnais. Clearly the alliance between the Bosonids and the Guillelmids had not held.[25]

The foundation of Cluny, then, came at a critical moment, when William and his retinue were being forced to retreat from Provence. By 910, the duke could not have been sorry that the pope had roundly scolded Amelius. Moreover, William had reason to think that the pope could be an effective protector of his interests. The Bosonids, in the person of Louis of Provence as Berengar's rival, had tried (and succeeded for a short time) in gaining Rome themselves. In February 901 Louis had come to a court hearing at Rome as a newly crowned emperor; about a month later, with the pope himself as intermediary, he confirmed the privileges of the church of Arezzo.[26] But, starting in 903, the new coalition at Rome (of which Sergius was a part) succeeded in establishing its independence from the imperial pretensions of the king of Italy. The next year, Berengar blinded Louis, who slunk back to Provence in defeat. The morals of Sergius notwithstanding, William had every reason to link his new monastic foundation to this very pope—"for protection, not domination."[27]

25. Documentation for these events may be found in Rosenwein, "Les bienfaiteurs."
26. For the *placitum*, DLouis III, pp. 18–21, no. 6; for the confirmation, pp. 22–24, no. 7.
27. It is true that there are no extant privileges for Cluny from Pope Sergius. Indeed, there are no extant privileges for Cluny whatsoever until 927, after Berno's death. But, as Cowdrey, *Cluniacs and the Gregorian Reform*, p. 16 n. 1, has observed, the so-called Testament of Berno, apparently written just before his death, says that Cluny had indeed received papal (and royal) privileges: "in eo statu, quo et per regalia praecepta, quin etiam et per apostolica privilegia dudum sancita sunt, et nunc a me decretum est, permanere consentiatis." The text

Cluny's Immunities

In the course of the next two centuries, the monks of Cluny used their contacts with the papacy, their local (and later universal) prestige, and their mastery of the transfigurative power of liturgical rites to negotiate the transformation of the property around them into sacred space. The first step in this process was to gain a *papal* immunity.

The first diploma to grant Cluny an immunity explicitly—using the very word—was a papal document, not a royal one, drawn up in 931.[28] This is also possibly the first time the papal chancery used the word "immunity" to refer to one its own privileges.[29]

The new-minted papal immunity for Cluny, issued by John XI (931–35), was not the same as a royal immunity, but it was neatly adapted to be reminiscent of one. It is not terribly long, and since we shall spend some time analyzing it, it is worth quoting in full here:

> Bishop John, servant of the servants of God, to Odo, venerable abbot of the monastery at Cluny built in honor of the blessed apostles Peter and Paul, situated in the *pagus* [district] of Mâcon, and through you to all your successors in that monastery, in perpetuity.
>
> It is fitting to the apostolic governance, moved by benevolent compassion, to answer the pious prayers of petitioners and offer assent to them with eager devotedness. For in this way we shall earn the greatest reward from God, Author of all. Therefore, because you have petitioned us to affirm said monastery in that state in which it was established by Duke William in his testament, subjected to the holy church of Rome, whose author is God, and which we serve, listening to your prayers, we concede it to you to rule. And thus let that monastery, with all its property and whatever it now has and will be given to it in future, be free from the control

of this Testament is printed in Joachim Wollasch, ed., *Cluny im 10. und 11. Jahrhundert* (Göttingen, 1967), pp. 12–13, and in PL 133, cols. 853–58.

28. Zimmermann 1:107, no. 64. Note, however, that the privilege of King Raoul of 927 for Cluny is reminiscent of an immunity even though it does not use the word itself. See *Raoul*, pp. 47–52, no. 12. Some of the material below has been published in Barbara H. Rosenwein, "Cluny's Immunities in the Tenth and Eleventh Centuries: Images and Narratives," in Constable, Melville, and Oberste, *Die Cluniazenser*, pp. 133–63.

29. I argue that this was the first papal immunity in Rosenwein, "Cluny's Immunities." Upon further reflection, however, I think it prudent to await critical editions of the earlier papal charters before pronouncing judgment. I would simply note that popes did not give out immunities between 896 and 931 (this is clear from the charters published in Zimmermann). The first two that were issued (both in 931) were to Cluny and to Déols, which was under Cluny's abbot; see Zimmermann 1:109–10, no. 65.

of any king, bishop, count, or any relative of William himself. Let no one presume to ordain a prelate for them there after your death against the will of the monks; but let them have the free right to ordain for themselves whomever they want without the consent of any prince according to the rule of Saint Benedict; unless perhaps, God forbid, they prefer to elect a person who will acquiesce in their vices; let whomever they choose prohibit this with the zeal of God.

Let the monastery called Romainmôtier, which the mother of our [spiritual] son King Rudolf gave to Cluny, be subjected to it, along with the villa Vaningo, just as she specified in her charter of donation. Moreover, if, at the request of those responsible for it, you consent to take over any monastery in order to improve it, you have our permission to do so.

Certainly we restore to you completely the tithes that once pertained to your chapels and which, by a pretended modern right or license, have been taken away by some bishop. And we concede chapels—if any have been built already or are to be built there—to remain such that none of the tithes from your churches is reduced. Certainly what our dear [spiritual] son, Bishop Berno [of Mâcon], conceded to you regarding your chapels we declare to be valid in perpetuity. Above all, we declare that whatever part of the tithes comes from the vineyards and fields should pertain to your monastic hospital and similarly for property that you will receive [in the future].

We confirm and restore to you by our apostolic authority that which Letbaldus gave and gave [yet] again to the monastery while he was dying; and similarly what ought to pertain to the monastery at Aine and elsewhere, and the chapel of Saint-Martin at *Maceio*.[30]

And because, as is proven, almost all monasteries nowadays swerve too much from their purpose, we grant that if any monk from any monastery wants to transfer to your way of life, purely out of zeal to improve his life, [since] his abbot clearly has neglected to enforce the rule against having private property, you are allowed to receive him until the way of life of his monastery is amended.

Certainly we concede immunity to you—as reverence is due to holy places everywhere—namely that no one may presume to distrain any of your dependents nor usurp any of your property in any way without your permission.

Let ten *solidi* be given every five years [as a *census* to the Apostolic See] as recognition that said monastery pertains to the holy Apostolic See to be protected and nurtured.

---

30. Zimmermann 3 : 1427 identifies this as Massy; Saint-Martin-de-Senozan is suggested in Maurice Chaume, *Les origines du duché de Bourgogne*, pt. 1, fasc. 3 (Dijon, 1931, reprint 1977), p. 1137 n. 8.

If anyone is tempted to go against this our very beneficial constitution or tries to overturn any of it and disobeys all that we decree in this privilege, let him know that, unless he repents, at the invocation of divine judgment, he will be bound eternally by the chains of anathema, alienated from the kingdom of God, and tormented without end alongside the devil. Certainly he who shows himself a custodian and observer of this our very beneficial decree should merit to attain here and in future the blessing of Christ, the Lord, and absolution from the holy apostles, judges of the world.[31]

Whereas royal immunities, as we know, forbade officials to enter immune land and seconded this with the promise of protection, the papal privilege of 931 substituted the general inviolability of Cluny's property.[32] Historiographical interest in the Gregorian reform, with its emphasis on the distinction between the temporal and the spiritual and its privileging of the latter, has obscured the close connection between matter and spirit in the tenth century. The privilege of 931 mingles the two. It affirms the free election of Cluny's abbot; then it subjects the monastery of Romainmôtier to the monastery of Cluny along with a villa. It restores lost tithes (which, strictly speaking, monasteries were not to have, but which they held quite routinely at this time).[33] It confirms and restores specific properties to Cluny and directly after that gives the monastery the extraordinary right to welcome monks from other houses. The next

31. Zimmermann 1:107–8, no. 64. See Appendix 7 for the text.

32. There was already an ecclesiastical tradition that used the word "immunity" to mean the general inviolability of church property. See the Council of Mainz of 847 in MGH Cap. reg. Fr. 2:174, no. 248: "Unde necessitas magna nos coegit pro hac re ad vos [Louis the German] reclamare et petere, ut, sicut apud antecessores vestros reges atque imperatores, qui ante vos fuerunt, honorem sancta Dei aecclesia habuit et per immunitatem eorum possessiones aecclesiasticae inconvulsae perstiterunt." Indeed, perhaps under the impulsion of such petititions, royal immunities were themselves becoming more general, along the lines of the papal document of 931. See, for example, Louis of Provence's concession of a villa to bishop Remigius of Avignon in *Louis III*, p. 93, no. 50 (908): "absque cujuslibet subtraccionis dumtaxat injuria seu qualibet injuste repeticionis calumnia. Hoc autem nostre immunitatis preceptum ut inviolabilem obtinead firmitatem." In 927, King Raoul granted a privilege to Déols, "ob immunitatis gratiam, ne quispiam ibi praeter abbatem ac monachos ejusdem coenobii unquam ab hac die deinceps aliquam de quacunque re haberet, vel in omnibus ejus possessionibus extendi potestatem"; see *Raoul*, pp. 54–55, no. 13. Both of these charters may have emanated from the Cluniac "circle": Louis of Provence's sister was Angilberga, who founded Cluny along with her husband, William of Aquitaine; Déols was one of the monasteries "bequeathed" to abbot Odo of Cluny in Berno's Testament.

33. See Giles Constable, *Monastic Tithes: From Their Origins to the Twelfth Century* (Cambridge, 1964).

clause—the one granting immunity—returns to property matters but explicitly justifies itself in terms of reverence for holy places. The clause that follows declares the pope's protection, but it is symbolized by a money payment.[34]

A similar "spiritualizing" of property was already apparent in Cluny's foundation charter. William gave the villa of Cluny and all its appurtenances to Saints Peter and Paul, transforming the property itself into a memorial to and reminder of the apostles. There, in this now implicitly sacred space, the monks were to carry out their life of prayer. To ensure the inviolability of their sanctuary, William turned to a temporal authority (the pope) for *defensio* even as he asked the apostles for *tuitio*. In the end he conflated their roles, calling upon Peter, Paul, and the pope together to be "protectors and defenders of said place, Cluny, and the servants of God living together there."

This emphasis on Cluny the place, based as it was on physical property belonging to Peter and Paul, was clear again in the way in which the foundation charter allowed for overlapping jurisdictions: Peter and Paul had *dominatio* over the property of Cluny; the abbot had *dominatio* over the same property and also of the monks there; the monks, meanwhile, were to possess, hold, have, and order (*possideant, teneant, habeant atque ordinent*) the very same property.

When other donors gave their own bits and pieces of property to Cluny, they added to the property of Peter and Paul; in effect, they sacralized the property that they gave away. And the charters quite matter-of-factly referred to Cluny's property as the "land of Saint Peter."[35]

Although the immunity clause of 931 was presumably meant to apply to Cluny's property in general (we know that, by the end of Berno's abbacy, Cluny had acquired property at more than thirty-five places), the papal text specifically mentioned only the following: (1) Romainmôtier and its villa; (2) lost tithes from unspecified chapels; (3) tithes from chapels given by Bishop Berno; (4) gifts from Letbaldus; (5) property at Aine; and (6) the chapel of Saint-Martin at *Maceio*. Why these properties and not others?[36] There are two answers. The first is that most of these

---

34. According to this immunity, the census paid by Cluny to the papacy signified the pope's *tuitio*. On the meaning of the census, which was sometimes independent of exemption, see Falkenstein, *La papauté*, chap. 1.

35. Barbara H. Rosenwein, *To Be the Neighbor of Saint Peter: The Social Meaning of Cluny's Property, 909–1049* (Ithaca, N.Y., 1989), pp. 75–77.

36. For the other places, see ibid., p. 215.

were places over which Cluny had been disputing or was still negotiating. "Our dear son Bishop Berno"(3 above) was Cluny's diocesan bishop. His predecessor, Gerard, had been involved in a dispute with Cluny over the proceeds from churches and chapels in the Mâconnais that had only recently (in 930) been given to Cluny by the couple Letbaldus and Doda (4 above).[37] That gift itself was the outcome of some overlapping claims: as the charter of donation notes, Letbaldus's chapels were handed over just as they had been "shared"between Abbot Berno and Letbaldus's father, Warulfus.[38] In 929, only two years before the 931 immunity, Bishop Berno awarded Cluny most of the dues and tithes from the churches, while he and his community were accorded exceptionally close *familiaritas*—privileged relations—with the monastery.[39] The villa of Aine (5 above) had been given to Cluny by Ava, the sister of Cluny's founder, Duke William; and subsequently William was instrumental in restoring this property to the monastery when it was claimed by one Anscherius.[40]

We have no early evidence about the chapel of Saint-Martin (6 above), but later, in 963, Ado, the newly appointed bishop of Mâcon, gave six chapels to Cluny, including that of Saint-Martin, assigning the monks the tithes as well.[41] At the end of the charter, the scribe wrote: "But if anyone asks why said bishop gave so many churches at the same time, let him know in truth that their properties [*beneficia*] [already] belonged to Saint Peter and the monks."[42] Very likely, then, the immunity of 931, "restor-

37. The dispute is discussed in a somewhat different context in Barbara H. Rosenwein, Thomas Head, and Sharon Farmer, "Monks and Their Enemies: A Comparative Approach," *Speculum* 66 (1991): 764–96, at pp. 774–75.

38. *Cluny* 1:368, no. 387 (930): "Has villas et ęcclesias, cum omnibus ad se pertinentibus servis et ancillis, terris cultis et incultis . . . sicut divisio facta fuit inter Bernonem, bonę memorię abbatem, et patrem meum Warulfum, ego et supranominata uxor mea tradimus monachis." In ibid., 1:278–79, no. 283 (927), the same properties and churches had been given to Cluny by Letbaldus and his wife, but this time they were given "sicut pater meus Vuarulfus cum Vuilelmo dividit, illam divisionem quę Vuilelmus accepit, hoc est duas partes," that is, as they were shared between Warulfus and Duke William.

39. *Cluny* 1:350–51, no. 373. Ulrich Winzer, "Cluny und Mâcon im 10. Jahrhundert," *Frühmittelalterliche Studien* 23 (1989): 154–202, at p. 158, has observed that this act either reveals or establishes "eine Gebetsverbrüderung zwischen dem Kloster und dem Domkapitel." The gift of the tithes of these same churches was made again by Bishop Maimbodus, Berno's successor, in 938, reiterating the terms of the 929 agreement; see *Cluny* 1:467–69, no. 484.

40. *Cluny* 1:179–80, no. 192, discussed in Rosenwein, *To Be the Neighbor*, p. 112.

41. For further discussion of Ado and this charter, see Winzer, "Cluny und Mâcon," pp. 175–76, 178–85, 198–200.

42. *Cluny* 2:230, no. 1139: "Quod si querit quis cur tot ecclesias simul dedit prelocutus pontifex, sciat veraciter quia beneficia earum proprii juris Petri et monacorum erant."

ing" Saint-Martin to Cluny, referred to property even then in dispute. It is just possible that its diplomatically vague reference to chapels taken away by "some bishop" (2 above) may have referred to the five other churches that Ado gave (or rather gave again) in 963: Saint-Julian, Saint-Germanus, Saint-Saturninus, another Saint-Martin, and Saint-Desiderius.[43] Pope John's immunity was part of ongoing property negotiations between Cluny and some of its most important donors and social contacts.

The monastery of Romainmôtier seems to have played no part in such negotiations and, after its donation to Cluny, pretty much slipped from the records until the mid-eleventh century. Rather, the mention of Romainmôtier in the papal immunity suggests a second answer to the question why certain properties were singled out in the immunity: many involved places of high spiritual worth. Romainmôtier itself had been founded as a miniature Cluny, while the chapels named in the immunity were properties of saints; that is why they were named after them.[44] The immunity of 931 was, among many other things, a public statement of Cluny's spiritual value as manifested through its property.

The papal privilege of 931 melded immunity with the sort of protection clause—prohibiting the usurpation of all earthly powers—used in Cluny's foundation charter and featured quite often in papal charters even before Cluny's day.[45] The charter of 931 grafted the term "immunity," now connected not to fiscal property but to sacred places, onto old prohibitions against disquieting the monks through misuse or abuse of their property. It was not only the monks of Cluny who were "chaste lambs" (*agni immaculati*), as they liked to call themselves; Cluny's property was "untouchable" as well.[46]

An Area of Peace

Toward the end of the tenth century these views about property and immunity dovetailed very well with a new policy, implemented by the ab-

43. The locations are discussed in Winzer, "Cluny und Mâcon," p. 200. Saint-Julian was given to Cluny (but perhaps not for the first time) in *Cluny* 1:673–74, no. 721 (c. 950); Ado himself sold half of Saint-Desiderius to Cluny in ibid., 1:708, no. 751 (949).

44. On Romainmôtier's imitation of Cluny, see *Cluny* 1:358–61, no. 379. The key passage is translated in Rosenwein, *Rhinoceros Bound*, p. 44.

45. Examples include Zimmerman 1:6, no. 2; ibid. 1:25, no. 13.

46. See Dominique Iogna-Prat, *"Agni immaculati." Recherches sur les sources hagiographiques relatives à Saint Maieul de Cluny (954–994)* (Paris, 1988).

bots of Cluny, to consolidate the monastery's lands and become a seigneurial lord.[47] That policy meshed in turn with a wider movement, just beginning at the end of the tenth century, called the Peace of God, in which
bishops and others met to declare an end to certain kinds of violence.[48] At
one of the earliest such councils, convened at Anse (near Lyon), the monks
of Cluny negotiated some astonishing privileges for their monastery. We
do not have the canons of the council (which apparently met twice, first
in 993, then again in 994), but we do have two documents that record its
proceedings, including one drawn up by the monastic scribes at Cluny
and copied into a cartulary (charter collection) in which they kept important privileges.[49]

The document begins by describing an assembly of bishops, before
whom came Odilo, abbot of Cluny 994–1049, along with a contingent of
monks.[50] The Cluniacs described how their monastery, that "most holy
place"(*sanctissimus*), was being oppressed by evil men. The fathers re-
sponded "out of reverence for Saint Peter . . . and most holy [*sanctissimus*
again] Abbot Majolus," conceding the monks a privilege "out of their inviolable episcopal authority." They granted protection to all the churches
and tithes pertaining to Cluny, its *burgus*—the settlement that had grown
up outside Cluny's walls—and its *potestas*, that is, Cluny's seigneury-in-
the-making: no booty was to be taken from these properties nor were any
of Cluny's churches, houses or cellars to be attacked. This privilege, the
document went on to say, applied especially to Lourdon, where Cluny
had a fortification (*castrum*), and to twenty-two additional places: the
council warned that no one should dare to violate (*infringere*) or plunder
(*depredare*) any of them.[51] Then (the account continued) the council ac-

47. Rosenwein, *To Be the Neighbor*, chap. 3; and see note 53 below.

48. See Thomas Head and Richard Landes, ed., *The Peace of God: Social Violence and Religious Response in France around the Year 1000* (Ithaca, N.Y., 1992).

49. For Cluny's document, see *Cluny* 3:384–88, no. 2255 = Cartulary C (Paris, BNF n.a.l.
2262), no. 135. For a recent discussion of this cartulary, see Rosenwein, "Cluny's Immunities."
The other account is printed in Paul-Émile Giraud, *Essai historique sur l'abbaye de S. Barnard
et sur la ville de Romans*, 2 vols. (Lyon, 1856–69), 1:28–31, no. 11. On the Council of Anse, considered as part of the "Vorgeschichte, nicht aber in die Geschichte des Gottesfriedens," see
Hartmut Hoffmann, *Gottesfriede und Treuga Dei*, Schriften der MGH 20 (Stuttgart, 1964),
p. 46. The problems involved in dating the council are clearly set forth in Dominique Iogna-
Prat, "Cluny à la mort de Maïeul (994–998)," *Bulletin de la société des fouilles archéologiques et
des monuments historiques de l'Yonne*, no. 12 (1995), pp. 13–23, at p. 14.

50. Including the bishop of Mâcon. But the account in Cartulary C appears to have substituted Bishop Letaldus (996–1018) for Bishop Milo (981–96); Iogna-Prat, "Cluny à la mort,"
p. 15, suggests that it did so because Milo was less favorable to the Cluniac cause.

51. For the list, see Rosenwein, *To Be the Neighbor*, Table 9.

corded Cluny a monopoly on regional defensive structures and (without using the term "immunity") proclaimed that no state agent, tax collector, count, or private army might dare to build a castle within or next to Cluny or on any of the properties of that "consecrated place,"nor might any magnate living near Cluny or near Charlieu (where Cluny had a monastery) plunder—here repeating the names of the key places—the *castrum* at Lourdon or the *burgus* of Cluny.

There then followed summaries of canons concerned with lay and ecclesiastical discipline, but the memorandum hurried through these matters to return to Cluny's property, ending with the council's final resolution that "violators be damned, anathema marantha, unless they repent and do penance and only after they have been absolved [*absoluti*] by the abbots and the brothers of that most holy place [*sanctissimus* again], namely Cluny."

This document has rightly been seen as an assertion and affirmation of Cluny's new seigneurial status.[52] There is no doubt that the timing of the council was perfectly coordinated with a major movement on the part of the Cluniacs—and, indeed, of many lay castellan families in the neighborhood—to consolidate their holdings and impose their ban, which was, in brief, the right to punish, collect taxes, and exercise jurisdiction.[53] But the council did more than ratify developments already under way. It emphasized inviolability, particularly for two places close to Cluny— Lourdon and the *burgus* just outside the monastery's walls.[54]

52. Iogna-Prat, "*Agni immaculati*," p. 347.

53. On castellan families, see Georges Duby, *La société aux XIe et XIIe siècles dans la région mâconnaise* (Paris, 1953; reprint, 1971), pp. 137–360; on Cluny's land consolidation, see Rosenwein, *To Be the Neighbor*, chap. 3. On the ban and current historiographical disputes about its meaning and significance, see Lester K. Little and Barbara H. Rosenwein, eds., *Debating the Middle Ages: Issues and Readings* (Oxford,1998), pt. 2.

54. It is, however, impossible to know how this *burgus* was conceived at the end of the tenth century. Did it coincide with the traceable bourg of the fourteenth century, largely built up to the south of Cluny? For the outlines of that later bourg, see most recently Didier Méhu, "La communauté d'habitants de Cluny et l'*ecclesia cluniacensis* (fin X^e–début XIIIe siècle)," in Constable, Melville, and Oberste, *Die Cluniazenser*, pp. 165–88. Émile Magnien, *Histoire de Mâcon et du Mâconnais* (Mâcon, 1971), p. 107, is brief but useful.

Or was the *burgus* imagined as a swath of territory encircling the monastery? Certainly one can trace a somewhat spotty tradition of monastic endowment in which a swath of land formed both the core of a temporal "living" and a barrier against the world. Already in 648 a charter of King Sigibert spoke of establishing circles of land (*dextros*) twelve miles in diameter around the monasteries of Stavelot and Malmédy: they were meant both to support the monks and to ensure their isolation ("ut absque inpressione populi vel tumultuatione seculari Deo soli vacarent"; see MGH Dip. Mer., p. 23, no. 22). I am extremely grateful to Theo Kölzer for sharing with me his views on this charter's (essential) authenticity along

The council claimed inviolability for Cluny's local properties because they belonged to a holy place. The words *sanctus locus* or *sanctissimus locus* were repeated no fewer than seven times à propos Cluny, and the same adjectives were reiterated to emphasize the sanctity and holiness of the council's own proceedings: the conclave consisted of "holy fathers" (*sancti patres*), all from "holy sees" (*sanctae sedes*). Saint Peter (*Sanctus Petrus*), the saint to whom Cluny was dedicated, was paired with "most holy Majolus" (*sanctissimus Maiolus*), the abbot of the monastery between 948 and 994.[55] The Council of Anse declared Cluny and some of its property to be as sacred, venerated, and inviolable as a relic. In the next century, the Cluniacs would "map"this property with precision.

Exemption and Liturgical Space

The provisions of the council of Anse were negotiated with bishops. But at just about the same time, Abbo, the abbot of Fleury, was discovering the advantages that came from negotiating exemptions with the pope. He apparently succeeded in getting Pope Gregory V to issue a privilege in 997 based on a charter that he had forged a few years earlier.[56] As we have seen, there had been a few seventh- and eighth-century papal ex-

---

with its problematic aspects. By the ninth century in Asturias and León, many rural churches were surrounded by a *dextros* of 72 or 84 paces in radius, within which was a cemetery of 12 paces, at the center of which was the church building. Conciliar texts prohibited the entry of those who would commit violence and rapine on the land; see Fernando López Alsina, "Millas *in giro ecclesie*: el ejemplo del monasterio de San Julián de Samos," *Estudos medievais* 10 (1993): 159–87; many examples quoted in Alfonso Garcia Gallo, "El concilio de Coyanza," *Anuario de historia del derecho español* 20 (1950): 439–44. Let me record my debt in this instance to James D'Emilio, who supplied me with plentiful bibliography and corrected my unfounded speculations.

55. This point about the extraordinary emphasis of the council and other Cluniac documents on the "sanctity" of place was made at about the same time by Rosenwein, "La question de l'immunité clunisienne," p. 6, and Iogna-Prat, "Cluny à la mort," pp. 15–16.

56. Zimmermann 2:656–57, no. 335, here counted as a forgery. But the latest scholarship vindicates this privilege as authentic, though based on Abbo's forged charter of Gregory IV. See Marco Mostert, "Die Urkundenfälschungen Abbos von Fleury," in *Fälschungen im Mittelalter. Internationaler Kongress der MGH, München, 16.–19. September 1986*, pt. 4, *Diplomatische Fälschungen*, pt. 2, MGH Schriften 33, iv (Hannover, 1988), pp. 287–318. This article also establishes the date of the papal diploma as 997 rather than (as Zimmermann has it) 996. See further Marco Mostert, *The Political Theology of Abbo of Fleury. A Study of the Ideas about Society and Law of the Tenth-Century Monastic Reform Movement* (Hilversum, 1987), pp. 58–59; Thomas Head, *Hagiography and the Cult of Saints: The Diocese of Orléans, 800–1200* (Cambridge, 1990), pp. 146–47.

emptions, but the general story line of exemptions bypasses the papacy until the tenth century. Indeed, even in the mid-tenth century, the pope was not thinking of exemptions. He wrote to his "fellow bishops" in Gaul, for example, to say that they were "the light of the world and the salt of the earth," asking them to be "protectors"of the monasteries committed to their rule. He even specifically begged Bishop Ado of Mâcon to be Cluny's particular protector, "as you are the faithful lover of Saint Peter."[57]

One could say that Abbo of Fleury simply revived and developed the idea of exemption.[58] But by the end of the tenth century, the role of bishops in blessings and consecrations had expanded and diversified; the "revival"of exemption in this environment and by the pope rather than bishops in fact introduced something radically new and defiantly anti-episcopal.[59] The new papal exemptions by-passed the diocesan bishop's increasingly important role without the bishop's consent.

Moreover, taken together, the privileges in the pope's charter for Fleury far surpassed any previous exemption. The pope gave Fleury's abbot the right to appeal to Rome (a right that, as we have seen, Fulrad had gained, quite exceptionally, in the eighth century); and he granted the abbot the right to "override" the local bishop's prerogative to bind and loose (the key power of a priest). The abbot himself was given the power to bind and loose the members of his order. Moreover, Fleury was exempted from any general interdiction: its monks could celebrate Mass even if the entire diocese was under anathema.[60] The Cluniac monks and the popes at Rome would soon discover useful variations on these themes.

Viewed in this light, the first papal exemption for Cluny, issued a year after the one for Fleury by Gregory V, was very conservative. It contained a list of properties, comprising both Cluny's fledgling seigneury and the churches and monasteries affiliated with the monastery (what modern

---

57. Zimmermann 1:372–73, no. 189 (968): "Quocirca Cluniensis monasterii semper esto protector, sicut beati Petri es fidelis amator."

58. Abbo gathered most of his "precedents" from the *Registrum* of Gregory the Great; other provisions, such as the guarantee of free abbatial election, came from royal diplomas. See Mostert, "Die Urkundenfälschungen," esp. pp. 301–4.

59. See, e.g., the discussion below at note 82, of the development of a new ritual for episcopal consecration of church cemeteries. The Romano-Germanic pontifical documents the extraordinary variety of blessings and consecrations that bishops were expected to carry out by the mid-tenth century; see *Le pontifical romano-germanique du dixième siècle*, ed. Cyrille Vogel and Reinhard Elze, 3 vols., Studi e Testi 226, 227, 269 (Vatican City, 1963–72). On such pontificals, see Éric Palazzo, *Histoire des livres liturgiques. Le Moyen Age, des origines au XIIIe siècle* (Paris, 1993), pp. 204–20 and, at p. 208 n. 2, bibliography on the growing liturgical duties of the bishop.

60. Zimmermann 2:656–57, no. 335.

historians call the *cluniacensis ecclesia*).[61] To this it added the most old-fashioned of exemption privileges: (1) that no bishop or priest might enter Cluny to ordain or consecrate its church, presbyters, or deacons or to celebrate Mass, unless invited by its abbot; and (2) that the abbots of Cluny could be consecrated by any bishop they chose.

It was only in 1024 that Cluny received a papal privilege that added the new and significant provision that none of its monks in any of its monasteries (*fratres ubicunque positi*) were subject to interdictions, excommunications, or anathemas declared by a local bishop.[62] If any grievances against Cluny arose, they would be determined by papal judgment. Though the text enumerated the virtues of Cluny as a *place* (*isdem locus*)—it was the "bosom of mercy," the "port of all piety and safety"—nothing in this privilege implied concern with the spatial dimensions of Cluny's property. The amalgamation of exemption with real—mappable and measurable—property came about only late in the century, with the privilege of Cardinal Peter of Albano (1080) and the sacred ban of Urban II (1095).

The circumstances under which Cardinal Peter accorded a special, protective privilege to Cluny are well known, and its main outlines were long ago made clear by Cowdrey.[63] The privilege was the outcome of a dispute among at least five parties: first were the canons of the cathedral of Mâcon; second, their bishop, Landricus; third, the archbishop of Lyon, Gebuinus; fourth, the monks of Cluny; fifth, Pope Gregory VII. In brief, in 1079 the canons at Mâcon, supported by Archbishop Gebuinus and represented by their bishop, Landricus, complained to the pope about Cluniac usurpations of their property. Finding the papal response temporizing, they upped the ante: Landricus excommunicated some of Cluny's chapels and chaplains, while Gebuinus excommunicated some of its churches and expelled Cluniac monks from their priory at Pouilly-lès-Feurs. Abbot Hugh of Cluny (1049–1109) sent his grand prior, Odo (he would later become

61. Ibid., pp. 682–86, no. 351 (998); the properties are tabulated and identified in Rosenwein, *To Be the Neighbor*, Table 9, pp. 163–68. On the *cluniacensis ecclesia*, see Dietrich W. Poeck, *Cluniacensis Ecclesia. Der cluniacensische Klosterverband (10.–12. Jahrhundert)*, Münstersche Mittelalter-Schriften 71 (Munich, 1998).

62. Zimmermann 2:1052–54, no. 558.

63. Copies of this privilege sometimes call it the *Carta Petri Albanensis Episcopi et Cardinalis Romani de immunitate cluniaci*, but the very earliest extant copy, that in Paris, B.N.F. n.a.l. 2262, does not have the title. The text of the privilege does not use the word "immunity." It is edited in H. E. J. Cowdrey, "Cardinal Peter of Albano's Legatine Journey to Cluny (1080)," *Journal of Theological Studies*, n.s., 24 (1973): 481–91. The outlines of the dispute that led to it are given there, and further discussion may be found in idem, *Cluniacs and the Gregorian Reform*, pp. 53–56.

Pope Urban II), to Rome to complain about these "attacks" (*infestationes*). Pope Gregory VII sent Peter of Albano to Cluny to resolve and settle the matter.

The ensuing meetings, both at Cluny and a few days later at Anse, have been well analyzed to show the community of interest that obtained toward the end of the eleventh century between Cluny and the reformed papacy.[64] What has not been much discussed is the relationship between the privilege accorded by Peter—a privilege delimiting a protected zone so precise that it may be mapped—and Cluny's liturgy.

Peter chose the charged moment of the Purification of the Virgin to arrive at Cluny.[65] This feast, characterized by processions with candles, had first been celebrated in the fourth century at Jerusalem. At that time, it was above all the celebration of the infant Christ's presentation in the temple after Mary's term of purgation had ended (Lk 2:22). But in the West, beginning already in the eighth century, the feast came to focus on Mary herself.[66] In the midst of its observance at Cluny in 1080, Peter declared a completely bounded circle around the monastery into which violators might enter only at peril of eternal damnation. Cluny's seigneury and the pure womb of the Virgin became thus allied.

Peter of Albano was not chosen for his job at Cluny by hazard.[67] A participant in the fight by the monks of Valombrosia against Pietro Mezzabarba, a Florentine bishop accused of simony, Peter had undergone a trial by fire (in 1068) to prove the truth of his accusations. It would be too much to say that the liturgy of this trial echoed the Feast of the Purification, but there were parallels. The four monks who lit the pyre carried the cross and twelve candles, and they directed their prayers to four people, including the Virgin Mary. Peter of Albano entered the flames and exited, spectacularly, without harm. Thereafter he was called Petrus

64. Cowdrey, *Cluniacs and the Gregorian Reform*, pp. 55–56.

65. At Cluny, even the deaths of abbots were "timed" to coincide with significant feast days; see Patrick Henriet, "Chronique de quelques morts annoncées. Les saints abbés clunisiens (X^e–XIIe siècles)," *Médiévales* 31 (1996): 93–108, at p. 102. Peace councils sometimes met on dates of particular significance; see, e.g., Hoffmann, *Gottesfriede*, pp. 34–35 (18 November at Limoges); and declarations of the Truce of God banned fighting at intervals defined by the liturgical calendar; see ibid., p. 95.

66. Eric Palazzo and Ann-Katrin Johansson, "Jalons liturgiques pour une histoire du culte de la Vierge dans l'Occident latin (V^e–XIe siècles)," in Dominique Iogna-Prat, Eric Palazzo, and Daniel Russo, eds., *Marie. Le culte de la vierge dans la société médiévale* (Paris, 1996), pp. 15–43, at pp. 23–32.

67. For the information below, see the account and source materials in Giovanni Miccoli, *Pietro Igneo. Studi sull'Età Gregoriana*, Istituto Storico Italiano per il Medio Evo, Studi Storici 40–41 (Rome, 1960). I thank Giancarlo Andenna for calling my attention to this study.

Igneus, "Fiery Pete," and must have gained a reputation for ousting bishops, for Pietro Mezzabarba thereafter fled Florence.

Our source for Peter's arrival at Cluny on February 2, "the day celebrating the Purification of the Virgin," and his subsequent acts is his own report. In it, he describes carrying out a series of major actions " both in the chapel of that same glorious Virgin and in the monastery." That the Virgin is the context of these acts invites our attention.[68] Mary was particularly important at Cluny; and the liturgy of the Purification was particularly elaborate there. Let us take up these points in turn.

Mary was a model of two virtues that, at Cluny, were closely linked: chastity and imperial rule. In Odilo's sermon on the Holy Cross, written at some point during his abbacy (994–1049), Mary was part of a holy triplet: she was the *genitrix* (mother), Mary Magdalene was the *peccatrix* (sinner), and Helena, mother of Emperor Constantine, was the *imperatrix* (empress). Helena, said Odilo, was the inspiration for the donation of Constantine, source of the "liberty" (*libertas*) and "privilege" (*privilegium*) of Rome: "Constantine, first among secular princes, with the advice and at the behest of . . . Helena, conceded the liberty and privilege of the Roman church."[69] This act made Helena the mother of Cluny's own liberty and privilege.

At the time that Cluny was founded there had already been a church on the property dedicated to Mary; a new church was dedicated to her ca. 1032; finally another was constructed 1083–85, just after Peter of Albano's visit.[70] The abbots were devoted to her: Odo was reported to have called her "mother of mercy," the epithet evoked in the widely used prayer "O domina et mater misericordiae."[71] Odilo claimed to be her servant; and certainly during his abbacy important writings about her were

---

68. The following is indebted to, and builds upon the argument in, Dominique Iogna-Prat, "Politische Aspeckte der Marienverehrung in Cluny um das Jahr 1000," in Claudia Opitz et al., eds., *Maria in der Welt. Marienverehrung im Kontext der Sozialgeschichte 10.–18. Jahrhundert* (Zurich, 1993), pp. 243–51, and in D. Iogna-Prat, "La croix, le moine et l'empereur. Dévotion à la croix et théologie politique à Cluny autour de l'an mil," in Michel Sot, ed., *Haut moyen-âge. Culture, éducation et société. Études offertes à Pierre Riché* (La Garenne-Colombes, 1990).

69. Odilo, *Sermo* 15, PL 142, col. 1032: "Constantinum, qui primus inter saeculi principes cum consilio et studio matris supradictae et saepedicendae Helenae libertatem et privilegium Romanae concessit Ecclesiae."

70. For the chapel of 1032, see Kenneth John Conant, *Cluny. Les églises et la maison du chef d'ordre* (Mâcon, 1968), p. 65 and plates XIV and XV; for references to the Mary church of the 1080s, see *Consuetudines cluniacensium antiquiores cum redactionibus derivatis*, ed. Kassius Hallinger, *CCM*, vol. 7, pt. 2, p. 171 n. 39, ll. 18a–20a.

71. H. Barré, *Prières anciennes à la mère du Sauveur* (Paris, 1963), p. 91.

copied by scribes in Cluny's scriptorium.[72] Abbot Hugh called her *apostola apostolorum*.[73]

The four Marian feasts—Nativity, Purification (or Hypapanti), Annunciation, and Assumption—were celebrated at Cluny with elaborate ceremonies and lessons.[74] Abbot Odilo wrote sermons for three of these feasts, including that of the Purification.[75] He emphasized two Marian virtues: her purity and her paradoxically wealthy poverty. The mother of God, Odilo said, was chosen from the lineage of the richest, wisest, and most powerful kings, David and Solomon, into whose temple she offered her son. "She was brought forth by a line of kings, yet was poor in temporal wherewithal."[76] But what happy poverty it was, since it enriched the world! In short Odilo's Mary projected an image of chaste and generous sovereignty; we shall see that it fit quite well with the image that the Cluniac monks had of themselves.

The liturgy of the Feast of the Purification at Cluny was described in detail in the *Liber Tramitis*, a customary written before 1040.[77] The entire oratory of Mary was adorned, and most of the offices of the feast were chanted there. It was brightly lit with candles, some of which were brought during a procession that began at the cloister. The congregation walked in carefully ordered ranks to the oratory "of the holy glorious Virgin" (the *Liber Tramitis* and Peter agreed on the same epithet). After various prayers, the priest blessed the candles and sprinkled holy water over them. Then they were lit in relay. The cantor began the antiphon, *Lumen ad revelationem*, echoing the words of Simeon upon seeing the infant

72. For writings about Mary, see Monique-Cécile Garand, "Une collection personnelle de saint Odilon de Cluny et ses compléments," *Scriptorium* 33 (1979): 163–80, esp. pp. 168–69. For Odilo's claim to be Mary's servant, see Jotsaldus, *De vita et virtutibus sancti Odilonis abbatis* 2.1, PL 142, col. 916: "ab hodierna die et deinceps me in tuo servitio habeto, atque in omnibus meis causis, misericordissima advocatrix, mihi semper adesto."

73. Quoted in Armin Kohnle, *Abt Hugo von Cluny (1049–1109)* (Sigmaringen, 1993), p. 45, with further evidence of Hugh's particularly marked veneration of the Virgin.

74. For the Nativity, see *Liber Tramitis aevi odilonis abbatis*, ed. Petrus Dinter, CCM 10:162–64, 198; for the Purification, pp. 40–43; the Annunciation, pp. 64–65; and the Assumption, pp. 148–55 and passim.

75. Odilo, *Sermones* 3, PL 142, cols. 999–1001. For the full set of sermons, see Jacques Hourlier, *Saint Odilon abbé de Cluny* (Louvain, 1964), pp. 108–9, no. 3 (on the Purification), no. 12 (on the Assumption), no. 12*bis* (on the Assumption), no. 13 (on the Nativity), and no. 14 (on the Nativity).

76. PL 142, col. 1000: "Erat progenita stemmate regali, sed pauper adeo stipendio temporali."

77. *Liber Tramitis*, pp. 40–43. The one change to this liturgy made later by Abbot Hugh was to have the monks not wear the *cappa* lest candle wax fall on it; see Kohnle, *Abt Hugo*, p. 44.

Christ. Carrying a picture of Christ and his mother, the monks returned to the cloister holding symbolic objects in an order most carefully described by the *Liber Tramitis*. Three are worth noting here: two crosses, symbols of Christ's imperial power (*imperium*); the imperial orb, given to Cluny by Emperor Henry II (1002–24) and a symbol of the royalty of Christ and the Virgin; and four candelabra, symbols of the Feast of Purification itself.[78] Mary's identification with light dated back to Isidore, in whose etymologies she became the *maris stella*, star of the sea.[79] But lighted candles had long been associated with the granting of immunities, as Paul Fouracre first noted, and the connection should be recalled here, given the nature of the declaration Peter of Albano was about to make.

At some point during this service, Peter of Albano began a ceremony of his own.[80] First, he displayed Cluny's papal privileges publicly; second, he lifted the excommunications that had been declared by Landricus; third, he admonished the bishop not to declare such excommunications ever again; fourth, he determined inviolable boundaries around Cluny, within which "no one of whatever dignity or power may rob, take booty, or make any attacks against the place, its inhabitants, or those fleeing into it."[81] Peter then described a bounded geographical entity: a circle of three or so kilometers in diameter around the monastery (see Map 5).[82] He threatened anathema against anyone who might violate these borders, and this became a sort of refrain in his report: those who infringed Cluny's sacred space would be prohibited from entering that other sacred space—the church—where the body and blood of the Lord was celebrated. In particular, laymen on horseback (*milites*; knights), above all those living at the *villa* of Cluny itself, were singled out and warned.

78. For the symbolism of the orb, see Iogna-Prat, "La croix, le moine" pp. 466–67.

79. See Jaroslav Pelikan, *The Growth of Medieval Theology (600–1300)*, vol. 3 of *The Christian Tradition: A History of the Development of Doctrine* (Chicago, 1978), p. 162.

80. He wrote in his report (Cowdrey, "Cardinal Peter," p. 488): "sermone perorato, auctoritate pontificum Romanorum per priuilegia huic loco attributa publice corroborans manifestaui," which suggests that a sermon had just ended when he began. *Liber Tramitis*, p. 40, speaks of "lectiones de sermonibus patrum" at the Night Hour; perhaps Peter began at this point.

81. Cowdrey, "Cardinal Peter," p. 488: "ut nulla persona cuiusque dignitatis uel potestatis rapinas, predas, siue aliquas infestationes loco isti, habitatoribus, atque confugientibus infra terminos subnotatas inferre presumat."

82. In Rosenwein, "Cluny's Immunities," Image 2, I depicted the boundaries of Peter's privilege as an irregular square. But the recent study of Didier Méhu, "La communauté d'habitants de Cluny au Moyen Age (X^e–XVe siècles)," (Ph.D. diss. Université de Lyon II, 1998) makes a convincing case for a circle. I owe most of the identifications of places and above all their map locations on Map 5 to Didier Méhu, whom I want to thank for sharing his work with me before its publication.

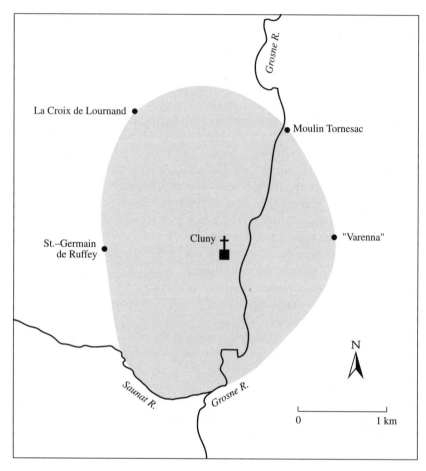

MAP 5. Cardinal Peter's Protected Zone for Cluny, 1080

In the hands of Peter of Albano, then, exemptions, protection, asylum, the Peace of God, and the liturgy of virginity came together in a declaration of confines. It was not much of a step from Peter's immunity to the sacred ban. But in the latter case, another liturgical rite, the new ritual for consecrating cemeteries, came into play,

The "hallowing"of burial ground had begun in the Carolingian period.[83] Indeed, the earliest evidence of a rite for the consecration of a

---

83. See Cécile Treffort, *L'église carolingienne et la mort. Christianisme, rites funéraires et pratiques commémoratives*, Collection d'histoire et d'archéologie médiévales 3 (Lyon, 1996), pp. 141–43. I am very grateful to Dr. Treffort for sending me a copy of her book and her dissertation, as well as supplying me with pertinent information over many years.

cemetery, or atrium, comes from the end of the ninth century. In the influential Romano-Germanic Pontifical of the tenth century, the bishop led liturgy that included singing the seven penitential psalms; marking the circuit of the cemetery by four lighted candles; sprinkling the ground with holy water; and chanting three prayers.[84]

By the eleventh century in Catalonia, for example, bishops demarcated *sagrera*, "cemeteries," when they consecrated their parish churches.[85] These were typically thirty paces in diameter. Originally designated for the dead, the *sagrera* came to function as a kind of attack-free population zone and were soon (if not from the start) linked to the Peace of God movement. Certainly after about 1030, whoever might try to assault or rob another within the hallowed and inviolable space of the cemetery was subject to excommunication and money compensation ten times the normal fine.[86] Such protected places could became densely populated with residences, farm animals, granaries, and tool sheds. Indeed, the *sagrera* became the nuclei of new villages, displacing and disrupting old settlement patterns.

Something similar to the *sagrera* may have existed in parts of southern France. In the Aude, for example, archaeologists have found churches girdled by inhabited ribbons of land fifty or sixty meters wide.[87] However, nothing comparable has yet been discovered in lower Languedoc.[88]

In 1095, then, when Urban II traveled to Cluny, consecrated cemeteries

84. *Pontifical romano-germanique* 1:192–93. For variants on this rite, see Treffort, *L'église carolingienne*, pp. 142–43 . On the use of this pontifical at Cluny, see Iogna-Prat, "La croix, le moine," pp. 467, 469.

85. See Karen Kennelly, "Sobre la paz de Dios y la sagrera en el condado de Barcelona (1030–1130)," *Anuario de estudios medievales* 5 (1968): 107–36; Pierre Bonnassie, *La catalogne du milieu du Xe à la fin du XIe siècle. Croissance et mutations d'une société*, 2 vols. (Toulouse, [1975–76]), 2:653–56; and Michel Fixot and Élisabeth Zadora-Rio, eds., *L'environnement des églises et la topographie religieuse des campagnes médiévales. Actes du IIIe congrès international d'archéologie médiévale, Aix-en-Provence, 28–30 septembre 1989*, Documents d'archéologie française 46 (Paris, 1994).

86. For excommunication, see Manuel Riu and Pilar Valdepeñas, "El espacio eclesiastico y la formación de las parroquias en la Cataluña de los siglos IX al XII," in Fixot and Zadora-Rio, *L'environnement des églises*, pp. 57–67, at p. 64. For the money compensation, Pierre Bonnassie, "Les *sagreres* catalanes. La concentration de l'habitat dans le 'cercle de paix' des églises (XIe s.)," in ibid., pp. 68–79, at p. 71.

87. Dominique Baudreu and Jean-Paul Cazes, "Les villages ecclésiaux dans le bassin de l'Aude," in Fixot and Zadora-Rio, *L'environnement des églises*, pp. 80–97, at p. 87.

88. Monique Bourin and Aline Durand, "Église paroissiale, cimetière et *castrum* en bas Languedoc (X^e–XIIe s)," in Fixot and Zadora-Rio, *L'environnement des églises*, pp. 98–106. Comparable developments seem to have taken place in Celtic cultures around this time; see Davies, "Protected Space"; eadem, "Adding Insult to Injury: Power, Property and Immunities in Early Medieval Wales," in Davies and Fouracre, *Property and Power*, pp. 137–64.

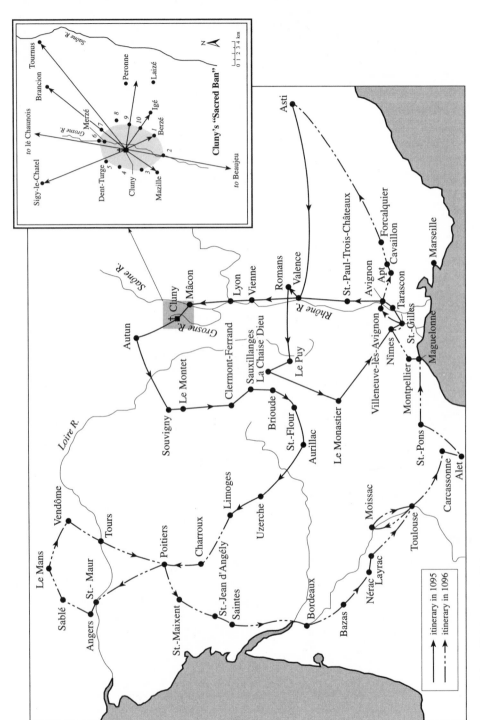

MAP 6. Urban II's Itinerary in France

may not have been very widespread. One purpose of Urban's trip seems to have been to popularize the ritual—and to associate it with the papacy.[89] When he came to Cluny, he did so as part of a year-long tour of France (see Map 6). Certainly, he was on his way to preach the First Crusade at Clermont. But before he got there, and then afterward as well, he spent his time following a well-chosen itinerary that allowed him to dedicate numerous cathedrals and monasteries, consecrate many altars, and bless many cemeteries. At Tarascon, for example, on his way to Cluny, the pope "blessed with his own hands" the place where a church was to be built—in the middle of a field already serving as a cemetery for poor pilgrims. The pope solemnly sprinkled consecrated water and made the sign of the cross over the field, whose boundaries were made clear by the author of the account. At the same place, Urban made a speech "to the people" (as he would later, at Clermont, when he preached the Crusade), promising God's indulgence for the sins of all who would keep the cemetery free and inviolate.[90] At Marmoutier, which he visited three months after Clermont, Urban confirmed the exemptions and immunities that he had previously given to the monastery; and there too he addressed "the people," this time from a podium constructed on the banks of the Loire. He excoriated the monastery's enemies and extolled the virtues of the monks.[91] Then he dedicated the monastery's new church, presided over a translation of its relics, and had his fellow bishops consecrate (*sacravit*) the altar. During the same visit, cemeteries—their bounds clearly noted—were consecrated by the pope and other bishops at his bidding.[92]

89. Élisabeth Zadora-Rio, "Lieux d'inhumation et espaces consacrés. À propos du voyage du pape Urbain II en France (août 1095–août 1096)," in André Vauchez, ed., *Lieux sacrés, lieux de culte, sanctuaires. Approaches terminologiques, méthodologiques, historiques et monographiques*, Actes de la Table-Ronde de l'École Française de Rome (2–3 juin 1997) (Rome, in press).

90. *Cartulaire de l'abbaye de Saint-Victor de Marseille*, ed. B. Guérard, Collection des cartulaires de France 8–9, 2 vols. (Paris, 1857), 1:243, no. 220. See the discussion in Zadora-Rio, "Lieux d'inhumation."

91. For the earlier exemptions and privileges, see *Papsturkunden in Frankreich*, n.s., vol. 5: *Touraine, Anjou, Maine und Bretagne*, ed. Johannes Ramackers, Abhandlungen der Akademie der Wissenschaften in Göttingen, 3d ser., no. 35 (Göttingen, 1956), pp. 83–84, no. 21 (1089).

92. The text in which all this appears, *Textus de dedicatione ecclesiae majoris monasterii*, in *Recueil de chroniques de Touraine*, ed. André Salmon, Collection de documents sur l'histoire de Touraine 1 (Tours, 1854), pp. 338–42, seems to have been written fairly close to the time of the events; the author bothers to include Urban's diatribe against the canons of the cathedral of Tours, with whom the monks of Marmoutier had contended over the issue of exemption during the late eleventh century. See Sharon Farmer, *Communities of Saint Martin: Legend and Ritual in Medieval Tours* (Ithaca, N.Y., 1991), pp. 46–49. However, Salmon could not find a manuscript of the *Textus de dedicatione*; rather (see *Recueil de chroniques*, p. cxx), he reproduced it as it had been printed in a seventeenth-century publication by Laurent Bochel,

There could be no more graphic way to demonstrate the meaning of "papal" exemption. Bypassing the local diocesan bishop, the pope was arriving at monasteries and churches to do blessings and consecrations himself. At Cluny Urban pointedly consecrated the altars of the new church and followed this exercise of episcopal *pontificium* by other consecrations, done at his order, by various archbishops and bishops from outside Cluny's diocese.[93] Then, in the midst of Masses and exhortations, he gave a sermon "to the people"in which he outlined the special status of Cluny: how it had been founded by William "the Pious" (this was the first time this epithet had been used for Cluny's founder) to be loved and cared for by the popes. He, Urban, who had been a monk and prior under Abbot Hugh, sought to aid and be useful to the monastery. That is why he consecrated the altars; and now he was pleased, and hoped his audience would be pleased as well, "to assign certain clear limits of immunity and security all around."[94] Within the boundaries that he described, "no man of whatever condition or power might dare to make an attack, whether big or small, or commit arson or pillage or robbery or rape or strike in anger or, which is much worse, commit homicide or cut off human limbs."[95] Violators would suffer excommunication.

Urban's sacred ban was circular and large—a *sagrera*, as it were, of eight kilometers or so rather than thirty paces in diameter—and it was described in such a way as to project outward, *toward* Brancion, *toward* Berzé, *toward* Beaujeu (see Map 6 inset). In this way it was always pushing beyond its limits. Unlike Peter's circle, which was truly bounded, the sacred ban thrust against its confines.

The term "ban" had a precise meaning in the eleventh century: the people living within a ban were under their lord's jurisdiction and subject to his penalties. But Cluny's ban was not ordinary. It was both sacred

Gregorii Turonensis, Historiae Francorum (Paris, 1610), pt. 2, pp. 125–29. Élisabeth Zadora-Rio informs me that this remains the earliest extant source.

93. Text in *Bullarium sacri ordinis Cluniacensis*, p. 25. For a discussion of its manuscript context, Cartulary C, see Rosenwein, "Cluny's Immunities."

94. *Bullarium sacri ordinis Cluniacensis*, p. 25: "quosdam certos limites immunitatis ac securitatis circum circa undique assignare." Didier Méhu, "*Burgus, immunitas, pax*. Les rouages de la seigneurie clunisienne du onzième au treizième siècle," International Medieval Congress, Leeds, 13–16 July 1998 further explores the implications of Urban's consecrations at Cluny.

95. *Bullarium sacri ordinis Cluniacensis*, p. 25: "nullus homo, cujuscumque conditionis ac potestatis unquam invasionem aliquam grandem vel parvam, aut incendium, aut praedam, aut rapinam facere, aut hominem rapere, vel per iram ferire, aut, quod multò gravius est, homicidium perpetrare, vel truncationem membrorum hominis."

(*sacer*) and consecrated (*sacratus*). The meanings that had come to inhere in immunities and exemptions were fully utilized in this declaration of sacred space so potent, dynamic, and inviolable.

⁂

The other side of this inviolablity was the monks' power to welcome in. We began the history of Merovingian immunities with a tale from Jonas's *Vita Columbani*: King Theuderic tried and failed to compel Columbanus to open the doors of his monastery to the surrounding populace. Not even the king could enter. But in the eleventh century, when monasteries had become enormously powerful institutions in their own right, they could not only shut their doors but also graciously open them when they wanted to.

The eleventh-century *Adventus* ceremony, by which monks carefully orchestrated and controlled the arrival of a king into a monastery, marked a triumphant obverse to Jonas's story. Cluny's *Liber Tramitis* is the earliest source we have for the *Adventus* ceremony.[96] It has elements in common with the liturgy for the feast of Mary's Purification.[97] Both include processions dominated by candelabra and both use the antiphon *Ecce mitto angelum meum*, the text that was chanted when bishops brought new kings to church to give them their blessing.[98] These rites expressed the sovereignty of the monks, who, chaste and paradoxically rich-poor, like Mary, went out from their church to "lead in" the king. In the eleventh century, Cluny considered itself so inviolable that it could welcome a king on its own terms.

96. *Liber Tramitis*, pp. 242–43. It is called the "premier *ordo* médiéval connu de l'accueil d'un souverain dans un monastère" in Iogna-Prat, "La croix, le moine," p. 468.

97. *Liber Tramitis*, pp. 40–43.

98. *Pontifical romano-germanique* 1:247.

9

"A Man's House Is His Castle":
Anglo-American Echoes

A FRENCH king is "permitted" to enter within the walls of a monastery; an Italian king assures men living within a castle that they are beyond the reach of public agents. When Americans read about such things, they think of the common-law adage implicitly embodied in the Fourth Amendment of the U.S. Constitution: "Every man's house is his castle; even though the winds of heaven may blow through it, the King of England cannot enter it."[1]

1. Labeled as a "common law maxim" in *Blackstone's Commentaries on the Laws of England* (1773), ed. Bernard C. Gavit, (Washington, D.C., 1941), p. 952. The source of the maxim in this form is likely William Pitt, Earl of Chatham (1708–1778), in his speech before Parliament of March 7, 1766 on behalf of repealing the excise tax on cider. According to the notes of James Harris, member of the House of Commons 1761–80, Pitt's speech invoked "the cause of liberty — that mens houses should not be violated . . . revenue matters not his province or passion . . . the loss might be 20,000 pounds a year—what that to a blemish upon liberty— every man's house his castle . . . the poor man's walls of mud and covering of thatch were his castle, where though the rains might enter, the king could not." Quoted in Jeremy Black, *Pitt the Elder* (Cambridge, 1992), p. 257. It took more elaborate form in Thomas M. Cooley, *A Treatise on the Constitutional Limitations*, 3d ed. (Boston, 1874), pp. 299–300 n. 4: "The poorest man may, in his cottage, bid defiance to all the forces of the Crown. It may be frail; its roof may shake, the wind may blow through it; the storm may enter; the rain may enter, but the King of England may not enter; all his force dares not cross the threshold of the ruined tenement." It is in this form that it is cited by the U.S. Supreme Court, as for example in *Miller v United States*, 357 US 301, 307 (1958) (Brennan, J.).

Did this adage arise from medieval immunities? Not exactly; not in any strict evolutionary sense. Yet when—in England, around 1500—the likening of house to castle was first expressed, it was understood in the context of English immunities and the institutions that had grown up around them. We shall see, in effect, that "house as castle" was only one part of a set of equations that, taken together, *never* entirely barred the "king" from entry.

The focus of this chapter necessitates a change in approach. Hitherto, I have explored a relatively short period of time in a fairly leisurely way; here I shall cover more than a thousand years of history in quick dispatch. Before, I was preoccupied with the contexts and negotiations surrounding the issuing of immunities; here such an inquiry is no longer germane. I have no doubt that immunities were negotiated in England, as they were on the Continent. But my primary purpose in this chapter is to discern how the English versions of immunities were embedded in that body politic and to comprehend what role they played in the notion of "house as castle." What the nature of English immunities had been, what happened to them in the early modern period, and what this led to in both England and the United States—these are the topics of this chapter.

Two points remain to be noted. First, in England, immunities were not called immunities very often; rather, they were called "franchises" and "liberties." This latter term may seem odd, since on the Continent (as we have seen) "liberties" referred most often to exemptions. To avoid confusion, I shall try to use the term "franchises" as often as possible to refer to English immunities; but "liberty" was the preferred term in the sources and must often appear when I quote them directly. Second, in England, many monasteries were attached to episcopal churches, so that franchises granted to bishops were meant to embrace monks as well.

The House in Western Tradition

It should be made clear at the outset that there was no long Western tradition of the house's inviolability against state incursions.[2] It is true that Cicero asked, "What is more sacred, what more hedged about by every

2. William Blackstone, *Commentaries on the Laws of England* 4.16, 5th ed. (Oxford, 1773), p. 223: "And the law of England has so particular and tender a regard to the immunity of a man's house, that it styles it his castle, and will never suffer it to be violated with impunity: agreeing herein with the sentiments of ancient Rome as expressed in the words of Tully [Cicero]: 'Quid enim sanctius . . . [etc]'" (see below, note 3, for the text).

restraint, than the house of each citizen?"[3] But Cicero was not referring to curbs on public authorities: his house had been razed by his political opponent, Clodius, acting under the sanction of a tribunican statute. In Cicero's day, unwanted access to a man's house was easy. Under the self-help rules of the early Roman Republic, a man who desired to search another's house for stolen goods, "should do so naked, girt with a 'licium' and holding a dish."[4] Writing in the second century A.D., well after these customs had fallen out of use, Gaius, our source for the practice, found the whole procedure absurd; but that was because by his time search and seizure needed no special accoutrements, not because homes were hedged about by prohibitions.[5]

Nevertheless, in Gaius's lost book on the Twelve Tables, he explained that "most thought that no one can be summoned [to court for litigation] from his house because the house is for each person the safest refuge and shelter [*quia domus tutissimum cuique refugium atque receptaculum sit*] and one who summons him from there is held to exercise force." The passage, extant today only in Justinian's *Digest* (published in 533), was followed there by another excerpt from Gaius and then one from the jurist Paulus:

Gaius, *XII Tables*, book 1: But also no one doubts that it is lawful to summon a person from the door of his house, the baths, and the theater.

Paulus, *Edict*, book 1: But although one who is at home can at times be summoned, yet no one ought to be dragged [*extrahi*] from his house.[6]

Taken together these comments suggest that the jurists of Justinian's day thought that the homes of ancient Romans had been shelters from public hurly-burly. But, once again, the context is important: a person who sum-

---

3. Cicero, *De domo sua ad pontifices oratio* 41.109, ed. Robert G. Nisbet (Oxford, 1939; reprint, 1979), n.p.: "Quid est sanctius, quid omni religione munitius quam domus unius cuisque civium?"

4. Gaius, *Institutionum iuris civilis commentarii quattuor* 3.192, in *The Institutes of Gaius*, trans. W. M. Gorden and O. F. Robinson (London, 1988), 377. I thank James Keenan for the reference.

5. The change is explained in J. A. C. Thomas, *Textbook of Roman Law* (Amsterdam, 1976), p. 358. The practice went out of use when the praetors established penalties "against an occupant who refused to allow his premises to be searched."

6. *Corpus iuris civilis*, vol. 1, *Digesta* 2, 4, 18–20, ed. Theodor Mommsen and Paul Krueger, 16th ed. (Berlin, 1954), p. 49; English translation in *The Digest of Justinian*, trans. Alan Watson, 4 vols. (Philadelphia, 1985), 1:46 (somewhat modified here).

moned another to court was not a government official but rather another private person. Paulus's prohibition against "dragging" a person out of his house to go to court was a restraint on that person's neighbors.

Continental Germanic law codes had provisions against housebreakers, burglars, thieves, and unwanted neighbors. The fact that penalties were stiffer when hedges, portals, and gates were violated than when thefts occurred in the open indicates a certain conception of close-peace.[7] But these laws had nothing to do with the entry of the king or his agents; their purpose, as with the Roman laws we have just discussed, was to regulate relations between neighbors.

When the king or public authorities—counts, for the most part—were invoked in these Germanic laws, it was not to respect the portals of a man's house. Entry seems to have been least likely in cases of debt: when all other remedies had failed him, the creditor was to call upon the count, who was obliged to go to the debtor's house with assessors (*rachimburgi*), request payment one final time, and then "take [the amount] from the debtor's property." There is no suggestion in this law code that the count *entered* the house (though, admittedly, there was also no prohibition against it).[8]

In other cases, however, entry was explicitly mandated. The Merovingian king Childebert II (596), for example, decreed "that every public agent who hears of a criminal brigand should go to his house and tie him up."[9] Under Ripuarian Frankish law, the royal agent was directed to go to the house of anyone who refused repeated summons to court, and "take from there the stolen property and give it to the complainant."[10]

---

7. The examples that follow are from *Pactus Legis Salicae*, ed. and trans. Karl August Eckhardt, vol. 2, pt. 1, 65 *Titel-Text* (Göttingen, 1955), cited here by title, section, and page numbers. For the theft of a boat the fine was 600 *denarii* (21 §2, 184); for the theft of a boat under lock and key, the fine was 1400 d. (21 §3, 184); the fine for a theft of something worth 2 d. outside a house was set at 600 d. (11 §1, 152); if the theft involved breaking and entering, the fine was 1200 (11 §3, 152); theft from an unlocked workroom was 600 d. (27 §29, 208), from a locked workroom, 1800 d. (27 §30, 208).

8. Ibid., 50 §3, 306. See also ibid., 56 §6a, 328: "ad casam suam ei nunciare debet precium aut debitum." Possibly the whole procedure was inspired by a passage in Deuteronomy 24:10–11. For the biblical education of Merovingian kings and their administrators, see Wood, *Merovingian Kingdoms*, pp. 235–54, with further bibliography. For Thomas Aquinas's use of the passage in Deuteronomy, see below, note 79.

9. *Childeberti Secundi Decretio* (596), c. 8, MGH Cap. reg. Fr. 1:17, no. 7.

10. *Lex Ribuaria* 32, §3, ed. Rudolf Sohm, MGH Fontes 6:62: "et sic iudex fiscalis ad domum illius accedere debet, et legitima strude exinde auferre et ei tribuere, qui eum interpellavit."

Destroying the houses of malefactors seems to have been fairly routine throughout the Middle Ages.[11] At Freiburg im Breisgau in 1120, "if [anyone] kills [another in the city], he will be decapitated. But if he escapes capture, his house will be razed."[12] In France, around 1183, Philip Augustus's privilege to the burgers of Roye declared that "if someone should kill another within the city, let the malefactor receive punishment wherever he is found and, if he has a house, let it be demolished."[13] Nor were the cities the only places in which this practice could be found. The *Österreichisches Landrecht* (territorial law) of 1237 had the regional law enforcement official (*Landrichter*) destroy houses that were centers of criminal enterprises.[14] The *Établissements de Saint Louis*, drawn up in France in 1273, said that lords may strip the vines and tear down the houses of murderers and other criminals under their jurisdiction.[15]

Some historians, however, insist that there was a sacrosanct housepeace, firm against even the incursions of state agents. These enclaves needed no legislation because they were based on custom dating back "time out of mind":

11. On this issue, see Alexander Coulin, "Die Wüstung. Ein Beitrag zur Geschichte des Strafrechts," *Zeitschrift für vergleichende Rechtswissenschaft, einschließlich ethnologischen Rechtsforschung* 32 (1914–15): 326–501.

12. Conrad von Zäringen's charter for Freiburg im Breisgau (1120), in *Deutsche Stadtrechte des Mittelalters*, ed. Ernst Theodor Gaupp (Breslau, 1851; reprint, 1966), p. 20, no. 10: "Si quis infra urbem pacem urbis infregerit . . . Si vero occiderit decollabitur. Si vero evaserit et non captus fuerit delebitur domus ejus."

13. *Ordonnances des rois de France*, ed. E. de Laurière et al., 21 vols. (Paris 1723–1849), 11:229, no. 10 (c. 1183): "Si quis alium intra villam interfecerit, ubicumque malefactor inventus fuerit, de ipso vindicta accipiatur, et si domum habuerit diruatur." In ibid., 3:294 (1358), the lord of Mautort (near Abbeville) was granted the right to remove the doors and windows of the houses of peasants who did not render him cens and corvées.

14. Ernst Schwind and Alfons Dopsch, eds., *Ausgewählte Urkunden zur Verfassungsgeschichte der deutsch-österreichischen Erblande im Mittelalter* (Innsbruck, 1895; reprint, 1968), p. 72, no. 34.

15. *Les Établissements de Saint Louis* 2.36, ed. Paul Viollet, 4 vols. (Paris, 1886), 2:460: "Et est en la volanté des seignors de tenir comme lor propre domoine ou de faire revage, c'est à savoir les vignes estreper, et les maisons abatre"; English trans. in F. R. P. Akehurst, trans., *The Etablissements de Saint Louis: Thirteenth-Century Law Texts from Tours, Orléans, and Paris* (Philadelphia, 1996), p. 159. Compare the provisions in *Ordonnances des rois de France* 11:232 (concession by Philip Augustus to eight named places in the region of Laon, 1184), c. 4: "Si [malefactor] infra ambitum Potestatis, possessiones domorum aut vinearum habuerit, à Domino . . . Major et Jurati de malefactore illo justiciam requirant: et si à Domino . . . submonitus, infra quindecim dies culpam suam emendare noluerit, . . . liceat Juratis omnem malefactoris illius substanciam destruere." See also ibid., c. 2, p. 235 (charter of the same king granting privileges to Crespy, 1184).

The purpose of the enclosure was to ward off violence. . . . Theft, arson, and murder committed by an intruder inside the enclosure were subject to twice the usual penalty. . . . On the other hand, if the criminal happened to be a person who normally resided within the walls, the magistrate could not intervene, could not enter the courtyard, unless invited by the head of household. In the early Middle Ages, court[yard]s were like islets dotting the territory, exempt from public law.[16]

Whence this view? It derives from a prewar historiography represented, for example, by Otto Brunner, whose work has recently come into vogue.[17] In Brunner's hands the inviolability of the private enclosure forms part of a larger thesis about the German idea of *Land*: that the rights of lordship, including jurisdiction, immunity, and coercion came ultimately from land ownership itself; they were not "given" or "usurped" from public power:

This status was enjoyed . . . by the houses in towns and villages, all of which were under the lordship, variously, of town lords, town communities, or seigneurs. Each of them was an enclave of peace, defined typically by the drip line of the rain coming off the roof. "His house is to be his fortress," as the town laws of Enns put it in 1212. This applied even to the peasant house in a village, whose drip line marked the end of the village lord's power.[18]

The sources that Brunner used to make this argument were, by and large, the *Österreichische Weistümer* (inquest reports), where Brunner found the "drip line," that is, the *Dachtrauf* or, in the Middle High German of the *Weistümer*, the *tachtropf*. But the *Weistümer*, which are filled

---

16. Ariès and Duby, *A History of Private Life*, 2:13.

17. Otto Brunner, *Land und Herrschaft. Grundfragen der territorialen Verfassungsgeschichte Österreichs im Mittelalter*, 4th ed. (Vienna, 1959), p. 256. See also Karl Siegfried Bader, *Das Mittelalterliche Dorf als Friedens- und Rechtsbereich*, vol. 1 (Weimar, 1957; reprint, 1967). The fact that Bader has been reprinted and Brunner recently translated (*"Land" and Lordship: Structures of Governance in Medieval Austria*, trans. Howard Kaminsky and James Van Horn Melton [Philadelphia, 1992]) is evidence of contemporary fascination with Brunner's work. For a critique of Brunner and an exploration of the relationship between his thesis and German fascist thought, see Gadi Algazi, "Otto Brunner—'Konkrete Ordnung' und Sprache der Zeit," in Peter Schöttler, ed., *Geschichtsschreibung als Legitimationswissenschaft, 1918–1945* (Frankfurt am Main, 1997). I thank Dr. Algazi for sending me a copy of this paper and the one cited below, note 21, in advance of their publication.

18. Brunner, *Land und Herrschaft*, p. 256 (*Land and Lordship*, pp. 212–13).

with such statements as "an honest man is to be secure in his own house," were not referring to warding off unwanted *lords*; they were talking about house-peace against criminal intruders.[19] Nor did the boundary of the *tachtropf* imply the "limits of the lord's power." In the *Weistümer* the *tachtropf* was simply associated with higher fines or punishments, which were to be paid if violence was done under the roof's overhang.[20]

In fact, however, it is of no importance whether or not the *tachtropf* of the *Weistümer* had the significance that Brunner attributed to it. For the *Weistümer* are too recent, and too problematic, to be considered witnesses to medieval practices. Gadi Algazi has elucidated their nature: in parts of Germany in the later Middle Ages certain peasants were sworn to "tell" the village custom in response to questions posed by their lord or his representative.[21] The result was hardly a true reconstruction of the past but rather a kind of negotiated memory composed in part of the lord's expectations and interests, in part of the hopes of the peasants, and in part (perhaps) of actual practice (or memories of it). Such sources cannot reliably be used as evidence for practices predating the late Middle Ages.

If we look at medieval sources alone, there is nothing that proves that local authorities were barred from private homes. The town laws of Enns, seemingly Blackstonian in implication, were nothing of the sort. Drawn up by Duke Leopold VI of Austria, they listed crimes and penalties. The section in which "his house is to be his fortress" is, in context, a bulwark against burglars, not dukes.[22]

Karl Bader, who picked up on many of Brunner's ideas, cited the case of Münchweier to show how inviolable the enclosure had become:

> When the advocate's agent comes [to the courtyard at Münchweier] wanting to lead out a thief, let him come to the door of the courtyard and ask for the captive, whom the bailiff [an official of Münchweier] will lead out. The latter, standing in the doorway, will hand over the thief with one

---

19. Brunner, *Land und Herrschaft*, p. 256 n. 6, referring to *ÖW*, vol. 2, pt. 2: *Die Tirolischen Weisthümer* (Vienna, 1877), p. 309 (Pfunds). Many such examples of house-peace are indexed under the words "Hausfriede und dessen Störungen," as, e.g., *ÖW*, vol. 9, pt. 3, *Niederösterreichischen Weistümer* (Vienna, 1909), p. 3: "iederman soll fridtwertig sein in seinem haus als der herzog in seiner burk."

20. E.g., *ÖW*, vol. 6, *Steirische und Kärnthische Taidinge* (Vienna, 1881), p. 24 (Pürg), p. 31 (Wolkenstein), p. 39 (St. Gallen).

21. Gadi Algazi, "Lords Ask, Peasants Answer: Making Traditions in Late Medieval Village Assemblies," in Gerald Sider and Gavin Smith, eds., *Between History and Histories: The Making of Silences and Commemorations* (Toronto, 1998), pp. 199–229.

22. Schwind and Dopsch, *Ausgewählte Urkunden*, pp. 42–46, no. 26.

hand, and receive five *solidi* . . . with the other. And thus the advocate will take the thief and will judge him according to law.[23]

But Münchweier was not a peasant's enclosure nor even a princely estate: it was part of an ecclesiastical immunity.[24] Bader tried to argue institutional continuity between ecclesiastical immunities and the inviolability of the house by conflating the two.[25] But he needed first to demonstrate that houses had in fact acquired a general impregnability against royal agents in the Middle Ages. We know that the homes of a few men living near Novara were granted this invulnerability in the tenth century.[26] They were exceptional.

The English Experience

King Alfred the Great of England drew up a set of laws sometime between 885 and 899. They suggest that in England a person could not just enter another person's house unbidden. But in a vendetta, the house played a very curious role: "We command [wrote the king] that the man who knows that his opponent is dwelling at home not fight him before he asks for justice for himself."[27] Here the law specified a ritual of notification consisting of a request for amends prior to doing violence. But the violence itself remained a threat. The law continued:

If he has sufficient power to surround his opponent and besiege him within [his opponent's house], he is to keep him inside for seven days and

23. Herman Bloch and Werner Wittich, "Die Jura curiae in Munchwilare," *Zeitschrift für die Geschichte des Oberrheins* 54 (1900): 391–431, at p. 423: "Cum nuncius advocati venerit volens educere furem, veniet ad portam curiae poscens ibidem captum, quem adducet praeco stansque in porta reddens furem cum una manu, recipiens V solidos . . . cum altera; sicque advocatus abducet furem iudiciabitque secundum legem statutam."

24. See Appendix 4, n. 3, for an example of the count demanding an immunist to deliver up a guilty party. In the case of Münchweier, the advocate's agent has taken the place of the count.

25. Bader, *Das Mittelalterliche Dorf*, p. 127, says that "der Hof [any Hof, not just monastic] eine Pforte habe, die der Vogt nicht überschreiten dürfe, wenn er den Dieb abholen will." See further, ibid., pp. 148–49.

26. See Chap. 7, n. 35.

27. *Laws of Alfred*, c. 42, ed. F. Liebermann, *Die Gesetze der Angelsachsen*, 2 vols. (Halle a. S., 1903–16), 1:75–76. Translations here generally follow, with modifications, those of *EHD* 1:415.

not fight against him, if he will remain inside; then, after seven days, if he will surrender and give up his weapons, he is to keep him unharmed for thirty days, and send notice about him to his kinsmen and his friends.[28]

Kin and friends were notified in order to initiate the process of compensation and amends. Other scenarios were possible. If the attacker did not have "sufficient power" to trap his opponent at home, then "he is to ride to the ealdorman and ask him for support; if he will not give him support, he is to ride to the king, before having recourse to fighting."[29] If the opponent did not give up his weapons, then the attacker might "fight against him."[30]

These laws suggest that in late ninth-century England the home was a key institution in the prosecution of a vendetta, serving half as place of siege, half as refuge. They do not suggest that a man's home was inviolable.[31] Nor was the public power barred. The king could be called in to help assault a house if the attacker was not powerful enough to do it himself. The idea of house-as-castle did not exist in the laws of Anglo-Saxon England.

The English Franchise

We are left, then, with the task of understanding the origins of the aphorism and explaining what English immunities had to do with it. It used to be thought that the story of English franchises began in the Anglo-Saxon period. Frederic William Maitland, the great legal historian of the last century, believed that when Anglo-Saxon kings gave out sake and soke, toll and team, *infangtheof* and *grithbryce*, they were conceding major jurisdictions.[32] He thought that the evidence from Domesday Book, a set of

28. *Laws of Alfred*, c. 42, §1, in Liebermann, *Die Gesetze*, 1:75–76.

29. Ibid., c. 42, §3, in Liebermann, *Die Gesetze*, 1:76–77.

30. Ibid., c. 42, §4, in Liebermann, *Die Gesetze*, 1:76–77.

31. Related to the high valuation of enclosed space by Anglo-Saxon kings are provisions against its pollution; amends, however, were based on the status of the parties involved rather than on the house itself: e.g., *Laws of Ine*, c. 6: "If anyone fights in the king's house, he is to forfeit all his possessions, and it is to be at the king's judgment whether he is to keep his life or not"; c. 6, §1: "If anyone fights in a church, he is to pay 120 shillings compensation"; c. 6, §2: "If anyone fights in the house of an ealdorman or other important councillor, he is to pay 60 shillings compensation and is to give another 60 shillings as a fine"; see Liebermann, *Die Gesetze*, 1:90–92, as translated in *EHD* 1:399.

32. "Sake and soke" is Anglo-Saxon for dispute and suit; "toll and team" refers to rights over market transactions; *infangtheof* means "catching of thieves"; *grithbryce* means breach

reports from a vast inquest held at the order of William the Conqueror c. 1086, proved that the sheriff (the English equivalent of the Continental *judex publicus*, or royal agent) had been barred from entering certain privileged territories.[33]

A postwar generation of historians, however, has effectively dismantled this view. Already in 1949 Naomi Hurnard downgraded the nature of the jurisdiction that Anglo-Saxon kings gave away: only *infangtheof* was "jurisdiction over the handhaving [redhanded] thief"; the rest were minor jurisdictions.[34] More recently Patrick Wormald has argued persuasively that the evidence from Domesday Book itself was sometimes tainted.[35] Zeroing in on the *seemingly* most unambiguous example of an Anglo-Saxon franchise, the "hundred" (shire subdivision) of Oswaldslow, which belonged to the church of St. Mary of Worcester, Wormald found evidence of contamination. The sworn testimony to the Domesday commissioners came hard on the heels of a dispute between the bishop of Worcester and the abbot of Evesham over customs and rights at Oswaldslow, an altercation that had led to forgeries and other evidence tampering. For the Domesday inquest, the same cast of characters was involved: the Domesday commissioners had earlier "presided over the dispute's final settlement" (where the bishop of Worcester got much of what he wanted), and the witnesses for Domesday Book were largely his men.[36] There *was* a franchise at Oswaldslow all right: it was created by the men of St. Mary's for themselves at the time of Domesday!

Dispensing with Oswaldslow means, in effect, dispensing with the evidence from Domesday. Are there other sorts of evidence for Anglo-Saxon franchises? No one would have placed such faith in Domesday had it

---

of peace. See Davies and Fouracre, *Property and Power*, glossary (pp. 272–84), for further information.

33. On the Anglo-Saxon king Edward giving out jurisdictional rights: Frederic William Maitland, *Domesday Book and Beyond: Three Essays in the Early History of England* (Cambridge, 1897; reprint, 1907), p. 260; on the evidence of Domesday, ibid., p. 88. On the sheriff, see William Alfred Morris, *The Medieval English Sheriff to 1300* (Manchester, 1927), and Patrick Wormald, "Charters, Law and the Settlement of Disputes in Anglo-Saxon England," in Davies and Fouracre, *Settlement of Disputes*, p. 163 and n. 71.

34. Naomi D. Hurnard, "The Anglo-Norman Franchises," *English Historical Review* 64 (1949): 289–327, 433–60. Julius Goebel Jr., *Felony and Misdemeanor: A Study in the History of English Criminal Procedure* (New York, 1937), pp. 370–73, to some degree anticipated Hurnard by arguing that the formulae granting sake and soke referred to fiscal privileges, not jurisdiction.

35. Patrick Wormald, "Lordship and Justice in the Early English Kingdom: Oswaldslow Revisited," in Davies and Fouracre, *Property and Power*, pp. 114–36.

36. Ibid., p. 125.

not been for charter evidence to back it up. The problem is that none of the charters is original, and assessments of their authenticity rely on assumptions about what was probable or even possible in the period they purport to come from. Wormald has recently dubbed all those that seem to be franchises as "dubious" or, worse, "largely or wholly bogus."[37] Even if a few may still be salvaged, we have to conclude that Anglo-Saxon kings did not have a tradition of curbing their agents' entry. They gave away rights, to be sure: but entry prohibitions did not constitute an important element of their conception of kingship.

It must have been the Normans who brought immunities with them when they conquered England in 1066.[38] Just as Norman dukes had adopted Frankish institutions in Normandy, so they assimilated some Anglo-Saxon forms when they arrived in England—and then added some of their own. They had never given away "sake and soke" in Normandy, for example, but they did so as English kings. Sometimes they appended a clause: "Let the monks [of Westminster] have the manors of Battersea . . . [etc.] with sake and soke, with toll and team . . . nor may anyone have any entry [intromissionem] at all at any time on the land or on the water except the abbot and monks, for the benefit of the monastery."[39] This privilege was granted in a charter dating between 1070 and 1082. In 1086, again in a grant to Westminster, the nec intromissionem clause appears.[40] Sometime after the Conquest and before 1087, King William gave to the bishop of Worcester (we know by now how much he wanted it!) a confirmation of his church's rights with, again, a noninterference clause.[41]

---

37. Ibid., p. 128. But for the opposite view, see Eric John, Land Tenure in Early England: A Discussion of Some Problems (Leicester, 1960). See further, idem, "The King and the Monks in the Tenth-Century Reformation," Bulletin of the John Rylands Library 42 (1959): 61–87. Anglo-Saxon charters are catalogued (as are opinions about their authenticity) in Peter H. Sawyer, Anglo-Saxon Charters: An Annotated List and Bibliography (London, 1968).

38. Goebel, Felony and Misdemeanor, p. xxv; Wormald, "Lordship and Justice," p. 132. On Norman immunities, see David Bates, Normandy before 1066 (London, 1982), pp. 190–208. Norman ducal charters are published in Recueil des actes des ducs de Normandie de 911 à 1066, ed. Marie Fauroux, Mémoires de la société des antiquaires de Normandie 36, 4th ser., vol. 6 (Caen, 1961); examples of immunities may be found on pp. 71–72, no. 3 (968), and pp. 73–74, no. 4 (990). For cautionary remarks about the nature and extent of Norman ducal immunities, see Charles Homer Haskins, Norman Institutions (Cambridge, 1925), pp. 25–26.

39. Regesta Regum Anglo-Normannorum, 1066–1154, vol. 1, Regesta Willelmi Conquestoris et Willelmi Rufi, 1066–1100, ed. H. W. C. Davis (Oxford, 1913), p. 44, no. 162 (full text on p. 123): "monachi habeant maneria Batriceseie . . . cum saca et socna, cum toll et team . . . nec ullus aliquam omnino habeat intromissionem aliquo tempore in terra siue in aqua nisi abbas et monachi ad utilitatem monasterii."

40. Ibid., p. 63, no. 235 (full text on p. 129).

41. Ibid., p. 66, no. 252.

Westminster, Worcester, and a few other churches received the first franchises in England.[42] More got the privilege under Henry I (1100–35).

Two important institutions developed around immunities, the first of which was expressed by the clause we have just seen. In English charters, the words *nec intromissionem, ne intromittat* or *nulla persona se intromittat* meant that sheriffs, royal justices, and sometimes others were prohibited from entering or "meddling" in franchises. The second institution took shape on the ground, as private courts developed within franchises.[43]

The King in the Franchisal Courts

In 1102–3, in a privilege to the monastery of Bury St. Edmunds, Henry I forbade all laymen and royal officials from meddling in its borough and added that "all the free tenants in the 8½ hundreds are to come to the great [private] courts of the abbot of [Bury] St. Edmunds, and those who refuse to do so may be distrained. And for this reason, let them be quit for all time from all suits and customs in the shire and county of Suffolk."[44]

This provision gave the abbot clear jurisdictional rights, and it expressly excused Bury's tenants from coming to the shire and hundred courts, presided over (or at least supervised) by the sheriff.[45] The sheriff was a royal functionary, subject to the exchequer and replaceable by the crown.[46] Henry's privilege seems to mark a "hands-off" policy. Yet even within this franchise, the king played an important role.

For example, when the abbot of Bury learned (at a convocation held in 1150 under the auspices of the king's steward) that two knights of his abbey were accused of betraying the king, he derailed the proceedings, arguing that "as is testified by the privileges and charters of our church, this allegation must be transferred and dealt with in the court of St. Ed-

42. See Helen Cam, "The Evolution of the Mediaeval English Franchise," *Speculum* 32 (1957): 427–42, at p. 434 n. 51.

43. Wormald, "Lordship and Justice," p. 132.

44. David C. Douglas, ed., *Feudal Documents from the Abbey of Bury St. Edmunds*, British Academy Records of the Social and Economic History of England and Wales 8 (London, 1932), pp. 62–63, no. 21: "ut omnes libere tenentes in VIIIto hundretis et dimidii ueniant ad magna placita abbatis sancti Eadmundi et qui uenire noluerit distringatur. Et per hoc sint quieti omnibus temporibus de omnibus sectis et consuetudinibus ad schyras et comitatus Suff'."

45. For a useful overview, see Helen M. Cam, "Suitors and *Scabini*," in her *Liberties and Communities in Medieval England: Collected Studies in Local Administration and Topography* (Cambridge, 1944), pp. 49–63.

46. Morris, *English Sheriff*, pp. 72–74.

mund and our church."[47] Accompanied by the "friends and monks and barons of his church," the abbot went straight to the king to show him charters proving Bury's franchise. At a county hearing on the matter, the abbot's rights were upheld. The king's justice transmitted the testimony to the king, and the king "ordered the abbot to fix a day in his court to do him right."[48] These words meant that the king himself would attend: "A few days later the king came to St. Edmunds where the abbot, with the counsel of the barons of the church and the aid of the barons of the king, reconciled his aforesaid knights with the king."[49] Here the abbot was acting as mediator in a time of civil war; his franchisal court served as a meeting place for the king and his potential enemies.

Even when the king's interests were not directly involved, his presence was felt. At some point between 1157 and 1180 one Albold Pulcin quit his claim to land at Manhall, property that Bury St. Edmunds considered its own: "Led by repentance [Albold testified], I went to the court of St. Edmund and publicly and by my free will confessed that I never had had any right in the aforesaid Manhall."[50] We learn at the same hearing that Albold had initially obtained a royal writ "by which I had unjustly sued [the abbot]."[51] The king was on everyone's mind. When in the 1180s a dispute arose over whether some land was a free fief of the church of Bury or not, the case first came to the king's court and then, "by leave of Ranulf de Glanvill [who was the royal Chief Justice, it was] held in the abbot's court."[52]

Thus, from the time of Henry I, non-royal courts were well in place, and yet the king's presence was felt within them. Bury St. Edmunds was not the only franchise where this was true. According to the Abingdon chronicle, for example, the abbot of Abingdon held a court at the house of one of his knights, where he succeeded in making Earl Walter (who held land claimed by the abbot) his knight.[53] But the same source points out that "all this was deraigned at the command of King Henry in Ox-

---

47. R. C. van Caenegem, ed. and trans., *English Lawsuits from William I to Richard I*, 2 vols., Selden Society 106, 107 (London, 1990–91), 1:289, no. 331. The case and its manuscript source are discussed in Helen M. Cam, "An East Anglian Shire-moot of Stephen's Reign, 1148–53," *English Historical Review* 39 (1924): 568–71.

48. Van Caenegem, *English Lawsuits*, 1:290.

49. Ibid., p. 291.

50. Ibid., 2:570, no. 519.

51. Ibid., p. 571: "regis breve, per quod eum injuste miseram in placitum" (my translation here).

52. Ibid., 2:651, no. 615.

53. Ibid., 1:128, no. 162 (1102).

ford." The close involvement of the king in the abbatial court at Abingdon is clear once again in a case involving William, the king's chamberlain, who "refused to do knight service or homage to the lord Abbot Faritius on his becoming abbot."[54] The account, again in the Abingdon Chronicle, turned on the theme of royal interests: "The abbot produced witnesses . . . that this service had now clearly been withheld from the reigning King Henry who needed it."[55] William came to terms with the abbot along the same lines as had Earl Walter. More interesting are the named witnesses who were present. There was a sheriff named William, probably of Warwickshire and Hugh de Bocland, the king's sheriff of Berks. There was Nigel de Oilly, who (as we learn from a different case) not only took a very long time to do homage to Faritius but, when he did, warned that "whenever the abbot has to plead in the king's court, he will be present on the abbot's side, unless the plea were against the king."[56] The final named witness was Ralph Basset, "justiciary under Henry I."[57] In short, attending this non-royal court were all the king's men.

Nor were Bury and Abingdon unusual cases. Abbot Bernard of the monastery of Ramsey brought claim in his court for the land of Stow and Girton against Pain Peverel, "who claimed to hold it from the church of Ramsey."[58] The court found in the abbot's favor. But the whole case was under the thumb of the king from start to finish. It was recounted in a royal charter: the court was held "before my [royal] justice, whom I had sent." The king warranted the deraignment and confirmed it "by my charter and therefore I will and order that the church of Ramsey and the abbot shall henceforth hold it in peace."[59] In short, the case took place in the abbot's court, but it was orchestrated by the king. Helen Cam's argument that franchise holders in England became, in effect, agents of the king, bears reiteration.[60]

In fact, the intimate way in which the identity of English kings was bound up with their control over litigation and policing meant that English franchises would bind kings to franchise holders even in franchisal courts. It is telling enough that Abbot Faritius made his claim against the

54. Ibid., 1:133, no. 164 (1101–3).
55. Ibid.
56. Ibid., 1:177, no. 206.
57. Ibid., p. 139, no. 172, n. 4.
58. Ibid., p. 151, no. 182 (1109).
59. Ibid., p. 152.
60. Cam, "Evolution," p. 438; see also eadem, "The King's Government, as Administered by the Greater Abbots of East Anglia," in *Liberties and Communities*, pp. 183–204.

royal chamberlain by stressing royal needs. But it is even more revealing that the only named witnesses at a franchisal court were sheriffs who were not "presiding," a king's justiciar, and a liegeman of the king. Sheriffs could not enter the franchise in their guise as royal agents, but they could and did enter as important men whose attachment to the king made their friendship and opinions matter.

By forbidding sheriffs to meddle in franchises, English kings articulated in a new way the Continental hands-off tradition that I have likened to Polynesian *tapu*. At the same time, however, they kept their hands in the franchise. They closely tracked events in franchisal courts, sometimes attended them in person, and summoned franchise holders into their own courts. Their agents and officers regularly attended franchisal courts. We shall soon see other ways in which they regularly "entered" the franchise.

The Sheriff and Entry

Until the fourteenth century (when Justices of the Peace—J.P.'s— gradually took over their job), the sheriff was the archetypical royal agent, even if he sometimes was looking out for his own interests as well.[61] To him fell the often onerous tasks of calling up jurors, collecting fines, summoning men to court, arresting accused criminals, and either making provision for their bail or keeping them under lock and key.[62] He did much of this because he was told to do so, by royal writs that set forth explicit instructions for each case. As the mechanisms of royal justice expanded and became more complex, so did the sheriff's job. The Assize of Clarendon (1166) gave him specific authorization to pursue fugitive criminals wherever they might go, and he was pointedly expected to enter all sorts of places, including castles:

> And let there be no one within his castle or without . . . who shall forbid the sheriffs to enter into his court or his land to take the view of frank-

61. For just one example of self-interest, see Van Caenegem, *English Lawsuits*, 2:672–85, no. 641 (1189–95): Gerard de Camville, sheriff of Lincolnshire, acted as part of a local faction seeking control of a marsh. On Justices of the Peace, see Cam, *Liberties and Communities*, pp. 197–98; and on their precursors of the thirteenth century, the *custodes pacis*, see Morris, *English Sheriff*, pp. 174–75.

62. Helen Cam, "Cambridgeshire Sheriffs in the Thirteenth Century," in *Liberties and Communities*, p. 30.

pledge and to see that all are under pledges[63] .... And let there be none in a city or a borough or a castle or without it ... who shall forbid the sheriffs to enter into their land ... to arrest those who have been accused.... Moreover, the lord king forbids anyone in all England to receive in his land ... or in a house under him any one of that sect of renegades [the Cathari].... And if anyone shall so receive them, he himself shall be at the mercy of the lord king, and the house in which they have dwelt shall be carried outside the village and burnt.[64]

With this legislation, houses and castles were explicitly open to entry and, indeed, demolition, in the interest of "the preservation of peace and the maintenance of justice."

After 1170, when King Henry II (1154–89) ordered an inquest of sheriffs, he made wholesale replacements in the shrievalty and gave new powers to his itinerant justices. At the Assize of Northampton (1176), these officials were to "see to it that the castles which have been destroyed are utterly demolished, and those which are due for destruction are razed to the ground."[65]

In the *Dialogue of the Exchequer* (1177–79), the sheriff's duties were set forth in detail. When he tries to recover a required payment from a burgess who is unable to pay "it is not enough for the Sheriff to pay in [to the Exchequer] such men's chattels ... or to offer his faith that he has sought them and found none, and so clear himself at the Exchequer. He must confiscate their houses and lands and town rents and let them out to others, so as to raise the money due to the King."[66] To the author of the

63. The sheriff was responsible for, and reaped the profits of, verifying periodically that the "frankpledge" system was working in his shire. By this system all or some men of a community were organized to produce any of their number accused of a crime.

64. Assize of Clarendon, cc. 9, 11, 21 (1166), in William Stubbs and H.W.C. Davis, eds., *Select Charters and Other Illustrations of English Constitutional History*, 9th rev. ed. (Oxford, 1921), pp. 171–73, English trans. in *EHD* 2:442–43, no. 24. I thank Sue Sheridan Walker for leading me to the proper edition of Stubbs and for other pertinent comments. For the special status of the franchise of Wallingford, see Michael T. Clanchy, *The Roll and Writ File of the Berkshire Eyre of 1248*, Publications of the Selden Society 90 (London, 1973), pp. xxviii–xxxiii.

65. Assize of Northampton, c. 8 (1176), in Stubbs and Davis, *Select Charters*, p. 180; translation in *EHD* 2:446, no. 25.

66. Richard FitzNigel, *Dialogus de Scaccario* 2.13, in *Dialogus de Scaccario (The Course of the Exchequer)*, ed. and trans. Charles Johnson, with corrections by F. E. L. Carter and D. E. Greenway (Oxford, 1983), p. 107. It is true that at this point in the *Dialogus*, the sheriff has not entered the house; but if he lets it out to another, clearly there is no entry prohibition. Similarly, if, in cases of debt, "aurum, argentum et ex hiis uasa composita, lapides quoque pretiosi et mutatoria uestimentorum et hiis similia" are sold off by the sheriff, the best guess is that these items are confiscated from the house: ibid., 2.14, p. 110.

Dialogue, Richard fitz Nigel, houses were "safe and secret places" where merchants hid their wealth.[67] This did not make them sacrosanct, though eventually, out of this context, the safety of the house would come to play a role in the idea of the home as castle. In the *Dialogue*, however, it simply made them prime targets for sheriffs. At the same time, however, because "the bulk of the possessions of those who have land and live by husbandry consists in sheep, cattle and grain," there was no point in entering the houses of countryfolk: their wealth was not within.[68] In the *Dialogue*, houses presented no more barriers to entry than did open fields.

Could the sheriff enter a franchise when pursuing a criminal or for other purposes? He could not, but that hardly meant that criminals could find sanctuary in franchises. Rather, the bailiff, an official of the *franchise*, was expected to deliver the accused to the sheriff upon receipt of a writ to that effect. But not all bailiffs (or their lords) were so cooperative. This seems to be why, by the time of King John (1199–1216), the sheriff was commanded to *enter* franchises where the bailiffs had not carried out the terms of the writ.[69] This command to the sheriff to enter was contained in a second writ, a royal order that contained the clause *non omittas propter aliquam libertatem*, which meant, "do not neglect [to carry out the first writ] on account of any liberty [i.e., franchise]."[70] The *non omittas* provision, which in effect overrode the *ne intromittat* clause of the franchise, would become a key medieval contribution to modern ideas about the house. That, however, is getting ahead of our story.

But the story does continue with kings increasingly apt to claim rights of entry. In the reign of Henry III (1216–72), which was preoccupied with rebellion, sheriffs were instructed to confiscate castles. In 1251, for example, the sheriff of Hereford was told to ride out with a posse, invest the

---

67. Ibid., 2.13, p. 108: "locis tutis et ignotis."

68. Ibid., p. 108.

69. Cam, "Evolution," p. 438.

70. According to Michael T. Clanchy, "The Franchise of Return of Writs," *TRHS* 5th ser., 17 (1967): 59–82, at p. 61, the earliest of these *non omittas* writs "seems to have been invented in the Norfolk-Suffolk shrievalty early in John's reign." Their purpose was precisely to give greater authority to sheriffs to override the boundaries of uncooperative franchise-holders. For an example of such a writ, see idem, *The Roll and Writ File of the Berkshire Eyre of 1248*, p. 447, no. a114, where, after the king greets the sheriff of Berkshire, "'Precipimus tibi quod non obmittas propter libertatem Windesour' [we command that you not omit (to carry out the first writ, printed ibid., p. 446 no. a113) on account of the franchise of Windsor]." For an example of a plea that a writ of *non omittas* be issued, see ibid., p. 236, no. 556; and for a general discussion of *non omittas*, see ibid., pp. xlvii–xlix.

castle of Penros, and arrest the people within.[71] Henry's son, Edward I (1272–1307), was from start to finish concerned with the duties of his sheriffs, generally understood as part of his program to control royal officials and bolster royal rights.[72] The Statute of Westminster I, drawn up in 1275, gave sheriffs a new remedy if lords impounded the beasts of their tenants "in a castle or fortress" in order to compel dues or services:

> If any from henceforth take the beasts of others, and cause them to be driven into a castle or fortress, and there within the close of such castle or fortress do withhold them against gages and pledges, whereupon the beasts be solemnly demanded by the sheriff, or by some other bailiff of the King's, at the suit of the plaintiff, the sheriff or bailiff, taking with him the power of the shire, should try to make replevin of [i.e., regain] the beasts from him who took them . . . [But if no delivery is made] the King . . . shall cause the said castle to be beaten down without recovery.[73]

This new remedy should be read alongside the second half of the same chapter: that sheriffs must enter franchises "without delay" to execute a writ if the bailiffs of the franchises themselves refuse to act. "And if that be done in the marches of Wales, or in any other place where the King's writs be not current, the King, which is sovereign lord over all, shall do right there unto such as will complain."[74] The Statute of Westminster implied that there was no need even to procure a writ of *non omittas*. The sovereign ruled and administered justice as and where he would—or, rather (in his view), when right needed to be done.[75] The fact that the same chapter in the Statute speaks of castles and franchises should alert

---

71. *Close Rolls of the Reign of Henry III Preserved in the Public Record Office*, vol. 6, *AD 1247–1251* Rolls Series (London, 1902–22, reprint, 1970), pp. 540–41.

72. Michael Prestwich, *Edward I* (Berkeley, Calif., 1988), pp. 92–98.

73. Statute of Westminster I, c. 17 (1275), in Danby Pickering, ed., *Statutes at Large from Magna Charta to . . . 1761* (Cambridge, 1762), p. 87: "qe le Roi . . . face abatre le chastel, ou le forcelette saunz relever." The translation given here is slightly modified from that in Pickering. The context of the provision is clarified in Theodore F. T. Plucknett, *Legislation of Edward I*, The Ford Lectures 1947 (Oxford, 1949; reprint, 1970), pp. 30–31, 52–59; on the "almost 1250 replevin cases" in the reign of Edward I alone, and their contemporary meaning, see Paul Brand, "Lordship and Distraint in Thirteenth-Century England," in *Thirteenth Century England*, Proceedings of the Newcastle Upon Tyne Conference, 1989, vol. 3, ed. P. R. Coss and S. D. Lloyd (Woodbridge, 1991), pp. 1–24.

74. Statute of Westminster I, c. 17, in Pickering, *Statutes*, pp. 87–88.

75. See Helen M. Cam, *The Hundred and the Hundred Rolls: An Outline of Local Government in Medieval England* (London, 1930), p. 214.

us to the fact that for contemporaries these could be confounded, since many franchises included fortifications.[76]

It is not surprising that immediately after his coronation Edward I initiated an inquest of sheriffs (resulting in the so-called *Hundred Rolls*). Soon thereafter he undertook a protracted *quo warranto* campaign (1278–94) designed to challenge rights to franchises.[77] The list of questions for this inquest set the tone for both contemporaries and later historians: they implied that franchises and royal interests were in opposition. Consider the tenth article of inquiry: "[Ask,] concerning franchises that have been given out—which impede common justice and subvert the royal power—by whom were they conceded and when."[78] This was a king who chafed at entry prohibitions.

The House as Franchise

By 1500, there was a long tradition of kings entering franchises, castles, and homes. It is at about this time, however, that the idea that a man's house is his castle appeared in print. The two matters were related, for it was a king's man, Chief Justice John Fineux (1441?–1527), who first made the equation in 1506:

> If someone is in his house and he sees that someone else wants to come to his house to fight him, he may certainly assemble some of his friends and neighbors to assist and aid him in safeguarding his person. But if someone threatened to fight him as he came from the marketplace or at some other place, in that case he may not assemble some people to assist him and go there to safeguard his person. For he is not compelled to go there, and he may have remedy to assure his peace. But a man's house is his castle and his defense [*la maison d'un est a lui son castel et sa defence*] and where he rightly ought to be, etc.[79]

76. See Norman J. G. Pounds, *The Medieval Castle in England and Wales: A Social and Political History* (Cambridge, 1990): Durham castle, pp. 42, 95; Leicester, pp. 133, 235; Lincoln, p. 91; Ely, p. 7; Winchester, pp. 91, 142; Wallingford, p. 235; at Newcastle-Upon-Tyne the castle had its own franchise (p. 211).

77. Donald Sutherland, *Quo Warranto Proceedings in the Reign of Edward I, 1278–1294* (Oxford, 1963), chaps. 2 and 3. On p. 2 Sutherland calls the campaign a "sustained, sixteen-year attack . . . aimed at franchises in private hands."

78. Cam, *The Hundred and the Hundred Rolls*, p. 248; the articles of inquiry are printed in Latin and English on pp. 248–57; here the translation is mine.

79. 21 Henry 7 in Year Book fol. 39, case 50. Fineux speaks here as if the idea that a man's home is his castle was already well known. And it well may have been so. For (see note 6 above) Justinian's *Digest* already contained the idea in a quotation from Gaius (*domus tutis-*

Within a generation the saying had become an aphoristic commonplace.[80] This occurred not because "house" and "castle" were simple and transparent terms, but on the contrary, because they represented whole worlds of meaning.

A "home" in Tudor-Stuart England, was, in the words of a recent interpreter of the period, "a material extension [of a man], through his physical house; a social seat, in the larger community; an economic center, for his business pursuits; a political body, of his co-occupant family and servants; a psychological structure, in the sense of place and belonging; and a moral force, as a restraining ethical influence."[81]

Let us add to this that, already by the late Middle Ages, the domestic family had become the locus of piety.[82] In the mid-thirteenth century Henry of Susa could use the word "religious" to speak of "people who live in a holy and religious manner in their own homes."[83] The notion that the home was the focus of spiritual life grew even stronger during the Reformation period. In the sixteenth-century English church the family was isolated as a unit within high enclosed box pews.[84]

---

simum cuique refugium atque receptaculum). Moreover, this very passage had been used by Thomas Aquinas in his discussion of the Old Law in the Summa Theologiae (a passage in Deuteronomy concerned with private debts): "When you shall demand of your neighbor anything that he owes you, you shall not go into his house [non ingredieris domum eius] to take away a pledge: But you shall stand without, and he shall bring out to you what he has" (Dt 24:10–11). As Thomas explained the practice, it was instituted "because a man's securest refuge is his house and so it is hard on him to have it violated" [tum quia domus est tutissimum uniuscujusque receptaculum, unde molestum homini est ut in domo sua invadatur]. Thomas Aquinas, Summa Theologiae 1a2ae Q105, art. 2, resp. 4, in Summa Theologiae, vol. 29, The Old Law, ed. David Bourke and Arthur Littledale (New York, 1964), p. 284. On Thomas's use of Roman Law, see Jean-Marie Aubert, Le Droit Romain dans l'Oeuvre de Saint Thomas (Paris, 1955), a general overview which does not, however, cite this passage. A modern commentator has taken the passage in Deuteronomy to be a precedent of the Fourth Amendment: Norman Lamm, "The Fourth Amendment and Its Equivalent in the Halachah," Judaism 16 (1967): 300–12. Choke (see note 90 below) may have had this maxim in mind, along with other considerations, when he spoke about sheriffs not violating houses for private debts.

80. See Morris Palmer Tilley, A Dictionary of the Proverbs in England in the Sixteenth and Seventeenth Centuries (Ann Arbor, Mich., 1950), M 473.

81. Lena Cowen Orlin, Private Matters and Public Culture in Post-Reformation England (Ithaca, N.Y., 1994), p. 18.

82. See Lawrence Stone, The Family, Sex and Marriage in England, 1500–1800 (New York, 1977), pts. 3 and 4; Ariès and Duby, A History of Private Life, vol. 2, pts. 4 and 5.

83. Henry of Susa, Summa aurea, bk. 3 (Venice, 1570), p. 193, quoted in André Vauchez, The Laity in the Middle Ages: Religious Beliefs and Devotional Practices, ed. Daniel E. Bornstein, trans. Margery J. Schneider (Notre Dame, Ind., 1993), p. 113.

84. For an extant example of sixteenth-century box pews, see the Church of the Holy Trinity, Goodramgate at York. I am grateful to Ian Wood for a tour of the church.

"House" also held a political dimension: "Every man is a king in his own house."[85] The household was likened to a commonwealth, the householder to its ruler. When, in the 1550s, Alyce Ardern was tried for killing her husband, her crime was not murder but rather petty treason.[86]

In this way a house was a castle; and calling it that emphasized its impregnability. But it was not a stronghold against the *king*. By 1500 there were few non-royal castles, and those that still existed were subject in numerous ways to royal will. We have already seen some of these devices, and there were others as well: castles could be entered by the sheriff if beasts were impounded there; they could be requisitioned to serve as jails for accused criminals; they could be destroyed if built without royal license.[87] At the same time castles were less and less to be distinguished from ordinary homes. Many had become little more than high-status domestic dwellings; whereas, perhaps with the addition of some decorative crenellation, simple houses, were fitted out to look like castles.[88]

There were thus many ways in which the king intruded into the equation of house and castle. Indeed, in its original formulation, the equation was a reminder that the doors of a man's home could be opened for certain purposes by the king.[89] This now-forgotten aspect of the home/castle linkage becomes clear when we read it in context. Beginning with the reign of Edward IV (1461–83) and extending into the seventeenth century, kings increasingly claimed to control the nature of English space. During this time, the question of entry—into sanctuaries, franchises, castles, homes, and enclosures—was being carefully parsed by men whose training was in the law and who, when they thought of the home as a castle, had no fear of maintaining the king's rights therein.

Richard Choke, a justice of the Court of Common Pleas at Westminster during the reign of Edward IV, explicitly drew the parallel between a franchise and a house. In the Year Books Reports for 1473,

it was held that for felony or for suspicion of felony, one may break open the house [*poit debruser meason*] to apprehend the felon, for it is for the

---

85. Tilley, *Dictionary of Proverbs*, M 123.
86. Orlin, *Private Matters*, pp. 85–86.
87. Pounds, *Medieval Castle*, pp. 99, 104.
88. Ibid., chap. 10.
89. Here, then, I differ with Cuddihy, "Fourth Amendment-Dissertation," p. 81: "English law defined a man's house as his castle in 1485 [namely, before the proliferation of occasions for searches and seizures during the Tudor period] and as his government's castle a century later." Even in 1485, a man's house was equivalent to a franchise and subject to the vicissitudes of entry that had grown up around the latter.

commonweal to apprehend him. And Choke said that the King has interest in the felony, etc. and where the king has interest, the writ is "do not fail [to do what this writ commands] on account of any franchise" [*non omittas propter aliquam libertatem*] etc.; thus, the franchise of his house [*le libertie de son meason*] will not hold true for him, etc. But it is otherwise for debt or trespass: the sheriff . . . may not break open the house to apprehend him, for those things are only in the interest of a private party.[90]

Thus Choke made the argument that the sheriff might break into a house by force in order to apprehend a felon or suspected felon. His argument, like Fineux's, was based on an equation: the house was a franchise.[91] Where the king's interest was at stake (as in cases of felony), the writ of the sheriff always implied a *non omittas* clause, whether there was one or not. On the other hand, in the case of debt or trespass, the sheriff might not forcibly enter a house. Although Choke's distinction turned on public vs. private interest, it was possibly even more compellingly based on a tradition of summons procedures: felons had long been summoned differently than trespassers.[92] Later the terms "civil" and "criminal" would define the difference.

J.P.'s had the same rights of entry as sheriffs. Not very well trained in the law, they were the intended audience of numerous handy pocket-sized manuals.[93] Through them and through other officials was implemented what William Cuddihy has called "a legal structure for door-to-door searches and mass arrests" that would last for the next five hundred years.[94] In Thomas Marowe's 1503 manual, for example, he spelled out

90. 13 Edward IV, Year Book, Easter Session, fol. 9, case 4.
91. On the "analogical thought of the Renaissance," which made such equations and their implications real and powerful, see Orlin, *Private Matters*, p. 71.
92. S. F. C. Milsom, "Trespass from Henry III to Edward III," *Law Quarterly Review* 74 (1958): 195–224; 407–36; 561–90, argues that cases of trespass were ordinarily heard in county (shire) courts but, during the course of the thirteenth century, were increasingly brought before the king's court, especially via the legal "fiction" that these cases were *contra pacem*—against the king's peace. Nevertheless, defendents charged with trespass might be brought to court following the least stringent procedure (starting with simple summons by the sheriff rather than attachment of property) which, already in the thirteenth century, was associated with "personal actions in which the king has no interest at all" (ibid., p. 573). Ibid., n. 68, Milsom cites a thirteenth-century treatise that treats debt as a form of trespass. Trespass normally involved such crimes as ploughing, digging, depasturing, reaping, and cutting trees on other people's property. See Morris S. Arnold, ed., *Select Cases of Trespass from the King's Courts, 1307–1399*, 2 vols, Selden Society 100, 103 (London, 1985–87).
93. For manuals, see below, at nn. 95–96. On Justices of the Peace, see Cam, *Liberties and Communities*, pp. 197–98.
94. Cuddihy, "Fourth Amendment-Dissertation," pp. 49–50.

what J.P.'s ought to do in case of riot: "If the rioters flee to a fortress or castle in the same county, if the Justices pursue them there, they may break into the fortress and take them out."[95] In William Lambarde's *Eirenarcha*, an expanded manual that glossed Marowe, the aphorisms of Choke and Fineux were neatly combined:

> If he that maketh an affray do flee into a house when the Justice[s] of Peace . . . cometh to arrest him, they may (in fresh suit) break open the doors, and take him . . . , or if he flees thence, they may make fresh suit and arrest him, though it be in another county . . . . And it should seem . . . that in this case also, they may break open the doors to apprehend him, because the Prince hath an interest in the matter, and then a man's house shall be no refuge for him, as it should be in debt or trespass, where the interest is but only to some particular subject.[96]

When Fineux formulated his famous dictum about the house as castle, then, it was in a context in which the royal right to encroach was expanding. Fineux himself was involved in the process. He was one of the justices who participated in the newly systematic *quo warranto* proceedings during the reign of Henry VIII. "As a result of a general summons that Fineux attested in June [1519] all of Henry VIII's subjects in Middlesex who claimed franchises or proprietary rights to royal offices had to submit and defend their titles."[97] At about the same time, Fineux participated in "a drastic reinterpretation of the law of sanctuary."[98] In effect, he denied the right of sanctuary anywhere beyond forty days. He also precisely delimited a new "circuit del'Meason," circumscribing the safety zone narrowly around the "house" of the church.[99] Less than ten years

95. Thomas Marowe, *De Pace Terre et Ecclesie*, in Bertha H. Putnam, ed., *Early Treatises on the Practice of the Justices of the Peace in the Fifteenth and Sixteenth Centuries*, Oxford Studies in Social and Legal History 7 (Oxford, 1924), p. 343: "si lez Riottourz fuount a vne Forcelett ou chastell deins mesme le countie, la lez Justices sils eux pursuount purront enfreindre le forcelett & prendre dehors & cetera."

96. William Lambard, *Eirenarcha: or of the Office of Justices of Peace* (London, 1582), pp. 143–44.

97. Harold Garrett-Goodyear, "The Tudor Revival of Quo Warranto and Local Contributions to State Building," in Morris S. Arnold, ed., *On the Laws and Customs of England: Essays in Honor of S. E. Thorne* (Chapel Hill, N.C., 1981), p. 238. Garrett-Goodyear disputes the view that the revival stemmed from the desire to eliminate franchises; he suggests it "may have been designed from the outset to raise money" instead (p. 237).

98. E. W. Ives, "Crime, Sanctuary, and Royal Authority under Henry VIII: The Exemplary Sufferings of the Savage Family," in Arnold, *On the Laws and Customs of England*, pp. 296–320, at p. 298.

99. Ibid., p. 299.

later, Henry VIII would initiate a campaign (connected to his break with Rome) that eventually resulted in the elimination of all franchises.[100] He also denied sanctuary to those who "do any ravishment of or to any woman, or which shall commit any manner of burglary, or which shall commit or do any manner of robbery," as well as to those accused of arson and sacrilege; limited what little of asylum remained to church buildings and their yards; and—inspired perhaps by the Bible, as well as by Wolsey's argument that "princes of the ancient world . . . were accustomed to set up places of refuge"—created eight new sanctuary cities for debtors.[101]

Among other things, these reforms suggest the new ways that the state was conceptualizing, organizing, and controlling space. During the sixteenth century and into the next, the occasions for search and seizure "proliferated from three to fifteen categories."[102] Not all searches meant breaking down doors; nevertheless, throughout the Tudor and early Stuart period, the king's men could enter another's house under a great many circumstances.

Two Images

By the seventeenth century, then, the house projected two powerful images: franchise and castle. There was no tension between them in the context in which they were first voiced. But images can have a life of their own. The first was associated with the sheriff's duty to enter, whereas the second implied a certain impregnability. A man like Edward Coke (1552–1634), whose writings are still cited by the Supreme Court of the United States, was sensitive to their different implications, especially since he assimilated the "castle" to the "safe refuge" of Roman law. In his comments

---

100. 27 Henry 8, c. 24 (1535–36), in *Statutes of the Realm*, 3:556, had all writs, indictments, and courts processes in every franchise and county palatine made out in the king's name. Further, the king might "tarry abide or make his repose" within or without franchises, and he and his ministers might keep their courts for justice "and exercise their offices" in all of his dominions.

101. For those denied sanctuary, see 32 Henry 8, c. 12 (1540), in *Statutes of the Realm*, 3:757. For the new limits on sanctuary space, see ibid., p. 756. For Henry's cities, see Isobel D. Thornley, "The Destruction of Sanctuary," in *Tudor Studies Presented . . . to Albert Frederick Pollard*, ed. R. W. Seton-Watson (London, 1924; reprint, 1969), p. 204, and further see Ives, "Crime, Sanctuary, and Royal Authority," in Arnold, *On the Laws and Customs of England*, p. 302, on Wolsey's argument for ancient precedents to sanctuary.

102. Cuddihy, "Fourth Amendment-Dissertation," p. 81.

on Semayne's Case (1604) we can see him pulled first by one image, then by the other. First he mused, à la Fineux,

> For a man's house is his castle, & *domus sua cuique est tutissimum refugium*
> [here quoting Gaius's commentary in Justinian's *Digest*]; for where shall a
> man be safe, if it be not in his house? [103]

Then again, the house was a franchise and thus could be breached for certain purposes by the king. Coke continued:

> In all cases when the King is party, the sheriff (if the doors be not open)
> may break the party's house, either to arrest him, or to do other execution
> of the K[ing]'s process, if otherwise he cannot enter.

However, since the house was a castle, it should be treated as one, as in the Statute of Westminster, where the sheriff had been required solemnly to demand the beasts held within a castle before battering it down. Coke universalized this procedure with a call for the sheriff to make a preliminary notification before *any* forced entry:

> But before he [the sheriff] breaks it [the door], he ought to signify the
> cause of his coming, and to make request to open doors; and that appears
> well by the stat[ute] of Westm[inster] 1 c. 17. (which is but an affirmance
> of the common law). [104]

Next, again considering the house as a franchise, Coke mused that even if a writ did not contain a *non omittas* provision, that is, a clause to enter a franchise, in cases of felony,

103. 5 Coke *Reports* 91b (Semayne's Case), *ER* 77:195. The Latin maxim is from Justinian's *Digest*; but perhaps it is via Aquinas as well (see note 79 above). Coke's misuse of sources has been emphasized since the time of Thomas Hobbes, "Dialogue between a Philosopher and a Student on the Common Laws of England," in idem, *The English Works of Thomas Hobbes*. ed. William Molesworth, 12 vols (London, 1839–45; reprint, 1992), 6:1–160. I thank Linda Hirshman for the reference. The charges continue: see Samuel E. Thorne, *Sir Edward Coke 1552–1952*, Selden Society Lecture, 1952 (London, 1957), p. 7, who speaks of "Coke's spurious Latin maxims, which he could manufacture to fit any occasion and provide with an air of authentic antiquity"; Donald O. Wagner, "Coke and the Rise of Economic Liberalism," *Economic History Review* 6 (1935): 30–44, points to Coke's incorrect citations, anachronistic interpretations, and faulty logic. But Coke's methods were deeply rooted in the *sic et non* tradition of scholasticism, where quotations were routinely ripped out of context with a view to heightening the terms of the argument and arriving at a moral truth.

104. *ER* 77:196. Interestingly, Coke's citation of the Statute of Westminster, c. 17, and his affirmation that this was part of "common law" was adopted by Justice Clarence Thomas in *Sharlene Wilson v Arkansas* (1995), to support his finding that a "knock-and-announce prin-

the King has interest, and where the King has interest the writ is *non omittas propter aliquam libertatem* [by definition]; and so the liberty or the privilege of a house [i.e., its franchise] doth not hold against the King.[105]

Thus Coke shuttled back and forth like a tennis ball on the court. The rules of the game were clear enough: the house was a castle *and* a franchise; it was the one place where a man had safe refuge *and* it was equally the place where the king's interest overrode inviolability.

William Cuddihy and B. Carmon Hardy have shown how the English system of house-search changed only very gradually, with the circumscription of the entry of *royal* but not *Parliamentary* agents the primary result.[106] The impetus for this development was less the equation of house and castle than it was the protests by members of Parliament against indiscriminate official entries into *their* households. For example, members of the Long Parliament (1640–53) who resisted royal taxation by decree found their chambers searched and papers seized by royal agents.[107] Though the legislators at first rested their protests on the claim of special Parliamentary privilege, by the mid-seventeenth century, they had begun to assert that such searches were "contrary to Law and the 'Liberty of the Subject.'"[108]

In the period after the Restoration (1660), a good many restraints on the powers of the government to enter and search homes were written into law. Indeed, Chief Justice William Scroggs was impeached in 1680 because, by his issuance of general warrants (types of writs) which allowed officials indiscriminate entry, searches, and seizures, "many of His Majesty's subjects have been vexed, their houses entered into, and they themselves grievously oppressed contrary to law."[109]

ciple" is part of common law. See *The United States Law Week* 63 (May 23, 1995), pp. 4456–59. However, in the Statute of Westminster, the whole process, including the "solemn demand," in fact added a new invasiveness to the sheriff's tasks; see above, note 73.

105. *ER* 77:197.

106. For what follows, see William Cuddihy and B. Carmon Hardy, "A Man's House Was Not His Castle: Origins of the Fourth Amendment to the United States Constitution," *William and Mary Quarterly*, 3d ser, 38 (1980): 371–400, and Leonard W. Levy, *Original Intent and the Framers' Constitution* (New York, 1988), chap. 11.

107. Cuddihy, "Fourth Amendment-Dissertation," pp. 19–20.

108. Ibid., p. 23.

109. *The History and Proceedings of the House of Commons of England*, vol. 2 (London, 1742), p. 66. See Cuddihy and Hardy, "A Man's House," p. 378 n. 39.

Yet general warrants much like Scroggs's were resuscitated in numerous contemporary acts of Parliament.[110] And even though at some moments in the mid-eighteenth century, such as when the printer John Wilkes was arrested, searches of homes were likened to illegal trespass, Parliament did not thereby give up its right to issue laws that authorized officials to enter homes.[111] When, in 1766, William Pitt made his impassioned plea against general warrants by invoking the rights of the poor man in his hut against the forces of the king—emphasizing the house's impregnability and conveniently leaving out the fact that it was a franchise as well—the motion was voted down because it limited *Parliament's* prerogatives. Indeed, James Madison argued for the Bill of Rights of the American Constitution by observing of English practices: "They have gone no farther than to raise a barrier against the powers of the Crown; the power of the Legislature is left altogether indefinite."[112]

Coda: The Fourth Amendment

The Fourth Amendment of the U.S. Constitution reads:

> The right of the people to be secure in their persons, houses, papers, and effects, against unreasonable searches and seizures, shall not be violated, and no Warrants shall issue, but upon probable cause, supported by oath or affirmation, and particularly describing the place to be searched, and the persons or things to be seized.

This Amendment and its particular wording grew only in part from the English experience. It derived more directly from events and politics connected with the American Revolution and the adoption of the Constitution. As in England, only when religious and political elites became the targets of searches and seizures did opposition become vocal and widespread. One turning point came in Paxton's Case (1761), when James Otis fired up the young John Adams and others by his arguments opposing the issuance of a type of general warrant known as a writ of assistance.[113] According to Adams's terse notes, Otis argued:

110. See Cuddihy and Hardy, "A Man's House," p. 384 n. 65.

111. On Wilkes, ibid., pp. 385–86.

112. *The Debates and Proceedings in the Congress of the United States*, vol. 1, Annals of the Congress 1 (Washington, D.C., 1834), col. 436 (June 8, 1789). See Cuddihy and Hardy, "A Man's House," pp. 386–87.

113. For a discussion of these writs and bibliography, see John Adams, *The Legal Papers of*

This Writ is against the fundamental Principles of Law. The privilege of a house. A man who is quiet is as secure in his house as a prince in his castle, notwithstanding all his debts and civil processes of any kind.—But for flagrant crimes, and in cases of great public necessity, the privilege may be [encroached?] on. For felonies, an officer may break upon process and oath—i.e., by a special warrant to search such an house, sworn to be suspected, and good grounds of suspicion appearing.[114]

Thus Otis claimed that only upon the issuance of *specific* warrants was the state's entry legal. It was, in effect, a new way to interpret the principle of *non omittas*, and it is worth noting that Otis drew on Choke's formulation (though likely via Coke) to distinguish (in the terms of *his* day) civil from criminal procedures.

At the time Otis spoke, few state constitutions mandated specific warrants.[115] The issue of warrants came to a head only with the new federalist movement represented by the Constitution. Samuel Bryan, writing as the "Centinel," for example, argued that the state of Pennsylvania should vote against ratification:

Your present form of government [the constitution of the State of Pennsylvania] secures to you a right to hold yourselves, houses, papers and possessions free from search and seizure, and therefore warrants granted without oaths of affirmations first made, affording sufficient foundation for them, whereby any officer or messenger may be commanded or required to search your houses or seize your persons or property, not particularly described in such warrant, shall not be granted . . . How long those rights will appertain to you, you yourselves are called upon to say, whether your *houses* shall continue to be your *castles*; whether your *papers*, your *persons* and your *property* are to be held sacred and free from *general warrants*, you are now to determine.[116]

Here, as with Otis, the image of impregnability took center stage, with that of franchise met by the institution of specific warrants. Similarly, Pat-

---

John Adams, vol. 2, *Cases 31–62*, ed. Kinvin L. Wroth and Hiller B. Zobel (Cambridge, Mass, 1965), pp. 107–12. On the circulation of Otis's argument, see ibid., p. 117.

114. Ibid., pp. 125–26.

115. Cuddihy, "Origins of the Fourth Amendment," pp. 397–98.

116. "Centinel" I, *Philadelphia Independent Gazetteer*, 5 October 1797, published in *The Documentary History of the Ratification of the Constitution*, vol. 2, *Ratification of the Constitution by the States, Pennsylvania*, ed. Merril Jensen (Madison, Wis., 1976), pp. 158–67, at 158, emphasis in the original. On the "Centinel" and his probable identity, see *Documentary History*,

rick Henry praised the Virginia Declaration of Rights, which provided against general warrants:

> There was certainly some celestial influence governing those who deliberated on that Constitution:—For they have with the most cautious and enlightened circumspection guarded those indefeasible rights, which ought ever to be held sacred.[117]

In the context that we have been discussing, the Fourth Amendment was a new way to deal with the implications of franchise and castle. It included one of the devices—warrants—that had been established to breach the franchise. Yet it was also a statement of impregnability. Let us recall that immunities had begun largely as a way to accommodate political power to a new sensibility about religious space. Some of the rhetoric supporting the Fourth Amendment invoked very old images: sanctuary, asylum, sacredness. We have just heard Patrick Henry speak of "sacred rights." Maryland's "Farmer" argued that every man's home was "the asylum of a citizen" and "the sanctuary of a freeman".[118] In the Fourth Amendment, medieval immunities and the institutions that conditioned them continued to reverberate.

---

vol. 13, *Commentaries on the Constitution Public and Private*, vol. 1, ed. John P. Kaminski and Gaspare J. Saladino (Madison, Wis., 1981), no. 133, pp. 326–37.

117. Patrick Henry, speaking before the Virginia Convention, 16 June 1788, in *Documentary History*, vol. 10, *Ratification . . . by the States, Virginia*, vol. 3, ed. John P. Kaminski and Gaspare J. Saladino (Madison, Wis., 1993), p. 1331.

118. "A Farmer," no. 1, *Maryland Gazetteer or the Baltimore Advertiser*, Fri., 15 Feb. 1788 (no. 351), p. 2, col. 2.

Conclusion

Political Theory on the Ground

WHAT WE have learned from the foregoing—at the least—is that immunities never had a single meaning. They functioned within and as part of numerous different political, religious, and social strategies. As documents, they seem repetitious, stiff, and dry; but behind their apparent formalism, their sober traditionalism, they hide social and political transactions of the liveliest and most up-to-date sort. I have tried to suggest the parameters of their usefulness and the outline of their evolution, but my discussion has necessarily been limited by certain linked conditions: the need for original—or at least authentic—documents whose context can be illuminated by other sorts of texts and which mark political and/or religious moments of some importance.

The traditional historical narrative separates immunities from exemptions. When treating exemptions, modern historians focus primarily on those issuing from the papacy. When, as happens rarely, episcopal exemptions are touched upon, two key figures come to the fore: Columbanus, who is said to have "created" episcopal exemptions, and Boniface, who is said to have ended them. For immunities, historians focus on kings.

In this book I argue that immunities and exemptions emerged and changed together, that both represented an outcome of negotiations between kings, courtiers, and their religious associates. The legislation and charters of Clothar II and his son Dagobert I invoked earlier precedents; whether or not such precedents existed in fact, their privileges were certainly built out of bits and pieces of Roman law and canonical regulations. At the same time, they were responses to growing sensibilities about the sacrosanctity of the altar, the independence of special monasteries such as Holy Cross at Poitiers, and the *secreta septa* of Columbanian houses. Once institutionalized—certainly by the time of Queen Balthild—as instruments of royal and state welfare ("for the salvation of the king's soul and the stability of his kingdom"), immunities and exemptions became a regular part of royal-aristocratic-episcopal-monastic relations. These relations were not static. Indeed, a dramatic change began in the mid-eighth century, when sensitivities to the "secret enclosure" were increasingly benumbed by the desire—expressed by kings, popes, bishops, and even abbots like Fulrad—to protect and control ecclesiastical property and monastic discipline. Thus, in the Carolingian period, immunities and exemptions remained part of the repertory of rulers, but they functioned rather differently. Both immunities and exemptions were accompanied by declarations of royal *mundeburdium, tuitio,* or *defensio.* Protected monasteries and churches might form clusters: for example, a whole *ecclesia* of chapels, monasteries, and churches was linked through immunities, exemptions, and protection across diocesan boundaries to the church of Saint-Denis, which was itself linked to the king by royal immunity and protection.

Popes, too, sometimes promised *ditio*—their own brand of protection—to churches; the implications of such protection were drawn forth by popes and monks in the course of the tenth and eleventh centuries. Immunities became part of this process when popes began to grant them in the tenth century; but in this context they again meant something far different from the original entry prohibitions against royal agents. Papal privileges of immunity intended, even from the start, to qualify certain properties as "holy." This was one of the "divergent paths" in the evolution of immunities. The other path was more secular, as immunities were subsumed into grants of rights of *districtus.* The two came together in 1095, when Urban II marked off an area of jurisdiction around Cluny and declared it to be sacred.

In England, immunities were "borrowed" from the Continent; by 1066 they must have seemed essential elements of any "modern" administration. They were rapidly incorporated into the royal legal system, *the* defining institution of English kingship. English "franchises" were off-limits to the king's sheriffs yet clearly subject to and participants in the royal legal system. Eventually that intervention was institutionalized, in the writ of *non omittas.* In the later Middle Ages, the principle of *non omittas* came to apply whenever the king had interest, as in cases of felony. In the Tudor-Stuart period, this policy converged with the new focus on the house as a miniature commonwealth. It became both a franchise and a castle: impregnable and yet subject to entry by the king.

All of this goes to show that there was an enormous range of thought and usage, strategy and intent, in the history of immunities. This should give us pause. It is very common to begin the story of the modern "liberal" state with John Locke.[1] Yet, as we have seen, King Berengar, for one, saw numerous advantages in limiting the potential intervention of his state in the affairs of individuals and corporations. It is equally common to write about medieval political thought by devoting a chapter to the patristic period and to skip immediately thereafter to the scholastics. Yet even if, with the exception of a few Carolingian thinkers, nothing much in the way of political theory was written between the fifth and twelfth centuries, that gives us no reason to ignore the years in between.[2] Political theory is not just what theoreticians say it is; it also lurks behind and within political *action*.[3]

If we drop the attempt to judge whether medieval kings were "strong" or "weak" and try instead to understand what assumptions they and their associates made about the uses and abuses of power, the early Middle Ages suddenly becomes extremely lively and inventive. And well it might be: First, its building blocks—the Mediterranean heritage—were enormously sophisticated. Second, the need to adapt them to new conditions was clear. Third, the clearly impoverished material conditions of the West in effect *forced* a rethinking of how to deploy scarce resources.

It was not necessary for Frankish kings, courtiers, and churchmen to postulate a "state of nature" in order to imagine that they nevertheless

1. But see the remarkable study by Brian Tierney, *The Idea of Natural Rights: Studies on Natural Rights, Natural Law and Church Law, 1150–1625*, Emory University Studies in Law and Religion 5 (Atlanta, 1997), which traces the origins of rights theory to the twelfth-century canonists.

2. Joseph Canning, *A History of Medieval Political Thought, 300–1450* (London, 1996), an excellent survey, nevertheless well illustrates this point: the first chapter, though in *title* extending from c. 300 to c. 730, in fact ends with St. Augustine. The second chapter picks up with the Carolingians. There is, however, a short discussion of the political implications of Germanic *mundeburdium*, "protection," in Walter Ullmann, *Medieval Political Thought* (Harmondsworth, U.K., 1975), pp. 56–58.

3. See Tierney, *Idea of Natural Rights*, p. 77: "The medieval concern for subjective rights in practical everyday life reshaped the language in which discourse about natural right was conducted." It is not Tierney's purpose to explore that "practical everyday life," but he clearly connects the language of the twelfth-century canonists to contemporary political practice.

constituted a community of interest.[4] Nor was a social contract necessary to elaborate a "hands-off" policy vis-à-vis favored monasteries. Asylum was the grudging concession by emperors to popular practice, and the "secret enclosure" represented a collusion of clerical and royal interests. We may conclude that one principle of early medieval political "theory" was that compromise and negotiation with powerful people were important mechanisms of power enhancement. We may also conclude that, as with Polynesian *tapu*, declaring a space off-limits was one way to control its demarcation and access to its resources, both of which demonstrated the power of the declarer. That immunities might at the same time undermine the ruler's resources was not noted theoretically, though Janet Nelson has shown that early medieval kings took care to replenish their resources when they could. But the *gesture* of giving out immunities could be continually renewed: all the confirmations of immunities show that this was the case. In that way, they constituted an inextinguishable resource. Only when social networks were ruptured did the system of ceaselessly replenished immunities stop working. And then it halted even when, as under the Carolingians, the notion of "protection" should have kept the recipients in the king's orbit.

Modern political theory, too, is implicit in practice. There is much to say about the origins of formal theories of rights and "uses of rights" language.[5] But it is not necessary to have theory to turn privilege into rights; they are largely the result of a democratization of earlier practices. At first the ruler gave out privileges to a chosen few. But as kings came to define themselves as sovereign and all others as their "subjects," privileges and exceptions were universalized.[6] We have seen this in the case

4. John Locke, *Second Treatise of Government*, chap. 2, in Peter Laslett, ed., *Two Treatises of Government: A Critical Edition* (Cambridge, 1960), p. 289. In fact the argument that Locke makes here depends on "one omnipotent and infinitely wise Maker," a political theology with which no Frankish king or churchman would quarrel.

5. See Tierney, *Idea of Natural Rights*, esp. pt. 1, and Richard Tuck, *Natural Rights Theories: Their Origin and Development* (Cambridge, 1979). I thank Lynn Hunt for the latter reference.

6. This is precisely the case for the "Privileges and Immunities" clause of the U.S. Constitution, which was part of a process of "universalizing" the notion of "immunities" as they were understood in the Tudor-Stuart period. See Bogen, "The Privileges and Immunities Clause of Article IV." The phrase "privileges and immunities" itself dates back to at least the fifth century; see *CT* 13.3.16: "We command that grammarians, orators and teachers of philosophy, and likewise physicians, in addition to the privileges and immunities [privilegia inmunitatesque] which they have obtained by the authority of sanctions formerly issued, shall . . . be vexed by no municipal tax payment." Bogan sees franchises as a medieval precedent to immunities, but in England the word "immunitas" was not used for franchises. Rather, the medieval usage that crept into the colonial charters probably derived from grants to privileged commercial entities. E.g., in the *Carta Mercatorum* of 1303, all foreign

of the *non omittas* clause, which applied first to franchises, then to whole territories such as Wales, and finally to everyone's private home.

This book has tried to show that immunities are best studied in their immediate historical context. Only then can we understand the roles that they played as flexible instruments of political life. Combining with the equally flexible institutions of asylum, protection, peace, and ritual, they were manipulated to serve the purposes of kings, monks, bishops, popes . . . and ultimately the American Founding Fathers. The history of immunities demonstrates, among much else, the enormous creativity of early medieval political life and thought.

---

merchants in England were granted liberties and free customs—here meaning certain rights of movement and trading privileges—as part of their *securitatis immunitas*: their "protection"; see Norman Scott Brien Gras, *The Early English Customs System* (Cambridge, Mass., 1918), charter printed pp. 259–64; discussed pp. 66–70.

Appendix 1

An Immunity of King Theuderic III (October 30, 688): *ChLA* 13:90–91, no. 570*

+ Theudericus, rex Francorum, uir inluster.

Dum et nobis diuina pietas ad legitema etate fecit peruenire et in solium regni parentum nostrorum sucedire, oportit nobis et condecit pro salute anime nostre cogitare dibiamus. Ideoque uestra cognuscat industria, quod nos, pro salute anime nostre, una cum consilio ponteficum uel obtimatum nostrorum, uilla noncopanti Latiniaco, que ponitur in pago Meldequo, qui fuit inlustribus uiris Aebroino, Uuarattune et Ghislemaro, quondam maiores domos nostros, et post discessum ipsius Uuarattune in fisco nostro fuerat reuocata, nos ipsa uilla de fisco nostro, ad suggestionem precelse regine nostre Chrodochilde seo et inlustri uiro Berchario, maiorem domos nostri, ad monasthirio sancti domni Dionisiae, ubi ipsi preciosus in corpore requescit, et uenerabilis uir Chaeno, abba, cum norma plurema monachorum, ad laudis Christi canendas, in ordine sancto ibidem adunata preesse uiditur, pro remedium anime nostri, plena et integra gracia, prepter rem illa, in loco, qui dicitur Siliacos, qui fuit Arulfo, quondam, et ibidem usque nunc ad ipso Latiniaco aspexit, quem apostholico uiro domno Godino episcopo per alia nostra precepcione concessemus; in reliquo uiro ad integrum ipsa uilla Latiniaco, ad ipso monasthirio domni Dionisiae ad die presenti uisi fuimus concessissae. Quapropter per hunc preceptum nostrum decernemus ordenandum et perpetualiter uolemus esse mansurum, ut ipsa uilla superius nomenata Latiniaco, cum terris, domebus, mancipiis, acolabus, uiniis, siluis, campis, pratis, pascuis, farinariis, aquis aquerumue decursebus, peculiis utriusque genere sexsus cum adiecenciis, adpendiciis uel reliquis quibuscum-

*See Chapter 4, note 42. I acknowledge with thanks permission from Urs Graf Verlag to reprint here the transcription in *Chartae Latinae antiquiores*.

que beneficiis, omnia et ex omnebus, rem exquisita, sicut ad suprascriptas per-
sonas fuit possessa uel postia in fisco nostro reuocata, cum omne integretate uel
soledetate sua, ad se pertenentis uel aspicientis prepter suprascripta rem in Si-
liaco, qui fuit ipsius Arulfo uel iam dicto pontefici, per nostra precepcione concessemus; in reliquo uiro predicta uilla Latiniaco ad integrum, sub emunetates
nomine, absque introitus iudicum, memoratus Chagno, abba, ad parte predicti
monasthiriae suae sancti Dionisiae per hanc nostram cessione, in lumenarebus
ipsius basilici, habiat concessa adque indulta; et deinceps in postmodum nec de
parte de fisci nostri nec ad quemcumquelibet persona nec per strumenta car-
tarum nec per quolibet ingenium, ipsa uilla de ipso monasthirio nullatenus ab-
straatur nec auferatur. Sed, sicut superius dixemus, pro nostra mercide ibidem
in perpetuo, in dei nomine, proficiat in augmentis; quo fiat, ut et nobis ad mer-
cidem perteniat et ipsis seruis dei, qui ibidem deseruire uidintur, delectit pro
anime salutem uel rigni nostri constancia adtencius domni meserecordia deprecare. Et ut hec precepcio cessio nostra firmior habiatur et melius per tempora
conseruitur, manus nostri subscripcionebus subter eam decriuemus roborare.
+ Uulfolaecus iussus optolit.
   + in Christi nomene Theudericus, rex, subscripsit
                              Bene ualete
Datum sub die tercio kalendas nouembris, annum xvi rigni nostri. Conpendio,
in dei nomine, filiciter.

Appendix 2

A Comparison of Key Clauses in *Gorze*, no. 4, and Marculf, no. 1*

To illustrate how the Gorze privilege in effect created an "anti-exemption" in part by using, in part by inverting the provisions of the standard formula for exemptions, a comparison of key passages from the foundation charter of Gorze (*Gorze*, no. 4) and the exemption represented by Marculf, no. 1, follows below. The order of clauses repeats that of the Gorze privilege, but the sequence of the Marculf privilege may be reconstituted by following the numbers before each clause.[1] Introductory comments summarizing the passages are in brackets. Identical words in the two documents are underlined.

Gorze

(1) [The purpose of the privilege is to provide monastic peace] Igitur <u>compulit nos affectio caritatis</u> atque dilectionis fratrum ipsorum, pro eorum <u>quiete</u> et ordine, qualiter, Deo juvante, valeant implere regulam et ordinem suum, et quod <u>nobis</u>, successoribusque nostris <u>maneant ad mercedem, et</u> a <u>recto tramite, inco[n]vulso limite terminare</u>, quod <u>perhennem deinceps, propiciante Deo, obtineant firmitatem</u>.

Marculf

(1) [The purpose of the privilege is to provide monastic peace.] <u>Conpellit nus affeccio Caritatis</u> Vestre, radio inflamante Devino, illa pro vestro <u>quieti</u> providere, quae <u>nobis maneant ad mercedem, et</u> ea <u>recto tramitae inconvulso limite terminari</u> que <u>perennem deinceps, propiciante Domino, obtineant firmitatem</u>.

---

*See Chapter 5, note 19.

1. The elements of Marculf no. 1 are analyzed in Ewig, "Beobachtungen zu den Klosterprivilegien," in Ewig, *Gallien*, 2:420.

(2) [Monasteries are "subiecta" to bishops]: Et ne quis, nobis detrahendo, estimet in id nova decernere, dum antiquitus, juxta considerationem pontificum, videant cetera sibi subiecta monasteria in omnibus esse conservata atque secura.

(2) [Monasteries are "sub libertatis privilegium"]: Et ne nobis aliquis detraendo estimet in id nova decernere carmina, dum abantiquitus iuxta constitucionem pontificum pro regale sanccionem monasteria sanctorum ... innumerabilia per omne regno Francorum sub libertatis previlegium videntur consistere.

(3)[2] [The diocesan bishop claims the right to bless the clergy, the altar and the chrism of the monastery] qui in vestro manastirio sancta debeat baiolarae officia, quem abba cum omne congregacione poposcerit, a nobis vel a succesoribus nostris sagros percipiat grados, nullum pro ipsorum onorem praemium perceptorum.

(3) [Prohibition against spoliation]: convenit nobis illis conservare, pro eorum quiete, et ordine, et tranquillitate, ut neque a nobis, neque archidiacono nostro, neque a ceteris ordinatoribus Sancti Stephani, vel a quolibet homine, inquietati nec condempnati, vel de rebus eorum expoliati, contra rationis ordinem, esse non debeant. Sed ... quieto ordine ipsas res teneant atque possideant; et de hoc quod nos ad ipsum monasterium dedimus atque firmavimus, vel a Deum timentibus hominibus donatum est atque firmatum, aut aliquid munere transmissum, vel in altario offertum, aut sacris voluminibus, seu quibuscumque speciebus, quod ad ornatum divini cultus pertinet, ad presens collata vel deinceps collatura fuerint, non auferamus.

(5) [Prohibition against exercising episcopal "potestas" and against spoliation]: Nullam paenetus aliam potestatem in ipso monastirio, neque in rebus nequae in ordinandis personis neque in vilabus ibidem iam conlatis aud deinceps regio munere aut privatorum conlaturas, vel in reliqua substancia monasterii, nos succesoresque nostri episcopi aud archidiaconi seu citeri ordinatores aut qualibet alia persona predicte civitatis habere non presumat, aut quodcumque de eodem monasterio sicut de parociis aut citeris monasteriis muneris causa audeat sperare aut aufferre, nec de hoc, quod ad Deum timentibus hominebus transmissum aut in altario offertum fuerit, aut sacris voluminebus vel quibuscumque speciebus, quod ad hornatum Divini cultus pertenit, ad presens conlata vel deinceps conlatura fuerint, aufferrae non presumat.

2. Ibid, p. 426. Ewig remarks regarding Chrodegang's privilege that "das Weiherecht des Bischofs ist anscheinend so selbstverständlich, daß es gar nicht erwähnt zu werden braucht."

(4) [Episcopal "mundeburdium" and "defensio" is one basis of monastic prayer]: Et sit ipsum monasterium subjectum sub mandeburde et defensione Sancti Stephani ecclesie Metensis . . . ut libeat eis pro vita et incolumitate regis, et stabilitate regni Francorum, et pro pontificibus suis suisque subjectis Domini misericordiam exorare.

(6) [Entry prohibition is basis of monastic prayer]: (see Marculf 6 below)

(5) [Choice of abbot with consent and will of diocesan bishop]: Et juxta dispensationem divinam, cum abbas de ipso monasterio ad Dominum migraverit, quem unanimiter omnis illa monachorum congregatio obtime regule compertum et vite meritis congruentem elegerint, una cum consensu et voluntate memorate urbis episcopi, ipsum sibi habeant abbatem. Et si in ipsam congregationem, quod absit! non potuerint talem invenire qui eos regulariter regat, tunc ipse pontifex, cum consensu et voluntate eorum, de alio monasterio eligat abbatem.

(4) [Free choice of abbot, who is to be installed by the bishop]: Et iuxta dispensacione Divina cum abba de ipso monastirio a Domino migraverit, quem unianimiter omnis congregacio illa monacorum ex semetipsis obtimae regola conpertum et vite meretis congruentem elegerint, sine praemium memorate urbis episcopus ipse promoveat abbatem.

(6) [Bishop's refusal of "munera" is another basis of monastic prayer]: Et si prefatus pontifex, pro lucranda oratione aut visitatione fratrum, quando ei placuerit, in ipso monasterio venerit, vel aliquam moram, pro lucrandis animabus fecerit, cum exinde in Dei nomine vult habere regressum, absque ullo munere terreno requisito revertatur, qualiter monachi, qui solitarii nuncupantur, de profecta quietis vel securitate valeant, Domino protegente, per longa tempora exultare, et sub sancta regula viventes, pro profectu ecclesie et salute regis vel patrie valeant plenius Domini misericordiam et attentius deprecari.

(6) [Entry prohibition is the basis of monastic prayer]: Et nisi rogitus a congregatione illa vel abba pro oracione lucranda nulli nostrum liceat monasterii adire secreta aut finium ingredi septa; et si ab eis illuc pontifex postolatus pro lucranda oracionem vel eorum utilitatem accesserit, caelebratu ac peractu Divino misterio, simplicem ac subriam benediccionem percepta, absque ullo requaesitu dono studiat habere regressum, ut quatinus monachi, qui soletarii noncupantur, de perfecta quieti valeant, duci Domino, per tempora exultare et sub sancta regula viventis et beatorum patrum vita sectantes pro statu aeccle-

siae et salutae reges vel patriae valeant plenius Dominum exorare.

(7) [Episcopal duty of secondary "correctio"]: Et si, quod absit! ipsi monachi, de eorum regula aut religione te-
pidi aut negligenter reperti fuerint,
secundum eorum regulam ab abbate
suo corrigentur. Sin autem ipse abbas
non prevalet, tunc prefatus pontifex
cohercere debeat.

(7) [Episcopal duty of secondary "correctio"]: Et si aliquid ipsi monachi de
eorum religione tepedi aut an secus
egerint, secundum eorum regulam ab
eorum abba, si prevalit, corregantur;
sin autem, pontifex de ipsa civitate
choercire debeat.

Appendix 3

An Immunity of Charlemagne
(December 6, 777):
ChLA 19:28–33, no. 679*

+ Carolus gratia dei rex Francorum et Langobardorum atque patricius Romanorum. Oportet serenitas nostra, ut ea, que a fidelibus nostris postulata fuerint iustae et racionabiliter, pro seruitio et fidelitate, que circa genetore meo Pippino rege et circa me habere uiduntur, eis inpertire debeamus. Notum sit omnibus fidelibus nostris tam presentibus quam et futuris, qualiter ueniens Foleradus, cappellanus palacii nostri et abba sancti Dyonisii, nobis retulit priuuilegium a partibus sancti Dionisii, quem senodalis concilius anno nono ad Patrisbrunna ex promisso Angalramno episcopo et Uuilhario archyepiscopo constituerunt de res proprietatis suae in loco qui dicitur Salona, que est constructus in honore sancta dei genetrice et beatorum martyrum et confessorum et uirginum, ubi sanctus Priuatus marthur et sanctus Ilarus confessor requiescere uiduntur; et in eo priuuilegio insertum inuinimus, ut neque Angalramnus episcopus neque successoris sui neque arcidiaconus neque missus ecclesiae suae Mediomatricis ibi in ipso cenubio pontificium habere non debeant, nisi si abbas sancti Dionisii expetierit ordinacionis faciendi, cresmetandi et tabulas benedicendi. Interrogauimus Angalramnum episcopum, si ipsum priuuilegium consentire debuisset; et ipsi nullatenus denegauit, nisi sicut a senodale concilio constituerunt, quo episcopi sui sic consentunt, sicut ipsi priuuilegius clariter innotuit. Propterea talem preceptum et confirmationem emennare precipimus a partibus sancti Dyonisii, ut post hunc diem nullus quislibet episcoporum neque Angalramnus aut successoris sui ipso cenubio non contingat, nisi sit sub emunitate et priuuilegium sancti Dionisii regulariter sicut ceteras ecclesias, que ad

*See Chapter 6, note 3. I acknowledge with thanks permission from Urs Graf Verlag to reprint here the transcription in *Chartae Latinae antiquiores*.

ipsa casa sancti Dionisii aspicere uiduntur, et terrolas, que Angalramnus et Folradus infra ipso agro Salona et fine commutauerunt. Simile modo ex nostrum
promissum et confirmationem absque episcoporum Metinsis ecclesiae inpedi-
mentum pars sancti Dionisii una cum ipso cenubio Salona sub nostram tuitionem et defensionem et procerumque nostrorum partibus sancti Dionisii debeant respicere et quicquid per commutacionis regum aut dationem aut conlata
populi ibidem additum aut conlatum fuerit et Folradus de suas res ipso cenubio ditauit, sub emunitate et defensionem sancti Dionisii omnique tempore
permanere debeant ex nostra auctoritate confirmatum, ut melius dilectet ipsa
congregatione sancti Dyonisii et sancti Priuati et sancti Ilari pro nobis et prolis
uxoreque nostra domini misericordia adtencius deprecare. Et ut haec auctoritas firmior habeatur uel per tempora melius conseruetur, manu nostra propria
subter eam firmauimus et de anulo nostro siggellauimus.

Signum [Monogram] Caroli glorioissimi regis.

+ Rado relegi et subscripsi.

Datum quod fecit december dies sex, anno X regnante domno nostro Carolo
rege. Actum Aquis, palacio publico. In dei nomen feliciter.

Appendix 4

Carolingian Immunities and Asylum*

We have seen that the idea of asylum, an inviolable space connected with each church, was indeed an ingredient in the conception of even the earliest immunities. But Timbal Duclaux de Martin argues that during the Carolingian period, asylum was confused with immunity.[1] Magnou-Nortier argues that this "confusion" signified the development of an utterly new "asylum-immunity" unconnected to the immunity of the charters.[2] The term "immunity" was used because "the perimeter covered by asylum was [like the immunity] also 'outside' ordinary penal laws." However, she allows, in the course of time this use of the word may have influenced the understanding of judicial immunities, especially by suggesting clear territorial boundaries.

The sources attesting to this amalgamation are not the charters (as Magnou-Nortier makes clear) but rather the Carolingian capitularies. The *locus classicus* is the *Capitulare legibus additum* (803), c. 2.[3] It stipulates that if someone commits a crime within an immunity, he is to pay a fine of 600 solidi, an incredible sum; and if someone commits a crime outside an immunity but flees into one, the count is to demand that the immunist render up the guilty party to him. If the immunist refuses, he owes 15 solidi; 30 solidi if he refuses a second time; and he must pay the full cost of the crime's penalty if he resists a third time. Meanwhile, the count has the authority to seek the criminal within the immunity.

But there are real problems in saying that the capitularies created a new meaning for "immunities" and that this meaning confounded areas of immunity with asylum. There is no reason to assume that the capitularies were not referring to judicial immunities, especially once *defensio* was associated with the

*See Chapter 6, note 61.

1. Timbal Duclaux de Martin, *Le Droit d'Asile*, pp. 147–51.

2. Magnou-Nortier, "Étude sur le privilège," p. 488.

3. MGH Cap. reg. Fr. 1:113, no. 39.

latter. This pairing meant that immunity at times became a synonym for protection and jurisdiction, as in the phrase "that all churches and priests should be under the immunity and privilege and ordination and disposition of the bishops of each parish in which they are found."[4] It also meant that Carolingian kings, guardians of Church order, would take *all* churches under their immunity, as Louis the German did in 865: "We establish that the churches of God founded within the borders of our entire kingdom remain secure under the protection of our immunity [sub nostrae inmunitatis tuitione]."[5]

Carolingian immunities were certainly understood to be special and protected spaces, a fact clear enough from the enormous sum demanded for a crime committed within one. However, this does not show a confounding of immunity with asylum. On the contrary: the very next chapter of the *locus classicus* (c. 3) contrasts the immunity with the atrium (= [often] cemetery) of a church: "If anyone flees to a church, let him have peace in the atrium of this very church, nor need he actually enter the church; and no one may presume to take him out by force." This is asylum; and it is quite different from the immunity, discussed just above it, where the count is obliged to enter if the immunist is not willing to bring out the criminal.

A capitulary of Louis the Pious on the "honor" of the Church may be helpful.[6] Here, if a dispute begins outside a church but one party flees into it and then kills the other, the killer is required to pay 600 solidi to the church "which he polluted by homicide" and, over and above that, pay the king's ban. If this same kind of homicide occurs in the atrium of the church "whose door has been consecrated by the relics of the saints [reliquiis sanctorum consecrata est]," then the perpetrator must pay as above (i.e., 600 solidi and the ban of the king), whereas "if the door has not been consecrated, he ought to pay the amend for the crime he committed in the atrium as [*sicut*] he ought to pay for a crime when an immunity has been violated." It is true that *sicut* is ambiguous: it can mean "as if," comparing the crime in the atrium to one in an immunity only because the fine is the same; or it can mean "as for example," meaning that the violated immunity is a case of crime in an atrium. But either way, the article proposes to fix fines for protected spaces, not to argue that an immunity is equivalent to an unconsecrated atrium *qua* place of asylum. (But see Chapter 8 for the *later*, eleventh-century identification of immunity and atrium.)

Nor can it be said that the "immunities" of the capitularies were more "territorial" than judicial immunities were. We have already seen that the immunity for Tussonval prohibited agents ingress onto its properties. There is nothing very different from this in the spatial implications of the *locus classicus*, where the adverbs *infra* (within) and *foris* (outside) abound.

I am grateful to Michel Lauwers for calling some of these texts to my attention.

4. *Capitulare missorum Suessionense*, 853, c. 4, MGH Cap. reg. Fr. 2:268.
5. *Capitula papiae optimatibus ab imperatore pronuntiata*, c. 2, ibid., p. 92, no. 216.
6. *Capitula legibus addenda*, 818, 819, c. 1, ibid., 1:281.

Appendix 5

A Concession of King Berengar (August 24, 906): DBer no. 65, pp. 177–78*

+ In nomine domini Dei aeterni. Berengarius rex. Noverit omnium fidelium sanctae Dei Ecclesiae nostrorumque presentium scilicet ac futurorum devota sollertia, Ardingum reverentissimum episcopum dilectumque archicancellarium nostrum suppliciter nostrae serenitatis exorasse clementiam, quatenus ob Paganorum incursionem concederemus nostra auctoritate Audeberto diacono sanctae Veronensis aecclesiae licentiam aedificandi castrum in loco ubi dicitur Nogaria inter curtes Duorum Roborum et villam quae nominatur Tillioano, super ripam videlicet fluvii qui Tartarum dicitur, circa quod etiam castrum et infra ipsum castrum negotia exercere et mercatum ędificare prefati episcopi precibus licentiam eidem diacono tribuere perpetualiter dignaremur. Cuius dignis impetrationibus acclinati, in prenominato loco et fundo eumdem Audebertum diaconum castrum ędificare permisimus eumque cum bertiscis, merulorum propugnaculis atque fossatis omnique monitione et argumento affirmare hac inscriptione decrevimus, quatenus ipsum castrum nostra regali fisus auctoritate bertiscis circumdet, propugnaculis muniat, omnique argumento corroboret, et mercatum ibique nostra licentia construat ad suam proprietatem, theloneum, palificturam, ripaticum, reddibitiones, cunctasque exhibitiones vel districtiones, sive quicquid per aliquid aut ingenium regie parti exinde aliquando pertinere potuisset prelibato diacono iure proprietario in integrum concedimus et largimur. nullus quoque comes, vicecomes, sculdassio, gastaldio, decanus vel cuiuslibet dignitatis aut ordinis magna parvaque persona in eodem castro placitum custodire, aut aliud aliquid inibi ad regiam partem exigere vel vindicare, aut mansionaticas facere potestative presumat, vel de eodem mercato publice

*See Chapter 7, note 22.

parti aliquid persolvere cogatur, sed liceat ei iure proprietario omnia possidere, remota totius potestatis inquietudine vel minoratione. Contra quod nostrae concessionis preceptum si quis temerario ausu insurgere temptaverit, ut inchoata perficere nequeat, triginta libras auri optimi solvere cogatur, medietatem camerae palatii nostri et medietatem prelibato Audeberto diacono aut cui ipse haec omnia habere concesserit. Quod ut verius credatur et diligentius observetur, manu propria roborantes anulo nostro insigniri iussimus.

Signum domni [Monogram] Berengarii serenissimi regis.

Ambrosius cancellarius ad vicem Ardingi episcopi et archicancellarii recognovi et subscripsi.

Data non. kal. septemb., anno dominicae incarnationis .DCCCCVI., domni vero Berengarii piissimi regis .XVIII., indictione .VIIII. Actum Veronae. in Christi nomine feliciter, amen.

Appendix 6

Foundation Charters of Cluny (B.N.F. Coll. Bourg. 76, no.5) and Pothières/Vézelay (Auxerre, Bibliothèque Municipale MS 227, 22–24v): Key Clauses Compared*

Introductory summaries are in brackets; italics are used for key words; underlining is used for passages of similar wording. The clauses of the Vézelay charter[1] are not in order but rather are placed to so as to correspond to passages in Cluny's charter. If organized in numerical order, however, they may be reconstituted as in the original charter (N.B. Protocol, *Sanctio*, and Eschatocol are not included).

Cluny	Pothières/Vézelay
(1) [The property of Cluny is handed over to SS Peter and Paul] Res juris mei sanctis apostolis Petro videlicet et Paulo de propria *trado dominatione,* Clugniacum scilicet villam, cum cortile [etc].	(3) [Properties pertaining to Pothières are listed]
	(4) [Vézelay is founded as a "habitaculum ancillarum dei" in the same way ("pari ordine") as Pothières, with list of properties pertaining to it.]
	(5) [All property is joined to these monasteries with reservation of usufruct for the founders] Totum ergo ex

*See Chapter 8, note 9.

1. It should be noted that the foundation charter of Vézelay, which was originally a house of nuns, was also the charter for the foundation of Pothières.

integro quicquid in supranominatis villis vel agris acquisivimus . . . sacratissimis locis et monasteriis coadunavimus . . . tantum nobis, dum manemus in vita carnis, *usu fructuario reservato.*

(2) [A list of those benefiting from intercessory prayers of the monks at Cluny]
Primum pro amore Dei, inde pro anima senioris mei Odonis regis, progenitoris ac genitricis mee, pro me et uxore mea . . . pro Avanae [etc].

(1) [A list of those benefiting from intercessory prayers of the monks at Pothières] Pro salute eorum [Emperor Louis, his wife, Judith, their son "senior atque domnus noster rex," Charles the Bald] exoratio . . . sed et dignam rependentes genitoribus atque parentibus honorificentiam.

(3) [A regular life is to be established] Ut in Clugniaco in honore sanctorum apostolorum Petri et Pauli monasterium regulare construatur, ibique monachi juxta regulam beati Benedicti viventes congregentur, *qui ipsas res perhennis temporibus possideant, teneant, habeant [atque] ordinent;* ita duntaxat ut ibi venerabile oracionis domicilium votis ac subplicationibus fideliter frequentetur, conversatioque celestis omni desiderio et ardore intimo perquiratur et expetatur, sedule quoque oraciones, postulationes atque obsecrationes Domino dirigantur, tam pro me quam pro omnibus.
(4) [The monks and all the property of the monastery are placed under Abbot Berno's power and control] Sintque ipsi monachi cum omnibus prescriptis rebus *sub potestate et dominatione* Bernonis abbatis, qui, quandiu vixerit, secundum suum scire et posse eis regulariter presideat.

(2) [A regular life is to be established] Fundatus . . . est locus devotionis nostrae in honore domini nostri Iesu Christi et veneratione beatissimorum apostolorum Petri et Pauli . . . ad villam quam ex antiquo Pultarias nominant . . . ut ibi venerabile orationis domicilium votis ac supplicationibus fidelium frequentetur conversatioque celestis sub regulari districtione et institutione beati Benedicti viventium.

(5) [When Berno dies, the monks have the right to choose their own abbot without interference] Post discessum

(10) [When the abbot or abbess dies, each community has the right to choose another, with the approval of

vero ejus, habeant idem monachi potestatem et licentiam quemcumque
sui ordinis, secundum placitum Dei
adque regulam Sancti Benedicti pro-
mulgatam, eligere maluerint *abbatem
adque rectorum, ita ut nec nostra nec
alicujus potestatis contradictione . . . in-
pediantur.*

(6) [A census is to be paid to Rome for
its protection] Per quinquennium autem <u>Rome</u> ad limina <u>apostolorum</u> ad
luminaria ipsorum concinnanda, x
solidos prefati monachi persolvant;
habeantque <u>tuitionem</u> *ipsorum apostolorum <u>atque</u> Romani pontificis <u>defen-
sionem</u>.*
(7) [The charity of the monks]
Prout oportunitas adque possibilitas
ejusdem loci sese dederit, cotidie misericordiae opera pauperibus, indi-
gentibus, advenis, peregrinantibus . . .
exibeatur.

(8) [The property of the monastery is
independent of all earthly powers] Ut
ab hac die *nec nostro, nec parentum nostrorum,* nec fastibus regie magnitudi-
nis, nec cujuslibet terrenę potestatis
jugo, subiciantur idem monachi ibi
congregati; neque aliquis principum
secularium, non comes quisquam, nec
episcopus quilibet, *non <u>pontifex</u>* supradicte sedis Romanae . . . invadat res ipsorum servorum Dei, non distrahat,
non minuat, non procamiet, non <u>*beneficiet*</u> alicui.

(9) [No one may place any prelate over
them against their will] Non aliquem
prelatum super eos contra eorum voluntatem constituat.

the pope] Ut quotiens abbas vel ab-
batissa de prefatis monasteriis . . . ex
hac luce migraverint, congregationes
ipse . . . habeant concessam sibi potestatem . . . alterum vel alteram . . . ex
suo consortio atque collegio electum
vel electam preficiendi, *prosequente
pontificis super hac re probatione.*

(7) [The monastery shall pay no dues
except a census to Rome, to which the
monastery is subjected] Pro benedictione annis singulis ad reverentissi-
mam sedem beatorum <u>apostolorum</u>,
cui loca eadem *subdidimus,* <u>Roma</u>e of-
ferantur beato pontifici Urbi librae argenti duae . . . ; liberi tamen ab aliis ex-
hibitionibus.

(6) [The founders are the protectors of
the monasteries] <u>Tuitionem</u> quoque
<u>atque defensionem</u> . . . *sub nostra cura*
habentes.

(9) [The monasteries and their properties are subjected to Peter and Paul at
Rome and to the control of the pope]
Hoc vero monasterium sive aliud su-
pranominatum cum omnibus rebus
ibi collatis beatissimis apostolis apud
Romam *subdidimus* et testamentario
libello dato aeterne sanctis <u>pontifici</u>-
bus Urbis illius, qui vice apostolica
annis sequentibus sedem *tenuerint ad
regendum, ordinandum* (non tamen ut
<u>benefici</u>aria potestate cuiquam dandi
aut procaminandi licentia sit) *disponendumque* perpetuo commisimus.

(10) [Peter, Paul and the Roman pope should loose from the society of the church those who disturb Cluny's property] (Petrus, Paulus, pontifex) alienetis a consortio sanctae Dei ecclesię. . . predones et invasores atque distractatores harum rerum.

(11) [Peter, Paul, and the pope should be protectors of Cluny] (Petrus, Paulus, pontifex) . . . sitisque tutores ac *defensores* jam dicti loci Clugniaci et servorum Dei ibi commanencium.

(12) [No one is to alter the founders' vow of piety or disturb it, else he be condemned by King Charles and by sentence of the pope] Inhibemus, ne cui pietatis nostrae votum liceat in perpetuum commutare vel prepostero ordine irrumpendo perturbare. Quod siquis . . . presumpserit . . . Karoli pii regis precepto damnatus . . . [atque] ex sententia sancti pontificis Urbis ut sacrilegus et sacrarum rerum fraudator a cetu populi dei extraneus penam aeternam . . . incurrat.

(13) [The pope is to be the ruler, consoler, and protector of the monks and nuns] Sit eis *rector*, assiduus consolator et tutor.

(11) [The number of entrants is restricted so as not to burden the monasteries]

Appendix 7

An Immunity of John XI (March 931): Zimmermann 1:107–8, no. 64*

Johannes episcopus, servus servorum Dei, Oddoni venerabili abbati monasterii Cluniensis aedificati in honore beatorum apostolorum Petri et Pauli, siti in pago Matisconensi, et per te in eodem monasterio tuisque successoribus in perpetuum.

Convenit apostolico moderamini benivola conpassione pie poscentium votis succurrere et alacri devotione his prebere adsensum. Ex hoc enim potissimum premium a conditore omnium Deo promerebimur. Igitur quia petistis a nobis, quatenus predictum monasterium in illo statu, quo a Uuilelmo duce per testamentum manere decretum est, nostra apostolica auctoritate in perpetuum constare decerneremus, sanctae Romane, cui Deo auctore deservimus, aecclesiae subiectum est, inclinati precibus tuis tibi ad regendum concedimus. Itaque sit illud monasterium cum omnibus rebus, vel quas nunc habet vel que deinceps ibi tradite fuerint, liberum a dominatu cuiuscunque regis aut episcopi sive comitis aut cuiuslibet ex propinquis ipsius Uuilelmi. Nullus ibidem contra voluntatem monachorum prelatum eis post tuum dicessum ordinare presumat, sed habeant liberam facultatem, sine cuiuslibet principis consultu quemcunque secundum regulam sancti Benedicti voluerint, sibi ordinare; nisi forte, quod absit, personam suis vitiis consentientem eligere maluerint; hoc quicunque voluerit, cum zelo Dei prohibeat. Cenobium, quod Romanis dicitur et quod mater filii nostri Rodulfi regis condonavit ad predictum Cluniacum, ita ei cum Uaningo villa subiectum sit, sicut illa per testamentum donationis decrevit. Si autem cenobium aliquod ex voluntate illorum, ad quorum dispositionem pertinere videtur, in sua ditione ad meliorandum suscipere consenseritis, nostram licentiam

---

*See Chapter 8, note 31. The sentence enclosed in angle brackets (⟨⟩) is an eleventh-century interpolation.

ex hoc habeatis. Decimas vero, quę olim ad vestras capellas pertinuerunt et per modernam quasi auctoritatem sive licentiam a quolibet episcopo subtracte sunt, vobis ex integro restituimus. Capellas autem, si aliquę iam facte vel faciende inibi sunt, ita manere concedimus, ut vestris ecclesiis nichil ex decimis minuetur. Hoc vero, quod dilectus filius noster Berno episcopus de predictis capellis vobis concessit, ratum esse decernimus in perpetuum. Preterea quicquid ex vineis vel culturis ad vestram partem pertinet, partem quoque decimarum ad hospitale vestrum pertinere sancimus, similiter et de his rebus, quas percepturi estis. Hoc etiam, quod Leobaldus ad predictum monasterium moriens reddidit et dereliquid, similiter et illud, quod in Agiona vel alicubi rebus, quę ad id monasterium pertinere debent, et capellam sancti Martini, quę est in villa Maceio, nostra apostolica auctoritate vobis confirmamus et restituimus. ⟨Monetam propriam sicut filius noster Rodulfus rex Francorum concessit, ita habeatis.⟩ Et quia nimis, sicut compertum est, iam poene cuncta monasteria a suo proposito prevaricantur, concedimus ut, si quis monachus ex quolibet monasterio ad vestram conversationem solo dumtaxat meliorande vitae studio transmigrare voluerit, cui videlicet suus abbas regularem sumptum ad depellendam proprietatem habendi ministrare neglexerit, suscipere vobis liceat, quousque monasterii sui conversatio emendetur. Immunitatem vero ita vobis concedimus, sicut locis sanctis ubique reverentia debetur, ut nullus vestra mancipia aut res quaslibet sine vestro consultu distringere aut invadere ullo modo presumat. Sane ad recognoscendum, quod predictum cenobium sanctae apostolicę sedi ad tuendum atque fovendum pertineat, dentur per quinquennium decem solidi. Si quis autem contra hanc saluberrimam nostram constitutionem resistendo venire temptaverit aut aliquid horum corrumpere conatus fuerit et omnia, quę in hoc privilegio sanccimus, non observaverit, sciat se sub divini iudicii obtestatione anathematis vinculo aeternaliter, nisi resipuerit, innodatum et a regno Dei alienandum et cum diabolo sine fine cruciandum. Qui vero huius nostre saluberrimae sanccionis custos et observator exstiterit, a Christo Domino benedictionem et a sanctis apostolis, mundi iudicibus, absolutionem hic et in futuro consequi mereatur.

Scriptum per manum Andreae scriniarii in mense Martio, indictione quarta.

Selected Bibliography

Manuscript Sources

Monza, Biblioteca Capitolare 7B 15/98 (Sacramentary of Berengar)
Paris, B.N.F. Coll. Bourg. 76 no.5 (foundation charter of Cluny)
Paris, B.N.F. n.a.l. 2262 (Cluny's Cartulary C)

Printed Primary Sources

Acta Sanctorum quotquot toto orbe coluntur. Edited by Joannus Bollandus et al. 69 vols. Antwerp, etc., 1643–1940.

Adams, John. *The Legal Papers of John Adams.* Edited by Kinvin L. Wroth and Hiller B. Zobel. Vol. 2, *Cases 31–62.* Cambridge, Mass, 1965.

Die älteste erreichbare Gestalt des Liber Sacramentorum anni circuli der römischen Kirche (Cod. Pad. D 47, fol. 11r–100r). Edited by P. Kunibert Mohlberg and Anton Baumstark. Liturgiegeschichtliche Quellen 11/12. Münster, 1927.

Andrieu, Michel, ed. "Réglement d'Angilramne de Metz (768–791) fixant les honoraires de quelques fonctions liturgiques." *Revue des Sciences religieuses* 10 (1930): 349–69.

Annales Fuldenses. MGH SRG. Hannover, 1891.

Annales Mettenses Priores. Edited by B. von Simson. MGH SRG. Hannover, 1905.

Arnold, Morris S., ed. *Select Cases of Trespass from the King's Courts, 1307–1399.* 2 vols. Publications of the Selden Society 100, 103. London, 1985–87.

Baudonivia. *Vita Radegundis.* Bk. 2. Edited by Bruno Krusch. MGH SRM 2:377–95. Hannover, 1888.

Bede. *Historia abbatum.* In *Venerabilis Baedae opera historica.* Edited by Charles Plummer. 2 vols. Oxford, 1896.

———. *Historia Ecclesiastica Gentis Anglorum.* Edited and translated by Bertram Colgrave and R. A. B. Mynors. In *Bede's Ecclesiastical History of the English People.* Oxford, 1969.

———. *Vita S. Cuthberti Prosaica.* Edited by Bertram Colgrave. In *Two Lives of*

Saint Cuthbert: A Life by an Anonymous Monk of Lindisfarne and Bede's Prose Life. Cambridge, 1940.

Beleth, John. *Summa de ecclesiasticis officiis.* Edited by Heriberto Douteil. Corpus Christianorum Continuatio Mediaevalis 41A. Turnhout, 1976.

Blackstone, William. *Commentaries on the Laws of England.* 5th ed. Oxford, 1773.

Boniface. *Epistolae.* Edited by Michael Tangl. In *Die Briefe des heiligen Bonifatius und Lullus,* MGH Epp. sel. 1.

Bullaire de l'Abbaye Saint-Gilles. Edited by Etienne M. Goiffon. Nîmes, 1882.

Bullarium sacri ordinis Cluniacensis. [Edited by Petrus Simon.] Lyon, 1680.

Caesarius of Arles. *Oeuvres monastiques.* SC 345. Paris, 1988.

van Caenegem, R. C., ed. and trans. *English Lawsuits from William I to Richard I.* 2 vols. Publications of the Selden Society 106, 107. London, 1990–91.

———, ed. *Royal Writs in England from the Conquest to Glanvill. Studies in the Early History of the Common Law.* Publications of the Seldon Society 77. London, 1959.

Cartulaire de l'abbaye de Cysoing et de ses dépendances. Edited by Ignace de Coussemaker. Lille, 1883.

Cartulaire de l'abbaye de Gorze, MS 826 de la Bibliothèque de Metz. Edited by Armand d'Herbomez. Mettensia 2. Paris, 1898.

Cartulaire de l'abbaye de Saint-Bertin. Edited by Benjamin Guérard. Collection des cartulaires de France 3. Paris, 1840.

Cartulaire de l'abbaye de Saint-Victor de Marseilles. Edited by Benjamin Guérard. 2 vols. Collection des cartulaires de France 8–9. Paris, 1857.

Cartulaires des abbayes d'Aniane et de Gellone. Vol. 1, *Cartulaire d'Aniane.* Edited by Léon Cassan and Edmond Meynial. Montpellier, 1900.

Cartularium saxonicum: A Collection of Charters Relating to Anglo-Saxon History. Edited by Walter de Gray Birch. 3 vols. London, 1885–93.

Chartae Latinae Antiquiores. Facsimile Edition of the Latin Charters Prior to the Ninth Century. Edited by Albert Bruckner and Robert Marichal. 46 vols. Lausanne and Dietikon-Zurich, 1954–1996.

Chrodegang. *Rule for Canons.* Edited by Jean-Baptiste Pelt. *Études sur la Cathédrale de Metz.* Vol. 1, *V^e–XIIIe siècle.* Metz, 1937.

Clanchy, Michael T., ed. and trans. *The Roll and Writ File of the Berkshire Eyre of 1248.* Publications of the Selden Society 90. London, 1973.

Close Rolls of the Reign of Henry III Preserved in the Public Record Office. London, 1902–22. Reprint, 1970.

Codex Lauréshamensis. Edited by Karl Glöckner. 3 vols. Darmstadt, 1929.

Codex Theodosianus. Edited by Theodor Mommsen et al. 2 vols., 1904. Reprint, Dublin, 1971. Translated by Clyde Pharr under the title *The Theodosian Code* (Princeton, 1952).

Codice diplomatico del monastero di S. Colombano di Bobbio fino all'anno MCCVIII. Vol. 1. Edited by Carlo Cipolla. Fonti per la storia d'Italia 52. Rome, 1918.

Codice Diplomatico Istriano. Edited by Pietro Kandler. Vol. 1, *Anni 50–1194.* Trieste, 1862. Reprint, 1986.

Columbanus. *Opera*. Edited and translated by G. S. M. Walker. Scriptores Latini Hiberniae 2. Dublin, 1957.

Concilia Galliae a.314–a.506. Edited by Charles Munier. CCSL 148. Turnhout, 1963.

Concilia Galliae a.511–a.695. Edited by Charles de Clercq. CCSL 148A. Turnhout, 1963.

Corpus Consuetudinum Monasticarum. Edited by Kassius Hallinger. 14 vols. Siegburg, 1963–.

Curia Regis Rolls (Great Britain). London, 1926. Reprint, 1971.

Desiderius of Cahors. *Epistulae*. Edited by Dag Norberg. Acta Universitatis Stockholmiensis. Studia Latina Stockholmiensia 6. Uppsala, 1961.

The Documentary History of the Ratification of the Constitution. Madison, Wis., 1976–93.

Donatus. *Vita Trudonis confessoris Hasbaniensis*. MGH SRM 6:264–98.

Douglas, David C., ed. *Feudal Documents from the Abbey of Bury St. Edmunds*. British Academy Records of the Social and Economic History of England and Wales 8. London, 1932.

Eigil, *Vita Sturmi*. In *Die Vita Sturmi des Eigil von Fulda*. Edited by Pius Engelbert. Marburg, 1968.

English Historical Documents. Vol. 1, *c. 500–1042*. 2d ed. Edited by Dorothy Whitelock. London, 1979. Vol. 2, *1042–1189*. 2d ed. Edited by David C. Douglas and George W. Greenaway. London, 1981.

English Reports. Edinburgh, 1900–1930.

FitzNigel, Richard. *Dialogus de Scaccario*. In *Dialogus de Scaccario (The Course of the Exchequer)*. Edited and translated by Charles Johnson, with corrections by F. E. L. Carter and D. E. Greenway. Oxford, 1983.

Fortunatus. *Vita Radegundis*. Bk.1. Edited by Bruno Krusch. MGH SRM 2:364–77.

Fredegar. *Chronicle*. Edited by Bruno Krusch. MGH SRM 2:1–193. Also J. M. Wallace-Hadrill, ed. and trans., *The Fourth Book of the Chronicle of Fredegar* (London, 1960).

Gallia Christiana. 16 vols. 1715–1865.

Gesta Berengarii imperatoris. Edited by Ernst Dümmler. Halle, 1871.

Gregory of Catino. *Destructio Monasterii Farfensis*. In *Il Chronicon Farfense di Gregorio di Catino*. Edited by Ugo Balzani. Fonti per la storia d'Italia 33. Rome, 1903.

Gregory of Tours. *Historiarum libri decem*. Edited by Bruno Krusch and Rudolf Buchner. 2 vols. Ausgewählte Quellen zur deutschen Geschichte des Mittelalters 2–3. Darmstadt, 1977.

———. *Liber in Gloria Confessorum*. Edited by Bruno Krusch. MGH SRM 1, pt. 2.

———. *Liber in Gloria Martyrum*. Edited by Bruno Krusch. MGH SRM 1, pt. 2.

Gregory the Great. *Registrum*. Edited by Dag Norberg. CCSL 140A. Turnhout, 1982.

I diplomi di Berengario I. Edited by Luigi Schiaparelli. Fonti per la Storia d'Italia 35. Rome, 1903.

I diplomi di Guido e di Lamberto. Edited by Luigi Schiaparelli. Fonti per la Storia d'Italia 36. Rome, 1906.

I diplomi Italiani di Lodovico III e di Rodolfo II. Edited by Luigi Schiaparelli. Fonti per la Storia d'Italia 37. Rome, 1910.

Isidore of Seville. *Synonyma.* PL 83, cols. 825–68.

Jonas. *Vita Sancti Columbani.* Edited by Bruno Krusch. MGH SRM 34. Hannover, 1902.

Jotsaldus. *De vita et virtutibus sancti Odilonis abbatis.* PL 142, cols. 897–962.

Justinian. *Digesta = The Digest of Justinian.* Edited by Theodor Mommsen and Paul Krueger. Translated by Alan Watson. 4 vols. Philadelphia, 1985.

Lambard, William. *Eirenarcha: or of the Office of Justices of Peace.* London, 1582.

Lapérouse, Jean-François de. *Voyage autour du monde sur l'Astrolabe et la Boussole (1785–1788).* Edited by Hélène Minguet. Paris, 1980.

Lex Baiwariorum. Edited by E. von Schwind. MGH Leges 5, pt. 2.

Lex Ribuaria. Edited by Rudolf Sohm. MGH Fontes. Hannover, 1883.

Liber Diurnus Romanorum Pontificum. Edited by Hans Foerster. Bern, 1958.

Liber Historiae Francorum. Edited by B. Krusch. MGH SRM 2:215–328.

Liber tramitis aevi odilonis abbatis. Edited by Petrus Dinter. CCM 10.

Liebermann, Felix. *Die Gesetze der Angelsachsen.* 3 vols. Halle a. S., 1903–16.

Liutprand. *Antapodosis.* Edited by Joseph Becker. MGH SRG. Hannover, 1915.

Manaresi, Cesare, ed. *I Placiti del "Regnum Italiae."* 3 vols. Fonti per la storia d'Italia 92, 96–97. Rome, 1955–60.

Marculfi Formularum libri duo. Edited by Alf Uddholm. Uppsala, 1962.

Marowe, Thomas. *De Pace Terre et Ecclesie.* In Bertha H. Putnam, ed., *Early Treatises on the Practice of the Justices of the Peace in the Fifteenth and Sixteenth Centuries.* Oxford Studies in Social and Legal History 7. Oxford, 1924.

Monumenta Vizeliacensia. Textes relatifs à l'histoire de l'abbaye de Vézelay. Edited by R. B. C. Huygens. Corpus Christianorum Continuatio Mediaevalis 42. Turnhout, 1976.

Odilo. *Sermones.* PL 142, cols. 991–1036.

Odo. *De Vita Sancti Geraldi.* PL 133, cols. 639–704.

Österreichische Weistümer. Edited by Akademie der Wissenschaften in Wien. 15 vols. Vienna, 1870–1960.

Pactus Legis Salicae. Edited and translated by Karl August Eckhardt. Vol. 2, *65 Titel-Text.* Göttingen 1955.

Papsturkunden, 896–1046. Edited by Harald Zimmermann. 2d ed. 3 vols. Vienna, 1988–89.

Papsturkunden in Frankreich. New ser., , vol. 5, *Touraine, Anjou, Maine und Bretagne.* Edited by Johannes Ramackers. Abhandlungen der Akademie der Wissenschaften in Göttingen, 3d ser., 35. Göttingen, 1956.

Pardessus, Jean Marie, ed. *Diplomata, chartae, epistolae, leges aliaque instrumenta ad res Gallo-Francicas spectantia*. 2 vols. Paris, 1843–1849. Reprint, 1969.
Passio Leudegarii Episcopi Augustodunensis I. Edited by Bruno Krusch. MGH SRM 5:282–322.
Paul Warnefrid [the Deacon]. *Liber de episcopis Mettensibus*. MGH SS 2:260–70.
Le pontifical romano-germanique du dixième siècle. Edited by Cyrille Vogel and Reinhard Elze. 3 vols. Studi e Testi 226, 227, 269. Vatican City, 1963–72.
Recueil de chroniques de Touraine. Edited by André Salmon. Collection de documents sur l'histoire de Touraine 1. Tours, 1854.
Recueil des actes de Charles II le Chauve, roi de France. Edited by Georges Tessier. 3 vols. Paris, 1943–55.
Recueil des actes de Charles III le Simple, roi de France. Edited by Philippe Lauer. 2 vols. Paris, 1940.
Recueil des actes de Louis IV, roi de France (936–954). Edited by Philippe Lauer. Paris, 1914.
Recueil des actes de Robert Ier et de Raoul, rois de France (922–936). Edited by Jean Dufour and Robert-Henri Bautier. Paris, 1978.
Recueil des actes des ducs de Normandie de 911 à 1066. Edited by Marie Faroux. Mémoires de la société des antiquaires de Normandie 36. 4th ser., vol. 6. Caen, 1961.
Recueil des actes des rois de Provence (855–928). Edited by René Poupardin. Paris, 1920.
Recueil des chartes de l'abbaye de Cluny. Edited by Auguste Bernard and Alexandre Bruel. 6 vols. Paris, 1876–1903.
Recueil des chartes de l'abbaye de Saint-Germain-des-Prés. Edited by René Poupardin. Paris, 1909.
Recueil des historiens des Gaules et de la France. Edited by Martin Bouquet and Léopold Delisle. Vols. 1–13. Paris, 1738–86. Vols. 14–24. Paris, 1806–1904.
Regesta Alsatiae aevi Merovingici et Karolini, 496–918. Edited by Albert Bruckner. Vol. 1, *Quellenband*. Strasbourg, 1949.
Regesta Regum Anglo-Normannorum, 1066–1154. Vol. 1, *Regesta Willelmi Conquestoris et Willelmi Rufi, 1066–1100*. Edited by H. W. C. Davis. Oxford, 1913. Vol. 2, *Regesta Henrici Primi*. Edited by Charles Johnson and H. A. Cronne. Oxford, 1956.
Regesto della chiesa cattedrale di Modena. Edited by Emilio Paolo Vicini. 2 vols. Regesta Chartarum Italiae 16 and 21. Rome 1931, 1936.
Regino. *Chronicon*. Edited by F. Kurze. MGH SRG. Hannover, 1890.
Regula Benedicti. The Rule of St. Benedict in Latin and English with Notes. Edited by Timothy Fry. Collegeville, Minn., 1980.
Les Reports des Cases . . . (Yearbooks 1307–1483). London, 1674. Reprint, 1981.
Sacrorum Conciliorum Nova et Amplissima Collectio. Edited by J. D. Mansi. Florence, 1757–98.

Schwind, Ernst, and Alfons Dopsch, eds. *Ausgewählte Urkunden zur Verfassungs-geschichte der deutsch-österreichischen Erblande im Mittelalter*. Innsbruck, 1895. Reprint, 1968.

Statutes at Large from Magna Charta to . . . 1761. Edited by Danby Pickering. Cambridge, 1762.

Statutes of the Realm. 11 vols. in 12. London, 1810–1828. Reprint, Buffalo, 1993.

Stubbs, William, and H. W. C. Davis, eds. *Select Charters and Other Illustrations of English Constitutional History*. 9th rev. ed. Oxford, 1921.

Thorpe, Francis Newton. *The Federal and State Constitutions, Colonial Charters, and Other Organic Laws*. 7 vols. Washington, D.C., 1909.

Versus de episcopis Mettensis civitatis quomodo sibi ex ordine successerunt. In *Die Gedichte des Paulus Diaconus. Kritische und erklärende Ausgabe*. Edited by Karl Neff. Quellen und Untersuchungen zur lateinischen Philologie des Mittelalters 3/4. Munich, 1908.

Vita Agili. AASS August VI. Pp. 575–87.

Vita Audoini Episcopi Rotomagensis. Edited by Wilhelm Levison. MGH SRM 5:536–67.

Vita Balthildis. Edited by Bruno Krusch. MGH SRM 2:275–508.

Vita Desiderii Caturcensis. Edited by Bruno Krusch. MGH SRM 4:563–69.

Vita Eligii Episcopi Noviomagensis. Edited by Bruno Krusch. MGH SRM 4: 663–741.

Vita Fursei Abbatis Latiniacensis. Edited by Bruno Krusch. MGH SRM 4:434–40.

Secondary Works

À Cluny, Congrès scientifique. Fêtes et cérémonies liturgiques en l'honneur des saints Abbes Odon et Odilon, 9–11 juillet 1949. Dijon, 1950.

Algazi, Gadi. "Lords Ask, Peasants Answer: Making Traditions in Late Medieval Village Assemblies." In *Between History and Histories: The Making of Silences and Commemorations*. Edited by Gerald Sider and Gavin Smith. Pp. 199–229. Toronto, 1998.

———. "Otto Brunner—'Konkrete Ordnung' und Sprache der Zeit." In *Geschichtsschreibung als Legitimationswissenschaft, 1918–1945*. Edited by Peter Schöttler. Frankfurt am Main, 1997.

Amann, Émile, and Auguste Dumas. *L'Église au pouvoir des laïques (888–1057)*. Vol. 7, *Histoire de l'Église*. Edited by Augustin Fliche and Victor Martin. Paris, 1948.

Andenna, Giancarlo. "Grandi patrimoni, funzioni pubbliche e famiglie su di un territorio. Il 'comitatus plumbiensis' e i suoi conti dal ix all'xi secolo." In *Formazione e strutture dei ceti dominanti nel Medioevo. Marchesi, conti e visconti nel regno italico (secc. ix–xii). Atti del primo convegno di Pisa, 10–11 May 1983*. Pp. 201–27. Rome, 1988.

Angenendt, Arnold. *Das Frühmittelalter. Die abendländische Christenheit von 400 bis 900.* Stuttgart, 1990.

———. *Kaiserherrschaft und Königstaufe. Kaiser, Könige und Päpste als geistliche Patrone in der abendländischen Missionsgeschichte.* Arbeiten zur Frühmittelalterforschung 15. Berlin, 1984

———. *Monachi peregrini. Studien zu Pirmin und den monastischen Vorstellungen des frühen Mittelalters.* Munich, 1972.

———. "Pirmin und Bonifatius. Ihr Verhältnis zu Mönchtum, Bischofsamt und Adel." In Borst, *Mönchtum, Episkopat und Adel,* pp. 251–304.

Anton, Hans Hubert. *Studien zu den Klosterprivilegien der Päpste im frühen Mittelalter.* Beiträge zur Geschichte und Quellenkunde des Mittelalters 4. Berlin, 1975.

Appelt, Heinrich. "Die Anfänge des päpstlichen Schutzes." *MIÖG* 62 (1954): 101–11.

Ariès, Philippe, and Georges Duby, eds. *A History of Private Life.* Vol. 2, *Revelations of the Medieval World.* Translated by Arthur Goldhammer. Cambridge, Mass., 1988.

Arnaldi, G. "Alberico di Spoleto." In *DBI* 1:657–59.

———. "Berengario." In *DBI* 9:1–26.

Arnold, Morris S., ed. *On the Laws and Customs of England: Essays in Honor of S. E. Thorne.* Chapel Hill, N.C., 1981.

Atsma, Hartmut, and Jean Vezin. "Cluny et Tours au Xe siècle. Aspects diplomatiques, paléographiques et hagiographiques" In Constable, Melville, and Oberste, *Die Cluniazenser,* pp. 121–32.

Atsma, Hartmut, ed. *La Neustrie. Les Pays au Nord de la Loire de 650 à 850.* 2 vols. Sigmaringen, 1989.

Bader, Karl Siegfried. *Das Mittelalterliche Dorf als Friedens- und Rechtsbereich.* Vol. 1. Weimar, 1957. Reprint, 1967.

Bates, David. *Normandy before 1066.* London, 1982.

Bergengruen, Alexander. *Adel und Grundherrschaft im Merowingerreich. Siedlungs- und Standesgeschichtliche Studien zu den Anfängen des fränkischen Adels in Nordfrankreich und Belgien.* Vierteljahrschrift für Sozial- und Wirtschaftsgeschichte, Beihefte 41. Wiesbaden, 1958.

Bergmann, Werner. "Untersuchungen zu den Gerichtsurkunden der Merowingerzeit." *Archiv für Diplomatik* 22 (1976): 1–186.

Berlow, Rosalind K. "Spiritual Immunity at Vézelay (Ninth to Twelfth Centuries)." *Catholic Historical Review* 62 (1976): 573–88.

Beyerle, Franz. "Das Formelbuch des westfränkischen Mönchs Markulf und Dagoberts Urkunde für Rebais a. 635." *Deutsches Archiv für Erforschung des Mittelalters* 9 (1951): 43–58.

Bitel, Lisa M. *Isle of the Saints: Monastic Settlement and Christian Community in Early Ireland.* Ithaca, N.Y., 1990.

Blackstone's Commentaries on the Laws of England (1773). Edited by Bernard C. Gavit. Washington, D.C., 1941.

Bloch, Marc. *Feudal Society*. Translated by L. A. Manyon. 2 vols. Chicago, 1961.

Bogen, David S. "The Privileges and Immunities Clause of Article IV." *Case Western Reserve Law Review* 37 (1987): 794–861.

Bonnassie, Pierre. *La catalogne du milieu du Xe à la fin du XIe siècle. Croissance et mutations d'une société*. 2 vols. Toulouse, [1975–76].

Bonnet, Charles. *Les fouilles de l'ancien groupe épiscopal de Genève (1976–1993)*. Geneva, 1993.

Borst, Arno, ed. *Mönchtum, Episkopat und Adel zur Gründungszeit des Klosters Reichenau*. Vorträge und Forschungen 20. Sigmaringen, 1974.

Brand, Paul. "Lordship and Distraint in Thirteenth Century England." In *Thirteenth Century England*. Vol. 3. Proceedings of the Newcastle Upon Tyne Conference, 1989. Edited by P. R. Coss and S. D. Lloyd. Woodbridge, 1991.

Breukelaar, Adriaan H. B. *Historiography and Episcopal Authority in Sixth-Century Gaul: The Histories of Gregory of Tours Interpreted in Their Historical Context*. Forschungen zur Kirchen- und Dogmengeschichte 57. Göttingen, 1994.

Brown, Peter. *The Rise of Western Christendom: Triumph and Diversity, AD 200–1000*. Oxford, 1997.

Brühl, Carlrichard. *Deutschland-Frankreich. Die Geburt zweier Völker*. Cologne, 1990.

———."Die merowingische Immunität." In *Chiesa e mondo feudale nei secoli X–XII. Atti della dodicesima Settimana internazionale di studio Mendola, 24–28 agosto 1992*. Pp. 27–43. Miscellanea del Centro di studi medioevali 14. Milan, 1995.

Brunner, Otto. *Land und Herrschaft. Grundfragen der territorialen Verfassungsgeschichte Österreichs im Mittelalter*. 4th ed. Vienna, 1959. Translated by Howard Kaminsky and James Van Horn Melton under the title *"Land" and Lordship: Structures of Governance in Medieval Austria*. Philadelphia, 1992.

Cam, Helen. "An East Anglian Shire-moot of Stephen's reign, 1148–53." *English Historical Review* 39 (1924): 568–71.

———."The Evolution of the Mediaeval English Franchise." *Speculum* 32 (1957): 427–42.

———. *The Hundred and the Hundred Rolls: An Outline of Local Government in Medieval England*. London, 1930.

———. *Liberties and Communities in Medieval England: Collected Studies in Local Administration and Topography*. Cambridge, 1944.

Canning, Joseph. *A History of Medieval Political Thought, 300–1450*. London, 1996.

Chaume, Maurice. *Les origines du duché de Bourgogne*. Part 1, fasc. 3. Dijon, 1931. Reprint, 1977.

Cheyette, Fredric L. "The Royal Safeguard in Medieval France." *Studia Gratiana* 15 (1972): 631–52.

Clanchy, Michael T. "The Franchise of Return of Writs." *TRHS*, 5th ser., 17 (1967): 59–82.

Clarke, H. B., and Mary Brennan, eds. *Columbanus and Merovingian Monasticism.* BAR International Series 113. Oxford, 1981.

Claussen, Martin. "Community, Tradition, and Reform in Early Carolingian Francia: Chrodegang and the Canons of Metz Cathedral." Ph.D. diss., University of Virginia, 1991.

Conant, Kenneth John. *Cluny. Les églises et la maison du chef d'ordre.* Mâcon, 1968.

Constable, Giles. *Monastic Tithes: From Their Origins to the Twelfth Century.* Cambridge, 1964.

Constable, Giles, Gert Melville, and Jörg Oberste, eds. *Die Cluniazenser in ihrem politisch-sozialen Umfeld.* Vita regularis. Ordnungen und Deutungen religiosen Lebens im Mittelalter 7. Münster, 1998.

Coulin, Alexander. "Die Wüstung. Ein Beitrag zur Geschichte des Strafrechts." *Zeitschrift für vergleichende Rechtswissenschaft, einschliesslich ethnologischen Rechtsforschung* 32 (1914/15): 326–501.

Coville, Alfred. *Recherches sur l'histoire de Lyon du Vme siècle au IXme siècle (450–800).* Paris, 1928.

Cowdrey, Herbert E. J. "Cardinal Peter of Albano's Legatine Journey to Cluny (1080)." *Journal of Theological Studies,* n.s., 24 (1973): 481–91.

———. *The Cluniacs and the Gregorian Reform.* Oxford, 1970.

Crozet, René. "Le Voyage d'Urbain II en France (1095–1096) et son importance au point de vue archéologique." *Annales du Midi* 49 (1937): 42–69.

———."Le Voyage d'Urbain II et ses négociations avec le clergé de France (1095–1096)." *Revue historique* 179 (1937): 271–310.

Cuddihy, William J. "The Fourth Amendment: Origins and Original Meaning, 602–1791." Ph.D. diss., Claremont Graduate School, 1990.

Cuddihy, William J., and B. Carmon Hardy, "A Man's House Was Not His Castle: Origins of the Fourth Amendment to the United States Constitution." *William and Mary Quarterly,* 3d ser, 38 (1980): 371–400.

Davies, Wendy. "'Protected Space' in Britain and Ireland in the Middle Ages." In *Scotland in Dark Age Britain: The Proceedings of a Day Conference Held on 18 February 1995.* Edited by Barbara E. Crawford. Pp. 1–19. St. John's House Papers 6. Aberdeen, 1996.

Davies, Wendy, and Paul Fouracre, eds. *Property and Power in the Early Middle Ages.* Cambridge, 1995.

———, eds. *The Settlement of Disputes in Early Medieval Europe.* Cambridge, 1986.

De Clercq, Charles. *La législation religieuse franque de Clovis à Charlemagne. Étude sur les actes de Conciles et les capitulaires, les statuts diocésains et les règles monastiques, 507–814.* Louvain, 1936.

Alain Dierkens. "Prolégomènes à une histoire des relations culturelles entre les îles britanniques et le continent pendant le Haut Moyen Age. La diffusion du monachisme dit colombanien ou iro-franc dans quelques monastères de la région parisienne au VIIe siècle et la politique religieuse de la reine Bathilde." In Atsma, *La Neustrie,* 2: 371–94.

Drew, Katherine Fischer. "The Immunity in Carolingian Italy." *Speculum* 37 (1962): 182–97.

DuBois, Jacques. "Sainte Bathilde vers 625–680, Reine de France 641–655, Fondatrice de l'abbaye de Chelles." *Paris et Ile-de-France. Mémoires* 32 (1981): 13–30.

Duby, Georges. *La société aux XIe et XIIe siècles dans la région mâconnaise.* Paris, 1953. Reprint, Paris, 1971.

Ducloux, Anne. *"Ad ecclesiam confugere." Naissance du droit d'asile dans les églises (IVe—milieu du Ve s.).* Paris, 1994.

Durliat, Jean. *Les Finances Publiques de Diocletian aux Carolingiens (284–889).* Beihefte der Francia 21. Sigmaringen, 1990.

Ebling, Horst. *Prosopographie der Amtsträger des Merowingerreiches von Chlothar II (613) bis Karl Martell (741).* Beihefte der Francia 2. Munich, 1974.

Engel, Arthur, and Raymond Serrure. *Traité de numismatique du moyen âge.* Vol. 1. Paris, 1891.

Ewig, Eugen. *Spätantikes und fränkisches Gallien. Gesammelte Schriften (1952–1973).* Edited by Hartmut Atsma. 2 vols. Beihefte der Francia 3/1–2. Zurich, 1976–79.

Fabre, Paul. *Étude sur le Liber Censuum de l'Église Romaine.* Paris, 1892.

Falkenstein, Ludwig. *La papauté et les abbayes françaises aux XIe et XIIe siècles. Exemption et protection apostolique.* Bibliothèque de l'École des Hautes Études 336. Paris, 1997.

Fanning, Stephen. "Bede, Imperium, and the Bretwaldas." *Speculum* 66 (1991): 1–26.

Farmer, Sharon. *Communities of Saint Martin: Legend and Ritual in Medieval Tours.* Ithaca, N.Y., 1991.

Firth, Raymond. *Economics of the New Zealand Maori.* Wellington, 1959.

———. *Tikopia Ritual and Belief.* Boston, 1967.

———. *We, the Tikopia: A Sociological Study of Kinship in Primitive Polynesia.* New York, 1936.

Fischer, Johannes. *Der Hausmeier Ebroin.* Inaugural dissertation. Bonn, 1954.

Fixot, Michel, and Élisabeth Zadora-Rio, eds. *L'environnement des églises et la topographie religieuse des campagnes médiévales. Actes du IIIe congrès international d'archéologie médiévale. Aix-en-Provence, 28–30 septembre 1989.* Documents d'archéologie française 46. Paris, 1994.

Fleckenstein, Josef. "Fulrad von Saint-Denis und der fränkische Ausgriff in den süddeutschen Raum." In *Studien und Vorarbeiten zur Geschichte des grossfränkischen und frühdeutschen Adels.* Edited by Gerd Tellenbach = *Forschungen zur oberrheinischen Landesgeschichte* 4 (1957): 9–39.

———. *Die Hofkapelle der deutschen Könige.* Part 1, *Grundlegung. Die Karolingische Hofkapelle.* Schriften der MGH 16/1. Stuttgart, 1959.

Fouracre, Paul J. "The Career of Ebroin, Mayor of the Palace, c. 657–680." Ph.D. diss., University of London, 1981.

———. "Eternal Light and Earthly Needs: Practical Aspects of the Development of Frankish Immunities." In Davies and Fouracre, *Property and Power*, pp. 53–81.

———. "Observations on the Outgrowth of Pippinid Influence in the 'Regnum Francorum' after the Battle of Tertry (687–715)." *Medieval Prosopography* 5 (1984): 1–31.

Fouracre, Paul J., and Richard A. Gerberding. *Late Merovingian France: History and Hagiography, 640–720.* Manchester, 1996.

Foviaux, Jacques. "Les immunités ecclésiastiques (IXe–XIe siècles)." *Histoire médiévale et archéologie*, no. 3 (1991): 47–67.

Frank, Hieronymus. *Die Klosterbischöfe des Frankenreiches.* Beiträge zur Geschichte des alten Mönchtums und des Benediktinerordens 17. Münster, 1932.

Freise, Eckhard. "Das Mittelalter bis zum Vertrag von Verdun (843)." In *Westfälische Geschichte.* Edited by Wilhelm Kohl. Vol. 1, *Von den Anfängen bis zum Ende des Alten Reiches.* Pp. 275–335. Düsseldorf, 1983.

Freud, Sigmund. *Totem and Taboo: Resemblances between the Psychic Lives of Savages and Neurotics.* Translated by A. A. Brill. Reprint, New York, 1946.

Fustel de Coulanges, N. D. "Étude sur l'immunité mérovingienne." *Revue historique* 22 (1883): 249–90; 23 (1883): 1–27.

Gäbe, S. "Radegundis: sancta, regina, ancilla. Zum Heiligkeitsideal der Radegundisviten von Fortunat und Baudonivia." *Francia* 16/1 (1989): 1–30.

Ganshof, François-Louis. "Les bureaux de tonlieu de Marseille et de Fos." In *Études historiques à la mémoire de Noël Didier.* Pp. 125–133. Paris, 1960.

———. *The Carolingians and the Frankish Monarchy: Studies in Carolingian History.* Translated by Janet Sondheimer. Ithaca, N.Y., 1971.

———. *Feudalism.* Translated by Philip Grierson. Rev. ed. New York, 1964.

———. "L'immunité dans la monarchie franque." In *Les liens de vassalité et les immunités.* 2d ed. Pp. 171–216. Recueils de la Société Jean Bodin 1. Brussels, 1958.

Garand, M.-C. "Une collection personnelle de saint Odilon de Cluny et ses compléments." *Scriptorium* 33 (1979): 163–80.

Gauthier, Nancy. *L'évangélisation des pays de la Moselle. La Province Romaine de la Première Belgique entre Antiquité et Moyen Age (IIIe–VIIIe siècles).* Paris, 1980.

Geary, Patrick J. *Aristocracy in Provence: The Rhône Basin at the Dawn of the Carolingian Age.* Monographien zur Geschichte des Mittelalters 31. Stuttgart, 1985.

———. *Before France and Germany: The Creation and Transformation of the Merovingian World.* New York, 1988.

Gennep, Arnold van. *Tabou et Totémisme à Madagascar. Étude descriptive et théorique.* Paris, 1904.

Gerberding, Richard A. *The Rise of the Carolingians and the "Liber Historiae Francorum."* Oxford, 1987.

Giraud, Paul-Émile. *Essai historique sur l'abbaye de S. Barnard et sur la ville de Romans.* 2 vols. Lyon, 1856–69.

Glöckner, Karl. "Lorsch und Lothringen, Robertiner und Capetinger." *Zeitschrift für die Geschichte des Oberrheins*, n.s., 50 (1937): 301–54.

Godelier, Maurice. *L'énigme du don*. Paris, 1996.

Goebel, Julius, Jr. *Felony and Misdemeanor: A Study in the History of English Criminal Procedure*. New York, 1937.

Goffart, Walter. *Barbarians and Romans, A.D. 418–584: The Techniques of Accommodation*. Princeton, 1980.

————. "From Roman Taxation to Mediaeval Seigneurie: Three Notes." *Speculum* 47 (1972): 165–87, 373–94.

————. *The Le Mans Forgeries: A Chapter from the History of Church Property in the Ninth Century*. Harvard Historical Studies 76. Cambridge, Mass., 1966.

————. *The Narrators of Barbarian History (A.D. 550–800): Jordanes, Gregory of Tours, Bede, and Paul the Deacon*. Princeton, 1988.

————. "Old and New in Merovingian Taxation." *Past and Present* 96 (1982): 3–21.

————. "Paul the Deacon's 'Gesta Episcoporum Mettensium' and the Early Design of Charlemagne's Succession." *Traditio* 42 (1986): 59–93.

Gray, Charles. "Reason, Authority, and Imagination: The Jurisprudence of Sir Edward Coke." In *Culture and Politics from Puritanism to the Enlightenment*. Edited by Perez Zagorin. Pp. 25–66. Berkeley, Calif., 1980.

Guérout, Jean. "Les origines et le premier siècle de l'abbaye." In *L'abbaye royale Notre-Dame de Jouarre*. Pp. 1–67. Paris, 1961.

————. "Le Testament de Sainte Fare. Matériaux pour l'étude et l'édition critique de ce document." *Revue d'histoire ecclésiastique* 60 (1965): 761–821.

Hallinger, Kassius. "Zur Rechtsgeschichte der Abtei Gorze bei Metz (vor 750–1572)." *Zeitschrift für Kirchengeschichte* 83 (1972): 325–50.

Hanson, F. Allan. "Female Pollution in Polynesia?" *Journal of the Polynesian Society* 91 (1982): 335–81.

————. "Polynesian Religions: An Overview." In *Encyclopedia of Religion*. 1987 ed. Pp. 423–32.

————, ed. *Studies in Symbolism and Cultural Communication*. Lawrence, Kan., 1982.

Hanson, F. Allan, and Louise Hanson. *Counterpoint in Maori Culture*. London, 1983.

Harries, Jill, and Ian Wood, eds. *The Theodosian Code*. Ithaca, N.Y., 1993.

Hartmann, Wilfried. *Die Synoden der Karolingerzeit im Frankenreich und in Italien*. Paderborn, 1989.

Haskins, Charles Homer. *Norman Institutions*. Cambridge, 1925.

Haubrichs, Wolfgang. "Fulrad von St. Denis und der Frühbesitz der Cella Salonnes in Lotharingien. Toponomastische und besitzgeschichtliche Überlegungen." In *Festschrift zum 65. Geburtstag von Hans-Walter Herrmann*. Pp. 1–29. Saarbrücken, 1995.

Hauck, Karl. "Die Ausbreitung des Glaubens in Sachsen und die Verteidigung der römischen Kirche als konkurrierende Herrscheraufgaben Karls des Grossen." *Frühmittelalterliche Studien* 4 (1970): 138–72.

———. "Paderborn, das Zentrum von Karls Sachsen-Mission 777." In *Adel und Kirche. Gerd Tellenbach zum 65. Geburtstag dargebracht von Freunden und Schülern.* Edited by Josef Fleckenstein and Karl Schmid. Pp. 92–140. Freiburg, 1968.

Head, Thomas. *Hagiography and the Cult of Saints. The Diocese of Orléans, 800–1200.* Cambridge, 1990.

Head, Thomas, and Richard Landes, eds. *The Peace of God: Social Violence and Religious Response in France around the Year 1000.* Ithaca, N.Y., 1992.

Heidrich, Ingrid. "Titulatur und Urkunden der arnulfingischen Hausmeier." *Archiv für Diplomatik* 11/12 (1965–66): 71–279.

———. "Die Verbindung von Schutz und Immunität. Beobachtungen zu den merowingischen und frühkarolingischen Schutzurkunden für St. Calais." *ZRG GA* 90 (1973): 10–30.

Heinzelmann, Martin. *Gregor von Tours (538–594). "Zehn Bücher Geschichte." Historiographie und Gesellschaftskonzept im 6. Jahrhundert.* Darmstadt, 1994.

Henriet, Patrick. "Chronique de quelques morts annoncées. Les saints abbés clunisiens (X^e–XIIe siècles)." *Médiévales* 31 (1996): 93–108.

Herity, Michael. "The Building and Layout of Early Irish Monasteries before the Year 1000." *Monastic Studies* 14 (1983): 247–84

Hiestand, Rudolf. *Byzanz und das Regnum Italicum im 10. Jahrhundert.* Zurich, 1964.

Hirsch, Hans. "Untersuchungen zur Geschichte des päpstlichen Schutzes." *MIÖG* 54 (1942): 363–433.

Hlawitschka, Eduard. *Franken, Alemannen, Bayern und Burgunder in Oberitalien (774–962).* Freiburg im Breisgau, 1960.

Hocquard, Gaston. "La Règle de saint Chrodegang. État de quelques questions." In *Saint Chrodegang. Communications présentées au colloque tenu à Metz à l'occasion du douzième centenaire de sa Mort.* Pp. 55–90. Metz, 1967.

Hoff, Erwin. *Pavia und seine Bischöfe im Mittelalter. Beiträge zur Geschichte der Bischöfe von Pavia unter besonderer Berücksichtigung ihrer politischen Stellung.* Vol. 1, *Epoche: Età imperiale.* Pavia, 1943.

Hoffmann, Hartmut. *Gottesfriede und Treuga Dei.* Schriften der MGH 20. Stuttgart, 1964.

Hourlier, J. *Saint Odilon abbé de Cluny.* Louvain, 1964.

Howard, Alan, and Robert Borofsky, eds. *Developments in Polynesian Ethnology.* Honolulu, 1989.

Hughes, Kathleen. "The Celtic Church: Is This a Valid Concept?" In *Church and Society in Ireland, A.D. 400–1200.* Edited by David Dumville. London, 1987.

Hummer, Hans Josef. "Monastic Property, Family Continuity and Central Authority in Early Medieval Alsace and Southern Lotharingia." Ph.D. diss., UCLA, 1997.

Hurnard, Naomi D. "The Anglo-Norman Franchises." *English Historical Review* 64 (1949): 289–327, 433–60.

Hyams, Paul. "Observations on the Charter as a Source for the History of the Early English Common Law." *Journal of Legal History* 12 (1991): 173–89.

Iogna-Prat, Dominique. *"Agni immaculati." Recherches sur les sources hagiographiques relatives à Saint Maieul de Cluny (954–994)*. Paris, 1988.

———. "Cluny à la mort de Maïeul (994–998)." *Bulletin de la société des fouilles archéologiques et des monuments historiques de l'Yonne*, no. 12 (1995): 13–23.

———. "La croix, le moine et l'empereur. Dévotion à la croix et théologie politique à Cluny autour de l'an mil." In *Haut moyen-âge. Culture, éducation et société. Études offertes à Pierre Riché*. Edited by Michel Sot. Pp. 449–75. La Garenne-Colombes, [1990].

———. "Politische Aspeckte der Marienverehrung in Cluny um das Jahr 1000." In *Maria in der Welt. Marienverehrung im Kontext der Sozialgeschichte 10.–18. Jahrhundert*. Edited by Claudia Opitz et al. Pp. 243–51. Zurich, 1993.

James, Edward. *The Origins of France: From Clovis to the Capetians, 500–1000*. London, 1982.

Jarnut, Jörg. "Ludwig der Fromme, Lothar I, und das Regnum Italiae." In *Charlemagne's Heir: New Perspectives on the Reign of Louis the Pious (814–840)*. Edited by Peter Godman and Roger Collins. Pp. 349–62. Oxford, 1990.

Jarnut, Jörg, Ulrich Nonn, and Michael Richter, eds. *Karl Martell in seiner Zeit*. Beihefte der Francia 37. Sigmaringen, 1994.

Jäschke, Kurt-Ulrich. "Die Karolingergenealogien aus Metz und Paulus Diaconus. Mit einem Exkurs über Karl 'den Kahlen.'" *Rheinische Vierteljahrsblätter* 34 (1970): 190–218.

Jensen, Merrill. *The Articles of Confederation: An Interpretation of the Social-Constitutional History of the American Revolution, 1774–1781*. Madison, Wis., 1963.

John, Eric. "The King and the Monks in the Tenth-Century Reformation." *Bulletin of the John Rylands Library* 42 (1959): 61–87.

———. *Land Tenure in Early England: A Discussion of Some Problems*. Leicester, 1960.

Jussen, Bernhard. "Le parrainage à la fin du moyen âge. Savoir public, attentes théologiques et usages sociaux." *Annales: ÉSC* 47 (1992): 467–502.

———. *Patenschaft und Adoption im frühen Mittelalter. Künstliche Verwandtschaft als soziale Praxis*. Göttingen, 1991.

Kapteyn, P. J. H. "De sociogenese van het woord 'Taboe' in West-Europa of: De 'Edele Wilde' en de 18de eeuwse burgerij." *Sociologische Gids* 22 (1975): 414–26.

Keesing, Roger M. "Conventional Metaphors and Anthropological Metaphysics: The Problematic of Cultural Translation." *Journal of Anthropological Research* 41 (1985): 201–17.

———. "Rethinking Mana." *Journal of Anthropological Research* 40 (1984): 137–56.

Kennelly, Karen. "Sobre la paz de dios y la sagrera en el condado de Barcelona (1030–1130)." *Anuario de estudios medievales* 5 (1968): 107–36.

Klauser, T., and R. S. Bour. *Un document du IXe siècle. Notes sur l'ancienne liturgie de Metz et sur ses églises antérieures à l'an mil.* In *Annuaire de la Société d'Histoire et d'Archéologie de la Lorraine* 38 (1929): 497–639.

Klebel, Ernst. "Zur Geschichte der Patriarchen von Aquileja." In *Festschrift für Rudolf Egger. Beiträge zur älteren europäischen Kulturgeschichte.* Vol. 1. Pp. 396–422. Klagenfurt, 1952.

Kohnle, Armin. *Abt Hugo von Cluny (1049–1109).* Sigmaringen, 1993.

Krahwinkler, Harald. *Friaul im Frühmittelalter. Geschichte einer Region vom Ende des fünften bis zum Ende des zehnten Jahrhunderts.* Vienna, 1992.

Kroell, Maurice. *L'immunité franque.* Paris, 1910.

Krusch, Bruno. "Die Urkunden von Corbie und Levillains letztes Wort." *Neues Archiv* 31 (1906): 337–75.

Labande-Mailfert, Yvonne et al., ed. *Histoire de l'abbaye Sainte-Croix de Poitiers. Quatorze siècles de vie monastique = Mémoires de la Société des Antiquaires de l'Ouest,* 4th ser., 19 (1986–87).

Laporte, Jean. "Les listes abbatiales de Jumièges." In *Jumièges. Congrès scientifique du XIIIe centenaire. Rouen, 10–12 June 1954.* Pp. 435–66. Rouen, 1955.

Laprat, R. "Les rapports de Saint Colomban et de la Gaule franque aux VIe et VIIe siècles." In *Mélanges colombaniens. Actes du Congrès international de Luxeuil, 20–23 juillet 1950.* Pp. 119–41. Paris, 1951.

Lebecq, Stéphane. *Les origines franques, V^e–IXe siècle.* Nouvelle Histoire de la France Médiévale 1. Paris, 1990.

Leblond, V., and Maurice Lecomte. *Les Privilèges de L'abbaye de Rebais-en-Brie.* Melun, 1910.

Le Goff, Jacques, and Jean-Claude Schmitt. "L'histoire médiévale." *Cahiers de civilisation médiévale, X^e–XIIe siècles* 39 (1996): 9–25.

Lemarignier, Jean-François. "La Dislocation du 'pagus' et le problème des 'consuetudines' (X^e–XIe siècles)." In *Mélanges d'histoire du Moyen Age dédiés à la mémoire de Louis Halphen.* Pp. 401–10. Paris, 1951.

———. *Étude sur les privilèges d'exemption et de juridiction ecclésiastique des abbayes Normandes depuis les origines jusqu'en 1140.* Archives de la France monastique 44. Paris, 1937.

Lesne, Émile. *La hiérarchie épiscopale. Provinces, métropolitains, primats en Gaule et Germanie depuis la réforme de saint Boniface jusqu'à la mort d'Hincmar, 742–882.* Lille, 1905.

———. *Histoire de la propriété ecclésiastique en France.* 6 vols. Lille, 1910.

Levison, Wilhelm. *Aus rheinischer und fränkischer Frühzeit. Ausgewählte Aufsätze.* Düsseldorf, 1948.

Levillain, Léon. "Un diplôme mérovingien de protection royale en faveur de Saint-Denis." *BÉC* 72 (1911): 233–44.

———. "Études mérovingiennes. La charte de Clotilde (10 mars 673)." *BÉC* 105 (1944): 5–63.

————."Études sur l'abbaye de Saint-Denis à l'époque mérovingienne." *BÉC* 82 (1921): 5–116; 86 (1925): 5–99; 87 (1926): 20–97, 245–346; 91 (1930): 5–65, 264–300.

————. *Examen critique des chartes mérovingiennes et carolingiennes de l'Abbaye de Corbie.* Mémoires et documents publiés par la Société de l'École des Chartes 5. Paris, 1902.

————. "Le formulaire de Marculf et la critique moderne." *BÉC* 84 (1923): 21–91.

————."Note sur l'immunité Mérovingienne." *Revue historique de droit français et étranger*, 4th ser., 6 (1927): 38–67.

Levy, Leonard W. *Original Intent and the Framers' Constitution.* New York, 1988.

Lynch, Joseph H. *Godparents and Kinship in Early Medieval Europe.* Princeton, 1986.

Little, Lester K. *Benedictine Maledictions: Liturgical Cursing in Romanesque France.* Ithaca, N.Y., 1993.

Longnon, Auguste. *Atlas historique de la France depuis César jusqu'à nos jours.* Paris, 1889.

López Alsina, Fernando. "Millas *in giro ecclesie*: El ejemplo del monasterio de San Julián de Samos." *Estudos medievais* 10 (1993): 159–87.

Lot, Ferdinand. *L'impôt foncier et la capitation personnelle sous le Bas-Empire et à l'époque franque.* Bibliothèque de l'École des Hautes Études 253. Paris, 1928.

MacCormack, Sabine G. *Art and Ceremony in Late Antiquity.* Berkeley, Calif., 1981.

Magnien, Émile. *Histoire de Mâcon et du Mâconnais.* Mâcon, 1971.

Magnou-Nortier, Élisabeth. "Étude sur le privilège d'immunité du IVe au IXe siècle." *Revue Mabillon* 60 (1981–84): 465–512

————."La gestion publique en Neustrie. Les moyens et les hommes (VIIe–IXe siècles)." In Atsma, *La Neustrie*, 1:271–320.

————. "Les *Pagenses*, notables et fermiers du fisc durant le haut moyen âge." *Revue Belge de Philologie et d'Histoire* 65 (1987): 237–56.

Maitland, Frederic William. *Domesday Book and Beyond: Three Essays in the Early History of England.* Cambridge, 1897. Reprint, 1987.

Manteyer, Georges de. *La Provence du premier au douzième siècle.* Vol. 1. Paris, 1908.

McKitterick, Rosamond. *The Carolingians and the Written Word.* Cambridge, 1989.

McLaughlin, Terence P. *Le très ancien droit monastique de l'Occident.* Poitiers, 1935.

Mead, Margaret. *Encyclopaedia of the Social Sciences.* 1934 ed. S.v. "Tabu."

Méhu, Didier. "La communauté d'habitants de Cluny au Moyen Age (X^e–XVe siècles)." Ph.D. diss. Université de Lyon II, 1998.

Metz, Wolfgang. "Miszellen zur Geschichte der Widonen und Salier, vornehmlich in Deutschland." *Historisches Jahrbuch* 85 (1965): 1–27.

Miccoli, Giovanni. *Pietro Igneo. Studi Sull'Età Gregoriana.* Istituto Storico Italiano per il Medio Evo, Studi Storici 40–41. Rome, 1960.

Milsom, S. F. C. "Trespass from Henry III to Edward III." *Law Quarterly Review* 74 (1958): 195–224; 407–36; 561–90.

Mitteis, Heinrich. *The State in the Middle Ages: A Comparative Constitutional History of Feudal Europe.* Translated by H. F. Orton. North-Holland Medieval Translations 1. Amsterdam, 1975.

Moreira, Isabel. "Provisatrix optima: St. Radegund of Poitiers' relic petitions to the East." *Journal of Medieval History* 19 (1993): 285–305.

Morelle, Laurent. "Moines de Corbie sous influence sandionysienne? Les préparatifs corbéiens du synode romain de 1065." In *L'église de France et la Papauté (Xᵉ–XIIIᵉ siècle)—Die französische Kirche und das Papsttum (10.–13. Jahrhundert). Actes du XXVIᵉ colloque historique franco-allemand (Paris 17–19 octobre 1990).* Edited by Rolf Grosse. Bonn, 1993.

———. "Le statut d'un grand monastère franc: Corbie (664–1050)." In *Le christianisme en Occident du début du VIIᵉ siècle au milieu du XIᵉ siècle. Textes et documents.* Edited by François Bougard. Pp. 209–15. Paris, 1997.

Morris, William Alfred. *The Medieval English Sheriff to 1300.* Manchester, 1927.

Mostert, Marco. *The Political Theology of Abbo of Fleury: A Study of the Ideas about Society and Law of the Tenth-Century Monastic Reform Movement.* Hilversum, 1987.

———. "Die Urkundenfälschungen Abbos von Fleury." In *Fälschungen im Mittelalter. Internationaler Kongress der MGH, München, 16.–19. September 1986,* pt. 4, *Diplomatische Fälschungen,* pt. 2. MGH Schriften 33, iv. Pp. 287–318. Hannover, 1988.

Murray, Alexander Callander. "Immunity, Nobility, and the Edict of Paris." *Speculum* 69 (1994): 18–39.

———. "*Pax et disciplina*: Roman Public Law and the Frankish State." In *Proceedings of the Tenth International Congress on Medieval Canon Law, Syracuse, August 12–18, 1996.* Forthcoming.

———, ed. *After Rome's Fall: Narrators and Sources of Early Medieval History. Essays Presented to Walter Goffart.* Toronto, 1998.

Nelson, Janet L. *Charles the Bald.* London, 1992.

———. "Making Ends Meet: Wealth and Poverty in the Carolingian Church." In *The Church and Wealth.* Edited by W. J. Sheils and Diana Wood. Pp. 25–35. Oxford, 1987.

———. "Queens as Jezebels: Brunhild and Balthild in Merovingian History." In Janet Nelson, *Politics and Ritual in Early Medieval Europe.* Pp. 1–48. London, 1986.

Nonn, Ulrich. "Merowingische Testamente. Studien zum Fortleben einer römischen Urkundenform im Frankenreich." *Archiv für Diplomatik* 18 (1972): 1–129.

Oexle, Otto Gerhard. "Die Karolinger und die Stadt des heiligen Arnulf." *Frühmittelalterliche Studien* 1 (1967): 250–364.

Orlin, Lena Cowen. *Private Matters and Public Culture in Post-Reformation England.* Ithaca, N.Y., 1994.

Palazzo, Éric. *Histoire des livres liturgiques. Le Moyen Age, des origines au XIIIᵉ siècle.* Paris, 1993.

Palazzo, Éric, and Ann-Katrin Johansson. "Jalons liturgiques pour une histoire du culte de la Vierge dans l'Occident latin (Vᵉ–XIᵉ siècles)." In *Marie. Le culte de la vierge dans la société médiévale*. Edited by Dominique Iogna-Prat, Éric Palazzo, and Daniel Russo. Pp. 15–43. Paris, 1996.

Paschini, Pio. *Storia del Friuli*. Vol. 1, *Dalle origini alla metà del Duecento*. 2d ed., Udine, 1953.

Paxton, Frederick S. "Power and the Power to Heal. The Cult of St. Sigismund of Burgundy." *Early Medieval Europe* 2 (1993): 95–110.

Pelikan, Jaroslav. *The Growth of Medieval Theology (600–1300)*. Vol. 3 of *The Christian Tradition: A History of the Development of Doctrine*. Chicago, 1978.

Pelt, Jean-Baptiste. *Études sur la cathédrale de Metz. La liturgie*. Vol. 1, *Vᵉ–XIIIᵉ siècle*. Metz, 1937.

Pennington, Kenneth. *Pope and Bishops: The Papal Monarchy in the Twelfth and Thirteenth Centuries*. Philadelphia, 1984.

Périn, Patrick. "Quelques considérations sur la basilique de Saint-Denis et sa nécropole à l'époque mérovingienne." In *Villes et campagnes au Moyen Âge. Mélanges Georges Despy*. Edited by Jean-Marie Duvosquel and Alain Dierkens. Pp. 599–624. Liège, 1991.

Perrin, Charles-Edmond. *Recherches sur la seigneurie rurale en Lorraine d'après les plus anciens censiers (IXᵉ–XIIᵉ siècle)*. Paris, 1935.

Pietri, Luce. *La ville de Tours du IVᵉ au VIᵉ siècle. Naissance d'une cité chrétienne*. Collection de l'École française de Rome 69. Rome, 1983.

Pivano, Silvio. *Stato e chiesa da Berengario I ad Arduino (888–1015)*. Turin, 1908.

Plucknett, Theodore F. T. "The Genesis of Coke's Reports." *Cornell Law Quarterly* 17 (1942): 190–213.

———. *Legislation of Edward I*. The Ford Lectures 1947. Oxford, 1949. Reprint, 1970.

Poeck, Dietrich W. *Cluniacensis Ecclesia. Der cluniacensische Klosterverband (10.–12. Jahrhundert)*. Münstersche Mittelalter-Schriften 71. Munich, 1998.

Pollock, Frederick, and Frederic William Maitland. *The History of English Law before the Time of Edward I*. 2d ed. Introduced by S. F. C. Milsom. 2 vols. Cambridge, 1968.

Poly, Jean-Pierre. *La Provence et la société féodale, 879–1166. Contribution à l'étude des structures dites féodales dans le Midi*. Paris, 1976.

Prestwich, Michael. *Edward I*. Berkeley, Calif., 1988.

Prinz, Friedrich. *Frühes Mönchtum im Frankenreich. Kultur und Gesellschaft in Gallien, den Rheinlanden und Bayern am Beispiel der monastischen Entwicklung (4. bis 8. Jahrhundert)*. 2d ed. Munich, 1988.

Pontal, Odette. *Histoire des conciles mérovingiens*. Paris, 1989.

Pounds, N. J. G. *The Medieval Castle in England and Wales: A Social and Political History*. Cambridge, 1990.

Remensnyder, Amy G. "Legendary Treasure at Conques: Reliquaries and Imaginative Memory," *Speculum* 71 (1996): 884–906.

Reynolds, Susan. *Fiefs and Vassals: The Medieval Evidence Reinterpreted*. Oxford, 1994.

Riché, Pierre. "Les bibliothèques de trois aristocrates laïcs carolingiens." *Le Moyen Age* 69 (1963): 87–104.

Rosenwein, Barbara H. "Association through Exemption: Saint-Denis, Salonnes, and Metz." In *Vom Kloster zum Klosterverband. Das Werkzeug der Schriftlichkeit*. Edited by Hagen Keller and Franz Neiske. Pp. 68–87. Akten des Internationalen Kolloquiums des Projekts L 2 im SFB 231 (22.–23. Februar 1996). Münstersche Mittelalter-Schriften 74. Munich, 1997.

————. "Les bienfaiteurs de Cluny en Provence (v.940–v.1050)." In *Saint Mayeul et son temps. Millénaire de la mort de saint Mayeul 4e abbé de Cluny, 994–1994. Actes du Congrès International, Saint Mayeul et son temps. Valensole 12–14 May 1994*. Pp. 121–36. Digne-les-Bains, 1997.

————."Cluny's Immunities in the Tenth and Eleventh Centuries: Images and Narratives." In Constable, Melville, and Oberste, *Die Cluniazenser*, pp. 133–63.

————. "L'espace clos: Grégoire et l'exemption épiscopale." In *Grégoire de Tours et l'espace gaulois. Actes du congrès international, Tours, 3–5 November 1994*. Edited by Nancy Gauthier and Henri Galinié. Pp. 251–62. Tours, 1997.

————. "The Family Politics of Berengar I, King of Italy (888–924)." *Speculum* 71 (1996): 247–89.

————. "Friends and Family, Politics and Privilege in the Kingship of Berengar I." In *Portraits of Medieval and Renaissance Living: Essays in Memory of David Herlihy*. Edited by Samuel K. Cohn Jr. and Steven A. Epstein. Pp. 91–106. Ann Arbor, 1996.

————. "Inaccessible Cloisters: Gregory of Tours and Episcopal Exemption." In *Gregory of Tours*. Edited by Kathleen Mitchell and Ian Wood. Leiden. Forthcoming.

————. "One Site, Many Meanings: Saint-Maurice d'Agaune as a Place of Power in the Early Middle Ages." In *Topographies of Power in the Early Middle Ages*. Edited by Mayke de Jong and Frans C. W. J. Theuws. Leiden, forthcoming.

————. "La question de l'immunité clunisienne." *Bulletin de la Société des Fouilles archéologiques et des monuments historiques de l'Yonne*, no. 12 (1995): 1–11.

————. *Rhinoceros Bound: Cluny in the Tenth Century*. Philadelphia, 1982.

————. *To Be the Neighbor of Saint Peter: The Social Meaning of Cluny's Property, 909–1049*. Ithaca, N.Y., 1989.

————, ed. *Anger's Past: The Social Uses of an Emotion in the Middle Ages*. Ithaca, N.Y., 1998.

Rosenwein, Barbara H., Thomas Head, and Sharon Farmer. "Monks and Their Enemies: A Comparative Approach." *Speculum* 66 (1991): 764–96.

Rossetti, Gabriella. "Formazione e caratteri delle signorie di castello e dei poteri territoriali dei vescovi sulle città nella langobardia del secolo X." *Aevum* 49 (1975): 243–309.

————. *Società e istituzioni nel contado lombardo durante il Medioevo. Cologno Monzese.* Vol. 1, *Secoli VIII–X.* Archivo della Fondazione Italiana per la Storia Amministrativa 9. Milan, 1968.

Sackur, Ernst. *Die Cluniacenser in ihrer kirchlichen und allgemeingeschichtlichen Wirksamkeit bis zur Mitte des elften Jahrhunderts.* 2 vols. Halle a. S., 1892–94.

Sahlins, Marshall D. *Social Stratification in Polynesia.* Seattle, 1958.

Santifaller, Leo. *Liber Diurnus. Studien und Forschungen.* Edited by Harald Zimmermann. Päpste und Papsttum 10. Stuttgart, 1976.

Sassier, Yves. "Les Carolingiens et Auxerre." In *L'École carolingienne d'Auxerre de Murethach à Remi, 830–908.* Edited by Dominique Iogna-Prat, Colette Jeudy, and Guy Lobrichon. Paris, 1991.

Sauerland, H. V. *Die Immunität von Metz von ihren Anfängen bis zum Ende des elften Jahrhunderts.* Metz, 1877.

Sawyer, Peter H. *Anglo-Saxon Charters: An Annotated List and Bibliography.* London, 1968.

Scheibelreiter, Georg. "Königstöchter im Kloster. Radegund (†587) und der Nonnenaufstand von Poitiers (589)." *MIÖG* 87 (1979): 1–37.

Schmid, Karl, and Otto Gerhard Oexle. "Voraussetzungen und Wirkung des Gebetsbundes von Attigny." *Francia* 2 (1974): 71–122.

Schmidinger, Heinrich. *Patriarch und Landesherr. Die weltliche Herrschaft des Patriarchen von Aquileja bis zum Ende der Staufer.* Graz, 1954.

Schulze, Hans K. *Die Grafschaftsverfassung der Karolingerzeit in den Gebieten östlich des Rheins.* Schriften zur Verfassungsgeschichte 19. Berlin, 1973.

Schwarz, Wilhelm. "Jurisdicio und Condicio. Eine Untersuchung zu den Privilegia libertatis der Klöster." *ZRG KA* 45 (1959): 34–98.

Semmler, Josef. "Chrodegang von Metz." *Theologische Realenzyklopädie* 8:71–74.

————. "Episcopi potestas und karolingische Klosterpolitik." In Borst, *Mönchtum, Episkopat und Adel,* pp. 305–95.

————. "Traditio und Königsschutz. Studien zur der königlichen monasteria." *ZRG KA* 45 (1959): 1–33.

————. "Zur pippinidisch-karolingischen Sukzessionskrise 714–723." *Deutsches Archiv für Erforschung des Mittelalters* 33 (1977): 1–36.

Senn, Félix. *L'institution des avoueries ecclésiastiques en France.* Paris, 1903.

Settia, Aldo A. *Castelli e villaggi nell'Italia padana. Popolamento, potere e sicurezza fra IX e XIII secolo.* Naples, 1984.

————. *Chiese, Strade e Fortezze nell'Italia Medievale.* Italia Sacra. Studi e documenti di storia ecclesiastica 46. Rome, 1991.

————. "Gli Ungari in Italia e i Mutamenti territoriali fra VIII e X secolo." In *Magistra Barbaritas. I Barbari in Italia.* Edited by Maria Giovanna Arcamone et al. Pp. 185–218. Milan, 1984.

Sharpe, Richard. "Some Problems Concerning the Organization of the Church in Early Medieval Ireland." *Peritia* 3 (1984): 230–70.

Shirres, Michael P. "Tapu." *The Journal of the Polynesian Society* 91 (1982): 29–51.

Shore, Bradd. "*Mana* and *Tapu.*" In *Developments in Polynesian Ethnology.* Edited by Alan Howard and Robert Borofsky. Pp. 137–73. Honolulu, 1989.

Sickel, Theodor. "Beiträge zur Diplomatik 1–3, 5. *Sitzungsberichte der Kaiserlichen Akademie der Wissenschaften, Philosophisch-Historische Klasse* 36 (1861): 329–402; 39 (1962): 105–161; 47 (1864): 175–277; 49 (1865): 311–410.

Smith, Julia M. H. *Province and Empire: Brittany and the Carolingians.* Cambridge, 1992.

Sprandel, Rolf. *Die merovingische Adel und die Gebiete östlich des Rheins.* Forschungen zur oberrheinischen Landesgeschichte 5. Freiburg, 1957.

Spreckelmeyer, Goswin. "Zur rechtlichen Funktion frühmittelalterlicher Testamente." In *Recht und Schrift im Mittelalter.* Edited by Peter Classen. Pp. 91–113. Vorträge und Forschungen 23. Sigmaringen, 1977.

Steiner, Franz. *Taboo.* 1956. Reprint. Middlesex, 1967.

Stengel, Edmund E. *Die Immunität in Deutschland bis zum Ende des 11. Jahrhunderts.* Innsbruck, 1910. Reprint, Aalen, 1964.

Stoclet, Alain. *Autour de Fulrad de Saint-Denis (v. 710–784).* École pratique des Hautes Études, Sciences historiques et philologiques 5. Hautes Études médiévales et modernes 72. Geneva, 1993.

———. "Fulrad de Saint-Denis (v. 710–784)." Ph.D. diss., Toronto University, 1985.

———. "Fulrad de Saint-Denis (v. 710–784), abbé et archiprêtre de monastères 'exempts.'" *Le Moyen Age* 88 (1982): 205–35.

Stone, Lawrence. *The Family, Sex and Marriage in England, 1500–1800.* New York, 1977.

Straw, Carole. *Gregory the Great: Perfection in Imperfection.* Berkeley, Calif., 1988.

Stumpf, Karl Friedrich. "Über die Merowinger-Diplome." *Historische Zeitschrift* 29 (1873): 343–407.

Sutherland, Donald W. *Quo Warranto Proceedings in the Reign of Edward I, 1278–1294.* Oxford, 1963.

Szabó-Bechstein, Brigitte. *Libertas Ecclesiae. Ein Schlüsselbegriff des Investiturstreits und seine Vorgeschichte, 4.–11. Jahrhundert.* Studi Gregoriani per la storia della 'libertas ecclesiae' 12. Rome, 1985.

Szaivert, Willy. "Die Entstehung und Entwicklung der Klosterexemtion bis zum Ausgang des 11. Jahrhunderts." *MIÖG* 59 (1951): 265–98.

Tabacco, Giovanni. "L'allodialità del potere nel medioevo." *Studi medievali,* 3d ser., 11/2 (1970): 565–615.

———. *The Struggle for Power in Medieval Italy: Structures of Political Rule.* Translated by Rosalind Brown Jensen. Cambridge, 1989.

Thomas, Nicholas. "Unstable Categories: *Tapu* and Gender in the Marquesas." *The Journal of Pacific History* 22 (1987): 123–38.

Thorne, Samuel E. *Sir Edward Coke 1552–1952.* Selden Society Lecture, 1952. London, 1957.

Thornley, Isobel D. "The Destruction of Sanctuary." In *Tudor Studies Presented . . .*

to *Albert Frederick Pollard*. Edited by R. W. Seton-Watson. Pp. 182–207. London, 1924. Reprint, 1969.

Tierney, Brian. *The Idea of Natural Rights: Studies on Natural Rights, Natural Law and Church Law, 1150–1625*. Emory University Studies in Law and Religion 5. Atlanta, 1997.

Tilley, Morris Palmer. *A Dictionary of the Proverbs in England in the Sixteenth and Seventeenth Centuries*. Ann Arbor, 1950.

Timbal Duclaux de Martin, Pierre. *Le Droit d'Asile*. Paris, 1939.

Treffort, Cécile. *L'église carolingienne et la mort. Christianisme, rites funéraires et pratiques commémoratives*. Collection d'histoire et d'archéologie médiévales 3. Lyon, 1996.

Ueding, Leo. *Geschichte der Klostergründungen der frühen Merowingerzeit*. Historische Studien 261. Berlin, 1935.

Ullmann, Walter. *Medieval Political Thought*. Harmondsworth, 1975.

Vacandard, Elphège. *Vie de Saint Ouen, évêque de Rouen (641–684). Étude d'histoire mérovingienne*. Paris, 1902.

Vaccari, Pietro. *Pavia nell'alto medioevo e nell'età comunale. Profilo storico*. Pavia, 1956.

Van Dam, Raymond. *Saints and Their Miracles in Late Antique Gaul*. Princeton, 1993.

Vehse, Otto. "Bistumsexemtionen bis zum Ausgang des 12. Jahrhunderts." *ZRG KA* 26 (1937): 86–160.

Verriest, Léo. *Institutions médiévales. Introduction au corpus des records de coutumes et des lois de chefs-lieux de l'ancien comté de Hainaut*. Vol. 1 of *Le Hainaut, Encyclopédie provinciale*. Edited by Léon Losseau. Mons, 1946.

Vieillard-Troiekouroff, May. *Les monuments religieux de la Gaule d'après les oeuvres de Grégoire de Tours*. Paris, 1976.

Wagner, Donald O. "Coke and the Rise of Economic Liberalism." *Economic History Review* 6 (1935): 30–44.

Wallace-Hadrill, J. M. *The Frankish Church*. Oxford, 1983.

Wemple, Suzanne Fonay. *Women in Frankish Society: Marriage and the Cloister, 500–900*. Philadelphia, 1981.

Wickham, Chris. *Early Medieval Italy: Central Power and Local Society, 400–1000*. Ann Arbor, 1981.

———. *The Mountains and the City: The Tuscan Appennines in the Early Middle Ages*. Oxford, 1988.

Wilmart, André. "Le Psautier de la Reine n. xi. Sa Provenance et sa date." *Revue Bénédictine* 28 (1911): 341–76.

Winzer, Ulrich. "Cluny und Mâcon im 10. Jahrhundert." *Frühmittelalterliche Studien* 23 (1989): 154–202.

———. *S. Gilles. Studien zum Rechtsstatus und Beziehungsnetz einer Abtei im Spiegel ihrer Memorialüberlieferung*. Münstersche Mittelalter-Schriften 59. Munich, 1988.

Woll, Ingrid. *Untersuchungen zu Überlieferung und Eigenart der merowingischen Kapitularien.* Freiburger Beiträge zur mittelalterlichen Geschichte. Studien und Texte herausgegeben von Hubert Mordek 6. Frankfurt, 1995.

Wollasch, Joachim. *Cluny — "Licht der Welt." Aufstieg und Niedergang der klösterlichen Gemeinschaft.* Zurich, 1996.

Wood, Ian N. "The Irish and Social Subversion in the Early Middle Ages." *Irland. Gesellschaft und Kultur VI.* Edited by Dorothea Siegmund-Schultze. Halle a. S., 1989.

———. "Jonas, the Merovingians and Pope Honorius: *Diplomata* and the *Vita Columbani.*" In Murray, *After Rome's Fall,* pp. 99–120.

———. "Letters and Letter-Collections from Antiquity to the Early Middle Ages: The Prose Works of Avitus of Vienne." In M. A. Meyer, ed., *The Culture of Christendom: Essays in Medieval History in Commemoration of Denis L. T. Bethell.* Pp. 29–43. London, 1983.

———. *The Merovingian Kingdoms (450–751).* London, 1994.

———. "The Secret Histories of Gregory of Tours." *Revue Belge de Philologie et d'Histoire.* Fasc. 2. *Histoire Médiévale, Moderne et Contemporaine* 71 (1993): 253–70.

———. "The *Vita Columbani* and Merovingian Hagiography." *Peritia* 1 (1982): 63–80.

Wormald, Patrick. "Charters, Law and the Settlement of Disputes in Anglo-Saxon England." In Davies and Fouracre, *The Settlement of Disputes,* pp. 149–68.

———."Lordship and Justice in the Early English Kingdom: Oswaldslow Revisited." In Davies and Fouracre, *Property and Power,* pp. 114–36.

Zadora-Rio, Élisabeth. "Lieux d'inhumation et espaces consacrés. À propos du voyage du pape Urbain II en France (août 1095–août 1096)." In *Lieux sacrés, lieux de culte, sanctuaires. Approches terminologiques, méthodologiques, historiques et monographiques.* Actes de la Table-Ronde de l'École Française de Rome (2–3 juin 1997). Edited by André Vauchez. Rome, forthcoming.

Index

Berlow, Rosalind, 159
Bermondsey/Woking, 107
Bernard, abbot of Ramsey, 197
Bernard, *fidelis*, 161–62
Berno, abbot of Cluny, 157–58, 161, 166–67
Berno, bishop of Mâcon, 164, 166–67
Berthefridus, bishop of Amiens, 79–81, 138
Bertilla, queen, 140
Bertulfus, abbot of Bobbio, 67
Bill of Rights. *See* U.S. Constitution
bishops: "monastic," 64; power of, over monasteries, 32–36
Bloch, Marc, 15
Bobbio, monastery of, 67, 106
Boniface, Saint, 99–101, 103, 110, 132, 213
Bosonids, 161–62
Brunhild, queen, 46, 48–51, 59, 66, 70
Brunner, Otto, 189–90
Bruyères-le-Châtel, monastery of, 89
Bryan, Samuel, 211
Burgundofara, founder of Faremoutiers, 62, 72
Burgundofaro, referendary, 62, 67–70, 72, 80
Burgundy, kingdom of, 49, 51, 59, 70. *See also entries for individual kings and cities*
Bury St. Edmunds, 195–96

Caesarius of Arles, 41, 56–57
Cam, Helen, 197
Cameri, license for fortification at, 149
Cancor, 113
Carloman, son of Louis the German, 140, 154
Carolingians, 84, 95–96, 126, 132, 140–42, 178. *See also entries for individual mayors and kings*
castles, 138–39, 198, 201–2. *See also entries for individual places*
cemeteries, consecration of, 178–81
Chagnericus, patriarch of Farones, 62, 72
Chagnoaldus, son of Chagnericus, 62
Chaino, 23, 87, 89–96
Chalcedon, Council of (451), 32–35
Chalon: Saint-Marcel at, 45–46, 48, 68; Council of, 77
Chambliois, 90, 94–95; aristocrats of, 90–96
Chardericus, abbot of Saint-Denis, 90, 94–95
Charlemagne, 111, 115–21, 124, 133–34, 140, 153
Charles Martel, 99–100, 102, 110

Charles the Bald, 137–38, 142
Charles the Fat, 141
Charles the Straightforward, 138–39
Charlieu, 170
Chelles, monastery at, 82–83
Chertsey, monastery at, 107
Childebert I, king, 43, 49
Childebert II, king, 46, 49–50, 56, 187
Childebert III, king, 89–90, 95
Childeric II, king, 83–84, 94
Chilperic I, king, 59
Chlodulfus, bishop of Metz, 126–29, 131
Choke, Richard, 204–6, 211
Chrodegang, bishop of Metz, 101–6, 112–14, 120, 124–26, 130–32
church councils. *See entries for individual councils*
Cicero, 185–86
Cilavegna, license to build fortification at, 150
Cittanova, castle at, 152
Cividale, 155
Classe, monastery of SS John and Stephen at, 47
Clermont, Council of, 1, 181
Clodius, 186
Clothar I, king, 49, 52–53
Clothar II, king, 50, 59–61, 70, 73, 213
Clothar III, king, 78–79
Clotild, princess, 53. *See also* Poitiers
Clotild, queen of Clovis I, 49
Clotild, queen of Theuderic III, 87, 89
Clovis I, king, 49
Clovis II, king, 64, 74–78, 94, 109
Clovis III, king, 92
cluniacensis ecclesia, 173
Cluny: *Adventus* ceremony at, 183; *burgus* of, 169–70; Cardinal Peter's privilege for, 173–78; foundation charter of, 157, 162, 166, 231–34; foundation of, 156–62; immunities of, 2, 163–68, 179–83, 235–36; papal exemptions for, 172–73; Urban's "sacred ban" for, 1–3, 179–83. *See also entries for individual abbots and popes*
Codex Theodosianus. See Theodosian Code
Coke, Edward, 207–9, 211
Columbanus, Saint, 51, 62–67, 70–72, 81, 183, 213
compater: relationship of, 146–47
Compiègne, Synod of, 103, 112, 120
Constantine, emperor, 175
Corbie, 82; exemptions and immunities for, 10, 79–81, 138
Cowdrey, Herbert E. J., 17, 173